D0561016

Eliot's New Life

Eliot's New Life

LYNDALL GORDON

FARRAR · STRAUS · GIROUX
New York

Copyright © 1988 by Lyndall Gordon
Originally published in Great Britain by
Oxford University Press, 1988
All rights reserved
Printed in the United States of America
First American edition, 1988

Library of Congress Cataloging-in-Publication Data
Gordon, Lyndall.
  Eliot's new life.
  Includes index.
  1. Eliot, T. S. (Thomas Stearns), 1888–1965.
2. Poets, American—20th century—Biography.
I. Title.
PS3509.L43Z6793   1988   821'.912 [B]   88-7235

Foreword

FROM 1970 to 1975 I wrote an account of T. S. Eliot's earlier life based on unpublished papers (his Notebook and early poems, his letters, his mother's poems, and his wife's diaries). *Eliot's Early Years* brought out the ties between his life and work. At the time, it went against the grain of Eliot studies, which had always stressed his impersonality. The idea that Eliot's poetry was rooted in private aspects of his life has now been accepted, and this has encouraged me to attempt a sequel on the years of Eliot's maturity and great fame.

Eliot's Early Years traced his journey across the 'waste land' to his conversion to Anglo-Catholicism at the age of 38. It emphasized the American influences of his youth—the moral fervour of a New England family and a mother who herself wrote passionate devotional verse—and it brought to light the shadowy period from 1910 to 1914 in Paris and Boston as a time of formative conflicts between body and soul. *The Waste Land*, although completed only in 1922, went back to this time, evolving from private, quasi-religious meditations that were overlaid by the contemporary scenes that made it appear so dazzlingly modern.

This first volume set out the external facts of Eliot's life—the ordeals that followed his impulsive marriage in 1915, the friendships with Ezra Pound and Virginia Woolf—as well as the 'unattended' moments, the definitive inward experiences that shaped the poetry. By avoiding the all-inclusive schema of 'official' biography, this more selective study showed the work and the life as complementary parts of one design, an insistent search for salvation.

Eliot's New Life, the sequel, begins with the renewal of his early relationship with a Bostonian, Emily Hale, who was to be vital to the religious poems and plays of his mature years. Her newly-discovered letters show an unfamiliar Eliot in a long-lasting but ultimately unfulfilled relationship which had to be subordinated to the unhappy fact of his marriage, his private penitence, and his public mission.

Eliot's New Life follows his last thirty-eight years, tracing the conflict between a capacity for love and a more compelling sense of sin, which was not resolved until the final eight years of his life. The structure of the book emphasizes the internal logic of Eliot's development rather than chronology which is, once again, no more than a prop for the way that he transmutes his own experience into great works of art. The climactic event of this life is the evolution of *Four Quartets* with its recurrent search for the form of the perfect life. A parallel feat is the extraordinary influence which Eliot built up as a critic until, in later years, he seemed to speak to his age as the timeless voice of judgement.

This second volume, like the first, is based on unpublished papers which reveal extensive details, so far unknown, about relationships with Vivienne Eliot and Mary Trevelyan as well as with Emily Hale. *Eliot's Early Years* brought out the importance of his first wife to his poetry, and I have continued to look at Eliot in part through the women in his life. In his mature years he had four quite different relationships with women who were all remarkable, and who entered his work in various ways. The last was his second wife, Valerie Fletcher, who brought relief after long trials. The new research continues to explore Eliot's religious life, central to his work, and his American past. I show here that the American ties, both personal and literary, became more, not less, important after he relinquished his nationality in 1927.

There is some overlap with *Eliot's Early Years*. This is intentional, because to bring out the curious single-mindedness of Eliot's life it is necessary to show recurrent links between its earlier and later stages, and also because *Eliot's New Life* was written to stand alone.

Contents

List of Illustrations

Eliot's New Life

1. A New Life

'NOTHING but a brilliant future behind me', Eliot said in July 1934. 'What is one to do?'

Behind him lay public triumph. As a young man from St Louis, Missouri, he had with a single poem, *The Waste Land*, become spokesman for the disillusioned post-war generation. Friendships with Ezra Pound, who proclaimed his Modernity, and the Woolfs, who published his poems, had established Eliot at the centre of London's literary society. But, for Eliot himself, public triumph was peripheral to private failure. There was the long-drawn-out failure of his marriage to an Englishwoman, Vivienne Haigh-Wood. There was sickness of soul, connected with that marriage, and, if anything, exacerbated by the way that Eliot freed himself in 1933. Sickly, uncertain, Vivienne could not fulfil her talents for dance, writing, or music. She alternated between moods of fitful exuberance and collapse. Neither she nor her husband were able to stay the deterioration of her mental health from the mid-twenties, and, in the years following their separation, Vivienne remained an emotional wreck, shut away for the rest of her life in a sanatorium. Though Eliot's new life was backed by friends and even Vivienne's brother, the past left a sense of contamination that shut him off, in turn, from any close relationship until the last eight years of his life. Those who believed themselves closest to Eliot, his faithful first love, Emily Hale, and his friends, Mary Trevelyan and John Hayward, all come to discover, after twenty, thirty, or fifty years, an inexplicable remoteness.

Eliot led a curious double life: publicly he was at the centre of a sycophantic buzz; privately there was the incommunicable life of a solitary that was all the stranger because it was not conducted in a monastery, but in the stir of the city, in the glare of fame. There was an inward silence and, at the same time, there was the speaker on platforms across Europe and America. Eliot's face acquired a sort of exposed reticence from the habit of looking down from a lectern over a sea of heads. His skin had a look of being drawn tightly across his face. His features, though sharp, were delicate, especially the softly indented mouth, and his eyes were introspective. It was his nature to have scruple within scruple, and to regulate his conduct on principles ignored by men of the world, as Lot in Sodom or Daniel in Babylon, who, Eliot told Pound, kept silence because they could do no good.

In his mature years Eliot often spoke of the 'unspoken'. In a solitude that was guarded by public roles he lived what was essentially a hidden life. It would be unreachable if he had not been a poet with a need to explore and define that life. Certain of his critical essays set up models, notably *Dante* (1929), 'Pascal' (1931), and *George Herbert* (1962), and autobiographical references to moral awakening and struggle pervade his unflagging critical output, which was not always criticism in the usual aesthetic sense but often bordered on moral debate and exhortation. He believed that literature and criticism had to have a social use. Through criticism—almost all of it in the form of talks in later years—and through the theatre, he channelled a private message to a wider public. Poetry, on the other hand, he made directly from the hidden life, and gave it a form quite different from that of standard biography. Eliot distils the inner life from its dross of biographic trivia so that what emerges is the coherent form of spiritual autobiography, direct, intimate, honest, and more penetrating than any outsider could dare to determine. *Eliot's New Life* will follow his own formulation, testing that against the facts of his actual day-to-day existence.

Eliot was a lone, last child of elderly parents, and he was alone, too, during his student year in Paris in 1910–11, when he walked the streets at night and conducted long philosophic vigils that brought him close to madness. He was alone even in marriage, longing to escape the emotional needs, tears, and demands of his wife. The interior solitude, then, was there from the start, but it took a new and deliberate shape from two events in middle age: Eliot's conversion at the age of 38, and his separation from his wife at the age of 44.

Eliot said that there is 'almost a definite moment of acceptance at which the New Life begins'. The primary story to be told is the drama of conversion; not the outward act so much as the hidden life of conversion which, for Eliot, was a bid to discover, or rediscover, the 'unread vision in the higher dream'. His poems of 1927–35 move towards a pulsating moment, a call coming through the New England fog, or a vision of radiant light in an English garden. What stimulated this crucial moment was a new, or renewed, relationship with Emily Hale, the beautiful, uplifted daughter of a Boston minister, Edward Hale, whom Eliot had known in his youth. Separated since Eliot's departure for Europe in 1914, and more decisively by his impulsive marriage in 1915, they renewed a steady contact from 1927. A few months before Eliot's conversion in that year, he defined what alone constitutes 'life' for a poet: it is the struggle to 'transmute his personal and private agonies' into something universal and holy. Emily Hale was vital to Eliot's new life because she had the power to stir a dream of beatitude through their mutual memory of pure love. First through memory, then through actual reunion, Eliot hoped for a renewed purity of feeling that would help him recover a visionary gift. In youth there had been hints and guesses, but during twelve years of a wretched marriage his life had become an inner waste, despite its overt success.

'Where is the Life we have lost in living?' Eliot asked. To recover a lost life meant not only to recover the power to dream but also to slough off the unwanted past, chiefly the wife who seemed to pollute the dream by her drugged proximity. As it turned out Vivienne refused to be dismissed, and with this complication the dream was all but destroyed. The marriage haunted Eliot like the memory of a sojourn in hell, leaving a residual taint from which he was not able to cleanse himself for more than twenty years.

This prolonged struggle gave another meaning to the new life; as Eliot put it: 'the recognition of the reality of Sin is a New Life.' It is as though two antithetical views fought for dominance: on the one hand the higher dream associated with Emily Hale; on the other, the sense of sin associated with Vivienne. Out of this conflict came the great works of Eliot's maturity, as he converts life into meaning in *Ash Wednesday*, *The Family Reunion*, *Four Quartets*, and the later plays.

The first stage of Eliot's new life was the higher dream, and the crucial but hidden part that Emily Hale played in its emergence. Later chapters will follow the struggle with the residue of the past. In the course of the thirties, Eliot came to perceive that the vision he longed for (what he called 'reality'), was blocked by his unworthiness, and, worse, by an inability to shake off a contamination, sexual in origin, but deepened by the horrific years of mental disturbance which he had shared with Vivienne. In a sense, he went on showing this disturbance during the subsequent years of separation, during which Vivienne tried to tug him back into a nightmare which, with even greater determination, he would shut off as the past. This trial of wills, in biographical terms a contest between the claims of past and future, in religious terms a contest between body and soul, remains a central drama in Eliot's story. It reappears in *The Family Reunion*, a play about a man who believes that he has destroyed his wife, and must pay a lifelong penance if his soul is to be saved. It is transmuted again into the more abstract terms of *Little Gidding*, in 1941–2, where the contest of past and future, body and soul, becomes a contest between the flames of hell and those of purgatory: 'Consumed by either fire or fire.' This contest must be central to any account of Eliot's life, while the cool Eliot or the gentleman joker, so frequently described, must be peripheral. The external facts are now well known, but the interior struggles remain in shadow, where profound events take place beyond record, and are reflected only in creative acts.

Eliot's greatest poetry sprang from the pain of some 'deeper failure', analysed most intimately in a draft of his last play (1958), where it is recognized that the public man

> ... who's been successful
> Isn't the real self—or that he has been striving
> All these years, for success, to conceal from himself
> Some deeper failure—or something he's ashamed of.

The record of Eliot's public life would be, from his own point of view, irrelevant to that 'real self', the solitary beneath the masks. Virginia Woolf could at times discern it where others could not. Suddenly, four years before Eliot's conversion, she caught sight of what would emerge:

That strange figure Eliot dined here last night. I feel that he has taken the veil, or whatever monks do.... Mrs. Eliot has almost died at times in the last month. Tom, though infinitely considerate, is also perfectly detached. His cell, is I'm sure, a very lofty one ...

Eliot's attraction to the lofty reaches of the religious life went back to childhood, and the model of the pilgrim in his mother's poems. Afterwards, as a graduate at Harvard, he read about the ordeals of the saints, and came to the idea of a lifetime burning in every moment. It occurred to him then that sainthood might be the only valid measure of attainment, but he perceived, too, the likelihood of self-delusion and personal unfitness, and this led him, for a decade, to discount this course of action, and direct his formidable gifts to worldly success. Conversion, I think, meant a return to the earlier, more overwhelming challenge. He was not simply joining the Church, but declaring himself ready to begin to close the gap between human frailty and perfection.

This dream, so fragile and daring, needed protection. A 'crowskin' must mask the approach to God's Kingdom: 'Let me also wear / Such deliberate disguises.' The interest of Eliot's life, as well as his work, has seemed to many readers to lie in a game of masks and unmaskings, yet it is not enough to see only an Eliot who changes inexplicably from one guise to another, according to his company. Hawthorne presents a New Englander, Holgrave, who shifts all the time yet 'never violated the innermost man' but 'carried his conscience along with him'. So, with Eliot, there is an inward certainty that inspires confidence, yet it remains elusive behind the many façades: 'I was still the same, knowing myself yet being someone other.'

As Eliot shed his American youth, he cultivated the front of an English gentleman. As a clerk in the department of foreign loans at Lloyds Bank (from 1917–1925) and as a publisher with Faber & Gwyer (later Faber & Faber) from 1926, he surrounded himself with the props of respectability: the correct City uniform, the dark suit and spats, the rolled umbrella, the deferential attentiveness, the voice so measured as to sound almost dead-pan. He liked to adopt an alias: visitors to his small, top-floor flat in the Charing Cross Road, a writing hideaway in the mid-twenties, had to enquire at the porter's lodge for 'The Captain'. Osbert Sitwell said that the feeling was nautical not military, but either way, Eliot was playing his favourite Sherlock Holmes role, living the life of mystery. The most long-lived role was an ageing man, first contemplated by Prufrock in a poem that Eliot wrote when he was 21: 'I grow old ... I grow old ...' By playing Possum, as Pound dubbed him, he could evade unwanted demands. To artistic Bloomsbury of the twenties, Eliot showed a face tinted green with powder to look cadaverous. To his publishing colleagues, he was a joker. He delighted to upset a solemn board meeting by setting off a firecracker (on the anniversary of American independence) under Geoffrey Faber's chair. He sent obscene verses to certain friends, about a Big Black Kween whose bum was as big as a soup tureen. But there was nothing spontaneous in this: the joker was another convenient role, a way of keeping these jolly chaps at a distance. (If any presumed to allude to the verses at the wrong moment, Eliot's respectability would slide into place, and, with frigid amazement, he would declare that no such verses existed.)

There is here an extreme dichotomy between the 'real', single-minded self and the public man of many faces. Eliot's visible life seems to invite standard biography, but that documentary form can convey only the shell of a character who was almost anti-thetical to his outward life. Eliot appeared mild and conventional, yet his hidden character was strenuous and daring. Outwardly he courted normality, while his hidden self refused all norms as it struck out for the frontiers of experience. To understand his life it is necessary to see the continuity of this venture through the poetry, so that it is futile to dab at individual poems. For Eliot said himself that an individual poem is not poetry—'That is a life.'

The multiplicity of Eliot's roles conceals an extraordinary singleness of mind. To follow the course of his development it is necessary to walk a narrow path: not to be dazzled by his fame, the myriad honorary degrees, or disarmed by the Old Buffer of the clubs, into a bland acceptance of Eliot's studied performances. It is essential, also, to resist the opposite temptation to crude exposé, for there is, in truth, a disturbing side to Eliot: the strange hatred of life, the early anti-Semitism, his apparent misogyny, and his treat-ment of the three women who gave their love to him during his most creative years. Yet these are partial truths, and must be seen in the perspective of a man who, while he carried out the routines of work, commuting, dining out, and committees in mid-century London, existed all the time, in his imagination, beyond the pale of civilization and within sight of eternity. No one in the rush-hour in a London tube train would have suspected that the immaculate gentleman with his carefully rolled umbrella, bowler hat, and white handkerchief poking from the breast pocket of a grey, sober suit was quietly praying when the train stopped between stations. This habit marks his remoteness from the urban setting in which he placed himself almost, it might seem, as cover. In early years, masked by apparent conformity, he had passed by in the midst of the workaday swarm, an anonymous Judgement ('The horror! the horror!') of innate depravity in the urban waste. In his mature years, still protected by anonymity, the soul at prayer infiltrated the crowded tube.

Eliot's admirers have tended to play up the masks, while his detractors have looked behind them only to find the faults. Both gloss over the new life beneath, the life that was so closely allied to the creative works as to be a reciprocal invention. The crucial problem is to discern the bonds between life and work in a way that will do justice to the poetry and plays which are, after all, central acts in his life. The obvious solution is to take Eliot's own point of view, to imagine a man with immortal longings, and to reconstruct the strategy by which he attained immortality. Eliot sets out the general lines in *Four Quartets*, and the plays demonstrate individual instances, the saint in *Murder in the Cathedral* and Celia in *The Cocktail Party*. In 1940 Eliot spoke of 'the poet who, out of intense and personal experience, is able to express a general truth'. In some sense his works do retain 'all the particularity' of private experience, though to work back from poetry to life may be done only with the utmost delicacy. The test of accuracy has to be Eliot's more prosaic statements in talks and critical essays. If the Eliot of this book appears unfamiliar, it is because many of these statements are drawn from buried pieces of uncollected criticism and also from unpublished papers: his numerous and widely scattered letters. Of particular use are the letters to his friend, Mary Trevelyan, between 1940 and 1956, and their casual conversations recorded in her unpublished memoir. The unfamiliar Eliot is reflected, too, in the faithful endurance of Emily Hale, whose commitment to him was lifelong. It is likely, as I shall explain, that most of her letters have been destroyed, but the few that remain are clear about the importance of this most long-lasting of ties outside his family. Her Bostonian restraint, her concern for discretion, and her acceptance (against her own wish) that Eliot's thousand letters to her should be sequestered until well into the next century, all persuade me that her available letters to friends speak the truth.

It is simple enough to collect facts, but to attempt to do justice to Eliot's immortal longings will mean that his own most subtle statements—his creative works—must be the central source, aided by drafts which show the evolution of his positions, as do the ten layers of his most confessional play, *The Family Reunion*, and the drafts of the poem he regarded as his masterpiece, *Four Quartets*.

To reconstruct Eliot's approach to the timeless from his particular position in his own time also means the exercise of imaginative sympathy for a man who was stranger than his disarming appearance would have us believe, and who grew harder to know during the more inscrutable years of his great fame.

In 1927 Eliot ventured to send Emily Hale the first of many gifts, his essay on *Shakespeare and the Stoicism of Seneca*. When she began to give Eliot's gifts away after 1944, she held this back till her death. Helen Gardner, the great Eliot scholar, suggested that this essay marks the date of the revival of their contact and that it revealed something personal to Emily Hale. 'What every poet starts from', he said, 'is his own emotions', which may be 'his nostalgia, his bitter regrets for past happiness'. These regrets might become, for a 'brave' poet, the basis of an attempt 'to fabricate something permanent and holy out of his personal animal feelings—as in the *Vita Nuova*'.

These words, delivered before the Shakespeare Association on 18 March 1927, three months before his conversion, suggest that his memory of Emily Hale was a spur to a new life. The words accompany an attack on readers who, Eliot said, fastened on the more superficial details of his work and invariably ignored 'my biography . . . in what I *did* write from personal experience'.

The tentative proposal in this essay was matched by the arrival of Emily Hale's first letter one fine May day about the time that Vivienne, after a year or more of deepening mental stress, left England for nine months' treatment abroad. At lunch hour Eliot walked around Russell Square with William Force Stead, an American priest who was his confidant in the years before and after his conversion, and who also had a disturbed wife. Looking at the sun on the new leaves, Stead said impulsively: 'it would be nice to be in love on a day like this.'

'Perhaps it is the weather,' Eliot replied, 'but I had a letter from a girl in Boston this morning whom I have not seen or heard from for years and years. It brought back something to me that I had not known for a long time.' He remembered, perhaps, a far-off girl singing 'May Morning' in a Boston drawing-room, and sending red roses from Merton College, Oxford (via Conrad Aiken) for her Saturday performance in a play in December 1914. Emily Hale was now 36, but to Eliot she was still the 'girl' of memory, with her dark hair, violet eyes, and fair skin.

Emily Hale had first met Eliot as a family friend, possibly as early as 1908. She epitomized the pre-war Boston of Eliot's youth, and, from about the time of his mother's death in 1929, became the focus for his nostalgia for his origins, the shades that now called and gestured behind the grey rocks of the New England shore. After fifteen years of exile, she provided the relief of old memories of a common past from which she had never been diverted, as Eliot had been diverted by what Henry James would have called, in short, Europe. Her years of teaching in Milwaukee and California hardly touched her, in that she remained always recognizably a Bostonian.

Emily Hale was born three years after Eliot, on 27 October 1891, into the same Boston Brahmin milieu as Eliot's family. She was actually born in East Orange, NJ, but her parents returned to Boston, and she spent her childhood on Chestnut Hill. Her father, Edward Hale, was an architect turned Unitarian minister, who became first assistant to Edward Everett Hale at the Southern Congregational Church in Boston. Emily later said that her father had been like another son to Edward Everett Hale, though they were not relations.

Early in her life came a series of tragedies. First, her mother took ill after the death of an infant brother, and remained a permanent mental invalid, unable to care for her child. Then, while Emily was still young, Edward Hale died, and she was sent to live with her mother's sister. The Revd and Mrs John Carroll Perkins were old friends of the Eliot family and stood, like them, at the very heart of Boston Unitarianism. Eliot once joked to Stead that his family's relation to Boston Unitarianism was like that of the Borgias to the Papacy.

Emily grew closer to her Aunt Edith and Uncle John, and they gave her the advantages that were then considered appropriate for well-bred young women. She was sent to Miss Porter's fashionable boarding-school at Farmington, Connecticut, where she probably met her lifelong friend, Margaret Farrand, who was to become a teacher at Smith College. For the rest of their lives they wrote to each other every fortnight, on alternate weeks. These letters were strictly confidential—after Margaret's marriage to Willard Thorp in 1931, she never showed them to her husband, and took care to destroy them before her death.

After completing high school, Emily was presented to Boston society. A portrait painted of her at this time shows a poised young woman, in a long, pink lace dress, seated with a posy of flowers on her lap. Her dark brown hair is drawn up, and her back straight and long. She was tall, with a poise even more arresting than her beauty.

It was now, at about the age of 17, that she became friends with Eleanor Hinckley, Eliot's first cousin (Mrs Hinckley and Eliot's mother, Charlotte Stearns, were sisters). In 1908 Eliot, a junior at Harvard, was a frequent visitor: with his parents far away in St Louis, this was a home from home. At first, Emily was no more than a family friend, while Eliot engaged in a flirtation with a more sophisticated older woman, Adeline Moffat, but after his return from Europe in 1911, a shared interest in drama brought them together.

Eleanor Hinckley, who wanted to be a playwright, and took the famous 'Drama 47' course at Harvard, also organized family theatricals, and on one occasion Eliot played the hypochondriacal Mr Woodhouse, and Emily the snobbish Mrs Elton, in a scene from *Emma*. Emily was keen to go on the stage professionally but her aunt and uncle would not allow it, so she had to content herself with private performances. She had a natural stage presence and a resonant voice that were to prove effective in commanding comic roles. Later, as a teacher at Smith College, she created a sensation one Valentine's day, when guests were invited to come to Laura Scales House dressed as books. Emily chose Edith Wharton's *A Backward Glance*. She put on an Edwardian gown of pale green silk that had belonged to her mother or aunt. Her hair was dressed; her neck bejewelled. Carrying an old silver mirror held at arm's length, and peering imperiously into it, she made a dramatic 'entrance'.

When Eliot did not return from Europe after his second visit in 1914–15, some of Emily's family connections concluded that he had not married her because her mother's mental illness might be hereditary. This seems unlikely. Even less likely was the noble fantasy with which Emily consoled herself, that with the outbreak of war Eliot, not strong enough to fight himself, took a schoolmaster's job in England in order to release a fighting man. The fact is that in London Eliot had met Pound, who turned him away from his prospects as Harvard philosopher with heady incitements to fame as Modern poet. Eliot's change of direction is evident in new poems in 1915 which look down on Bostonians ('Cousin Nancy' and 'Aunt Helen') and Harvard academics with scathing contempt. It was then that he met and suddenly married the flamboyant Vivienne Haigh-Wood.

In 1915 a curtain drops on Emily's life. In that year she moved to Seattle, and it was perhaps then that she enrolled at the Cornish School of Drama. She had to find a way of earning her living. Although she had a good home with her uncle she also had, I would guess, a degree of independence, and a continuing need to express her talent for the theatre. If she could not go on the stage, she could teach and, accordingly, took several courses, one of them at the Leland Powers School of Dramatic Art in Boston, and one at the Speech Institute in London. Because her formal qualifications to teach drama were meagre, she was forced to find her way into colleges as an administrator. In 1918 she took up her first post as Assistant Matron of the dormitories at Simmons College, Boston. Unofficially she was a drama coach, while as a matron she nursed efficiently in the influenza epidemic that followed the war. Calling her a 'superior type', the college authorities appointed her Director of Dormitories from 1919 to 1921.

In 1921, when she was 30, she took a combined post as administrator and Assistant Professor of Speech and Dramatics at Milwaukee Downer College (which eventually became part of the University of Wisconsin). There she acted in the plays she produced, and a splendid collection of photographs shows her as a highly painted, arrogant French marquise. She remained in Milwaukee through the twenties, and it was during her last two years there, 1927–9, that she began writing to Eliot.

When she ventured to approach him after thirteen years, she asked no more than advice on what modern literature to use in her classes. She was a conscientious teacher who prepared carefully before presenting her material, and in 1929 she was concerned about a lecture that she was to give on modern poetry. Eliot sent her Hulme's *Speculations*, and asked her to send him the text of her lecture. Emily made light of these formal first exchanges, but on Eliot's side an immediate picture of a woman's spiritual presence is evident in *Shakespeare and the Stoicism of Seneca* (1927), *Dante* (1929), and *Ash Wednesday* (1927–30).

Their eventual reunion was propelled by a dream that was given the space of long separation to take hold. To dream of meeting an old love, after many years, was a replay of Dante's reunion with Beatrice on the verge of Paradise, as Eliot saw it the recrudescence of old passion in a new emotion, in a new situation which 'comprehends, enlarges, and gives meaning to it'. Like Beatrice, Eliot's Lady forgives the poet his defection. In an essay on Dante, which he owned to be autobiographical, Eliot quotes and translates these moving lines:

Olive-crowned over a white veil, a lady appeared to me. And my spirit . . . without further knowledge by my eyes, felt, through the hidden power which went out from her, the great strength of the old love. As soon as the lofty power struck my sense, which already had transfixed me before my adolescence, I turned leftwards . . . to say to Virgil: 'Hardly a drop of blood in my body does not shudder: I know the tokens of the ancient flame.'

Eliot once discussed with Stead the way that Dante's love for Beatrice passed over into love of God in the *Vita Nuova*. 'I have had that experience', Eliot said eagerly and rather shyly, and then lapsed into silence.

Emily Hale came to England in the summer of 1930, and stayed, at least some of the time, in Burford, near Oxford. A few months later, Eliot confided to Stead that he had found a certain happiness that made celibacy easy for the first time. Emily did not disappoint Eliot's dream of beneficence. She was a warm, loyal person, and found it easy to pity him. She later told an ex-pupil: 'A very dear friend of mine was involved, early in life, with a weak and selfish and seriously unstable partner. For many years I observed the blighting effect of this marriage on my friend.' To Eliot, she had a kind way and a nice smile, as he described her in one of his unpublished Cat poems, where Miss Hale is the one Old Morgan (the Faber office cat) would most like to see.*

It was in the summer of 1930 that Eliot identified Massachusetts as his real ancestral habitat. This assertion to Stead on 20 June follows his completion of the final part of *Ash Wednesday*, where the higher dream moves to the New England shore. The poet's

---

* T.S.E. wrote two Cat poems to Emily Hale. The one referred to above is untitled. The other is called 'Morgan Tries Again'. He wrote her one other comic poem, called 'A Country Walk'. She dated the Cat poems about 1937 or 1938. All three are in Princeton University Library.

wings, which were collapsed in the opening section, and then strengthened by the quiet presence of the 'life-giving' Lady, now fly seaward, as his memory stirs of sailing off Cape Ann, a scene he always associated with divine intimations. Across space and time he hears the whisper of ancestral voices of New England divines who spoke the Lord's Word. Eliot sees these family figures not as individuals, but collectively as shades who beckon him to the exalted state for which he is destined. Then he must return to his own time where he must live in 'exile' from the promised land that he sees is still, after all, his inheritance.

Exile's dreams bring back the granite rocks of the New England shore, the bent golden-rod, and the salt smell of the sandy earth. Once more, he hears the distant call of ghostly forebears as they drift back into the fastness of their own time, and, with that, his resolve hardens. He too must speak the Word everlasting. And over this resolve presides the blessed woman, nameless, faceless, known only in a series of subordinate clauses, 'Who . . . / Who . . .', who walks with the 'new years', who restores his power to write 'new verse', who bends her head in silent acceptance, and gives the all-important sign that the Word would come (an answer to Gerontion's hopeless cry in 1919: 'We would see a sign!'). The spirit of his creative fount, of the shaping scenes of his New England youth, she alone can bring him back to the New World. In *Marina*, written in July 1930 and published in September, while Emily was still in England, Eliot effected his imaginative crossing. He resigns his present stale life for 'the new ships' as he homes in hope, lips parted, towards a pure woman. The lone voyager battered, almost broken as he crosses from one life to another, comes at last to a haven of domestic love—but it is not ordinary love, and the woman is not human in the ordinary sense. In this meeting, some emotions have been purified away so that others, ordinarily invisible, become apparent. The woman on the New England shore appears as the embodiment of a divine call. So, he returns to where he belonged. In a draft of this poem the old forms re-form in a New World.

After so many years in London, Eliot said in August 1930, he had to go back to Massachusetts and Missouri for natural imagery. *Marina*'s setting is actually Casco Bay, Maine, with the fog in the fir trees that crowd the Maine shore. He explained that he felt enough of a Southerner to be somewhat alien in Massachusetts so that, even in his youth, the New England of his associations existed more in Maine, the destination of his most ambitious sailing ventures. It is there, in imagination, that his voyager is 'awakened' as the longed-for call comes through the fog, and suppressed emotion for the long-lost yet familiar woman breaks out in a cry of recognition.

The demands of the higher dream were twofold. It meant the recall of New England, with the native's nostalgia for what Robert Lowell called 'that short moment when the New World and God were one'. For Eliot this fused with nostalgia for Emily Hale, who appeared to all who remember her as the very embodiment of old Boston, from the clear, precise diction of her old Boston accent to the conscious perfection of her manners and conduct. She was, though, only a convenient focus for Eliot's evolving idea of love.

He refined his idea of love to pose an almost unattainable ideal. It began as early as 1910 with a ruthless rejection of the body's uncleanness, with the same old New England rigour of Emerson who said plainly, 'the sublime vision comes to the pure and simple soul in a clean and chaste body'. Long before Eliot made his commitment to Christianity, a fierce disgust for the flesh, its masturbations and defecations, appeared in his unpublished 'First Debate between Body and Soul', in the violence of the three martyr poems of 1914-15, and again in *The Waste Land*'s ruthless 'Burning burning burning burning' of the sexually polluted flesh. Yet, all the time there was an incipient feeling of reverence, easily bruised by rude contact with the meanness of twentieth-century urban squalor, but surfacing again in response to the radiant young Emily Hale with her long, shining hair. Eliot's imagination dwelt on a beloved woman's hair, the light on it in 'La Figlia' (1912), wet in *The Waste Land* (1922), loosened in *Ash Wednesday* (1930), sweet brown hair blown over the mouth: in this post-conversion poem, desire returns, but is feared now as a distraction.

For the only way that Eliot could admit a renewed love was with reverence and chastity. On this basis, the sudden emotional fertility that came to Eliot between 1927 and 1930 was like an unlooked-for blessing after years of hollowness. In imagination the Lady 'of memory' took shape. She is veiled from sight (they did not meet for some time); veiled too to protect the senses. And after the gap of sixteen years, she is unknown, except as the one who made strong the fountain—of this power Eliot was certain—whatever else might have changed.

Emily replaced Vivienne as Eliot's muse in *Ash Wednesday*, the long conversion poem written between 1927 and 1930. Looking at this as the pivotal poem in Eliot's career, A. V. C. Schmidt suggested that it is too often seen as a poem about penitence, and not enough as a poem about love. In the earliest section, published in December 1927, a man sheds his past with his flesh. Reverence replaces diseased forms of love: frustration and, worse, the satiety of barren lust. The poem forecasts the vow of chastity that Eliot took, soon after, in March 1928:

> Terminate torment
> Of love unsatisfied
> The greater torment
> Of love satisfied.

His idea of love does not fit our usual categories, sexual and romantic. 'The love of man and woman', he said in 1929, 'is only explained and made reasonable by the higher love, or else is simply the coupling of animals.' He wished to transform the energy of desire into something absolute and lasting. The contemporary word 'sublimation' bore some relation, but he had to go back to the late Middle Ages for an exact state of exalted feeling which, he insists, we no longer experience. Dante said of Beatrice, *imparadisa la mia mente*. So Eliot's Lady will direct him to the paradise of 'the garden'. In an epigraph to a draft, the poet declares, as he waits on his Lady: 'The hand of the Lord was upon me.'*

Eliot wanted nothing less than perfect love, part of his longing for 'the impossible union'. This is how he explained it in 1935 in one of his numerous buried essays: 'I mean the turning away of the soul from desire . . . of drugged pleasures, of power, or of *happiness*. I mean "love", in the sense in which "love" is the opposite of what we ordinarily mean by "love" (the desire to possess and to dominate or the desire to be dominated by).'

In the second half of his life Eliot was more concerned with love

---

* Ezekiel 1: 3. 'The hand of the LORD was there upon him.'

than in his early years: love's essence in memory that inspired the poetry of the new life; divine Love; and, much later, the discovery of marital love. The automatic disgust with almost all women in the early poems came from hardly seeing them as they slot into given roles: inciters or prey of low desire. Eliot remained 'frightened' of women through his middle years (he used this phrase often in conversation with his friend, Mary Trevelyan). To unbend, he needed the reassurance of many unthreatening contacts. Frequent church-going, Mary prescribed for their friendship, after it was shaken by her proposal of marriage in 1949.

Emily Hale was exempt from low desire. Though not ethereal herself, and not in the least silent as a teacher of speech and drama, she became the model for silent, ethereal women in Eliot's poetry, La Figlia, the hyacinth girl, the Lady, who all elevate the poet's spirit. To consummate such a love might tarnish the dream that made the art, or more accurately, art's climax. So she was set to play the roles of Virgin and kinswoman waiting faithfully for the battered traveller. This was hard on Emily Hale, for as no real woman fits Eliot's reductive image of rank temptress, so no real woman could approximate his dream of purity.

After ten years of teaching, Emily allowed herself a three-year interim from 1929 to 1932. This, she said in July 1931, 'has given me an excellent opportunity to review the past, as well as to plan for the future, in my work'. On a visit to England she took the opportunity to go to Dublin to learn about the Irish theatre. By 1931 she needed to find work again—perhaps she had to support her sick mother as well as herself—and put out tentative feelers to President Ernest Jaqua of Scripps College in Claremont, California. It was newly founded in 1926, and one of only two colleges for women west of the Mississippi. Emily was at first hesitant about leaving her mother in the East, but in January 1932 she accepted Jaqua's offer of a two-year appointment as Assistant Professor of Oral English (she insisted on professor, not instructor). Her courses (she named them) were to be 'Dramatic Interpretation' and 'English Speech and Diction'. In preparation, she began to study phonetics.

At this time Eliot was deciding to come to America for the first time since a brief visit in 1915. He accepted the Charles Eliot

Norton professorship at Harvard for the academic year 1932/3. Emily would have preferred not to be on the other side of the continent, but they did plan to meet, for, on 15 May, she wrote rather apologetically to Jaqua for an advance College calendar for the fall of 1932, as 'others' plans beside my own, are dependent upon your dates'.

The two years at Scripps, 1932–4, were the climax of Emily Hale's life both in her relationship with Eliot and in her work where, for the first time, she was able to concentrate on teaching drama. As Head of House at Toll Hall, elegant and gracious, Emily (now 41) was admired by her pupils, who imitated her style and manners (they noticed how she made a ceremony of a refectory meal), and visited her constantly. She maintained a firm balance between cordiality and reserve, with a look that said 'don't intrude further' which her pupils respected. Laurabel Neville (Hume) recalled Emily as

a vivid interesting person who attracted a large following of stage-struck girls; I was one of them. Part of her charm was her dignity and gaity, and her Bostonian accent. And the weekly letters that came to her in blue envelopes with British postage from the great poet. She had a leather folder in her room with two pictures of Mr. Eliot, autographed to her. . . . She lived on campus, and her living-room was a mass of color. She wore a black silk dressing-gown (you can see that we visited her informally and often) covered with gold brocaded Chinese dragons. Her many bookshelves were covered with photographs, some of her appearing in plays in Boston—*non*-professional productions, she assured us. Evidently her family had not approved of Emily going on the stage at all, but she persisted in her slightly shocking activities anyhow. She was an excellent director.

Emily made friends also amongst the faculty, with Ruth George, an English teacher who wrote poetry (Emily later sent her book to Eliot), and with Paul Havens, also teaching English, and his intelligent wife, Lorraine, who became one of Emily Hale's lifelong correspondents. Several Americans, now in their seventies, eighties, and nineties, remember her clearly at this happy time. One of her most perceptive students was Marie McSpadden (Sands), who designed sets for her productions, and came to know her well. She remembered a pretty woman who seemed young, with her soft features, but who could be authoritative as a drama coach:

She was a lonely person, highly sensitive and prone to attach herself to a few students. I think she considered most of us 'primitive', a viewpoint often held by New Englanders. Young Californians are prone to be active in the out-of-doors. My friends and I were absorbed in studies only fifty percent of the time. This confused and amused Emily but she liked to share our activities and meet our 'dates'. . . . I remember her directing a Molière play very successfully.

I cannot remember her having men friends—perhaps because of her caring for Eliot, perhaps being shy and lacking the opportunity to meet other men on a women's campus.

Financially she had to be careful. I don't think that she had independent funds, although her aunt in Boston was close to her. However, she did purchase a small Ford roadster and on one spring vacation she and I drove to Yosemite National Park, the beauty of which deeply impressed her. She also was fond of attending concerts and plays in Los Angeles, a forty-minute drive from Scripps.

Drama began to take a more prominent place at the college. Under Miss Hale, the languishing Siddons Club sprang to life with her first production, *La Locandiera* (*The Mistress of the Inn*), an eighteenth-century comedy by Carlo Goldoni. The girls were soon abandoning themselves to grandiloquent bows and Italian oaths on a moonlit balcony. Later that year she put on Lady Gregory's *The Dragon*, accompanied by weird music and magic whistles, carrying a delighted audience 'through the world in a dream'. Another review praises Emily Hale's performance as Lady Bracknell in the Padua Players' production of *The Importance of Being Earnest*:

Miss Hale as Lady Bracknell dominated the play with one sweep of her lorgnette. She provided the motivating character, and combined social rapacity with a most imposing glare. Her make-up failed to give her the requisite years for the part, but her dignity of bearing compensated to some degree.

It was not long before the small faculty became aware of her friendship with Eliot. She spoke of him often, always as 'Tom', and was obviously in frequent touch. There was much excitement when she announced that the poet would actually arrive to see her in the winter of 1932/3, and would speak to the students on Edward Lear. Early in December, in preparation for his visit, Emily Hale made Eliot the subject of the weekly book talk in the Toll Hall browsing room. It was noticed that she spoke more about the man, whom she knew personally, than about the poet, but she did read some of his poems, and spoke of 1922–8 as his 'bitter period'. She saw him as 'a man of extremes, a man of undoubted faults and highest virtues'.

Meanwhile, Eliot was making a 3,000-mile train journey across the continent. Back in London, Vivienne lost touch at this point with the movements of a husband who had decided never to see her again. Only Virginia Woolf asked awkward questions. 'And you are now on the Santa Fe Railway', she wrote. 'But why? Where are you off to?'

Emily was waiting on the West Coast platform when, at 6.20 in the morning, the train arrived. What made the next few weeks different from all the subsequent years of Emily Hale's attachment to Eliot, is that, for once and once only, it was not a secret. Thousands of miles away from the centres of their lives in Boston and London, they relaxed their vigilance. In any case, everyone knew that Eliot had come all this way to see only one person. 'How else could he have been attracted to our campus?' said Margaret Ann Ingram. She recalled 'a flurry of undergraduate speculation of "something" between Emily Hale and Eliot'. Marie McSpadden Sands said that she frequently mentioned their correspondence to her pupils, and it remained her practice to share carefully selected excerpts with those who were interested.

Her new friends rallied round, and helped in Eliot's entertainment. Some gave him tea. Mrs Havens drove him to church, and, with the determined pride of a young mother, marched him upstairs to view the baby. Surrounded by so many well-wishers, there was little privacy. One day Marie took them to her mother's cottage on Balboa Island (between Los Angeles and San Diego), then a quiet place in winter, reached by a car bridge or small car ferry from Balboa Beach. She sailed them round the harbour, and left them on a sandy beach called Corona del Mar at the harbour's mouth. Eliot seemed delighted with the Pacific seascape, and afterwards, sent Marie a copy of *Marina*.

Back in Cambridge, Mass., Eliot gave Pound strictly private word that the US had done him good. There was a moment that spring of 1933 when he felt torn between America and England. From America he wanted, specifically, domestic affection; from England, something else he did not spell out, as well as a degree of anonymity impossible in America. In America he was still exasperated by the small-minded materialism of the virtuous; but in

England there was the eighteen-year nightmare of his private life—
like a bad novel by Dostoevsky, he confided to Paul Elmer More, a
Princeton theologian who had also come from St Louis, and had
followed a religious path that Eliot felt to have been much like his
own, in its striving, in its awareness of the barbarism of the times,
but above all in the fact that, as a convert, More had arrived at his
conclusions from 'somewhere else'. Both had emerged from
American Calvinism, a journey which, Eliot felt, no English
theologian was in a position to understand.

Drawn alternately to America and England, Eliot felt like Alice
passing through the looking-glass of a two-sided life. Fortunately,
the time of choice was long gone. Or was it? As he raced about,
from New York to Princeton, Virginia, Haverford, Yale, Smith,
Mount Holyoke, Bryn Mawr, Vassar (where *Sweeney Agonistes* had
its first performance), Providence, Buffalo, Pasadena, Minneapolis,
and St Louis, he tossed off jaunty letters to Virginia Woolf,
describing the Cabots and Sedgwicks of Boston and a wild woman
of Providence, the first ever to make eyes at him. She replied to
every one of his remarks, 'My! What a line you've got!' He seemed
delighted to be back on home ground, responsive to women
students at Mount Holyoke, amused by a restaurant shaped like a
bowler hat, and keen to pick up the latest popular songs. He liked
to sing:

> I met you first at Spring Street,
>   And then upon my word
> I thought I'd known you all my life
>   When we reached 23rd.
> I won your heart at Harlem,
>   At the Bronx you murmured Yes:
> We lost no time
> On that ride sublime
> On the Subway *Express*.

Eliot prolonged his stay in America into June. As soon as the
spring semester was over, Emily Hale returned to Boston where
her uncle was now minister of the historic King's Chapel. Eliot was
fond of the Perkinses, and called them, as Emily did, 'Aunt Edith'
and 'Uncle John'. They welcomed him to their home where, in the
hall, hung the portait of Emily as Eliot would have remembered
her, a rather regal young woman. Eleanor Hinckley was still living

Emily Hale's presentation portrait: 'Footfalls echo in the memory . . .'

Emily Hale at Scripps College, California, where Eliot visited her in 1932–3.

'So we moved . . . / Along the empty alley.'

'And the pool was filled with water out of sunlight'.

THE GARDEN AT BURNT NORTON

'Twenty years and the spring is over' ('New Hampshire'): Eliot at
Mountain View House, Randolph, New Hampshire, June 1933.

in Boston. According to Eliot's older brother, Henry Ware Eliot, jun., family reminiscences made for one of the happiest periods Eliot had known since childhood.

In the midst of family, in a city where Eliot was a celebrity, he and Emily were less free than in California. Dorothy Elsmith, a friend who lived at Woods Hole, provided a retreat, as she recalled: 'Emily and Mr Eliot made several visits to the anonymity of my home here [Ros Marinus], where they walked the beach, in quiet retreat from Cambridge publicity.' Mrs Elsmith also joined them, together with the Revd and Mrs Perkins, for a weekend in the Berkshires. Then, in early June, there was a family vacation which included Emily Hale, at Mountain View House in Randolph, New Hampshire. Eliot's poem, 'New Hampshire', is patently autobiographical. 'Twenty years and the spring is over': the poet 'grieves' for lost opportunity, but enjoys a moment of soaring happiness before his departure for England. He is 'between the blossom- and fruit-time', and experiences, briefly, a domestic idyll as imaginary children 'Swing up into the apple-tree'. The final glimpse of Eliot and Emily Hale together at this time is on 17 June when, with Dorothy Elsmith and members of the Eliot family, she attended his address at his old school, Milton Academy.

According to Lorraine Havens, Emily was actually in England during Eliot's hideaway summer of 1933. She returned to Scripps with an elk-hound, a present from Eliot, and wearing a ring that he had given her, although there is no mention of her presence in Frank Morley's detailed account of that summer, when Eliot stayed with his family at Pikes Farm in Surrey.

When Eliot visited Virginia Woolf in early September, he appeared rejuvenated: 'He is 10 years younger: hard, spry, a glorified boy scout in shorts & yellow shirt. He is enjoying himself very much. He is tight & shiny as a wood louse. ... But there is well water in him, cold & pure.' She saw it bubble with unexpected life. When she asked about Vivienne, he replied with some asperity, resenting 'all the past waste and exaction'. For too many years he had seen 'nobody'. Now, at 46, he wanted 'to live, to love'.

On 7 December, Eliot was tramping the pavements of Clerkenwell looking for cheaper lodgings. His foray into Kensington in October had proved it to be too expensive: three guineas a week

for one room. In Clerkenwell the bathrooms were uninviting, but
he could rent a room at one guinea a week, with suppers at one-
and-sixpence each, and half-a-crown a week for coals. The new life
was no longer a dream. Eliot's most pressing needs were to
restructure his outward life, and to avoid Vivienne. Before his
return to England he had toyed with a policy of incognito, not
without relish—it had amused him to imagine meeting Pound, also
incognito (shades of Eeldrop and Appleplex*), at some pre-
arranged and sequestered spot like Cliftonville or Reigate—but on
his return to London, soon found adequate containment in a
clergyhouse as a paying guest of his vicar, the Revd Eric Cheetham,
in his club (the Oxford and Cambridge in Pall Mall), and back at
work at Faber & Faber.

As a publisher who was also a good businessman, Eliot set
himself the challenge of making poetry pay and the phrase, Faber
poetry, a by-word. By the time that he stated this aim in 1955,
Faber was publishing the foremost English and American poets of
the age, including Auden, Spender, Day Lewis, Pound, Muir,
Robert Lowell, Marianne Moore, Ted Hughes and, later, Sylvia
Plath. Back in the mid-thirties, Faber & Faber was still a relatively
new firm and Eliot's publishing ambitions still in the making. The
tedious aspect comes out in letters to Pound. As Eliot toiled
patiently over Pound's disorderly manuscripts, struggling (with
help from Geoffrey Faber) to emend error-filled quotations from
obscure Greek texts, he reflected how relatively little publishers
have to show for their efforts to act as psychiatrists, labour
exchange, school of journalism and authorship, spiritual, legal and
medical advisers, and soup kitchen. The tedium is emphasized also
in his 1935 report for the Harvard class of 1910: 'I spend a great deal
of time talking to authors whose work I do not want to print. And
I have read a great many manuscripts, most of which are uninteresting. . . . I forgot to say that I am obliged to spend a great
deal of time answering letters from Ezra Pound, but my firm pays
for the stamps.'

It eventually became necessary to distance himself from the
infection which emanated from Pound, whose values became
wildly pro-Fascist, and, on 12 March 1934, he warned Pound

---

* Assumed imaginary identities of Eliot and Pound in Eliot's 1918 prose fiction
about two investigators of the obscurer London streets. See *Eliot's Early Years*, ch. 4.

against Mosley, the leader of the British Fascists. As Pound's publisher, Eliot also tried to curb the cryptic allusions in the *Cantos*. How could Pound expect Britons to be excited about a president like Martin Van Buren when they were unaware of Jefferson and John Quincy Adams?

Eliot was quick and decisive in his rejections of manuscripts— 'all out', he would often say at Wednesday afternoon meetings— yet his letters of rejection were kindly and hopeful. One such letter to a young poet and translator, Edouard Roditi, who was about 18, advised him to ignore both praise and censure but to criticize himself, painful as this is. Eliot advised the young Allen Tate to cut down on strong words for, he said, a strong word ought to be led up to and followed by words which do not demand so much attention. Years later, in 1943, he joked that the bulk of his literary criticism was buried in letters and in marginal comments on manuscripts. He set before young poets a standard of civilization against barbarism, as Kathleen Raine put it. He was attentive, too, to authors' needs. Stead once witnessed his anxiety to discover the address of an author who had faded into obscurity and poverty.

It was part of Eliot's job to help with general submissions, many of which were, of course, unsolicited. Brigid O'Donovan, his secretary from 1934 to 1936, recalled that, at the time, everyone in the firm took part: 'blood and thunder' went to the office boy; 'novelettish' novels to the secretaries; and those few manuscripts that might actually be publishable to the directors, Faber himself, Richard de la Mare, Eliot, and the other American settled in England, Frank Morley.

A fair share of Eliot's time went on his quarterly journal, the *Criterion*, founded in 1922 to establish an international current of ideas which, he believed, was a necessary medium for great art. As sole editor, he wrote regular Commentaries, commissioned articles, and selected books for review (doing many of the reviews himself). For almost two decades everything he read was shaping itself in his mind as, potentially, a judgement that would, in turn, shape public opinion: in the mid-thirties it might be doubts about Dylan Thomas, or admiration for Cocteau's theatrical ability and Saroyan's fiction—it was difficult in 1935 to get good fiction for the *Criterion*. It was altogether a prodigious undertaking which lasted until 1939, when divisiveness between European countries put a stop to cross-cultural exchange.

The social centre of Eliot's life, on his return to London, was the
Faber–Hayward circle. John Davy Hayward was to play an
important role as literary adviser and flat-mate in Eliot's later
years. He was a younger man who had made his first approach to
Eliot when he was an undergraduate at Cambridge in the mid-
twenties. The son of a surgeon in Wimbledon, he went to
Gresham's School, Holt, and from there won an Exhibition to
King's College, Cambridge in 1922. By the time he went up in 1923
he was already disabled by the progressive paralysis of muscular
dystrophy. His contemporaries thought that he had not long to
live, but he defied fate with his wit, his bright eyes, his resonant
bass voice in musical societies, and, not least, his comic imitations
of people and puffing trains.

For that generation of students, the seventeenth century was the
favoured age: Donne was their poet and Webster their dramatist.
George Rylands recalled John Hayward as the Fourth Madman in
The Duchess of Malfi, at once comical and macabre. He loved doing
all the madmen, especially the line in iv. ii: 'I have found out his
roguery: he makes allum out of his wife's urine, and sells it to
Puritans, that have sore throats with over-straining'. In another
play he acted behind the scenes a bevy of prisoners under torture,
producing 'some of the most blood-curdling noises ever heard in
Cambridge'.

While still an undergraduate, he edited Rochester's poems for
the Nonesuch Press. After he went down in 1927, he settled in
London as a professional man of letters, editor, anthologist, critic,
and bibliographer. In the twenties and thirties he published
admirable editions of Donne and Swift (including the first correct
recension of *Gulliver's Travels* since the eighteenth century), and
also a short life of Charles II. In his wheelchair, he went about
London with unconcerned ease. He would allow himself to be
lugged up to the second floor of a London restaurant for a book
collectors' dinner—he joined a dining club founded by Michael
Sadleir called 'The Biblioboys'—and then pushed into a taxi to go
home alone.

On Eliot's return to London, a group gathered round Hayward
whose members had a passion for Sherlock Holmes, and also
exchanged witty repartee in the form of light verse. Identities of
the Coot (Geoffrey Faber, who was bald), the Tarantula (John
Hayward, who had, as his friends were aware, a lethal bite), the

Whale (Frank Morley, who was large), and the Elephant (Eliot, with his notable memory) were assigned. The style of exchange between these characters has now dated. Their digs read like the kind of after-dinner jollity of men who avoid expressiveness. Their verbal play was a feeble emulation of the poetic star, Eliot, who was, at this low point, parodying himself.

His lyrical impulse had temporarily dried up. At the end of 1933 Vivienne refused to sign the Deed of Separation, and it became obvious that she would never consent to her husband's freedom. As he began to compose *The Rock* it was like cranking a machine. Then, too, with the rise of a new generation of poets, Eliot feared that he would soon appear an old fogey, and he began to play a caricature of that role, presenting himself as a man who tended to fall asleep in club armchairs.

What was happening at Hayward's flat at 22 Bina Gardens was the formation of a court circle around Eliot. His courtiers were tactful enough to make no emotional demands. As gentlemen, they refrained from intruding on Eliot's private life, and showed themselves content to engage with the limited personality of the joking Old Buffer. This was not the new life; it was merely its cover, a strategy for living in a public world. It was a world of men without women. Emily Hale was teaching 6,000 miles away. The wives, Mrs Faber and Mrs Morley, were out of it, at home. No woman in the thirties could hope for high promotion at Faber's, according to Brigid O'Donovan, an Oxford graduate who left the firm for this reason.

In this all-male clique, Eliot now took up Henry James's mantle as the Master. When facilities at Cheetham's temporarily broke down, Hayward conveyed to Morley the exciting fact that the Master had 'to shave and shit' at his Club. And the Master, no doubt aware of instant relay, went into little beyond the banalities of day-to-day routines. Any one entry in Virginia Woolf's diary, after one of her unafraid talks with Eliot, tells us more than Hayward's mountain of trivia. A devotee, hanging on Eliot's lips, Hayward seems not to have recognized the Master's inscrutable distance. Eliot's outermost casing was his formal public image of formidable authority. Beneath this was the secondary casing of the Director's daily routine at Faber & Faber, and the night-time jollities at Bina Gardens. Most people who write memoirs of the Eliot they 'knew' seem to feel a certain triumph to have got past the formidable façade to the comic performer and kindly, patient publisher, but I think they were nowhere near the hidden life. Its inner casing was another set of rituals: daily prayers at St Stephen's Church in the Gloucester Road, and, from 1934, duties as Vicar's Warden. This was the visible chrysalis for the invisible life that was now in the making. When the saint-to-be enters in *Murder in the Cathedral*, he speaks enigmatically of 'the pattern'. Eliot believed that there was an eternal pattern of action; but could even the highest human intelligence perceive it through the veil of Time?

The first logical step must be to shed the illusions of Time and all the useless schemes of the temporal order: the deceptive attainments of ordinary human love, worldly ambition, and political power, the vanities of all the fools under the sun. To replace these, Eliot needed a rigorous programme that would carry him across the perhaps impassable gap between time and eternity. The pattern of all such crossings lies in the Bible, which resonates through Eliot's new verse.

In one way the new life was not new: the model for spiritual venture Eliot had always known. It was conceived before his birth by a mother who, in poem after poem, plotted the course from the wilderness of this world to the Celestial City; and not only by his mother but, generations back, by the American Puritans who saw their task in a New World in terms of a Promised Land, and, in particular, in terms of Nehemiah who in 444 BC left Persia to govern Jerusalem, establish religious order, and rebuild the walls. Eliot himself picked on Nehemiah as model builder in *The Rock*, his pageant history of the Church in Britain.

Eliot had a mock competition on ancestors with Virginia Woolf. He set against the numerical importance of her Venns (Evangelicals, connected with the Clapham Sect), such weighty New England figures as the Revd Daniel Greenleaf, the Revd Obadiah Smith, and the Revd Dr Asahel Stearns,* the last a descendant of Isaac Stearns who had migrated from England to Salem in 1630. For these home models of migrant and preacher Eliot found more prestigious parallels in Europe. In 1927 he translated *Anabase* which

---

* (1774–1839). He served as state senator, and became Professor of Law at the newly established Harvard Law School. His book *The Revised Statutes of the Commonwealth of Massachusetts* (1836) became a standard text. The Stearns family had many distinguished clergymen and teachers, with names such as Isaac, Samuel, Abigail, and Ebenezer.

prefigures *Marina* in section ix where St-John Perse recounts a voyage to the New World: 'Such a long time now we were making westward . . .—Young woman! and the nature of a land all scented therewith.' Dante more than any other writer marked out the route from 'depravity's despair' to 'the beatific vision': a complete schema. What all Eliot's models have in common is the pattern of a life in which failure is linked to beatitude. He was attracted, for this reason, to Pascal, and the biographical essay Eliot wrote in 1931 reflects an image of himself: 'His despair, his disillusion . . . are essential moments in the progress of the intellectual soul; and for the type of Pascal they are the analogue of the drought, the dark night, which is an essential stage in the progress of the Christian mystic.' This is a stage of patient waiting on the Lord. It demands that one shed personality so as to concentrate on a mystery beyond the self. Eliot's model here was the seventeenth-century Anglican divine, Lancelot Andrewes, in whose sermons, Eliot said, one 'is finally "alone with the Alone"'.

Eliot's first success at sustained contemplation had come in the last (and, to him, most important) section of *The Waste Land*. There, for the first time, attention does not flit distractedly, but concentrates in a dogged way on the absence of water, the symbol of spiritual fertility. The concentration is so intense that water is, at times, imagined, and though it proves a mirage, the speaker does make some way towards a new poetic language of longing and prayer, using the biblical imagery of thirst and journey for a modern pilgrimage away from the sterile site of urban despair.

This act of concentration was hard to recapture, as the mental struggle shows at the end of 'The Hollow Men' (1925). In 1926, in 'Lancelot Andrewes', Eliot acknowledged the gap that still remained between the limitations of poets with self-centred emotions (Donne is his prime exemplar), and the austere holiness of Andrewes: 'Donne . . . belonged to that class of persons, of which there are always one or two examples in the modern world, who seek refuge in religion from the tumults of a strong emotional temperament which can find no complete satisfaction elsewhere.' Donne had something in common with the Jesuits or Calvinists in their understanding of sin, but Andrewes had the purer concentration. So Eliot reminded himself that there were still higher places 'in the spiritual hierarchy'.

Right action comes from right feeling, not from a given set of ideas. Eliot stressed the poet's commitment to emotion, 'precise' not sloppy emotion, and he tried to train it on a perfection beyond human limits. Only saints could aspire to such perfection, and in December 1934 Eliot fixed on Thomas à Becket, an Englishman in the twelfth century who became the most popular saint in Western Europe in the late Middle Ages.

In the eight years between the essay on Andrewes and the play on Becket came Eliot's new life, and with it some shortening of that formidable gap. In Becket he found a model who was not so different from himself. Here was a man to all appearances not born for sainthood, a man of the world, the able and all-powerful Chancellor of Henry II, who moved from worldly success into spiritual danger. Following his investiture as archbishop of Canterbury in 1162 (a wholly political move on the part of the king), he at once resigned his chancellorship, and declared allegiance to a Higher Power. So acrimonious was the dispute with an outraged Henry II, who stripped Becket of his properties, that he fled from England in 1164. For six years he found refuge in abbeys in France. When, in 1170, he returned to reclaim his see, he came to face almost certain death.

Eliot's play stresses the fact that Becket's sainthood was not achieved without struggle. This was no noble-minded Thomas More, but a man exalted out of a fair share of worldly dross and political ambition. Eliot said that a bit of the author may be the germ of a character, but that, too, a certain character may call out latent potentialities in the author. *Murder in the Cathedral* was a biographical play that had its impact on Eliot in shifting the balance of his new life from the shared course of love to the lone course of religious trial.

Eliot chose this subject despite the fact that the Canterbury Festival, for which the play was commissioned, had had (as might be expected) almost too many Beckets in recent years. But he was determined. Martin Browne, who directed the play, said that not once did Eliot consider anything else.

The external action is minimal: its focus is the last days of Becket's life, in December 1170, as he awaits his murder. His destruction, and the dismay of his priests and people, set off the inward triumph of the saint in the making. The crude act of murder is no more than the occasion for this inward action. He must make perfect his will as he moves in measure towards a death that is

God's will. When the abusive knights arrive to kill him, stumbling, drunk, and rowdy, what Thomas hears is the steady oncoming measure of his destiny: 'All my life they have been coming, these feet. All my life . . .'

We, the audience, are privileged to witness that rarest of all actions, when a man crosses the gap between the human and the sublime, shedding the last temptations of his humanity, and, at the last, living by a divine order. His defiance of his killers, there in Eliot's earliest pencil notes, is an unswerving intent to hold to his assigned role to the end, to give his life 'To the Law of God above the Law of Man'.

The novelty of this action is that Eliot dares to fix the spotlight on what is normally invisible: the inward moments of transformation and resolution. In his review, F. O. Matthiessen noted that the play's inwardness is 'of the sort that shows Eliot even more clearly than ever in the tradition of Henry James, and, more especially here of Hawthorne'. The temptations that beset Becket are exactly like the evil whisperers in Hawthorne's eerie allegories. Virginia Woolf, more hostile, called the play, 'the pale New England morality murder'. The one sees Eliot succeed, the other fail to solve the obvious problem: how on stage to make interior action visible? This was to be the problem of all Eliot's plays, and later he tried to solve it by shortening the reach of the interior action, but here his solution is the bold and effective one of embodying the whispers of Becket's past as four visible Tempters, who play on him with increasing subtlety.

The last and most dangerous is the whisper of spiritual pride: to die for immortality on earth, to envisage the saint's tomb and pilgrims in the centuries to come, or, even more insidious, to die to stand high in heaven. These dreams are the 'higher vices', and Eliot, projecting them through Thomas, knows well that to seek glory is the route to hell. To want sainthood is to undercut it. This is the divide, narrow but plummeting, between saint and sinner. At an early stage of composition, Eliot saw Thomas as a 'lap ahead' of all four Tempters, but in the final draft the fourth Tempter is unexpected, and this because Thomas has not yet achieved his necessary distance from spiritual pride. The closeness of the fourth Tempter to the saint in the making must be shown in production as a mirror image. Eliot told his brother that this Tempter should be a man of the same stature and the same type as the archbishop, and like him, clad as a priest and tonsured. He added that it was more important that this part be played competently than any of the others.

Eliot was offered the part of Becket in the film but preferred the role of the fourth Tempter, which he did as a voice echoing in Becket's head. Spiritual pride is the temptation that lingers in the mind of the elect, who is vulnerable to it precisely because of his unavoidable awareness of the possibility of election. Eliot once remarked that characters in plays should be 'dramatizing, but in no obvious form, an action or struggle for harmony in the soul of the poet'.

The way that Eliot spoke as a voice in the mind after a series of external Tempters, suggests the closest of self-encounters, and, possibly, Eliot's own relation to the saintly model: a flawed other-self, left behind on the wrong side of the gap between frailty and perfection. The meeting was perhaps where Eliot stood in December 1934–April 1935 as he wrote this play: still in danger of taking the right solitary course for the wrong reason, still fighting the last temptation of success, immortality. He certainly did fear damnation (he told P. E. More that he walked in daily terror), and at the same time he was blessed just enough to be able to imagine the crossing Becket made. His own recent quickening in a shaft of sunlight, in a Cotswold garden in September 1934, made it possible to conceive the absolute conviction of Becket: 'I have had a tremor of bliss, a wink of heaven, a whisper . . .'

Martin Browne has suggested that Eliot did not think of Tempters until Browne and Rupert Doone conceived them. This is not borne out by Eliot's preliminary pencil notes. It is true that the label 'Tempters' did not appear in these notes, but on the back of the fourth of the eighteen pages of notes, he jotted down the names of certain contemporary authors, numbering them one to four. These were, I propose, the germ for the four Tempters. It seems that Eliot (like Dante) worked from living models to frame his hierarchy of sin.

The first name that occurred to him was that of his ex-teacher, Bertrand Russell, and next to this name he put a two: this was the germ for the Tempter to power who speaks with persuasive reason. In the twenties and thirties, Eliot had attacked Russell repeatedly. In a 1927 *Criterion* review of Russell's *Why I Am Not a Christian*, he had stated that Russell's radicalism was merely a

variety of Whiggery, as his non-Christianity was merely a variety
of Low Church sentiment. Russell, he said in 1931, preached 'the
enervate *gospel of happiness*', bolstered by popular catchwords of
emancipation which may have been advanced in Russell's youth,
but were by now eminently respectable: 'What chiefly remains of
the new freedom is its meagre impoverished emotional life.'

The second name was H. G. Wells, and against it Eliot put a one.
A noted philanderer, Wells was the germ for the first and most
easily-dismissed of the Tempters. He represents the facile charms
of the senses and good-fellowship. In the first production, the first
Tempter wore a top hat to show the man-about-town.

Number three was D. H. Lawrence, the germ of the blustering
boor. In terms of social status, the third Tempter, who is a restive
baron, does not fit with Lawrence's working-class origins, but
what they share is rebellious heat. Becket is tempted to bring down
the whole social edifice. 'Samson in Gaza did no more', he muses,
and then, abruptly, turns from what would be the 'desperate
exercise of failing power'. If he breaks, he must break himself alone.

Next to number four are two curious names: Huxley and
Babbitt. Their connection with the fourth and most dangerous
Tempter is difficult. To which of the grandsons of the Darwinist,
Thomas Huxley, did Eliot refer? Did Julian or Aldous represent,
for Eliot, a substitute religion* which is how he regarded the
humanism of Irving Babbitt? In the *Criterion*, Eliot called Babbitt
(another ex-teacher) a 'real' atheist as opposed to Russell, and, as
such, to be taken more seriously. In a letter to the *Bookman* in 1930
Eliot wrote that his chief apprehension about Mr Babbitt was lest
his humanism be transformed by disciples into the hard-and-fast
dogma of an ethical church, or something between a church and a
political party.

What all four numbers have in common is that they are writers.
Eliot was pitting himself against rival opinion-makers a year after
his *Primer of Modern Heresy* which distinguished Lawrence as arch-
heretic. 'I am concerned with the intrusion of the *diabolic* into
modern literature', Eliot had said. '. . . It may operate through men
of genius of the most excellent character.'

The Tempters conduct Becket round his own past so that he

---

* See Julian Huxley, *Religion Without Revelation* (London: Ernest Benn, 1927) and
Aldous Huxley, *Do What You Will* (London: Chatto, 1929).

becomes a spectator of himself. As a chorus of the women of
Canterbury witness Becket inspecting his life, so we, as audience,
observe in turn as Eliot sets up before us an introspective structure
of watching within watching: the visible form of the play exhibits
the inner life as an act of detection.

The audience is compelled to abandon its passivity as spectators.
Goaded by the knights who come forward through time to justify
their murder as it fades swiftly from our sight, we are tempted to
deny what we have seen. Just as Thomas à Becket faced his four
Tempters, so the modern audience is tried by four killers who tell
us comforting lies, bolstered by our favourite catchwords of
commonsense, and by deft appeals to our insidious envy of
superiority, our secret delight at its collapse. The killers regret it,
they say politely, but violence is sometimes necessary. They were
only doing their duty. Eliot wrote this play in a period of the rising
duplicity and violence of fascist regimes. Just before the play went
on in America in 1936, he discussed with his brother the difficulty
of conveying his intended satire on the totalitarian state to a
country where the problem did not exist as in Europe.

Eliot gave here his clearest exposition of his essential political
position, which was to attack all forms of political power and
rhetoric. He implies that the only way the business of the world
might be conducted with any safety is on the basis of moral principles that derive from strict belief. For the mass of people, voluntary altruism, the humanist dream of the nineteenth century, will
not work, for altruism is, alas, not built into human nature. Eliot's
view of human nature is like that of Hawthorne, in his lurking kinship with Puritan New England, and his recoil from the optimism
of latter-day America. Both share the Calvinist presumption—
Hawthorne regretfully, Eliot savagely—that man's nature is
fundamentally depraved. The second Knight, the prime agent of
power, veils his depravity (as did the second Tempter) with the
plausible rhetoric of reasonable expediency.

The beguiling argument of the last killer, like that of the last
Tempter, is the most difficult to resist. It is the excuse of
psychology. The fourth knight, Richard Brito, puts it to us that
Thomas à Becket willed his death, actually provoked it, and was, in
fact, a suicide not a saint. Again, Eliot challenges the audience's
immunity, for we know this to be the very opposite of the truth,
and yet it happens to be just the sort of cleverness to which the

twentieth century has been particularly susceptible. It would be so much simpler to accept this glib interpretation that would relieve us from contemplating what is, anyway, beyond our compass. Should we let the saint recede to his usual hazy distance from modern memory? The poetic suggestiveness of the medieval drama is turned into our own blunt prose. The very language that attracts us with its comforting familiarity—hard, deceptively conclusive— is called into question. As witnesses, in our capacity as audience, we simply cannot swallow its lie. We are compelled to act, but what exactly should our role be: jury? Sleuth?

The most challenging role is to become an investigator of the inner life, the Watson to Eliot's Holmes, and this is, I think, the inevitable response of the active reader to all of Eliot's works. The title, *Murder in the Cathedral*, itself spoofs the act of detection as it invites us to it, for gory murder, a reliable box-office attraction of Jacobean tragedy, is precisely *not* what we're to detect. Martin Browne presented the murder in a stylized way that swerved from historical fact, as Eliot was fully aware: he mentioned to his brother that, in actual life, Becket, a powerful man (he was over six foot), knocked the killers about a bit before they got him down. No doubt, there were practical reasons for cutting out sensational action—the stage in the Chapter House of Canterbury Cathedral was awkwardly shallow—but everything in the play points to a conception of sleuthing that shifts deliberately from murder to the inner life. The culprits themselves are obvious and not very interesting—Eliot called them pathetic—beside the subtle moral dilemma of their victim and his sublime solution. For Becket, and for us, detection becomes what Poe called 'that moral activity which disentangles'.

Murder in the Cathedral was written for a special audience of church-goers on whom Eliot could rely to carry through this moral action. He told his brother that he thought its run would terminate with the Canterbury Festival in June 1935, but within a few months it opened in a small theatre in London, the Mercury in Notting Hill Gate. It was taken there by Ashley Dukes, who had acquired the theatre for the incipient ballet company of his wife, Marie Rambert.

Eliot never expected the popular success that the play at once achieved, because he tended to underrate the popular audience. The chorus of women of Canterbury reflect Eliot's regard for the select Canterbury audience for whom he wrote: sensitive to the Void beyond death, attracted to the archbishop, and fearful of the momentousness of God's hand in a drama that comes so close to their own small lives. The advantage of writing for the select audience was that Eliot did not talk down, as in his subsequent West-End plays. Conrad Aiken was struck by the women's language of humanity: 'That is perhaps the greatest surprise about it—in the play Eliot has become human, and tender ...' The chorus—partitioned between varied individual voices—represents all who confront the mystery of corruption and the mystery of holiness. Their humanity, which the saint's vocation precludes, draws the audience into the play in another way, through common feeling.

A young OUDS* actor, Robert Speaight, created the part of Becket. He was 31 where Becket was 56, and of middle height where Becket was tall, but Speaight's elocutionary skills shone in a play that was mainly speech. He had immense acclaim for his restrained eloquence, and soon became a leading actor in the West End. Martin Browne's production brought out the allegorical side of the play, and on occasion he himself played the fourth Tempter, stealing a seat on Becket's throne through the darkness cast over the stage. Browne presented the play as a medieval tapestry: one can imagine the static tableaux set off by the flexible exploratory verse that would bring the tapestry to unexpected life.

After an American tour, where there were full houses but unfortunate mishaps in arrangements, the play re-opened at the end of October 1936 at the Duchess Theatre, Aldwych, a few yards from the Strand. *The Times* hailed it as 'the one great play by a contemporary dramatist now to be seen in England'. Excerpts from the 1936 production were televised that December (when television was still in its preliminary stages), before an audience of three hundred.

As the years passed it became clear that *Murder in the Cathedral* was attracting a new audience for the serious theatre. Queen Mary came to see it in February 1937, and after nearly four hundred performances it toured the provinces. In Leeds the audience sat silent for a full thirty seconds after the final curtain before breaking into rapturous applause. During the war, in March 1941, the

* Oxford University Dramatic Society.

Pilgrim Players, with Martin Browne as Becket, presented the play in an air-raid shelter to an earnest and attentive East-End audience. Settings, props, and movements had, of course, to be simplified to the utmost to suit the shelter. They continued to play this emergency version for three years in shelters, cathedrals, and village schoolrooms. One performance was given in the basement of Lloyds Bank in Leadenhall Street to a deeply stirred audience, mainly from Hackney. The basement was fitted with bunks, and held over two hundred sleepers. Henzie Raeburn (an actress with the Pilgrim Players and wife of Martin Browne) recalled that for the first ten or fifteen minutes the form and language of the play seemed strange to the audience, but when they got caught up 'it was one of the most "shared" performances I have ever known'.

After the war, the play became popular for school and college productions. Eliot's old school, Milton Academy in Massachusetts, put it on in May 1948, and it was also produced at Eliot's retreat, the house of the Sacred Mission, Kelham, in Nottinghamshire. This was a training college for future Anglo-Catholic priests who could not afford a university education. The Kelham Brethren ate little and did their own housework. Their production of *Murder in the Cathedral* was rather bleak, to judge from photographs.

The full possibilities of the play were not realized until Robert Helpmann's highly theatrical production at the Old Vic in April 1953, which, as Brooks Atkinson observed in a superb review, proved that a play of literary and spiritual distinction could be made to fit the commercial theatre. Helpmann, an Australian who had made his name with the Royal Ballet (he was the first long-term partner of Margot Fonteyn), used his dance experience to keep the chorus in motion in a way that clarified its feelings: huddling in casual throngs, frightened, gossiping about the archbishop, or sweeping lightly across the stage like withered leaves blown around the walls of Canterbury by the winds of political violence. Helpmann managed to make the chorus dramatic, and also brought out the contrasting tones and tempos of different characters. The blustering entrance of the killers shook the play out of its thoughtful preoccupation with spiritual problems. Becket's Christmas sermon, when he perceives that he must act solely as God's instrument, was wonderfully pure, like a sweet interval in a storm. This was Robert Donat's great moment. Standing alone, downstage, outside the frame of the main drama, he delivered his intimate lesson with kindly simplicity in a patient voice that was very moving. 'He never intrudes on the part personally', wrote Brooks Atkinson. 'He brings to it his own humility as an artist. He sees in the part the devout exaltation of Mr. Eliot's view.'

Eliot himself thought Donat the best of the three Beckets he had seen. He remarked to Mary Trevelyan, who accompanied him to the performance, 'Speaight was an actor being an Archbishop; Groser [in the film] was a priest trying to act; Donat is an actor failing to be an Archbishop, yet the only one who gives some idea—too much perhaps—of what the Archbishop and Chancellor was like.'

This production brought out the balance between different parts of the play: the lamentation of the women; the anxious questions of the priests; the belligerent assertions of the Tempters; the simplicity of the sermon; the barbaric hostility of the knights, and their whining appeals to the audience. It was, said Atkinson, 'a grand design'. Everything, he said, in Mr Eliot's character and experience had prepared him for this work.

Here, then, was the given plan: a model life acting its part in a grand design. But where, exactly, did Eliot stand in relation to this design? Was he facing the difficulties of the fourth temptation? Or was he less advanced, still at the phase of waiting? I think he could imagine, but did not himself know with the certainty of Becket, the moment that pierces one with a sense of God's purpose.

A new life is the perception of a plan; it is also the tentativeness of the interior work of conversion. In contrast to the play on a saint's life, which took Eliot no more than four months, some poems took much longer, years even, because they depended so closely on the yield of his own life. His repeated honesty about hesitation and waiting is what makes these poems so true: lips that would—but can't quite—pray, and the convert who declares belief before the world but denies it 'between the rocks'. It was necessary for Eliot's life to authenticate the poems' progress. He had to accept the gap or Shadow* (as he called it) between, on the one hand, a programme so grand that he could not state it, and on the

---

* Eliot was interested in P. E. More's sense of a deep fissure in his work between what More called actuality of form and actuality of content. In a letter of 20 June 1934 he asked More if the fissure was less evident in *The Rock*.

other a weak, hollow man waiting and waiting for a call, for the message of the thunder ('DA ... *Datta* ...'), or at least for a fount of renewed feeling. Eliot always foresaw the difficulties: the process of transformation could be lifelong and agonized by fear of Judgement.

'I am afraid of the life after death', Eliot had said to Pound in 1919.

'This beats me,' Pound replied, 'beats me.' Pound was drunk on the beauty and culture of Italy, which was life enough. In Verona in 1923 they sat with Bride Scratton at the Caffè Dante towards sundown by the arena. Eliot, in some theatrical get-up with a little (not very clean) lace falling over his knuckles, was in the role of *il decaduto* (the decadent), but also, Pound recognized, Arnaut Daniel suffering in Dante's Purgatory for his sins.

In each successive poem Eliot told the conversion story from the angle of a further state: irresolute in 'The Hollow Men' (1923–5); ill-at-ease in the 'old dispensation' after his conversion in *Journey of the Magi* (August 1927); waiting in *Ash Wednesday* (December 1927–April 1930). Here he exhibits the remains of the old life: dry bones, scattered in the desert, waiting to be re-composed. This was the second ordeal after fear: to surrender all expectation. The warped old self has now taken that course so feared by hollow men, and what has made it possible is the consoling presence of the 'Lady of silences'. The bones 'chirp' in her imagined presence, content to put themselves in her power to make the man anew. 'When I find my own heart wrought upon, then I can best discover it to another', said Thomas Hooker in a sermon, *Saints Dignitie*. Like the American Puritans, Eliot assumed that verbal expression would validate the genuineness of religious experience. Some 'new verse' would rise from chirping bones if they could prove, by sheer endurance and by their gratitude to the Lady, that they deserved to live. According to the Revd John Cotton, the man with a new mind and new affections would have 'new Language. ... By these causes you may clearly discern whether God hath given you a new life or no.' From the pulpit of King's Chapel, Boston, in 1932, Eliot said that words had to wait on religious experience which one could not will. A godly and devout life would not suffice, only the strongest and deepest feelings helped by moments of insight, clarification, and crystallization which come but seldom.

Such depth of feeling came to Eliot in 1930 when he was granted the grace to declare his slow but sure regeneration. At the end of *Ash Wednesday* a lyric emotional climax was wrung from the preceding ordeals. *Marina*, written soon after, sustained that climax, and carried it to the point of spiritual birth. The most effective charge of new feeling came from Emily Hale—or a dream she inspired; the other charge from intense regret. Eliot's essays of this time seem to vibrate with personal import as in 1931 when he fastens on certain lines 'which surely no man or woman past their youth can read without a twinge of personal feeling:

> O God! O God! that it were possible
> To undo things done; to call back yesterday . . .

In his youth Eliot had shown, in unpublished poems, a curious avidity for the agonies of martyrdom. This was directed now through proper moral channels—Eliot spoke repeatedly about the need to discipline one's emotions—but, still, something idiosyncratic remained that was alien to mild Anglican traditions. He was what Jean Stafford said of Robert Lowell, 'a puritan at heart' in his liking for certain aspects of Catholicism: fasting and penance. Both would have worn hair shirts if they could have found them. In the absence of Puritanism, both sought a religion of equal rigour. The *Church Times* did recognize in *Murder in the Cathedral* 'a smack of the Puritan temper'. It is most noticeable in the awakening of the women of Canterbury to the pervasiveness of corruption. They smell death in the rose and a 'hellish' sweet scent in the woodpath, and they feel a pattern 'of living worms' in their own guts. Their senses are overcome by a flood of vileness—rat tails twining in the dawn, incense in the latrine, the taste of putrid flesh in the spoon—until they recoil from all living things in a swoon of shame.

They say: 'We are soiled by a filth that we cannot clean, united to supernatural vermin.'

Stevie Smith noticed how Eliot's poetry mounts with each touch of contamination. This horror is private, she said briskly, peculiar to the author who 'enjoys feeling disgust and indulges this feeling with the best of his poetry' and she went on to deprecate the way that Eliot touched that nerve 'which responds so shockingly to fear and cruelty, which Dante touched most surely of all, and one might have hoped for all time.'

There was a telling controversy between Eliot and P. E. More on the cruelties of hell, in which More, in the friendliest way, accused Eliot of Calvinism, and Eliot, equally friendly, accused More of heresy. More had declared that God did not make hell. This shocked Eliot: to him, hell was *giustizia*, *sapienza*, *amore*, the words over the entrance to Dante's *Inferno*. More thought eternal damnation too cruel to be a divine plan. Is your God Santa Claus? Eliot demanded. He perceived something above morals and human happiness, and worse than ordinary pain: it was the very dark night or desert. He spoke in June 1930 as though he had been or still was there. Then, later that summer, he wrote that people only stay in hell because they cannot change. Perhaps it was in the summer of 1930 that he began to feel the possibility of God's blessing, as in the lines he quoted from Psalm 130 in King's Chapel, Boston, on 1 December 1932:

> I wait for the LORD, my soul doth wait, and in his word do I hope.
> My soul *waiteth* for the LORD more than they that watch for the morning: *I say, more than* they that watch for the morning.

It seemed to Eliot that Providence had led him from one point to another: he said this to Stead who watched him become 'a man with a mission'. In *The Rock*, a pageant history of the Church in Britain (performed at the Sadler's Wells from 28 May to 9 June 1934), he hoped that a 'new life' would energize the spoken word, but not in the ordinary way. He looked to the dramatic speech of the prophets, Isaiah and Ezekiel. In his own Bible he marked God's call to Isaiah: 'Fear not: for I have redeemed thee, I have called *thee* by thy name; thou *art* mine.'

To take up the role of God's spokesman was, of course, daunting in so secular an age. 'CRY what shall I cry?'* was the refrain of 'Difficulties of a Statesman' (1931), as a leader tried to turn from power to prophecy. Riding away from the sycophantic throng who admire only the image and trappings of fame, he tries out Isaiah's voice: 'All flesh is grass . . .'. But, as with the effort at prayer in the mid-twenties, the will fails. Eliot needed, perhaps, the verbal

---

* Isaiah 40: 6–8:
The voice said, Cry. And he said, What shall I cry? All flesh *is* grass, and all the goodliness thereof *is* as the flower of the field.
The grass withereth, the flower fadeth: because the spirit of the LORD bloweth upon it: surely the people *is* grass.
The grass withereth, the flower fadeth: but the word of our God shall stand for ever.

licence of an expansive scenario, like that of *The Rock*, to free a prophetic voice:

> The Word of the LORD came unto me, saying:
> O miserable cities of designing men,
> O wretched generation of enlightened men,
> Betrayed in the mazes of your ingenuities . . .

The icy brilliance of Eliot's early years is replaced here by a new image of

> The Witness. The Critic. The Stranger.
> The God-shaken, in whom is the truth inborn.

As early as 1923, Eliot had told a fellow-American, Richard Aldington, that he had 'an inherited disposition to rhetoric' from innumerable ancestors who had occupied themselves with the church. But his most direct model came from the poems of his mother, like 'Saint Barnabas: A Missionary Hymn' which begins:

> Let me go forth, O Lord!
> How burns within me the unuttered Word.

There is a connection between the ludicrous Prufrock, wondering in 1911 if he dare disturb the universe, and the deadly stabs of Eliot's prophetic voice in 1934, castigating the decent, godless people whose only monument will be a thousand lost golf balls, and alerting them to the vacancy of the desert in their souls: 'The desert is squeezed into the tube-train next to you.'

Eliot said that 'the American writing in English does not write English poetry'. The difference did not lie fundamentally in local subject matter but in 'the different rhythm in the blood' which made it impossible for him to enjoy the kind of English verse that fell into 'an ecstatic contemplation of a peaceful landscape'. Eliot fell into a more judicial note. His old friend, Sir Herbert Read, said that one always had a slight uneasiness in his presence, fearing that he might at any moment assume the judicial robes. Whitman defined the American poet as a seer: not just an arguer, he is judgement itself. 'High up out of reach he stands turning a concentrated light . . . he turns the pivot with his finger.' And behind Whitman stands Emerson on his lecture platforms, saying: 'Let us affront and reprimand the smooth mediocrity and squalid contentment of the times.' He stands in the same New England tradition of moral earnestness as the Eliot forebears: Andrew Eliot in the eighteenth century, who preached to Boston society on 'a generation of vipers', meaning his audience; and in the nineteenth century William Greenleaf Eliot, the admired grandfather, of whom a classmate at Harvard Divinity School said: 'His eye is single. . . . There is something awful about such conscientiousness. One feels rebuked in his presence.'

The grandson's own 'cry' was the imminent decline and fall of civilization. This is the classic American sermon, the Jeremiad, developed by settlers in the seventeenth century in order to re-possess their dream of perfectibility. On the lecture platform, Eliot spoke less as literary critic than as moralist. 'I speak as a New Englander', he told his Virginia audience in 1933, and, as such, tried to re-introduce words like 'heresy', 'Original Sin', and the 'diabolic' into modern discourse. He believed that the disappearance of belief in Original Sin meant the disappearance of 'real' people who undergo moral struggle. Looking towards 'the dark ages before us', he predicted a time 'of cords and scourges and lamentation', of war and 'maternal sorrow'. Only saints would prevail, holding to 'the ultimate vision'. To this vision, Eliot could not personally lay claim. He was witness to its existence, but the reality of what exactly it was that he witnessed faded amidst the clamour of secular society, faded into the flatness of record:

> . . . set down
> This set down
> This . . .

The prophetic role was part of a larger programme. The two completed parts of 'Coriolan' were sketches for a progress that was to move from empty shows of power to a prophetic role, and then on towards a state of mystical elevation based on St John of the Cross. On 20 October 1931 Eliot told the critic, Middleton Murry, that he doubted that he could write the fourth part on the state of the saint, and on 17 February 1932 he wrote to P. E. More that he wished to discuss St John of the Cross when next they met. Of the third part he says no more than that it was writable. My guess is that it would have been about the recovery of spiritual power, still 'hidden' from the would-be prophet of part two, something like the recognition scene in *Marina*. Desmond MacCarthy, a Blooms-bury friend and astute literary journalist, thought that *Marina* indicated the nature of a longer poem that Eliot might write. It is as though, in 1930–1, Eliot were sketching possibilities without an assured sense of their outcome. This was the course of composition for all his long poems: he would write pieces which, later, he would pull together with some dramatic resolution that depended, to a degree, on developments in his own life. The unfinished 'Coriolan' is a rare case of a 'hidden' possibility, that hovered in Eliot's consciousness, but remained undeveloped.

In order to 'cry', a public figure must arm himself with renewed feeling for something hidden in his life that he cannot easily retrieve. Bombarded by images of his patrician family with their stern sense of public duty—authoritarian, hard-nosed men like Charles William Eliot, President of Harvard from 1870 to 1909, who once urged Eliot not to stay abroad and be a fool like Henry James—his mind instinctively turns away to thoughts that have no public importance. When he asks himself what should he cry, all he can hear are the sounds of small creatures, the firefly, the dove, emblematic of some lost emotion tucked under the soft wing of memory. An unpublished fragment, 'Hidden under the heron's wing', which Eliot wrote as a graduate student, supplies the elusive memory: it is of a woman crossing the lawn towards the writer. Consciously or unconsciously, Eliot did retrieve this memory, for he used its exact terms as Emily Hale advanced, once more, out of the past.

The climactic scene of the new life took place in Gloucestershire in the late summer of 1934. Preparations began at Scripps College on 19 February when Emily Hale asked President Jaqua for a year's leave to go to England. Jaqua (who was regarded by his faculty as a difficult, rather devious man) would not guarantee to keep her job open, but she went all the same. She must have been confident of Eliot's attachment to risk a job with scope for her dramatic talents, and where colleagues and students had become friends. The students' enthusiasm enabled her to stage four plays that year, apart from her courses. In November 1933 she put on an Indian legend; the Christmas play was a symbolist drama of Paul Claudel; in March 1934 she directed Shaw's satire, *Great Catherine*; and finally, in June, *Comus* in one of the college courts to mark the three-hundredth anniversary of its presentation at Ludlow Castle.

Meanwhile, Eliot was in increasingly difficult circumstances with Vivienne's continued refusal to accept their separation. In fear of her pursuit, he kept his address a secret from almost everyone. After a guest house in Courtfield Gardens, his hideout was the clergyhouse at 9 Grenville Place in the Cromwell Road. His rooms were drab, with hideous purple covers in the small, angular sitting-room, and meagre dribbles from the hot tap (he shared a bathroom with the curates). It was not a home. He had only a few of his books, piled on top of one another, for the bookcases had shelves missing. The District Line ran under his bedroom, and sherry and glasses had to stand on the sill. The only light relief seems to have been provided by the unknowing Sisters of St Elizabeth, who washed for the Vicar and Eliot: they carefully took out their pyjama cords for ironing, but always forgot to put them back.

Behind these dreary conditions lurked a fear that the years with Vivienne had scarred him permanently. There were times when he wondered if his present course, 'Denying the importunity of the blood', living solely for the afterlife, would destroy, not save him. He might lose all substance, and become 'a spectre in its own gloom'. Emily Hale was vital to him, not just as the Beatrice-figure of his poetry, but because she gave back the 'simple soul' of youthful innocence. Her staunch love had, if only intermittently, the power to restore his capacity to feel.

On 15 July, Emily sailed from Boston. On arrival she joined the Revd and Mrs Perkins who were already installed at Stamford House, Chipping Campden, in Gloucestershire. Emily was to have the adjoining Stanley Cottage. Eliot went there at once: on 30 July, he wrote to Mrs Perkins to thank her for the hospitality.

Eliot was a frequent visitor, according to Jeanette McPherrin, a Scripps student who stayed at Stamford House *en route* to France. Edith Perkins was a dedicated gardener and a keen photographer of local gardens. Sometimes Eliot accompanied her on these visits. When he presented her lantern slides to the Royal Horticultural Society in 1948, he recalled that Hidcote Manor was 'the one I loved the best'. His more tentative ventures with Emily Hale into the open countryside are recorded in an unpublished comic verse 'A Country Walk: An Epistle to Miss E—— H—— with the humble compliments of her obliged servant, the Author'. It is mainly about the Author's terror of cows. Emily added at the bottom: 'we often took long walks in the country about Gloucestershire.'

Eliot's New Life

The Perkinses had leased Stamford house from Mrs Sunderland-Taylor, who went to Yugoslavia in the summers. It was a graceful, early eighteenth-century house, built on a grassy bank towards one end of the High Street, with cottages on either side. The front bedrooms looked out on the church tower. Downstairs, a vast stone fireplace stretched the length of the sitting-room. That and the dining-room across the hall were well-proportioned without being too grand. The back window of the sitting-room looked out on what must have been Mrs Perkins's joy, a charming garden, rising in three tiers, each with flowers. It was an intimate, genial house and Eliot told Aunt Edith in 1935 that he came 'to feel "at home" in Campden in a way in which I had not felt at home for some twenty-one years, anywhere'.

Emily Hale wrote to Scripps in August that she was 'optimistic' under the supervision of a 'doctor' in London who was to make some decision in the autumn—this may actually be Eliot—and she describes her life in Campden with delight:

> Stamford House,
> Chipping Campden,
> Gloucestershire.
> August 27, 1934

Dear Dr. Jaqua:

Your very kind letter of over a month ago brought me very much pleasure and comfort: it happened to come on the morning when I was going up to London to see the doctor who is to supervise my care over here, and I left Campden feeling no matter what the doctor said your kind words and generous [statement] about my work at Scripps, would be the best tonic for me.

On the whole, his report was encouraging, although I can not know about his final decision until the autumn when further examinations will be made. I note with appreciation what you say of the year's appointment for Mr. and Mrs. Lange, and I shall hope that I can give you a definite statement about year after next in time enough for your own convenience in planning for that future day.

... Amid the beauty of these surroundings in which we are living at present, I am bound to be optimistic, and optimistic I wish to remain [as] to the final decision. If Mrs. Jaqua and you could but come in for tea this afternoon, you would find your way up the long curving street of Chipping Campden, which is the one street the town has, and on which stands houses dating as far back as the early 15th century ... made from

the beatiful Cotswold stone, for which this region of the Cotswold hills is
as famous as its once far famed sheep and wool markets. . . . We live and
keep house in quite a modern building, 1705 being the date over the door,
and a fine type of dignified domestic architecture which represented the
house of the well to do farmer at that time. . . . Back of the house lay
originally the farmyard and outbuildings—these are transformed into a
very lovely garden and garden sheds respectively, the garden rising in
three terraces—on one of which I now sit, looking thru' a superb old pear
tree, over the *stone tiled* roof of such warmth of grey, to the famous
church tower which rises in its glory at the *top* end of the street—a
landmark for miles around. We live a very quiet—to some a too quiet life
perhaps—as the residents in a town of 2,000 citizens. . . . All marketing
purchases are delivered by hand, the bread comes out of a large basket on
the arm of a man too small to carry it, or the milkman stands like a
reincarnated Roman charioteer, in his two-wheeled cart, driving his gay
sage pony, who knows at just which house door he shall wait, or the quiet
voiced butcher hands you a leg or a shoulder in a quite callous manner!

.   .   .

I walk two or three times a week to some spot of interest or charm not
too far away, and any stroll along these Cotswold woods or even the
wolds is its own reward.

Jean McPherrin joins us today until she goes to France. . . .

The political news in the papers is of course wholly centered on
Germany. . . . As yet we have no 'inside' news on German affairs as there
are few men who move in state circles here but my uncle, Dr. Perkins,
feels very sure much is going on in Germany of which we know nothing.
. . . The constant correspondence and articles related to war talk is
depressing to say the least.

.   .   .

My kind regards to Mrs. Jaqua, please, and believe me

Very sincerely yours
Emily Hale

It is not known exactly when in 1934–5 Eliot and Emily paid a
visit, so momentous for Eliot's poetry for the next eight years, to
Burnt Norton, two miles outside Chipping Campden, but all the
facts would fit late August–early September 1934. On 4 September,
Eliot wrote to Aunt Edith: 'My weekend, apart from being twice
the length, gave me still more happiness than the previous one.' In
Burnt Norton it is a time of 'autumn heat' both literally—the roses
in their second flowering—and as a metaphor for a mature love
which recalled the lingering, regretful desires for 'La Figlia' where,

long before, in 1912, Eliot had rehearsed an autumn departure from the garden of young love. The garden at Burnt Norton presented the temptation to replay that scene, that past, those other selves that might have been. 'Footfalls echo in the memory', Eliot wrote in *Burnt Norton*, 'Towards the door we never opened . . .' Their love was still unconsummated but, here, it was easy to renew.

Burnt Norton is owned by the Earls of Harrowby. Two years later, in 1936, the 6th Earl and Countess took up residence, but at the time of Eliot's and Emily Hale's visit, it was mostly unoccupied. It was the garden, not the house, that they explored: a formal, timeless garden with box hedges and a processional path leading to two great pools set squarely in the centre of a sweeping semi-circle of lawn. The 'brown edge' of the pool in Eliot's poem is its covering of old green moss. The pools were empty (as they still are), the larger slightly shaded by overhanging gold-green branches, so that the light fell on it in dappled fragments.

When Eliot says that the roses had the look of flowers that are looked at, it was not poetic fancy. The straight path to the pools leads through two lines of rose-bushes (the present ones are red) which lean out along the path, in attitudes of attention as one advances through an eighteenth-century arch or arrives, as Eliot and Emily, down a flight of steps, round the corner of the box hedge, to pass slowly down the path, in the heady scent of the full blooms. The faces of the roses, turned towards the walker and leaning slightly into the path, give one an extraordinary sense of advancing as in a procession through a divided crowd towards the arena of the pools. Birds call from the wild part of the estate below a brick wall to the right of the pathway.

To go to Burnt Norton is like discovering a lost, forgotten world, like the haunted garden in Kipling's 'They'. The entrance is about three-quarters of a mile's walk from Chipping Campden along the Stratford road. It is easy to miss the unidentified turn-off to a private track, which bumps along and curves across several fields until you come to the arched entrance, and beyond that a rose-garden, and beyond that other gardens laid out in the eighteenth century in the expensive taste of Sir William Keyt, a dissipated baronet who eventually became insane, and burnt the house and himself in it—hence the name. The garden has remained as it was, immaculate and silent, except for birdcalls. This hidden garden was the scene of Eliot's divergence into a lost world of experience.

Some momentous experience at Burnt Norton is reshaped into three accounts in Eliot's writings: the 'Bellegarde' sketch which he sent in the spring or early summer of 1935 to his brother in Cambridge, Mass.; *Burnt Norton* itself; and the rose-garden encounter in Eliot's second play, *The Family Reunion*. Each work relates an experience of love from a different angle. 'Bellegarde', written first, is the most physical of the three versions: a man experiences 'leaping pleasures' that release him from a mood of futility, and reach a 'matchless' moment, then fade all too fast, 'impaired by impotence'. There is a dramatic arousal, and an even more dramatic collapse that seems psychological, not physical, for pleasure is almost at once eroded by a self-lacerating mind that worries over the experience until it is virtually destroyed. The poetry is so intensely self-absorbed that a reader might well wonder if there was any partner at all, but the title, 'Bellegarde', does imply the presence of a woman, both beautiful and good, as in the novel to which Eliot alludes. This is *The American*, an early work by Henry James. The American in Europe, Christopher Newman, falls in love with a mature, gentle, aristocratic woman, Claire, who is guarded by her strict French family. Ruthlessly, and to the visiting American inexplicably, they abort the love affair, virtually an engagement, just as it appears to succeed. As usual, Eliot swerves from his source (as in his 'Portrait of a Lady'), overlaying James with his own idiosyncratic mood. In James, the pure woman retreats into a convent, where she immures herself beyond Newman's reach; in Eliot's 'Bellegarde', the object of love is again invisible (as the Lady of silences, behind her veil), but, here, more completely deprived of her agency. For it is the writer—stricter than the Bellegardes themselves—who shuts off the woman.

Two details in 'Bellegarde' suggest that it was a source for *Burnt Norton*. The woman is a silken, joyous, and not unwelcome apparition from the past: this may be the origin of the footfalls that 'echo in the memory' in *Burnt Norton*. There is, too, the matchless moment. The poet distils love's essence in memory, and then the evanescent moment slips from the mind when memory fingers it too freely. It is as though the poet examines the experience at progressively farther removes. The pleasure, first recalled, contains an element of imagination, a self-expansion which the poet longs to grasp, but it remains inapprehensible. Then, more detached, he sees greed and vanity in his delight. The human aspect of the experience proves all too easy to dismiss. All that finally remains is the act of recollection, and, not least, the great poetry into which Eliot transmutes this experience in *Burnt Norton*. The fragment, not much itself in the way of poetry, is solely of autobiographical importance, for, in it, Eliot explored arousal with an intimacy that is not likely to be found in any other of his papers.

The opening and conclusion of *Burnt Norton* rework the rudimentary 'Bellegarde' material as a deeply emotional encounter with a first love. The rapport is so acute that the ghosts of their former selves seem to walk towards a moment that transcends love with a glimpse of eternity, the still point of the turning world, as literally they walk the aisle of roses towards a pool filled with sunlight. This moment fulfils Eliot's dream in 1921 of 'Memory and desire', of a girl who had once inspired a moment of unspeakable bliss 'Looking into the heart of light, the silence'. In 1934 this same woman, now in the flesh, provoked once again that particular vision as the pool's unfolding lotus glitters 'out of the heart of light'. The man is drawn from 'un-being' into full being. Whatever actually happened at Burnt Norton, the poem records the darting, breathless, unforgettable bliss: 'Quick now, here, now, always—.'

Writing this about nine months after the event, Eliot addresses his now-silent companion with intimate certainty that she shared the rapport that called up the ghostly selves of their youth. As their footfalls continue to echo in their memories, so, now, 'My words echo / Thus, in your mind'. It is the most moving of love letters: the experience was over—it seems they will never know such bliss again—but the poetry recreates the experience for her, he tells her, as well as for others. His gift to her, perhaps his consolation for fading feeling, was to recreate their experience with such verbal sublimity that it will outlast time, as Shakespeare did when he says that time will wither his beloved, but the record will remain:

> So long as men can breathe or eyes can see
> So long lives this, and this gives life to thee.

Eliot's final record of this scene, in his play (its scenarios go back to 1934-5), gives more identity to the man and woman, as well as a psychological explanation for fading emotion. Two women are associated with the sunlit moment, the virginal, waiting Mary who is destined to become what Agatha is, a middle-aged college teacher. Mary brings Harry 'news' of a door that opens to 'Sunlight and singing' but it was, for Harry, 'only a moment, it was only one moment / That I stood in sunlight, and I thought I might stay there'. Mary remains bereft and resigned. The other sympathetic woman, Agatha, has actually had an affair with Harry's father, and awakens some replay of attraction in Harry. For Agatha, the feeling is simple nostalgia for love and unborn children, followed by solitary endurance.

> I only looked through the little door
> When the sun was shining on the rose-garden:
> And heard in the distance tiny voices
> And then a black raven flew over.
> And then I was only my own feet walking
> Away, down a concrete corridor . . .

For the man, Harry, it was a phantasmal union, and necessarily incomplete:

> And what did not happen is as true as what did happen
> O my dear, and you walked through the little door
> And I ran to meet you in the rose-garden.

Agatha replies that this 'is the beginning'. She means that, having passed through this door, there is no going back. The silent woman of *Burnt Norton* is here granted a voice and when she speaks of 'relief from what happened', she speaks for both. For her, the 'relief from that unfulfilled craving' is the simple release of natural love. For Harry the words apply differently: the mystical rapport fulfils a craving for visionary communion which had fed his dreams, until this moment to no apparent purpose. It is, at the same time, a release from his private nightmare.

Eliot explained further to Martin Browne in a letter that resonates with personal implications: Harry, he said, was partially de-sexed by the horror of his marriage. He could be 'stirred up' by a lovable woman but, because of his state of mind, was unable to develop this feeling into a stable commitment. His attraction to a particular woman warred with his general idea that all women are 'unclean creatures'. His solution is to find refuge in an 'ambiguous relation'.

In 2019, when Eliot's letters to Emily Hale are opened, we shall know better how he saw her. I imagine that with the Emily of his poetic dream and the old familiar Emily of his Boston youth, he was entirely at ease, but that he did not know what to make of an offer of natural love from a virtuous woman. He once remarked to P. E. More that the good were to him more bewildering than the bad, for they have an easy and innocent acceptance of life that he simply could not understand.

Compared with the inevitability of Dante's approach to Paradise through reunion with Beatrice (Eliot said that when they meet in the last cantos of the *Purgatorio*, Dante is already in the world of Paradise), his own reunion with Emily Hale in the paradisal garden left behind it a trail of uncertainty and introspection. Was it not impossible to recover the might-have-beens of the past? Had not all possibility of renewed love turned to dust in present marital circumstances? And then there was the quite different appeal of martyrdom. A few months later, when Eliot began *Murder in the Cathedral*, spiritual crisis became more compelling than the matchless moment.

So Emily Hale continued to wait, while Eliot put off a decision. She could not give an answer to President Jaqua that autumn, as arranged, and so lost her job. She was still in England in the summer of 1935 while, for Eliot, the exhilaration of the new life faded into a protracted ordeal. He had to atone for his abandonment of Vivienne, and try to expunge the taint left by their marriage. There was an increasing conviction that nothing must impinge on this ordeal. What Emily perhaps did not fully measure was Eliot's concern with pain, and his need, more pressing than the need to love, to recast pain as a dark night of the soul.

All through the thirties Eliot repeatedly met Emily Hale, and in his next most autobiographical play, *The Family Reunion*, he posed his continued dilemma: should a man at the end of a tormenting marriage seek salvation through natural love, or through a lone pilgrimage across a whole 'Thibet of broken stones' that lay, fang up, a lifetime's journey?

2. The Mystery of Sin

A NEW life sheds the old. The problem for Eliot was that the old life, in the form of Vivienne, refused to go away. From 1932 to 1938 she haunted him: there were her insistent attempts to see him at Faber & Faber; there was her continued presence in his memory; but worst was some obscure miasma of evil, the residue of years of wrong. He never solved what he called 'the Mystery of Iniquity'. It was, he said, 'a pit too deep for mortal eyes to plumb'.

A simple view, endorsed by all his friends, was that, since Vivienne was (in Virginia Woolf's phrase) a 'bag of ferrets' around Eliot's neck, and a bar to further progress, he must leave her. But, in September 1932, when he had tried to separate, Vivienne had run 'amok' through London. Distraught, she had seen him off at Southampton when he sailed on 17 September to take up his year's post at Harvard. From Boston, in February 1933, he had sent a letter to his London solicitor to prepare a Deed of Separation. He had enclosed a letter for Vivienne, and then had to face his return to England in June. He told a friend that the interim was like 'a phantasma or a hideous dream'.*

In the spring of 1933 arose the germ of a conflict that was to persist for some years. On the one hand was his renewed love for Emily Hale, sealed by the visionary promise that came to him in her presence in 1930, and was to come again in 1934: this would seem to initiate a new life of spiritual power fuelled by the goodness of love. Yet Eliot retreated from this promise into a further period of moral agony. The plan to leave Vivienne was foiled, not in actual fact, but in Eliot's mind, by his own scruples, his fear that he had been, still was, and must continue to be implicated in Vivienne's disturbance. As the years passed, he was drawn deeper into the mystery of sin through contemplation of the choices he had made. At some stage it became unthinkable to Eliot to pursue what to the ordinary man would have seemed an obvious solution, and accept the comfort that Emily Hale offered. By the mid-thirties the new life was no longer directed by the

---

* Brutus in *Julius Caesar*, II. i.

Lady of the *Vita Nuova*; it was dominated by 'the reality of Sin'. He said in April 1933 that only when we are awakened spiritually are we capable of real Good, but the danger is that, at the same time, we 'become first capable of Evil'.

The need to explore, diagnose, and eradicate evil was the prime motive for several great works which all had their origin in the gravest moral crisis of his life from 1934 to 1938. There could be no pat conclusions of guilt or innocence, but there could be literary re-creations of Eliot's dilemmas, with the complex suggestiveness of imaginative works. From a social, legal, and even priestly view, Eliot did no wrong in leaving his wife. In fact, a common view was surprise that he had not left her long before. But Eliot's works explore feelings that preceded and accompanied his dismissal of Vivienne; feelings that were not only socially inadmissible, but beyond the usual limits of prose. The earlier years of Eliot's marriage were the background to the macabre, unfinished play, *Sweeney Agonistes* (1926) and the later years of separation the background to the introspective nightmare of *The Family Reunion* (1939). These plays are complementary, for both expose a man's horror, almost possession, at the discovery of his capacity for violence. The strange feeling is not guilt, but a curious contamination that bonds Sweeney and Harry with their victims—or imagined victims. Even more curious is a certain pride that they should suffer so acutely for potential wrongs. Eliot described this more precisely in an essay where he says that it could be one's glory to be man enough for damnation. In April 1936 Eliot asked P. E. More if he could recommend a good treatise on Original Sin, and all his works from the mid-thirties to the mid-forties are preoccupied with private sin, the acute sense of which came to the surface during his prolonged struggle to be free of Vivienne.

From late April to mid-May 1933, Eliot was in Charlottesville, Virginia, and it was there that his resolve hardened. Where New England meant the quickening of new life (in 'New Hampshire' and 'Cape Ann'), the South, with its 'red' river, brought out the other, disturbing side to the complicated emotions of that critical year. His ominous poem, 'Virginia', spells the necessity for destruction that had to be the counterpart to renewal. 'Iron thoughts came with me / And go with me', he wrote of that Southern spring, as he waited to leave a wife who would certainly

Sept. 1932: Vivienne Eliot (on the right) and her husband visited Virginia Woolf at Monks House just before their separation.

Sweeney: 'Any man might do a girl in'. Rupert Doone's *Sweeney Agonistes* (1935 revival).

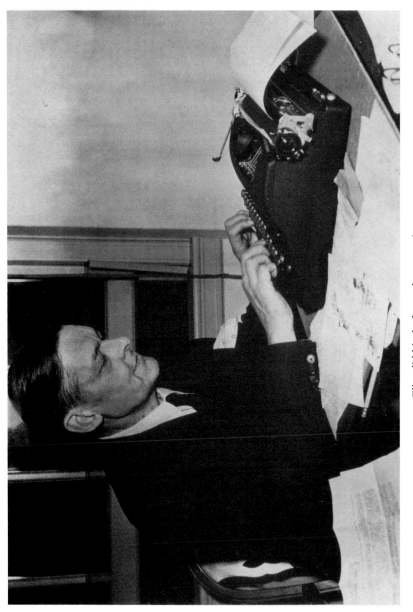

Eliot did his drafts on the typewriter.

The temptation of spiritual pride. *Murder in the Cathedral*, Canterbury, 1935 (with Robert Speaight as Becket).

fight separation with all the weapons of the weak. He became determined to remove Vivienne from his life at whatever human cost.

This decision was sufficient basis for a disturbed future. Eliot had always feared that to leave Vivienne would destroy her, but his difficult position was that to go on with her would have damaged himself. In future, he would provide for Vivienne, but refuse any form of contact even when she appealed to him in distress. It was this withdrawal from responsibility that Vivienne was to find unbelievable. She was, in effect, under sentence, though its exact nature would not emerge until 1938.

Eliot's judicial nature came, he perceived, from the witch-hangers of his family history. In December 1933 he told Pound wryly that one ancestor (either Andrew Eliot or, on his mother's side, 'hanging' Judge Blood) had sat on the same condemning witch-jury with Hawthorne's ancestor at the notorious Salem trials of the 1690s. Both writers inherited the need to inspect evil. Eliot owned to Pound that he just naturally smelt out witches, couldn't help it. But, as Hawthorne was aware, to venture on this activity is to risk misjudgement and worse. 'It shall be yours to penetrate ... the deep mystery of sin', the devil promises the impeccable Puritan in Hawthorne's most telling fable of the New England mind. As witness to acts of depravity, including his own, the Puritan then takes on a hypersensitivity to sin that will cut him off from human ties. For Eliot, the 'red' mood that he associated with Virginia was a strange, isolating state, beneath the rectitude of his manner.

Already, he was haunted by future torments. He went on to write a play in which Furies gain possession of the hero. The Furies lurk first in an epigraph that Eliot chose for *Sweeney Agonistes* in October 1926 ('*You don't see them, you don't–but I see them: they are hunting me down ...*'). As late as 1953, Eliot spoke of the poet 'haunted by a demon, a demon against which he feels powerless, because in its first manifestation it has no face, no name, nothing; and the words, the poem he makes, are a form of exorcism of this demon'. All through these fraught years of Eliot's middle age he seems to struggle against demonic possession, that disease of the soul that had so gripped early New England. Like *The House of the Seven Gables* (Eliot's favourite of Hawthorne's novels), where the family is haunted by 'the violent death ... of one member of the family, by the criminal act of another', *The Family Reunion* turns on a curse which is a compulsion to murder. In Hawthorne, the curse emanates from a wizard, and festers in a well, emblem of the inner life. Oddly, a well appears in Eliot's drafts as a possible scene of murder, and here too the curse emanates from a witch. As Harry may have been tempted to break away from the Furies through the natural love of the waiting Mary, so Eliot was tempted to break out of the nightmare of his psychic bond with Vivienne through an emotional commitment to Emily Hale.

Though the Eliots were physically incompatible from the start, they shared something that, at a deeper level, bound them: a mutual susceptibility to horror. 'As to Tom's *mind*, I am his mind', Vivienne wrote to Jack Hutchinson. His dark muse, she carried him beyond the normal: her nerves, like her hair, are stretched out tight; she fiddles whisper-music on the strings; she is ready to throw off decorum. In 'Hysteria', 'Ode', and *The Waste Land*, the woman's shadowy companion stares appalled—and fascinated. Already in 'Hysteria', written in Oxford in 1915, just before Eliot's marriage, an embarrassed man in a tea-garden tries to stop the shaking of a woman's breasts, while he feels drawn into the pulsating tunnel of her throat. In 'Ode' a bridegroom finds himself with a 'succuba eviscerate' who lies on the bed. Again, a man makes a vain effort at a semblance of decorum: the bridegroom, smoothing down his hair, is trying to detach himself from the creature who has claimed him for her own. The creature is not without her own outrage: she is cut open, her entrails exposed. The couple, like the Eliots, discover a mutual nightmare with their first damaging contact. For Eliot, horror mounted swiftly to a vision of hell: he spoke of 'horror of life' as 'a mystical experience'. For Vivienne, horror came from hidden motives. Women rattling prams behind her in the street might be 'dying to propagate their own loathesomeness'. Their menace complements Eliot's red-eyed scavengers creeping from Kentish Town and Golders Green.

Hope Mirrlees was one of the few of Eliot's friends who took trouble with Vivienne. She had come to know them through Virginia Woolf, who described Hope as impulsive, ecstatic, odd. She was attentive to her thyroid gland and her dachshund but not too absorbed to be attentive also to Eliot's troubles. She recalled that any ordinary remark could provoke from Vivienne a barrage of questions, her eyes staring at some hobgoblin of the mind:

She gave the impression of absolute terror, of a person who's seen a hideous ghost, a goblin ghost. . . . Her face was all drawn and white, with wild, frightened, angry eyes. An over-intensity over nothing, you see. Supposing you were to say to her, 'Oh, will you have some more cake?' she'd say: 'What's that? What do you mean? What do you say that for?' She was terrifying. At the end of an hour I was absolutely exhausted, sucked dry. And I felt to myself: Poor Tom, this is enough! But she was his muse all the same.

No date is given, but this mental nightmare, with its bombardment of impressions (as in schizophrenia), went back to the mid-twenties. In about 1924 Vivienne was having hallucinations in which a glaring figure would appear in chains or on crutches, with strange looks, shrieks, and imprecations, a frightful other self which, she told her friend, Sydney Schiff*, she must learn to accept. For Eliot, Vivienne may have been the one character in *The Waste Land* who is *not* projected from the poet's inner world of nightmare. The fact that she did exist validated the poem's mood of horror, for she enacted that swift conversion of fact into nightmare that was an essential strategy of Eliot's poetry.

'Perhaps not even you can imagine with what emotion I saw the Waste Land go out into the world,' Vivienne told Sydney Schiff in October 1922, 'it has become a part of me (or I of it) this last year.' Pound wrote 'photography' on the draft of the first marital scene in *The Waste Land*. It originated in a fragment called 'The Death of the Duchess', in which a woman plays a scene from a love-drama while her mate devises a more sinister plot of life and death. He longs to escape from her room, though this would end her. As the scene developed it was called, at one point, 'In the Cage', for the woman beats against the bars of mental isolation. The man, by contrast, craves solitude. Entrapped, he shuns the physical proximity of his wife by refusing to notice her barrage of anxious questions: 'Why do you never speak? . . . What are you thinking of? What thinking? What? . . . What is that noise now? What is the wind doing? . . . You know nothing? Do you see nothing? Do you remember / Nothing? . . . Are you alive, or not? Is there nothing in your head?' The gaps are filled with silent denial of her frantic plea for communication. He will remember only his own dream of metamorphosis: 'Those are pearls that were his eyes.' This secret

---

* Schiff wrote under the name, Stephen Hudson.

commitment is a drama which he must enact alone, as voyager or pilgrim. What did Vivienne make of that silent retort? At any rate, she applauded the frenzy of the woman: 'wonderful, wonderful'.

The prestige of normality since the Enlightenment, which isolates frenzy as a form of deviance, must not deceive us, said Foucault, as to its 'original exuberance'. Eliot gave Vivienne's voice a measure of expression in so far as it complements his own breakdown at the time of *The Waste Land*. Before the wife speaks, she brushes her hair before the fire, and it stands out around her head in fierce burning points, like the burning words that alternate with the savage stillness of non-communication. It is an uncompromising exhibition of temperamental violence: partners so evenly matched that their powerplay must end in deadlock. The husband's withdrawal is disguised as gentlemanly forbearance. Mockingly, he drowns out her voice in the syncopated rhythms of ragtime. The silent vehemence of his refusal to hear is matched by the outspoken threat of the wife to expose their torment in public:

> 'I shall rush out as I am, and walk the street
> With my hair down, so.'

Vivienne's feverish energy and Eliot's languor, what he called his *aboulie*, were perhaps short of manic and depressive extremes, yet, brought together, they formed a bond that Eliot had to escape but continued to use creatively. Theresa Eliot put it neatly when she said that 'Vivienne ruined Tom as a man, but made him as a poet'. The pair were strangely like the Ushers in Poe's tale of mental breakdown. The artistic Usher tries to bury his frenzied twin, the Lady Madeleine, in the vaults of the subconscious, but becomes enervated without her. She returns to haunt him, recalled by a mind that cannot be whole without her. So, in *The Family Reunion* and *The Cocktail Party* (1949), the wish to be rid of a woman is countermanded by her hold from beyond the grave—the insidious, still-living tie of prolonged intimacy. Its final damage is when a man finds himself reduced to death-in-life without it.

Vivienne, with her swift hatred and lashing words, was a grotesque caricature of what disturbed Eliot in his own nature. He was, Virginia Woolf saw, 'thrown like an assegai into the hide of the world'. His violence, controlled by the perfection of his manners, appeared in the early poetry as disgust with sexual licence, intellectual pretension, rotting cities, and Jews fallen from moral grandeur into avarice. This fallen world Eliot transmutes into *The Waste Land*'s vision of hell, of which Vivienne, with her anarchic abandon, was arch-embodiment. She was a deviser of tortured situations and also their victim. All this I think she saw, like a clever bad child. Eliot told Bertrand Russell that she had an uncanny astuteness, and in Vivienne's copy of *Poems 1909-1925*, he wrote that only she would understand them. 'He is a Prophet', she declared, recognizing the exact character of his vehemence.

After he left her she said that he had made her feel 'a sort of super-being'. His poetry displays her in overweening roles, playing Duchess, Cleopatra, or the lady of situations, conspicuously vocal compared with the ideal Lady of silences. Vivienne was not disposed to be her husband's inferior. Creative, febrile, perpetually sick, she had needs of her own. These Eliot met with conscientious patience and an inward detachment that made her, perhaps, the more demanding. In intermittent dramas between 1923 and 1925 the tension rose: Vivienne's explicit; Eliot's repressed.

In April 1925 he confided to Virginia Woolf that he had spent three months mewed-up in Vivienne's room. Vivienne's doctor had opened up her childhood fears of loneliness, and she would not let her husband out of her sight. If he did go out, he would come back to find her staging a faint. It is as though the scenario which he had set out years before in 'The Death of the Duchess' were coming to life: the wife's fear of abandonment; the husband's wish to escape from the room. The open terror of the woman may actually be a response to that unspoken but desperate wish.

Over the next few years Virginia Woolf watched him 'drown, wrapped in swathes of dirty seaweed'. So the mermaid sang to Eliot, a deformed muse who dragged him down into her dark, underwater world. It was, in part, the distorted drama of a woman who was not developing her own talents; in part, a struggle for survival. In 1923, when Eliot proposed leaving the bank in order to give more time to poetry, Vivienne argued that this would leave her without financial protection, and she refused to allow it. It is possible that Eliot's resentment provoked the virulence of *Sweeney Agonistes* which he began in about September 1923:

> I knew a man once did a girl in
> Any man might do a girl in
> Any man has to, needs to, wants to
> Once in a lifetime, do a girl in.

When Vivienne eventually saw this play performed by the Group Theatre on 2 October 1935, she wondered how she had managed not to faint at the 'absolute horror of the thing'.

While the play took shape in Eliot's mind between 1923 and 1926, marital trouble sharpened. It had its origin, ironically, in Vivienne's determined effort between February 1924 and July 1925 to collect herself, and take up writing. She worked hard at stories and poems which Eliot published regularly in the *Criterion*, but another severe illness was followed by a collapse of morale in 1925, which seems to mark the start of irreversible mental decline.

'Am ill (*still* ill) not ill again (always ill)', she told Pound, with insistent, rhythmic cries.

Illness may have been fomented by current opinion that a woman who showed signs of strain should be stopped from writing. The case was similar to Virginia Woolf's, and Eliot duly went to Leonard Woolf for advice. Vivienne, he explained, was naturally immoderate, and had never been trained in regular habits of work. When she got an idea, she wanted to work it out at once. When she was not allowed to write, she would think and think the whole time. Should her writing be curtailed, he wanted to know, or should she have a free hand?

Vivienne stated her protest in a draft of a letter which she pasted into her writing book. She might be speaking here for all who are struggling to find a voice. It was 'torture' to follow standard ways of writing at appointed times. She argued that her material could not be regulated, because it came, not from books, but from some 'very overgrown and hidden inner spirit':

When this begins to spurt, it is intolerable to choke it up, & will lead to my going mad. It is agony either way, of course, but I think at first, until one has got the spout of this long disused fountain clear, it is better to let the water burst out when it will & so *force* away the accumulation of decayed vegetation, moss, slime & dead fish which are thick upon & around it.

Eliot defined Vivienne's case as a nervous rather than mental breakdown. He made this scrupulous distinction, granting that there were reasons for her collapse: her loneliness in their marriage, and her fear that he would leave her. Eliot implied that it was he, if anyone, who was in need of mental treatment, and asked Leonard Woolf to recommend a doctor with psychoanalytic knowledge. Leonard sent him to Sir Henry Head, a curious choice, since Virginia Woolf had attempted suicide immediately after consultation with this man in 1913. Eliot merely found him not modern enough.

Vivienne became more obviously disturbed following a curt rejection from the *Dial*. There were wild accusations of her old friend, Lucy Thayer, who had encouraged her to submit the work, and she called on Eliot to 'curse out' Marianne Moore and the *Dial*. Vivienne became increasingly prey to lightning switches of mood in which she would pounce at random on a scapegoat for self-despair. Often she was clever enough to hit the mark, as with doctors whose tampering usually did her more harm than good. She told Pound that she was 'crying with rage' against one Dr West who was convinced that all her ills lay in a rock-hard liver. She hammered poor Pound with sarcastic questions:

Is West alrite?
Do you *know*?
Do you believe in Vichy [for cures of the liver]?
Do you believe in Liver?

There is an element in this of hilarious enjoyment, even pride in her drama. At this time she 'took to' trances. 'Spouse all of a dither', she boasted. 'Am very *hypnotic*, *always was*. Could be 1st class MEDIUM.'

Eliot, worn out, went away to Rapallo at the end of 1925. He left Vivienne at a Health Institute in Watford, Herts. From there she sent an SOS via Pound: 'All I can utter are abstract yells.' Ezra must make Tom 'rescue' her at once. When Eliot rushed back to England, he found her fairly normal. She was affectionate, but he could not respond. He wrote to Pound that her behaviour left much to be desired, and returned forthwith to Italy, threatening Vivienne half-jokingly that he might turn vampire if not allowed some respite. Vivienne took on the role of a doomed Little Nell, and declared herself 'anxious to die'.

Such dire exchanges lead easily into the threatening world of *Sweeney Agonistes*, which Eliot published in two fragments in October 1926 and January 1927. The epigraph to a typescript scenario quotes the same words of Brutus which Eliot used to refer to the coming end of his life with Vivienne:

> Between the acting of a dreadful thing
> And the first motion, all the interim is
> Like a phantasma or a hideous dream.

The play is about a dream of murder which has rooted itself in Sweeney's mind, and which he is compelled to relive. In the published version, Sweeney speaks of murder as by some other man, but in the typescript scenario Sweeney himself appears to shoot Mrs Porter (the Madam of the brothel which he frequents in *The Waste Land*). Mrs Porter is carried out for dead, but is resurrected. Her voice coming from the next room taunts Sweeney with a bawdy ballad about the sexual prowess of a hero of the red-light district. Murderer and victim accept the roles assigned by fate, and the victim returns to take her place beside Sweeney, so that the sequence may repeat itself *ad infinitum*. Man and woman are locked by their natures in a savage, inescapable ritual, propelled by unceasing drum taps.

Sweeney is a type of brute innocence who stumbles into a complex drama. In 'Sweeney Among the Nightingales', it is a conspiracy in a low dive; in *Sweeney Agonistes* it is a fatal tie to a woman, either Mrs Porter or Doris, the prostitute of 'Sweeney Erect'. Doris has a moment of horror in the first scene, an intimation of her death which is matched, in the second scene, by Sweeney's horror at what murder—or it may be the intent to murder—does to a man. The main difference between Eliot's scenario and final draft is that in the latter sin itself is not dramatized: what interests him, like Hawthorne, is the aftermath of sin in the lives of sinners. As Sweeney's undeveloped nature awakens to moral consequences, he finds himself trapped in the toils of remorse, pursued by 'hoo-ha's', and waiting for Judgement. The fragments end with a chorus of Hoo's followed by nine loud knocks.

Sweeney is haunted like Sykes after his murder of Nancy in *Oliver Twist* where the real nightmare is not the pursuit of the police but the resurrection of his victim. Her eyes are upon him wherever he flees. Eliot, too, was haunted by eyes in the 'Dream Songs' of this time. There is a drowning face that 'sweats with tears'. There are the remembered tears of the rejected La Figlia che Piange: the speaker is afflicted by his separation from these eyes, which have since dried and become eyes of judgement. As the lost violent soul becomes a mere hollow man he comes to fear the eyes of his victim, and dares not meet them in his dreams. Yet, at the same time, he holds to a distant, fading image of other eyes that could restore his soul and revive poetic sight. These eyes, which he must not approach, are sublime, a 'perpetual star'. This is the futile dream of empty men: the 'Multifoliate rose' of good love.

The dreaming that connects *Sweeney Agonistes*, 'Doris's Dream Songs', and 'The Hollow Men' seems to veer between supernatural terror and grace, that have their source in Eliot's contrasting ties to his wife and Emily Hale. What Eliot's mind made of these relations—the dreaming itself—is unfathomable. We are drawn into some underlying and unspeakable emotion, and at the same time distracted by the restless activity of visionless characters, prostitutes and noisy transatlantic visitors to London, ex-soldiers on a spree, nudging one another into bravado, and propping their meagre personalities with stale phrases. 'We did our bit,' they say loudly, 'got the Hun on the run.'

Into this routine patter explodes Sweeney's tale of murder. The killer keeps the woman's body in a bath of lysol while he maintains a façade of respectability. He pays the rent and takes in the milk. Inwardly, though, he is dead, more truly dead than his victim, since he is damned for all eternity. The play, at one stage called 'The Marriage of Life and Death', had at its core this buried state of death-in-life which will bind killer to victim more completely and permanently than in life. And this tie will cut him off from all humanity. Sweeney's story had its origin in a prose piece which Eliot wrote in 1917, where Eeldrop, a bank clerk, analyses a man in Gopsum Street who has murdered his mistress: 'The important fact is that for the man the act is eternal, and that for the brief space he has to live, he is already dead. He is already in a different world from ours. He has crossed the frontier.'

In Eliot's dream-poetry, the antithesis to the hollow lives of dead souls are stars, like heavenly eyes, which recall a lost purity of feeling. A golden foot 'I may not kiss or touch' glows in the shadow of the bed, and the eyes appear in a 'golden vision'. The dreamer swings 'between two lives' as he strains towards the angelic touch or breath, and then wakes alone, trembling with tenderness, with lips that would kiss or frame prayers to the broken image of a girl once loved. Her fading memory stirs the dreamer to contemplate 'death's other Kingdom', what Dante called 'that second kingdom where the human spirit is purged and becomes fit to ascend to Heaven'.

Eliot was at his most obscure in these poems with their strong personal emotions about which the reader cannot be sure. My guess is that in the early twenties he suffered in two ways: looking up, he saw a star-like purity he had lost; looking down, he saw his wife drowning in her river of tears. Could he cross that river? Could he face, on the farther bank, the savage spears of guilt which shook in the distance? Strung between loss on the one hand and fear on the other, there is a sense of hopeless stasis.

Through Sweeney, Eliot dramatized the prospect of spiritual fear. Desmond MacCarthy, at the first London production, saw 'a man under a lamp sitting at a table . . . speaking out of himself, out of his inner terror. He is addressing the girl opposite him, but he is also addressing us: it is half a sinister soliloquy, half a confession— or perhaps a threat to her.'

What is not explained is the motive for murder. Eliot's letters to Pound, with their undisguised misogyny, might help us to understand that the play was rooted in the peculiar circumstances of his own life. This kind of link, though, could easily become reductive, for the point of Eliot's career is how he managed to transmute almost maddening states of mind into a universal drama. The best commentaries here are his essays, especially his description of the horror that is 'projected from the poet's inner world of nightmare'. This nightmare—and it is here that Eliot makes his dazzling leap to a spiritualized view of his career—'is a triumph; for hatred of life is an important phase—even, if you like, a mystical experience—in life itself'. The essays also analyse a mind that becomes moral by becoming damned. Eliot was fascinated by Middleton's play about a strange sexual tie in which the unwilling partner becomes 'habituated' to the repulsive partner:

> Beneath the stars, upon yon meteor
> Ever hung my fate, 'mongst things corruptible.

Twice, Eliot's essay quotes these lines of the damned mate.

Eliot's friends—the Woolfs, Ottoline Morrell, and Hope Mirrlees—attended a masked performance of *Sweeney Agonistes* by the experimental Group Theatre in its upper studio at 9 Great Newport Street in November 1934. 'I sat by Tom', Virginia Woolf reported in her diary. 'Certainly he conveys an emotion, an atmosphere: . . . something peculiar to himself; sordid, emotional, intense—a kind of Crippen in a mask.' Eliot once said that the author may put into a dramatic character 'some trait of his own' which may be 'some tendency to violence or to indecision, some eccentricity even, that he has found in himself. Something perhaps never realized in his own life, something of which those who knew him best may be unaware.'

Sweeney Agonistes is unfinished and baffling, and almost never produced. Eliot set it up on two distinct levels. Sweeney's state of spiritual terror was to address itself to what Eliot envisaged as a small receptive élite in the audience, while, theoretically, the 'literal-minded and visionless' sector would share the response of their counterparts on stage: for them, the fortune-telling games of the tarts, the party songs of the Jazz Age, and murder as mere thriller. This superficial action is a cover for the fact that the core of the play is non-dramatic or, rather, pre- and post-dramatic: foreboding and remorse.

The lack of visible action is often seen to be a flaw in Eliot's plays, but interior action can be dramatic in its own way. In his 1935 revival, Rupert Doone made all the characters projections of Sweeney's mind: they were his bogies on a darkened stage. Even when they unmasked at the end, they were scarcely human. Sweeney alone did not wear a mask, but appeared as a sinister clerk in pin-striped trousers and steel spectacles.

The real problem may be the cover-action, the extensive card-game of the tarts and the boring high-jinks of the Americans, Krumpacker and Klipstein. In his poetry Eliot had dismissed Burbank and Bleistein with one lethal glance. It was an effort, now, to extend attention to the soulless—in later plays, to platitudinous aunts or cocktail natter—but Eliot prolongs these scenes as a sop to what he takes to be the conventional portion of a theatre audience.

'If the audience gets its strip-tease it will swallow the poetry', he told Pound. 'IF you can keep the bloody audience's attention engaged, then you can perform any monkey tricks you like when they arent [*sic*] lookin, and its what you do behind the audience's back so to speak that makes yr play IMMORTAL for a while.'

Such a line was bound to be self-defeating. Eliot wanted to reach a popular audience, but looked down on it. Not even the thickest playgoer is likely to be engaged by Krumpacker and Klipstein, whose pointless antics serve only to set off Sweeney from his milieu.

Still, there was one dramatic advantage to a play on two levels. Here, and again in *The Family Reunion*, Eliot jolts the audience from one level of reality to another, giving his covert pre-eminence to psychic or supernatural horror. This jolt should be played up in performance, to undercut the banalities of naturalistic action. Martin Browne, who directed all Eliot's subsequent plays, often missed the point when he begged for more action of the ordinary kind, and his predecessor, Rupert Doone, made the same mistake in his staging of *Sweeney Agonistes*. He set up a final scene of actual murder which is not in the text: Sweeney, holding a razor, raised his arm, and Doris screamed off stage. A razor chase, done in slow motion, was retained in the Morley College production in the mid-fifties. Such crude action only obscures further the hidden life of penitential torture.

The Eliots' misery was more or less hidden for the first ten years. Until his brother's visit in 1926, Eliot kept Vivienne's addictions from his family, and later said that the worst of it was there being 'nobody to hold one's hand and nobody to tell about it'. There was the odd confidence to Bertrand Russell or the Woolfs, but to them, too, he never mentioned drugs. Vivienne herself was initially even more discreet. The only diary that she kept during her time with Eliot says little beyond the fact that his moods depressed her vivacity. (She liked tea-dances and seemed happy outside literary circles, which she satirized in her sketches.) A veiled confession to Sydney Schiff suggests that she was disturbed by the violence of her husband's distastes. These, she thought, stemmed from a lack of vigour which he could not admit.

After 1925 the unhappy pair could no longer conceal the deterioration of Vivienne's mental health. The description of the wife in *The Family Reunion* is an accurate picture of Vivienne as others saw her at this time: an excited, irresponsible woman who would never leave her husband alone. A student called Wynyard Browne, who came to see Eliot in 1930, had the door slammed in his face: 'Why, oh why, do they all want to see my husband', Vivienne wailed. In the play, it is said that the wife wanted to keep her husband to herself to satisfy her vanity. She didn't want to fit herself to his relations or friends, but to bring him 'down to her own level'. As Vivienne became more disturbed she would take wildly against this person or that, and drag Eliot into vendettas against the Sitwells or Marianne Moore. At this time, too, she began to complain of her husband.

'She used to go about a great deal with me,' Eliot recalled in 1954, 'and I was afraid of the dreadfully untrue things she said of me and afraid that my friends believed her. I couldn't say anything—a kind of loyalty perhaps and partly a terror that they would show me that they believed her and not me. . . . Happy? NO, I was never happy . . .'

In these particular unhappy circumstances, it would be unfair to assign blame. Vivienne cannot be held responsible for mental illness and her husband suffered with her. Though he may have blamed himself, he did do what he could over very many years. His emotional withdrawal may have deepened Vivienne's distress but he had to protect himself. No-one else could bear Vivienne's company for long. The worst of it was, I imagine, the endless uncertainty: the long episodes of illness, physical and mental; the odd hopes of recovery. Doctors never succeeded in diagnosing Vivienne's problem, but pumped her freely with all sorts of drugs, with opium as a girl, later with alcohol-mixtures for headaches, and morphine in various forms. In 1932 both Edith Sitwell and Virginia Woolf noticed an overwhelming smell of ether as Vivienne entered a room. In fact she used to rub it all over her body, so it is not surprising that she often appeared to be half-dazed, fighting dim obstacles.

In 1927 two events exacerbated the mental damage of the collapse in 1925. In March her father, a successful artist, died at the Warrior House Hotel, St Leonards, in Sussex. In her diary she remembered 'how his dying eyes lingered on the sea & the sunsets, sitting up in bed in room no. 9 poor, poor darling Father. I remember how he always begged me to stroke his head . . . & how I wish there were still *someone* who needs the touch of my hands which are the best part of me.' She returned to the hotel after Eliot left her, in 1934, and walked the beach with her memories:

. . . a lovely clear night, with a low sloop down in the East, & the illuminated trams dashing up & down the front. It was cold & sharp & clean & very tempting to stay out. *Full* of memories, Father & Tom, Tom & Father—those two of my heart. *The sea is so much in it all.*

Vivienne broke down after her father's death. For nine months she went from one sanatorium to another in France, ending up at Malmaison outside Paris. About a month after Vivienne's departure, the second and more far-reaching event took place: Eliot's conversion in June 1927. With her quivering sensitivity, Vivienne at once perceived Eliot's rejection when he came to bring her back from Malmaison to London in February 1928:

My dear Tom brought me back with him but he did not want to. I was *out of my mind*, & so behaved badly to Tom & got very excited. It seemed everything he said was a *sneer* & an *insult*. . . . My *first* night in England was a very *un*happy, lonely night, sick & *frightened*.

The next month, Eliot took his vow of celibacy. I've wondered whether, at this point, he conceived his plan to leave Vivienne, which, perhaps, only a monastic code could justify. As Eliot detached himself, Vivienne never knew who would abet him. This was the reason for her suspicious scrutiny of Conrad Aiken, and her resistance to other visitors. There were times when she gave up, and, like the tortured wife of *The Waste Land*, walked the streets at night. Sometimes she did not return, and stayed the night in a hotel. Most of her actions between 1928 and 1932 were desperate, ill-judged claims on her husband's attention, literally plucking at his sleeve while he talked. These claims were always underlined by her frail health, and illness seemed to strike particularly at times of mental crises. She nearly died of colitis in 1923, when Eliot tried to leave his job; in June 1929 she had pleurisy when Eliot's mother was dying and he was on edge. 'A *terrible* time for my poor angel boy', she recalled.

Vivienne's long fear that he would leave her led to wild accusations of other women, Ottoline Morrell and Virginia Woolf. She clung to her husband, listened to his phone calls, and insisted on accompanying him on visits to the Woolfs, who found her sinister. Her conversation was challenging, explosive. At Monks House, in November 1930, Virginia, proud of her honey, asked Vivienne: 'Have you any bees?'

'Not bees', Vivienne answered. 'Hornets.'

'But where?'

'Under the bed.'

Vivienne's outrageousness aroused pity for Eliot. 'You're the bloodiest snob I ever knew', she said loudly to him at a party.

Conversation stopped. Eliot drank heavily. He was never sure how far she would go.

Once, when the Eliots invited the Fabers, the Joyces, and Osbert Sitwell to dinner, Vivienne, with a twisted smile, picked an argument with her husband across the table.

'It's been lovely, Vivienne,' Enid Faber thanked her at the end of the meal.

'Well, it may have been lovely for you, but it's been dreadful for me.'

'Nonsense, Vivienne, you know it's been a triumph,' said poor Mrs Faber.

'A triumph! . . . Look at Tom's face!'

Eliot remained, for the most part, imperturbable. Only those who knew him well could detect the merest flicker of exasperation when he stressed the last syllable of her name: 'Vivi*enne*.' He treated her, Willard Thorp recalled, like a patient father with a fractious child. Evie Townsend, Faber's secretary, also noticed Eliot's patience when his wife would ring him soon after his arrival at the office, and demand his return. He would apologize for interrupting his dictation, and leave.

When Conrad Aiken came to lunch in the autumn of 1930, he saw a woman like a scarecrow on thin legs who attacked her husband in front of an old college friend.

'There's no such thing as pure intellect', Eliot remarked.

Vivienne laughed. 'Why, what do you mean? . . . You know perfectly well that *every* night you tell me that there *is* such a thing: and what's more, that *you* have it, and that nobody *else* has it.'

'You don't know what you're saying', Eliot retorted rather lamely.

Father Underhill took it upon himself to advise separation. Did he realize that this would mean the virtual extinction of Vivienne? Beneath the Eliots' repartee lay this issue of life and death, and Aiken sensed the violence of their emotion. Hatred, he thought it. Vivienne was 'shivering, shuddering' like the wife in *The Family Reunion*: 'A restless shivering painted shadow.'

Between 1928 and 1932 there must have been times when Vivienne's claim prevailed. She had, Eliot acknowledged, a gift for argument which he called coercive. His letters to Ada Leverson*

---

* Mrs Leverson, known as 'the Sphinx', had been a loyal friend to Oscar Wilde. She was the sister of the Eliots' friend, Mrs Schiff.

present a domesticated couple, accepting middle age and loss of initiative. In 1930 he dedicated *Ash Wednesday* to Vivienne. It must have been a placatory gesture, no more, for the poem looks away from her towards a promised land. With its longing memories of New England, it turns towards the remote, idealized muse of Emily Hale.

Vivienne was Eliot's muse only so long as he shared her hell. There was no place for her in the purgatory of *Ash Wednesday*, in the sainthood of *Murder in the Cathedral*, and in the introspective ordeals of *The Family Reunion*. As Eliot's works put aside the distractions of worldliness for self-contemplation, real women are replaced by abstractions, ideal beneficence or hellish torment. A new phase of religious poetry was contingent on Vivienne's dismissal. The conversion, in short, spelt her doom.

To Vivienne, this must have seemed the more threatening for not being at once clear. Her verbal assaults on Eliot all had to do with his façades and prevarications, as though she would force him to declare—something. When Virginia Woolf noticed that Eliot looked 'leaden' and 'sinister' in 1930, she blamed Vivienne, who was a 'torture'. But, to be fair, Vivienne's frantic scenes are not inexplicable if she did sense a future for Eliot that did not include her. Her scenes were not so much protests but, increasingly, try-outs for a doomed role, a reckless, perverse performance that contributed to her ruin, as though, in a strange mocking way, she played—to the hilt—some scenario imposed upon her.

Edith Sitwell, meeting Vivienne by chance in Oxford Street in the summer of 1932, called out, 'Hullo, Vivienne.'

'No, no: you don't know me', Vivienne replied. 'You have mistaken me *again* for that *terrible* woman who is so like me. . . . She is always getting me into trouble.'

Eliot's poetry repeatedly contemplates the end of a woman, and the earliest instances precede Vivienne's appearance in Eliot's life. Men in the early poems despise women as the 'eternal enemy of the absolute', and cope with inhibition by dreams of power, a godlike power to end women's lives. What is disturbing is the unreality of the female victim. She is punished, it would seem, for the fact of her sex. Her existence has served its purpose as foil for the man's moral drama. Veiled with irony, a delicious brutality slips through in 'Portrait of a Lady' ('Well, and what if she should die some day . . .?'); unveiled, in 'The Love Song of Saint Sebastian', a man throttles a woman as a mode of possession. An additional quatrain to the second draft of 'Whispers of Immortality' once again contemplates the end of a woman. When the female soul departs, then men turn up their eyes, and become, repeatedly, Sons of God.

On 4 March 1932 Eliot wrote a formal letter to Vivienne, promising to return to England following his Norton professorship at Harvard for the academic year 1932/3. Clearly Vivienne, fearing that he would remain, made him state that his appointment at Harvard was not renewable, and that he would return in May 1933.

Just before Eliot's departure in September 1932, they paid their last visit as a couple to the Woolfs at Rodmell. A photograph shows Eliot standing beside Virginia Woolf, while Vivienne stands apart, drooping, her white hat pulled down over her eyes. Dressed in white satin in the rain, her handkerchief exuding ether, she behaved weirdly. Virginia saw her as a wild Ophelia: 'alas no Hamlet would love her, with her powdered spots.' The Woolfs tried to be kind: Virginia gave her a jar of home-made raspberry jam, and Leonard some flowers. 'We had tea', Vivienne recalled, '& as I was *very nearly insane* already with the Cruel Pain of losing Tom . . . I paid very little attention to the conversation. . . . We got back to the Lansdowne [Hotel, Eastbourne] I felt *very ill* & *was in a fever*. Tom also *seemed very strange*.' As she wrote these lines, she toyed with the pathetic illusion that, if she had clung harder, he could not have left her. She berated herself for not having had the nerve to accompany him to America: '& so am damned for ever—.'

Two years later, Vivienne Eliot sat in the waiting-room at Faber & Faber, her hands screwing up her handkerchief as she wept. She asked for her husband, whom she had not seen since his departure for America. This was a routine visit, and there was a routine to deal with her. Eliot's secretary, Brigid O'Donovan, herself in love with the poet, would phone Eliot who would slip out of the building. He was not in, Brigid told Vivienne, who would then leave. For the rest of the day Eliot would be distant and on edge, speaking with cautious slowness.

Vivienne Eliot was cast off by those who aligned themselves with her husband, and this meant almost everyone whom they had known as a couple. At this time she joined the Fascists though her diary shows not the slightest interest in politics, simply a dim wish to belong to some form of social existence. She clung to formal ties, sending handkerchiefs to Eliot's sister Marian, who replied coolly. Everyone to whom Vivienne appealed took Eliot's part, refusing to make any move to bring them together. It baffled Vivienne that people behaved as though her husband hardly existed; they told her that they rarely saw him.

Virginia Woolf found her in September 1933 sitting 'under a crowned effigy', Eliot's photograph by Elliot Fry with a wreath of daisies. It appears that Eliot wrote to Vivienne on 27 November 1933, and in December she did acknowledge to Virginia Woolf that he would not come back to her.

'I would give a good deal to see him', she wrote in her diary on 20 January 1934. She refused to sign 'any blackmailing paper relinquishing all rights to him for anybody', though she would put '*all* in Tom's hands, if he wld. honestly come back to me'. She felt unfit to live alone and care for herself: 'I look like the little *ghost* of a *street child*.' Slowly, that year, she packed up and sold household goods, sometimes blanking out on the day's activities. 'The rest of the day', she wrote on 11 August, 'must have been unspeakably wretched, for, I cannot remember anything at *all* about it.' Her ruin was not sudden; it was the slow accumulation of lost days:

17 September 1935

... I just slowly grope my way through Limbo, sometimes accelerated by a kind of artificial fury, which rages for a time, *during* which I can perform great tasks, & after which I am utterly spent & dry & sick. I think I feel more & more as *Tom* used to feel, & I suppose still does. I shd. understand him so much better now.

To follow the full story from 1933 to 1938 it is essential to allow, for the first time, the voice of Vivienne's diaries to sound freely so as to record a situation of maximum moral density. The mills of God, she wrote, had ground her to powder. Or had someone sinned against her? The sin, she adds, was *not* her husband's. She could not bring herself to believe that it was his own choice to have left his 'true companion'. Yet on 11 December 1934 five or six men forced their way into Vivienne's flat to remove Eliot's books and copies of the *Criterion*. They pulled shelves off the wall, damaged a clock, and went off with some of Vivienne's books. The raid left her in a 'state of nervous collapse'. A second raid followed on 15 July 1935 to get Eliot's files and photographs.

She wrote to Dr Miller: 'It hurt me so terrible [*sic*] that they took away all those photographs of the Eliot family which I have had round me all the last twenty years, and of which many were sent to me.'

Despite recurrent collapse, Vivienne could rally. Her imagination was formidable, which is why Eliot feared to meet her, feared even—in his work—that she would haunt him always. Her major act of woman in distress was interrupted by a more dashing one of woman to the rescue. She sallied forth in blue serge cape and waistcoat, flourishing a cigarette-holder or in a black velvet coat and black angora turban, determined to pierce the mystery of her husband's disappearance. 'At last the *courage* had *come* to me . . .' she wrote in her diary. A daring and, for Eliot, humiliating phase of pursuit was initiated on 13 September 1934 when Vivienne placed an advertisement in the personal column of *The Times* for 17 September (though it was not printed):

Will T. S. Eliot please return to his home 68 Clarence Gate Gardens which he abandoned Sept. 17th, 1932.

Her rationale was to check whether her husband was alive, but the real purpose was to test or, at least, expose barriers to communication. Another scheme was to offer to hand over to Eliot some silver and his deed box, and to ask the bank to secrete her in the room when he came to collect them. When she visited Faber & Faber, Miss Swan and Miss O'Donovan received her kindly, but told her that Eliot's presence was erratic.

'Tom never *was* erratic,' she mused. 'He was the most regular of men.'

In March 1935 she took courage to protest loudly at the office: 'It is too absurd, I have been frightened away too long. I am his wife.'

She played with the notion that Eliot was a prisoner of sorts, which sounds absurd, but he was, in fact, guarded by various stalwarts. To his wife his invisibility was a mystery. It was, therefore, a day of triumph when, on 18 November 1935, after more than three years, she finally faced him at the *Sunday Times* Book Exhibition at the Dorland Hall.

A friend sent Vivienne the newspaper announcement that Eliot was to talk at 3.30. She dressed in what she called in her diary her 'Fascist' uniform, a black beret, a large black mackintosh cape,

and a penguin pin that Eliot had given her in 1927, and, armed with
Polly their dog, confronted Eliot as he arrived:

I turned a face to him of such joy that no-one in that great crowd could
have had one moment's doubt. I just said Oh *Tom*, & he seized my hand,
& said how do you *do*, in quite a loud voice. He walked straight on to the
platform then & gave a most remarkably *clever*, well thought out lecture.
. . . I stood the whole time, holding Polly *up* high in my arms. Polly was
very excited & wild. I kept my eyes on Tom's face the whole time, & I
kept nodding my head at him, & making encouraging signs. He looked a
little older, more mature & smart, much *thinner* & *not* well or robust or
rumbustious at *all*. No sign of a woman's *care* about him. No cosy
evenings with dogs and gramophones I should say.

During the applause, Vivienne pushed her way to the platform and
let Polly off the lead. The dog tore round Eliot's feet, jumping for
joy. Eliot took no notice, but Vivienne, undaunted, leapt up beside
him on the platform.

'Will you come back with me?' she demanded quietly, leaning
forward with her hands on the table.

'I cannot talk to you now', Eliot said. He signed three books for
her and left quickly with Richard Church.

'Come back' was the essence of Vivienne's plea. In this phase she
indulged in dotty dreams of offering Eliot protection. She
imagined giving him two rooms, with lock and key, so that he
might work in the flat unmolested. She would treat him, she
planned, like a grown-up son. Another plan was to let him know
that she would leave the door open from 10.30 to 11 every night.
'Here is your home,' she wrote, '& here is your *protection*. *Which
you need*.'

To Vivienne's fevered imagination, Eliot's few words at the
Dorland Hall implied a promise of contact. 'Everything was
perfectly allright between us', she wrote to Messrs. James & James,
her solicitors. It seemed important to her that the large audience
constituted 'many witnesses'. Witnesses to her joy? To their
reconciliation?

Vivienne also sent excited letters to her bank manager and
to Eliot himself, which initiated her last role—that of a suicide.
A physical accident, she whispers to Eliot, might befall her at any
moment. She cast herself as a doomed wife, the living replica of the
doomed wife of Eliot's next play. When the play opens, she has

gone overboard during a voyage, and Harry, the husband, is not sure if he tipped her over. He is guilty, anyway, of wishing to do so.

Sir Herbert Read, whose friendship went back to the early days of the marriage, and who could remember Vivienne as sweet and lively, thought that posterity would judge her harshly, but from the vantage point of half a century the harshness, it seems, came from her contemporaries. Though a feminist ideology would now rescue Vivienne's reputation, to take an angle in this story—to focus on one partner rather than the other—is to evade the whole truth, which must acknowledge, at least in this phase of the marriage, the unhappy effects of schizophrenia, and the fact that, even when Vivienne was not ill, she was, like some pathetic people, insensitive to others. It appears of less moment that she broke social decorum and embarrassed her husband, than that her own strong feelings were so absorbing that she became unaware of how others thought and felt. All the same, this inattentiveness is contradicted by the acute observation of her sketches. In her good spells she could be fun, with a daring critical intelligence and a quickness of engagement that would be appealing. A romantic, she abandoned herself to the mood of the moment without the faintest notion of right feeling.

Vivienne was also a snob. She was agog about royalty, and sent Eliot's poem *Marina*, about a spiritual journey, to Marina, Duchess of Kent. She fantasized descent from the houses of Carnarvon and St Germain to the extent of using their crests. But in such silliness, and in her wilder states, she was never dangerous to anyone but herself; and these states were, in any case, episodic. It is likely that Eliot was never quite sure whether she was mad or not, but did always know that, since no one else would look after her, he alone was in a position to save her. Curiously, in his play, the end of the wife was a side issue. What interested him was if the husband could save himself through protracted penance.

Though Harry is not conceived as a likeable character—Eliot later called him a prig—the play does sanction self-contemplation in the name of moral trial. Pride was the recurrent concern of Eliot's maturity, in the form of the final Tempter of Becket, in *Four Quartets'* need for humility, and in the humbling of the Elder Statesman. In *The Family Reunion*, though, pride is treated far less critically. It may be that Eliot identified too closely with Harry to judge him with customary detachment while he planned and wrote this play in the heat of marital crisis.

Edward Fox has played Harry looking exactly like Eliot, impeccable, reserved, but forced by inner necessity to fragmented disclosure. The play gains in urgency in the light of Eliot's life: it is the text of his public confession as part of his private bid for salvation. The intimacy of the testimony is painfully honest. Harry is condemned for his wife's end by no one but himself, yet that very admission is, of course, his salvation. Harry's testimony, with its emphasis on sin, conforms to the set pattern of the personal narrative, as it was called in New England. There, persons wishing to join a church had to relate publicly the story of their salvation. These narratives were often anxious and open-ended, for success lay not in formal measurement of sin but in quality of repentance: it had to be desperate and uncertain enough to prove genuine abasement. Formal confession in the Anglican Church was, for Eliot, rather too mild a ritual. His scrupulousness demanded more unflinching introspection.

What was Vivienne's part in this inner drama? Did she, like the wife in the play, provoke it? She was always the actress, quick to seize a part, and her diaries show that the long-drawn-out process of separation was, for her, a melodrama of pursuit and escape, in which pursuer and victim could change places. On 19 June 1935 she expected something like an arrest. Though the day passed uneventfully, she set off for France with fears for her life. Was this wholly a deranged fantasy? In July she sent Eliot wild letters pleading with him to return. She visited Faber & Faber, and Miss Swan told her that Eliot was rarely there, a lie that Vivienne accepted, temporarily, with despair. Fits of resentment alternated with fits of fear, neither unreasonable in her circumstances. Effort after effort to reach her husband—through the passport office, through their dentist—was blocked, and then, in the summer of 1935, she became physically afraid, with perhaps an inkling of the asylum ahead: 'I am a fugitive. From whom, I know not (precisely, *yet*)', she wrote on 4 August. Between then and the middle of 1938, her position changed from pursuer to pursued.

In June 1936 she pretended to have gone to America. She gave as her forwarding address 83 Brattle Street, Cambridge, Mass., an apartment block which was the home of Eliot's favourite sister, Marian Cushing Eliot, and also of a distant relative, Elizabeth

Wentworth, who had been the only member of the family to meet Vivienne in London after Eliot left her, and who subsequently wrote her a few friendly letters. Vivienne gave out that she had gone to be with her husband's people—her own improbable family reunion—but there was another motive: to imitate Eliot's disappearance following his departure for America. She lost his track, she says, in December 1932, which was of course the time that he crossed the continent to see Emily Hale. Vivienne's Day Book states her motives:

> to reduce the strain on my brain, & at the same time to see if I could succeed in disappearing so completely & baffling all attempts to trace me as my husband has. And, at the same time I have in my mind such an undying resentment against all those who had any part in this business that I want them to know what it is like to suffer in the same way.

> *Tiresias*

At this point I became Daisy Miller.

She gave out that she had let her flat to a student at the Royal Academy of Music, called Daisy Miller, who would answer correspondence in her supposed absence. This was the self she now chose to be. *Daisy Miller*. The very name reverberates with unstated suggestion. There, amidst embittered ramblings, Vivienne implied a brilliant reading of her position.

Daisy Miller is James's story of a reckless woman who dies misunderstood. Her liveliness does not conform to the dictates of the correct but corrupt Roman society where she is placed. Accompanied by a shallow, neglectful mother and an offhand younger brother, she assumes a freedom of behaviour that brands her as ill-bred. This freedom becomes flamboyant in the face of the chill caution of Winterbourne, who pays her passing court. Winterbourne, a Europeanized American, who is even more rigidly correct than Europeans, aligns himself with public outrage at Daisy's behaviour. We hear Daisy's story, after her death, filtered through the distorting consciousness of Winterbourne, and our challenge is to reconstruct it so as to perceive inexpressible emotion in Daisy's wildness, and, more difficult, to discern the source of her tragedy in the peculiar character of Winterbourne: his withholding of the self. Hawthorne, who understood, said James, the 'deeper psychology', called this the Unpardonable Sin: a habit of spectatorial detachment, rooted in pride, which severs his New Englanders from the 'human heart'.

The last year of the records that Vivienne kept for posterity's judgement was 1936. It was her wish that they be published verbatim: she felt herself to be a victim of a 'fantastic' conspiracy to keep her husband beyond her reach. What she did not realize is that the papers show not only her pathos but the warping effect of protracted suffering: she was haughty and demanding to employees, quick to fault and denounce others, and the politically dim sort of Fascist who enjoyed the excitement of a rally where public denunciations provided an outlet for private fury. In 1977 *Eliot's Early Years* redressed the balance of sympathy somewhat in Vivienne's favour but, reading through her papers again, I am convinced that we must not simplify the picture of this erratic woman. To read her cold instructions to her servant or her vituperative letters is to realize that Virginia Woolf was not being unfair when she exclaimed 'Vivienne! Was there ever such a torture since life began!—to bear her on one's shoulders, biting, wriggling, raving, scratching, unwholesome, powdered, insane, yet sane to the point of insanity ...' Her mother alone sustained some fondness for 'my little Vivy', but late in 1936 the already ailing Mrs Haigh-Wood had a stroke. She became a helpless invalid, and Vivienne's last shred of support was gone.

Shortly before this, she made a valiant effort to take up a career in music. On 26 September 1935 she passed the pianoforte entrance examination and enrolled as a student at the Royal Academy of Music. She took up singing with Miss Gale, and exulted in her '*huge*' voice. She seems to have been one of those people with almost too many talents who are unable to focus any one of them in a sustained way. She meant to work hard, but there were endless distractions. What kind of piano should she hire? A long, exhausting fuss followed. She went repeatedly to see *Murder in the Cathedral*; in January and February alone, seven times. She failed her Elements of Music examination that winter, and then in the spring had a 'poisoned' foot. That summer, when she had three more examinations, she kept up her round of grand receptions, and dashed about to furbish up her elaborate wardrobe. How could she practise when she had to think about her leopard coat and model gowns?

The public engagements, of course, filled a social gap. Daisy

Miller was called upon to state that Mrs Eliot 'has had very great friends, & she prefers to mourn their loss, than to fill the gaps they leave'. Her thoughts turned to Bertrand Russell or to Osbert Sitwell: what had happened to those distinguished friends of the early days of her marriage? She reminded Geoffrey Faber that he had often been her guest, but he kept her at bay with the placatory notes of a busy gentleman. Vivienne also wrote to Theodora Eliot and the Henry Ware Eliots, and urged them, for form's sake, to keep in touch with her, but she wrapped this pathetic plea in haughty, resentful words.

On 5 August, Daisy Miller explained that Mrs Eliot was 'apt to lose her wits and go all to pieces'. A letter to her solicitor on 10 August hints that she will soon be dead. She was still brooding over Eliot's disappearance and in September hunted up the cables (to do with his return) that she had received in July 1933. That September she also wrote to 'The Literary Manager' at Faber & Faber to offer her own illustration for *Marina*. Eliot's secretary rejected the offer politely.

She still made her futile journeys to the office. She began to believe that she was being followed, and on 10 December wrote to Geoffrey Faber to protest, but he denied any knowledge of this. The last we hear of Vivienne's voice was her intention to send Christmas cards to Eliot and to her American sisters-in-law, Marian, Theodora, and Margaret. She insisted on this connection to the end, and refused to be addressed by any other name than 'Mrs T. S. Eliot'.

From the beginning of 1937 she fell silent, and there is a gap in her story. Then, on 14 July 1938, a letter from her brother to Eliot announced her doctor's recommendation to have her certified. The procedure would have taken place before a magistrate who, on the basis of a certificate from Dr Reginald Miller, would have made an order for Vivienne's reception and detention in Northumberland House, a private Home in London authorized to take certified patients. This order would have had to be signed by two relatives or close friends. There is a report that, when Maurice Haigh-Wood was close to death, he confessed that he, with Eliot, had signed this order, much to his later regret, for when, after some years abroad, he saw his sister again in 1946, he was convinced that she was as sane as he was.

Maurice wrote again to Eliot on 17 August 1938, to say that

Vivienne was installed in the asylum, was fairly cheerful, and reading a certain amount. It sounds as though he felt obliged to tell his brother-in-law only what he would wish to hear. Unless Vivienne were drugged, it is inconceivable that she should have accepted this tamely, particularly in view of a later attempt at escape, when she was caught, and forced back.

Vivienne behaved, we recall, as though she saw a 'goblin ghost'. Harry, in Eliot's play, is also haunted by ghosts, but here the family doctor is patently unfit to judge them. If Eliot did sign the order, he must have held an ambiguous attitude to such official judgements. For Vivienne, mental disturbance led to the asylum; for Eliot's hero, disturbance was a sign of superior destiny.

It is as though Eliot were living out a tale by Poe or James in which superficial order is forced upon a wrong which lurks beneath the surface, becoming the ghosts of the mind. Vivienne receded into the background of Eliot's consciousness, a phantom of anguish and reproach. He put himself so totally beyond her reach that it was as though he had vanished or she were no more.

In 1936 Eliot wiped out the dedication of *Ash-Wednesday* 'To my Wife' from the new *Collected Poems 1909-1935*. After Vivienne was certified she was made a Ward in Chancery, and Eliot never visited her in the asylum, where she remained for the rest of her life. That one moment when they shared the platform at the Dorland Hall in November 1935 was the last she saw of him. Soon after that meeting, she recalled with pleasure her husband's clean-cut mouth, his fine head, his keen deep eyes. She was still in love with him, the hopeless kind of love that feeds off exaggerated trust.

'I *trust* the man', she told her friend, Louie Purdon. 'He has some very strong reasons. You do not argue with God, or question his ways.'

Released from Vivienne, Eliot travelled more, and the places he visited—Massachusetts, Virginia, New Hampshire, Scotland, Wales, the Cotswolds, Somerset, and Huntingdonshire—became the poetic focus for certain states of mind. The scenes that Eliot visited with Emily Hale—New Hampshire in June 1933, and Burnt Norton the following summer—are seen with an ecstatic quickening of lyrical emotion, while a more lasting implacability found a locus in the 'red river' of Virginia, and in the Scottish moor where clans had battled for generations.

In November 1933 Eliot drove with Frank Morley, Donald Brace (his American publisher), and George Blake from Glasgow to Inverness and back, across Rannoch Moor. The landscape of 'Rannoch, by Glencoe' tells of a pride that, despite personal humiliation, holds on in shadow, outlasting death. Gazing at that barren landscape of death, Eliot declares that even in the relics of embattled lives, the bones, that withholding pride will remain forever: 'No concurrence of bone.' Eliot's sense of constriction reflects all mortal creatures, waiting for death in the 'long pass' of the lifespan, suspended in the inexorable movement of time. There seems no way out of this passage as the road winds to no apparent purpose in 'Listlessness of ancient war / Langour of broken steel'. The wretched stories of history, like Eliot's struggle with Vivienne, are stale, with their repeated 'Clamour of confused wrong'.

As it turned out, Eliot's 'Landscapes' were rehearsals for *Four Quartets*. These begin with four different landscapes, linking scenes with states of mind, from which rise generalizations about all lives. Though *Four Quartets* was completed during the second world war—it was published as a complete work in 1943—it is rooted, with 'Landscapes', in the mid-thirties, in scenes that Eliot visited between 1934 and 1937. In other words, these years prior to Vivienne's certification marked not only his upheaval but also the stir of a new and great phase of creativity. He jolts his writing to life with a startling candour in 'Virginia', 'Rannoch', and above all in his most ambitious play, *The Family Reunion*.

Eliot settled to write this play after an actual family reunion in 1936. After two summers in England (1934-5), Emily Hale did not return in 1936, for Eliot went to New England where, I assume, he saw her. Nothing so far is known of this visit, except that it was not a public one. There are photographs of a family vacation in rural New Hampshire, Eliot in a cloth cap, his sisters comfortable in their rockers on the porch of Mountain View House. This might have been another time for decision. Eliot was, as he put it years later, very much in love with Emily Hale, and would willingly have sacrificed everything for the possibility of marrying her. A professorship at Harvard was on offer. It would have been logical to consider a return to Massachusetts as an obvious solution to the pursuit of Vivienne, who had always feared to cross the Atlantic.

In *The Family Reunion* Harry looks into the possibility of
returning to his old home after years abroad. There he meets Mary,
who shared his youth and is still 'Waiting, waiting, always waiting'.
But return proves impossible, for Mary's appeal is blotted out by
the pursuit of Harry's dead wife in the form of Furies.

'I cannot tell you when or whether there will be more of
Sweeney,' Eliot wrote to Hallie Flanagan on 9 February 1934, 'but
in any case I hope to begin something new of the same kind as soon
as I have finished with a dramatic pageant [*The Rock*] . . .' In 1936
he still thought *Sweeney Agonistes* the most original thing he had
done, but twelve years had made too great a difference for him to
finish it in its old form. Eliot's most ambitious works gestated for
several years during which he tried out fragments or sections, then
there would be an enormous effort to unify and complete. No
work gestated longer than *The Family Reunion*, with its roots in
the *Sweeney* fragments of 1923–6. The first four of ten discernible
layers of composition date back to 1934–5, and precede or coincide
with *Murder in the Cathedral*. The commissions for *The Rock* and
Murder interrupted a plan for a play which grew out of the facts of
his life: a family who had disapproved of the hero's marriage, who
had not attended it, and were glad it was over; a marriage linked
with exile; a wife, possessive, shivering with nerves, doomed,
closely modelled on Vivienne; and a waiting woman, no longer
young, with close ties to the hero's family, who would have been
the legitimate choice.

The timing of the play's composition forecasts events in Eliot's
life with remarkable closeness. In the play Harry is said to be
'psychic', in that he knows in advance that his wife will be
destroyed. Eliot completed his second Working Draft in the spring
of 1938. On 7 June a letter from his secretary, Anne Bradby (later
Ridler), to Ezra Pound implies that the play was nearly ready for
performance. During the next two months, July–August, Vivienne
was institutionalized. The play was due to go on that autumn,
though it was eventually postponed a few months. Michael
Redgrave, who played Harry in the first production, said that Eliot
sat with his head down during rehearsals, revising until the last
moment.

Writing at the very time of his wife's crisis, Eliot conveys the
torment of the questions that gnaw at Harry. Did he push his wife
over the rails, or did she, as she had threatened, destroy herself?

Harry is struggling to escape the shadows of his marital past. He is haunted, like Sweeney, by his own latent violence, except that the Hoo Ha's are now visible as Furies. No longer funny, they appear the essence of evil to the man at whom they look with terrible complicity.

At the same time memories of youth return, as in Eliot's Cape Ann poem of 1935, and with it hopes of simplicity and innocence. The problem for Harry, as for Eliot himself, was how to cope with two separate lives: the stained years abroad and the distant past at home.

The first scene that he worked out in any detail centred on the waiting Mary as she offers Harry new hope. The date of this scene, 1934–5, puts it exactly in the period that he was most engaged with Emily Hale, then making her prolonged stay in England. Mary urges Harry to open a door just to hand. All that is wanted is a simple turn, and she pictures the smell of new-cut grass under sunlight. The door opening into a garden of love was to be the opening scene of *Burnt Norton*, but had its origin in this early, unfinished draft of the play, written soon after the visit to Burnt Norton in September 1934, which may have provided the initial impetus for both *The Family Reunion* and *Four Quartets*. The biographical link of these two works is possibly earlier than the standard link of the opening lines of *Burnt Norton* with an abstract, discarded passage from *Murder in the Cathedral*.

In *Burnt Norton*, the woman is faceless, subsumed in 'we'. Here she is the leader into new experience, with all the charm of assurance. Mary, in draft, may be closer to Emily Hale than the toned-down Mary of the final play. She is allowed to take a more diagnostic view of Harry than in the revised version of their exchange: a corrective, not flattering view. To her, Harry is a man who creates his own torment and prefers it. This torment is a form of pride which masks his fear of taking up a new part, in case he might not appear so well in it.

The next phase of composition, also 1934–5, was an additional scenario in which Harry explains the double nightmare that now became the central drama of the play. One nightmare is a state of possession which goes back to the ancestor who was cursed by a witch: in this state Harry cannot see his wife as human. The other nightmare seems to be a state of mental isolation in which he feels divided from the self he had been in his youth. This explanation is something of an answer to Mary's simple cure of natural feeling. Harry, if not mad, is on the brink of madness. 'O that awful privacy / Of the insane mind!' Harry exclaims in the play, and these are the very words Eliot himself was to use in describing his life with Vivienne, years later, to his friend, Mary Trevelyan. He said: 'I used to find that, once I got out of the atmosphere, I recovered normality surprisingly quickly. But at the time it seemed as though it would never end.' Harry needs another, more daring cure than natural love, which is offered by the other beneficent woman in the play, the older Agatha: her cure is a process of de-possession, what the play finally calls 'exorcism'. Harry must translate his isolation into the deliberate solitude of a special destiny: he must cross some frontier into another world. This again brings Harry into line with Eliot's own states of extremity and religious trial.

Next come three pages of pencil notes for a scene between Mary and Downing, Harry's chauffeur, as watchers of Harry's fate. Downing tells Mary that Harry's is to be a lone journey, and he confirms the notion that it is destined in some way. His lordship's marrying was 'a kind of preparation for something else'. The three pages are on the same paper as the manuscript of *Murder in the Cathedral*, and were kept with it. This was the last of the fragments of 1935. There followed a gap of about eighteen months until late 1936 when Eliot began again.

The autobiographical basis of the earliest fragments give to this play the emotional intimacy of Eliot's early work, as though we were looking at a man with his back to us, who abruptly turns and speaks with low, confessional urgency, and then, as abruptly, turns away once more. The confessional manner is not very English, though Harry is an English lord. Martin Browne misconceived the play from the start, when he praised the reality of the family and criticized non-realistic scenes (the Furies and the trances when characters speak beyond themselves). The weakness, as with *Sweeney Agonistes*, lies rather in Eliot's naturalistic cover: the idle chatter of obtuse people, who in this play are certain members of the family. They seemed to Virginia Woolf stiff pokers. For the sake of a theatre audience that Eliot was to underrate for the rest of his career, he forced himself—and us—to attend to dullards' chit-chat. Their platitudes roll forth, even from the wise Agatha in her (to Eliot) dull capacity as Principal of an Oxford women's college.

As Helen Gardner noted, this aspect of Agatha is not convincing, especially when she complains of thirty years of trying not to dislike women. (In the 1950s, when Janet Adam Smith* was proposed as Principal of a women's college, Eliot sent her a warning postcard of a stately hen, with the message: 'This card should help you to remember how to behave.' The card also refers to Agatha as 'a most tiresome woman'.)

Between the platitudes of a family reunion, Harry must select the right drama from three alternatives on offer: his family's drama of return; Mary's drama of renewal through love; and the still-obscure drama of the Furies. In all the years that Harry remained abroad, he had come to think of family life as substantial and simple, but he discovers on his return that the simplification had taken place in memory. Most members of the family are rigid with lifelessness, and precisely because they have changed so little, the change in Harry is more manifest. Martin Browne told Eliot that he found Harry baffling. In reply, Eliot sent that long analysis of Harry that sounds like a private testimony. He covered his tracks, characteristically, by telling Browne that he identified with Charles, an uncle of slightly modified dimness, but Harry is patently Eliot, as Virginia Woolf saw at once: 'the chief poker is Tom'. The letter reveals 'a horror of women'. What might well be a reasonable wish to be free of an impossible wife calls out an extreme pattern of feeling, an old pattern for Eliot that goes back to the murder of a woman in 'Saint Sebastian', revived in *Sweeney Agonistes*, and connected with a predisposition to see women as creatures of sexual sin who dare men to consort with them and so receive their ineradicable taint.

As this mind pursues itself, the external world comes unstuck. Harry talks past his expectant family, saturated with his awareness of something present to his mind but not visible. As a student, Eliot had noted that what appears as paranoia, delusional insanity, may be a diabolical mysticism. More than thirty years later, his play contrasts a state of demonic possession with the blinkered state of Harry's aristocratic family. The social setting is that of the English country house comedy of manners, yet the feeling of moral

* Janet Adam Smith (now Mrs John Carleton) was Assistant Editor of the *Listener* (1930–5), and then worked for the *New Statesman and Nation* (1949–60), in the last eight years as Literary Editor. Her first marriage, in 1935, was to Michael Roberts, a contributor to the *Criterion*, and Eliot was godfather to one of their three children.

horror—Harry's alertness to incursions from the unknown—is
pure New England. Eliot was consciously following Henry James,
whom he praised in 1933 for 'his curious search, often in the
oddest places, like country houses, for spiritual life'. The play
jolts us successively from the familiar to the strange, domesti-
cating, as James does, dangers 'that look like nothing and that can
be but inwardly and occultly dealt with, which involve the
sharpest hazards to life and honour and the highest instant
decisions and intrepidities of action'. The familiar aunts and
uncles are out of English detective fiction from Conan Doyle to
Christie: the old buffer of the club, the retired Indian army
officer, the spinster of the vicar's teas. The deeper drama is the
mystery of sin and redemption explored with a strenuous rigour
that came to Eliot most directly through his mother. All through
the play, Eliot sustained this parallel of native core and English
rind that derived, ultimately, from himself. Externally, he was an
English gentleman; internally, as he now and then admitted, a
Puritan—and perhaps the more Puritan for not having been born
in Massachusetts.

For the three generations that the Eliots had lived on the
Mississippi they had continued to look upon New England as
their spiritual home, and after Eliot's father died members of the
family gradually filtered back to Cambridge, Massachusetts. The
exile often cultivates the spirit of place, which becomes more real
to him than the place where he actually lives. It gains imaginative
wholeness through memory and distance, like James's Boston, or
Joyce's Dublin, or Eliot's Cape Ann. His possession of ancestral
destiny actually grew stronger after he relinquished his nationality, not just in the use of American locale in his later poems,
but in a more deep-reaching retrieval of the New England
conscience. Eliot may have claimed English tradition, but it may
be that English tradition cannot wholly claim Eliot, for he
brought into English tradition not only a native habit of introspection but also a state of mind that survived and flourished in
the relative isolation of New England in the seventeenth century:
inflexibility. 'It is as radical as any form of Calvinism', wrote a
reviewer of *The Family Reunion* after the first Edinburgh Festival
production of 1947.

There was a rumour in America that when Eliot once gave a
friend letters of introduction to certain Bostonians, he also

Eliot returned to New England in 1936. A family outing.

Mary (Ruth Lodge) tries to shut out the Furies in *The Family Reunion*, 1939 (with Michael Redgrave as Harry).

Emily Hale at Smith College, 1939. She suggested revisions
to *The Family Reunion*.

Eliot at Shamley Green, Surrey, where he wrote the last two *Quartets*. From l. to r.: Constance Moncrieff, Lina Mirrlees, Hettie James (back), Ellen James (holding wool), Hope Mirrlees, T. S. Eliot.

identified them through their characterizations in *The Family Reunion*. Eliot's family, like Harry's, had looked on his marriage as an aberration. His father had said that he had made a mess of his life, and Charles William Eliot had written a stiff letter urging his nephew's return to the fold, but Vivienne had refused to cross the Atlantic. A letter from Eliot's sister Margaret to their brother Henry had expressed 'the family's anxiety, when Tom went back to England' after a brief visit in August 1915 to explain his actions. *Time* magazine reported that some of Eliot's relations regarded him as the black sheep, and quoted their saying 'his poetry still fuddles a lot of us'. Henry Ware Eliot retorted on 21 March 1938 that some of the family regarded themselves as being in a uniquely favourable position to understand the work 'some of which is unintelligible unless you know the man'.

In returning to his family, Harry imagines an escape from one life to another. Mary offers the subtlest encouragement to escape when she assures him that she remembers, and can return him to, the 'real' Harry. With her, he tries out the view that his marriage has been the 'accident of a dreaming moment' when he was someone else. The early unfinished draft gave more attention to Mary's offer of natural happiness, and the light, singing, and water that Harry glimpses through her are the metaphors Eliot always uses for his rare fertile moments of renewal. Her voice sounds like a waterfall, and in her silence—always a potent word for Eliot—is the sound of nature, of ordinary life persisting between the two storms of marriage and Furies. In the unfinished draft, Mary urges Harry to stay in one place, and acquire the rhythms of recurrent seasons. The routine surface life wouldn't matter because there would be stillness in its depths. In all subsequent drafts, Mary counsels what Eliot was to consider again, in more abstract form, in *East Coker*: a life which would take its place in the ancestral round, in time's scheme, where there is necessary union of man and woman, and couples hold each other by the hand. For Eliot himself, as he conceived the play in 1934–5, the future hung in balance. To go on with Emily Hale could bring him a late spring of natural happiness, corresponding to the upswing of their time together in New Hampshire in early June 1933.

The Family Reunion was set in late March, and on one title-page Eliot jotted the words 'vernal equinox'. Could Harry accept the spring? The alternative, as Harry puts it to Mary, is to turn back into wintry darkness, a timeless dark night of the soul. Against natural love is Harry's horror of women which, Eliot explained to Browne, made Mary repulsive, though there remained a normal bit of Harry that was still attracted to her personally. In Mary's favour is her power to bring him 'a new world, in the deep, in the abyss of light, a *new* world'. The earlier drafts have this excited, deep rhythm of emotion. Harry is quickened by her glimpse of new life, her repudiation of the shadows around him, but at the very point of accepting what she has to offer, the Furies claim him more completely than ever before. All else fades into unreality. Mary herself appears obtuse because, at first anyway, she can't see them. Furiously, he rejects her: 'You're of no use to me.'

This decisive moment is all the more dramatic in earlier drafts for the strength of the alternative emotion that precedes it. From this moment, Mary becomes peripheral to the drama. When Martin Browne and Frank Morley questioned this, Eliot made a note to himself to fill out her part by having her arrange flowers. Morley said flatly that this was no solution, but the flower-arranging remained. Emily Hale, too, urged Eliot to make more of Mary. In 1938 he gave Emily his Working Draft which contained, near the end, a long speech of protest from Mary, indignant that her feelings are never consulted, and saying that she wants her turn to live. The speech follows a suggestion that it is from Mary, specifically, that Harry's destiny takes him. Emily Hale wanted Eliot to intensify this idea earlier in the play, and advised him to shift the speech to the beginning. The effect, which she tactfully did not spell out, would have given more play to Mary's feeling. But though Eliot agreed to the shift, he would not be drawn into Mary's drama. He toned down all protest so that she emerges from revision quiet, controlled, polite. Mary's fate was to go on waiting, together with Agatha, in the shadowy space between the worldly life of the women's college (Emily herself started teaching at Smith in 1936) and the otherworldly, directed life reserved for Harry alone.

Emily Hale played her special part from about 1930–5, when Eliot's sense of two lives hung in balance. She belonged to one of these lives, the American past, which revived in the later poetry. I think that she held to her memory of a more innocent Eliot (as Mary to the 'real' Harry) but then, like Mary, had to accept a man damaged by his more recent past, and accept too the penitential 'lifetime's march' that took him away from her.

The Furies bring evil home with inescapable terror. They show Harry that there is no untarnished self to which he can return for the taint of his flesh has reached his marrow. Are the Furies (as in one draft) the origin of evil or are they divine messengers? The uncertainty comes from the obscurest recess of Eliot's mind, what he called the octopus or angel with which the poet struggles. Like Jacob wrestling with the angel, Harry is 'chosen', but this means a lifetime of trials.

The crucial trial is the Furies, who are real in the terms of a play in which the real and unreal change places. The apparent reality of the family comes to appear precarious, and is finally extinguished when their clock stops in the dark of the last scene. The insubstantiality of reported phantoms should be confounded by a dramatic shock when they enter. The spectacle should be overwhelming as in the most successful production to date, in London in 1978, when they appeared suddenly at every entrance of the round Camden theatre, at about twice the human size, hooded in white like the Ku Klux Klan, to a grinding noise unendurable to the ear. They loomed over the audience on every side in the sudden darkness, blocking all exits. Such terror was never achieved in Eliot's lifetime by all accounts of productions on both sides of the Atlantic. In fact, reviews mention the Furies surprisingly little, which itself suggests their feeble impact. Most of these productions were constrained by Eliot's fear of a sceptical audience. In Martin Browne's productions, the Furies were safely contained in a side window. In fact, Browne's final view was that they should not appear at all, only their effect on Harry, but this solution would underscore the obtuse family view that Harry is mad. It is essential to persuade the audience that Harry is a man of destiny, and visible Furies achieve this with maximum economy and drama.

On the other hand, it would be all too easy to raise a laugh. When Gielgud read the script in 1938 (to consider the part of Harry), he saw that if the Furies were crudely visible they might seem ridiculous. After a performance at the end of 1948 in Sweden, Eliot reported that the Furies had appeared as a sort of rugby team of fifteen huge leprous giraffes, swarming out when the bookshelves parted in a library that looked like St Pancras Station. In an Illinois production in 1949, the Furies looked like toy puppets or jacks-in-the-box: not scary, rather fun. In October 1958, at the Phoenix Theatre in New York, they had red pupils glaring from enormous white eyes, as they peeped coyly through the draperies of the living-room. The programme gave the cast list side by side with a large advertisement for 'MY SIN . . . a most provocative perfume'.

Hell must have real sin and sinners, Eliot told Pound, people like himself. (He advised Pound to put *him* into the *Cantos* if he wanted a proper Hell, rather than mere types like the financiers, Beaverbrook, Mellon, and Rothermere.) In the hell of *The Family Reunion*, Eliot has a man like himself, caught in moral problems like his own. The challenge for Harry is to move from hell to purgatory, and this depends on his courage to face the Furies who are projections of his changing state of mind.

On one level this is a ghost story like 'The Jolly Corner' by James where an exile, returning to New York after years abroad, meets his deformed other self lurking in the old family home. As Agatha predicts from the start, Harry will have to face his ghost, down the corridor that led to the nursery, and 'it will not be a very *jolly* corner'. On a deeper level, Harry is moving according to a predestined pattern. His wish to kill is not, he finds, his own wish only, but a 'curse' passed down the generations of his family. Deeper than the individual, psychological drama lies this universal drama of innate depravity. Calvin said: 'we are so . . . perverted in every part of our nature that by this great corruption we stand justly condemned and convicted before God, to whom nothing is acceptable but righteousness, innocence, and purity.' Harry comes to realize that if he faces the depravity in himself and his family (who epitomize the whole human family), he can play a part in a pattern of redemption.

This is the right drama. In taking up the moral burden of the family, Harry is more truly responsible than if he were to take up a local public role as its leading member. He is to rescue its spirit, not preside over its daily doings. Obtuse members of his family see only the psychological drama, following the traumatic end of his marriage. To them, the Furies are signs of his disturbance. Eliot's eldest sister, Ada, may have exemplified such a view when she feared that her brother's 'dramatism' would endanger his sanity.

But in the play there is one member of the family, Agatha, who recognizes the Furies to be real. She tells Harry that his nightmare is the real purgatorial fire, and so sanctions his departure as an essential move in a predestined pattern. Eliot told Martin Browne that Harry follows the Furies like the Disciples dropping their nets. This, then, is the biblical pattern: to leave one's family for the religious life. Agatha and Mary, who can see paradise as well as purgatory, bless his way: 'Follow follow.'

One of Emily Hale's suggestions (on the second of the two drafts that Eliot sent her) was that Harry's mission be brought to a stronger climax. She wrote at the end of the penultimate scene: 'chance for Harry's explanation of Furies as he *now* sees them . . .' The result was an important additional dialogue beginning with Amy's question, 'But why are you going?', and ending with Harry's announcement of his 'election'. He means to purify himself through solitude, envisaged in terms of the remote lives of desert saints: the heat of the sun, thirst, the icy vigil. There is some talk of 'care over lives of humble people' who are ignorant and have 'incurable diseases', but this is not very convincing. Harry is no Father Zossima, with compassion for the sufferings of the people. He is absorbed in his own soul, and through him Eliot explored the nature of a hermit in the making.

Some people will leave the theatre bewildered about Harry, and, to an extent, disappointed. Amy's death on Harry's departure was Eliot's attempt to give such members of the audience a dramatic finale of an obvious sort, but the real end is the prayer of the two women who will imaginatively 'follow' Harry wherever his pilgrimage takes him, as we, the audience, should ideally 'follow'. In the end, Eliot did not act on the pleas of Martin Browne and Emily Hale to close the play more explicitly. In Emily Hale's draft he tried to predict Harry's sanctification, but this he cut. The play was so close to his own experience that it had to remain as open as his own fate.

Eliot's new life turned on choices that he made in the mid-thirties: to turn from the path of renewed love and family reunion, choosing the lone path of religious ordeal. Specifically, this meant to stand by that form of High Anglicanism which made divorce impossible. It meant that though, at some point, he did wish to marry Emily Hale, their relationship could remain no more than an understanding—I think something more than friendship. This

decision to hold back may have been reinforced by the fact that
Eliot's closest friends in London did not take to Emily Hale or
grant her entrée. John Hayward dismissed her in slightly mocking
tones, as though she were some fad of Eliot's, an unwelcome
diversion from the male club. To Virginia Woolf, she appeared
too proper, an impeccable Bostonian. In a flight of inaccurate
malice, Virginia Woolf wrote her off as Eliot's 'rich American
snob lady'.* Eliot, though, was not a man to be influenced
inordinately by his friends. It is more likely that his was a moral
decision.

It may be that Emily Hale's fate was sealed by the time that he
first conceived the play in 1934–5. Mary, unlike the wife, is at least
visible, but like the wife she is barely a character, and even less so in
Eliot's revisions. It is a one-man show. The dead wife represents his
polluted soul; Mary a rather perfunctory temptation. The country
house, with its decayed family, is a naturalistic front for what is, in
essence, a morality play in which figures move in set patterns, as
they try in different ways to free the house from the curse of its
decline.

Eliot plays up the difference between this momentous drama
and the paltry disaster of Harry's brother John, who has drunkenly
reversed his car into a shop window in Ebury Street, and told the
police: 'I thought it was all open country about here.' The
Wodehouse-ish joke comes from the *Evening Standard* on 14 April
1937, which reported that the young Viscount Forbes of Halkin
Street, SW, drove at 52 miles an hour in Beddington Lane, near
Croydon, on 4 February. When stopped, he said, 'I thought it was
all countrified'. Eliot also kept the *Standard*'s May 1937 report on
Robert Edgar, aged 21, a graduate of Christ Church, Oxford, who
was charged with drunken driving in the High Street on
Coronation night. When arrested, he refused to be examined by a
doctor. 'I have always refused to do so because I distrust their
efficiency', he told the court. This very English comedy of manners
sets off the quite different moral drama where Furies lead Harry
'across the frontier'. At the end, Harry fades out of clear-cut
English society into the dim distance of a far frontier. The
accidents of such as John are nothing to the danger that Harry is to
face, of being alone with his flawed self.

* See ch. 4 for Emily Hale's marvellous letter describing this visit to the Woolfs.

The Family Reunion poses outward accident versus internal danger as a challenge to the audience: which matters? The one is patent; the other a mystery. The play teases us with the superficial mystery of murder, especially when a policeman arrives on the scene, but that drama is undercut by the profounder mystery of guilt. Harry did not push his wife overboard, but—as Eliot pointed out in a letter to Martin Browne—he didn't call for help, nor did he jump in after her. Is passivity culpable? Hawthorne said: 'It was the policy of our ancestors to search out even the most secret sins, and expose them to shame.' The repressed puritan world of secrets and sudden breaches of decorum is half-concealed within the tame setting of English society. The shock comes when extreme containment is broken by disclosure: 'I pushed her.' The unexpected confession is the tactic of Eliot's early dramatic monologues: Prufrock's expectation of 'a hundred visions . . .' or the hope that an unwanted Lady 'should die some afternoon . . . / Should die and leave me sitting pen in hand'. These are the disclosures of a mind approaching some frontier of vision or horror.

Agatha's function is to direct Harry across that frontier. It was a difficult, perhaps impossible part, Eliot remarked to Mary Trevelyan after seeing Sybil Thorndyke in Peter Brooke's production in 1956. She must be a soothsayer as well as a normal, warm-hearted woman. Agatha had to have a measure of spiritual power, and this was lacking, again, in Lilian Gish in New York in 1958. Agatha's formidable task is to make the frontier real, and this can happen only if the production prepares for it. The country-house setting has to seem by contrast increasingly unreal, so that we shift from watching a predictable drama of strains and manners to one that is beyond us.

Eliot's aim was what he termed the ultra-dramatic. In two unpublished talks in 1937 he said that poetic drama could awaken the audience to a hidden pattern of reality which may supersede what is conventionally dramatic. He believed that an audience would accept this so long as there was something more ordinary to attend to. The characters in such a play have a double existence: they must appear living creatures like ourselves, and at the same time they must make us see through the usual classified emotions into a world of which we are normally unaware, which comes from the depths of the playwright himself. A poet, once he has found his way into these strange lands of more than polar darkness and more than equatorial light, may gradually lose interest in the normal world, and his characters may come to be, in the normal sense, less real. Such a poet has crossed the frontier from dramatic action to the spiritual action that transcends it. Eliot spoke repeatedly of a poet who has crossed into a world where we cannot follow him— somewhere *beyond* the dramatic.

Eliot had a rationale, then, for his unwillingness to be explicit about Harry's future actions. Under pressure, he told Michael Redgrave that Harry would take a job in the East End, but this was a sop to an actor: it was never in the script. The statement elicited by Emily Hale, 'I have this election', was as far as clarity could go.

Eliot moves beyond drama through his use of seasonal change. The greenhouse flowers that Mary brings on stage were not just to give her some feeble action; they bear out a precise time, late March, in the north of England: just too early for garden flowers. The metaphoric reach of the poetry—the strongest poetry in all Eliot's plays—suggests that the spring that is on the way is not to be a natural awakening, but a time of pilgrimage that will take Harry outside time's scheme to the polar regions of extreme trial where the life of the senses will freeze.

The vernal equinox might be said to be the fulcrum on which Eliot himself moved and had his being, swinging into the 'cruellest' month of April or swinging back the other way into the dark night of winter, when only the soul's sap quivers. The seasonal cycle at which the play stands poised is superseded when a man abandons seasonal change for the perpetual winter of the poles. Spring, to Harry, excites us with 'lying voices', and is, therefore, 'an evil time'. He repudiates the stir of the senses so as to see himself as part of a larger pattern: some monstrous aberration of all men, of the world 'which I cannot put in order'. Order is the clue to his true mission—and to Eliot's. It is not to be a missionary in any literal sense, but to create order in the form of a perfect life. The autobiographical crisis of the play propels Eliot into the abstract order of the *Quartets*. The condition of this venture was nothing less than what Mary called, in the early unfinished draft, perpetual exile.

Eliot abandoned the theatre for the next eight years. The reason he gave was the difficulty of putting on plays with the outbreak of

war. Yet *Murder in the Cathedral* was revived successfully throughout the war in a variety of improvised theatres. It is possible that
the apparent failure of *The Family Reunion* daunted Eliot, for the
first production at the Westminster Theatre closed after five
weeks. But there may have been some more compelling reason: his
need to retrieve the grace glimpsed at Burnt Norton five years
before. 'I must follow the bright angels' is Harry's exit line, a
difficult one for an actor to deliver with any conviction. Harry
exits from the explicit medium of the theatre into the invisible
drama of spiritual autobiography, for the only cure of demonic
possession lay in further exploration of what *Burnt Norton* had
called the way down. This slow, painful transformation of a flawed
self had been the formal alternative to an immediate experience of
bliss which Eliot had called the way up. In the two sequels that
Eliot planned in 1940, bliss was to remain only a memory. The way
down now took over, culminating in an imaginary journey across a
vast and terrible sea. The only landmark was the treacherous rocks,
the Dry Salvages, off the coast of Cape Ann. In closing with this
ordeal, Eliot renews the crossing of Andrew Eliot, in 1669, to the
New World. It meant that he had to distance himself, at least
temporarily, from the comfort of love and family. In a sense, he
was exchanging the present-day reality for the dream of New
England. The ancestral journey loomed out of the past, that
crossing that was driven by the loftiest dream of a purified life, and
was, at the same time, a surrender to the severest of trials.

3. The Perfect Life

STARTING from 'acute personal reminiscence'—reunion with an old love or 'things ill done and done to others' harm'— *Four Quartets* recounts Eliot's struggle to recast his lot during his years in the clergyhouse in Kensington. This is reflected in the original title, 'Kensington Quartets', which Eliot had in mind until he completed the poems in September 1942. Looking back, he seemed to have lived on the edge of a 'grimpen', a dangerous mire.* The period of trial in his life from 1934 to 1938 then came to epitomize the grim ordeal of a whole society under fire from 1940 to 1942. Yet in the midst of danger, both personal and public, there is a promise of renewal in a shaping idea of the perfect life.

Although only one of the four poems is set in New England, the entire sequence revives the American Puritans' resolve to establish the perfect life on earth. In the seventeenth century they set out the signs of election as an exact sequence, and because communication of this took precedence over art, they eschewed more imaginative forms of writing for the plain style. Eliot, too, set out the inward sequence, often in terms so deliberately prosaic ('The poetry does not matter', he said in 1940), that some admirers of his earlier pyrotechnics accused him of flatness.

In earlier days, Virginia Woolf had seen Eliot as 'a New England schoolmaster', and Pound had complained about his blood, 'the thin milk of ... New England from the pap'. His own unwillingness to acknowledge his native tradition until late in his career was not snobbery, but a fear, repeated in the essays, of 'provincialism'. From the start he wanted to be a universal writer, not local like Hawthorne with whom he had much in common. Yet, far from abrogating his native tradition, Eliot renews the idealism, the strenuousness, and moral power of colonial New England as he brought to greatness its distinctive literary forms, sermon and

---

* Eliot derived 'grimpen' (*East Coker*: II) from Conan Doyle, *The Hound of the Baskervilles* (1902): 'Life has become like that great Grimpen Mire, with little green patches everywhere into which one may sink and with no guide to point the track.' Conan Doyle, in turn, derived the word from Grimspound Bog, near Widecombe, on Dartmoor.

spiritual biography. At the same time, through his use of parallels from European and Eastern traditions, he rescued native tradition from 'provincialism'.

Andrew Eliot, who crossed the sea as an act of faith, is the work's ancestral exemplar, like the first fathers in Cotton Mather's *Magnalia Christi Americana*. Eliot's parallel tradition came from books he had read first at Harvard, the *Upanishads*, *The Divine Comedy*, *Samson Agonistes*, and the mystics of the late Middle Ages, St John of the Cross and Dame Julian of Norwich, all of whom set out a similar progress towards perfection.* This he undertook to renew for his own time, the dispirited years of the second world war. 'Now', he said in 1940, 'under conditions / That seem unpropitious.'

The form of life that Eliot both inherits and renews is quite simple. His long poems often look formidable because of their profusion of bookish allusions, but these serve only to repeat and support, in different terms, a simple proposition, say the prevalence of spiritual sterility in *The Waste Land*, or the emotional demands of 'turning' or conversion in *Ash Wednesday*. The epigraph to *Burnt Norton* proposed two equally valid ways to perfection: the way up and the way down are the same.

The 'way up' is a life directed by a visionary moment in which the mind perceives a timeless 'reality'. Eliot begins with his own intuition of the way up in the garden of Burnt Norton. He gives no other examples of people who followed this way, though it is easy to think of candidates: Henry Vaughan, perhaps, who could write with sublime casualness, 'I saw eternity the other night / Like a great *Ring* of pure and endless light' or Emily Brontë whose boldness invited what seem to have been nightly visitations: 'And visions rise and change that kill me with desire.'

Walking with Emily Hale through the rose-garden at Burnt Norton, Eliot experienced a startling access of emotion that awakened him momentarily to 'the heart of light'. It seemed no less than a miracle that he should be allowed to experience once again a moment when, through human love, he could apprehend divine love, and that this should not be reserved for the innocence of

---

* As a graduate student T.S.E. took notes on St John of the Cross and Dame Julian from Inge's *Christian Mysticism*, and noted, too, the Dark Night mentioned in Evelyn Underhill's *Mysticism* (he took extensive notes from this book) soon after it was published in 1911.

youth, as he had thought, but should come in middle age to a man who felt contaminated by marriage. For, as the speaker comes from the rose-garden, across the lawn towards an empty pool of dry concrete, it seems to fill with water out of sunlight. He feels the same indescribable ecstasy recalled in *The Waste Land* where, leaving a garden, rapt by the 'hyacinth girl' whose arms were full of flowers, a man stares suddenly 'into the heart of light, the silence', only to collapse, in bitter frustration, into the sterility of present life, with its abortive sexual relationships in a polluted London. So, too, at Burnt Norton, the moment passes: a cloud shuts off the sun, the pool is dry once more, and Eliot is left to lament 'the waste sad time / Stretching before and after'. But the collapse in *The Waste Land* is not quite the same. In that poem, a man is flung from sublimity to futility; in *Burnt Norton* he turns from sublimity to perceive—though still only in theory—an alternative course by which we may transcend our imperfect existence. The 'way up', in fact, provides the incentive to pursue the 'way down'.

Although in his early years Eliot had aspired, at least inter-mittently, to the way up of the chosen, those who live perpetually in the light of grace, after his imaginative encounter with the Furies of 1934-8 he aligned himself, in the later *Quartets*, with the other party, the flawed beings who must be remade if they are to become worthy of sublime insight. 'Sin is Behovely': Christ's words to Dame Julian of Norwich in the fourteenth century confirm what was sharply apparent to Eliot's conscience. The way down, which dominates the central two poems, *East Coker* and *The Dry Salvages*, is an operation on Original Sin, a radical excision of all one feels, knows, and is. Assuming the otherness of the divine spirit, that it is utterly beyond human feeling, knowledge, and identity, Eliot comes to realize that the seeker must divest himself of all attributes most precious to him if he is to come to know God.

The initial publication of *Burnt Norton* as an isolated poem in 1936, the gap that followed while Eliot wrote *The Family Reunion*, and the separate publication of the subsequent three poems, encourage us to read the *Quartets* as separate units, but they are unified, not merely by the formal repetition of their five-part structure, but by a profounder strategy of repetition. It is the strategy of Emerson's essays, where each sentence is self-contained but repeats, in different terms, the same idea. It is also the tactic of the sermon: each unit, whether homely or poetic, is designed to awaken the audience, on different levels, to the same revelation. Eliot, like Emerson or Whitman, is writing a form of scripture. His poetry seeks the Word, not mere words, but the Word 'Swaddled with darkness'. As the reader must launch into the chasm between Emerson's sentences, or follow Whitman's trail of dots, so must he fill the blanks on Eliot's page. Eliot, like Whitman, also emulates the repetition of the Bible and the alternation of the prosaic and poetic that he thought essential to the long poem.

Repetition is the very message of *Four Quartets*: to try again and yet again for the perfect life, and not to look for the fruits of action, an end to the pilgrimage. What appears to be the end—it may be a climactic personal effort, it may be the end to a poem—becomes, in the model life that Eliot devised, a new beginning. In this way, *Burnt Norton*, with its idyllic garden, which might have seemed the *Paradiso* at the end of Eliot's 1936 edition of *Collected Poems*, turns out, in the course of his continued existence, to be only the beginning of a much longer poem which demands recurring effort. Each subsequent poem must repeat the cycle of moral and artistic effort in changed circumstances and new terms. In *East Coker* there is an effort to submit to surgery; in *The Dry Salvages* to 'fare forward' across a battering sea.

Although the beginning of effort repeatedly succeeds the end, Eliot does suggest the possibility of progression: 'In my end is my beginning', he says, but also 'In my beginning is my end'. In one sense he refers simply to the inexorable course of the life-span which ends in death. But then, for some, death itself is the beginning of eternal life (as Emily Dickinson's death-carriage rides her triumphantly past children playing in a ring, past the offer of love, as she perceives that she moves 'toward Eternity'). Eliot, too, lives with an eye to eternity: that supreme possibility of progression is implied when he longs for 'the unimaginable / Zero summer', for a fullness of being that lies outside the round of the seasons, outside time's scheme.

Eliot sets himself the question: how do we live in time so as to conquer time? Each of the *Quartets* explores a point of intersection of time and timelessness which he draws initially from his own life. In *Burnt Norton* there is the moment of love, fixed in memory, but here, at the outset, Eliot will not sustain that feeling that could most naturally close the gap between flawed and ideal life. In leaving a promising love to wither, Eliot may seem perverse to the

point of idiosyncrasy. To Emily Hale it remained a 'mystery' for
the rest of her life. Yet Eliot's commitment in *Four Quartets*, as in
The Family Reunion, to the solitary burden of the soul is not out of
line with a standard American plot where the middle-aged New
Englander, awakening to life, renounces love out of a finer moral
passion 'to be right', or where Melville spurns the ease of the shore
to confront the nature of creation, or Huck Finn lights out for the
Territory ('there is no more solitary character in fiction', said
Eliot), or the Lone Ranger turns his back on the homestead, and
rides into the horizon to confront dangerous facts that lie beyond
the limits of domesticity. The frontier, in Eliot's case, is that of
time and eternity.

To consort with his own kind was only a respite from this lone
journey. For most of his life Eliot was a solitary who yet saw it as
his duty (as public figure or as Christian performing acts of charity)
to partake in the world. Love did not come easily, for, until the last
eight or nine years of his life, he reserved his emotional energy for a
higher object than woman, much as Aeneas left Dido for his higher
destiny to found Rome. He identified with the moment when the
gods call Aeneas, urging a further voyage, and promising him
imperium without end. Eliot cultivates the *pietas* of the classical
hero when, in the wake of old Andrew Eliot, he renews the
ancestral voyage in *The Dry Salvages*: 'fare forward, voyagers.'

The word 'destiny' resounds with unmistakeable import in the
essays Eliot wrote while he composed *Four Quartets*. The woman
who provokes the vision of the heart of light remains unidentified,
no more than a dim shade of the past who is allowed to impinge on
the hero's consciousness only in so far as she inspires, once again,
his great destiny. For here, in the first *Quartet*, he is more the hero
planning a private future, than the exemplar who speaks to us. We
may overhear, but we cannot share his exclusive moment. Nor is it
explained why love must turn so entirely to 'dust'. The same
abrupt denial recurs in the summer night when couples dance,
holding each other by the hand, feet rising and falling in rhythmic
concord. For some time the poet lends an eye to this recurrent
festival of coupling and earth's fertility, but then, like a shot, comes
his dark judgement that it amounts to nothing but 'dung and
death'. The stern voice of denial is like that of the Puritan killjoy in
Hawthorne's tale, who rebukes and breaks up the nuptial frolics in
'The Maypole of Merry Mount'. Hawthorne was, in fact, more

aware than Eliot of the moral ambiguity of the killjoy position: that so grave a sense of human corruption, of 'dust' and 'dung', is itself warping. A recoil in horror may be realistic, but it does wither the bonds of feeling.

Not love then but, in the end, art is one certain point of intersection with the timeless: a Chinese jar, created at some point in time, which 'still/Moves perpetually in its stillness'. Eliot's room-mate at his school, Milton Academy, used to boast of a grandmother who had collected Chinese jars brought by the Salem clippers. In Eliot's maturity the jar comes to represent the classic art to which he now aspires. As the jar epitomizes the achievements of Chinese civilization, and as the garden, blending formality with mystery, epitomizes the achievements of English civilization, so Eliot must fulfil his own heritage from New England divines who tried to convey the Word. Ordinary words 'slip, slide, perish,/Decay with imprecision, will not stay in place', but against the perpetual decay of language in the course of time Eliot has as his model 'The Word in the desert', language that has the permanence of scripture, as though graven on tablets of the law. In Christian terms, the Word is the deity whose holiness was proven in the face of temptation. Eliot sets up here the highest challenge that language can present: to make shoddy words approach the perfect Word.

The initiating impulse for this enterprise came from the silent, faceless companion at Burnt Norton: not the woman as a person, but love's transforming power. The whole sequence begins with 'we', a shared experience, but the woman's power to generate this rarefied feeling in Eliot worked largely through memory and imagination. It did not depend on frequent meetings, and may have flourished at some distance. Whatever Emily did to re-initiate the 'heart of light' was part of Eliot's hidden life, a crucial source of creativity as well as religious striving, which comes to the surface only momentarily at high points in the poetry. The drafts of the later *Quartets* suggest that she continued to preside over his imaginative life, as he came to see how their love might be used to sustain religious effort.

Yet the public face of Eliot's poetry obliterates Emily Hale, not only by an appropriate conversion of personal life into impersonal art, but by deliberately subsuming her unvoiced appeal in the 'voices of temptation' at the end of *Burnt Norton*. Temptation, for Eliot, meant love's sensual dross. From his earliest juvenilia, he showed a distrust of sensuality, a belief that love was too delicate to be enjoyed. What looks like misogyny in the early poems is more a disgust with women like Grishkin, the predator in 'Whispers of Immortality', or Fresca, the scribbling socialite in *The Waste Land* manuscript, who travesty love by the abuse of their bodies.

Eliot was, I think, tacitly asking of Emily Hale an extraordinary feat: that her feeling should match his own need to transmute love into 'Love', a distilled concentrate that would never evaporate. Language cannot convey this feat: 'I can only say, *there* we have been: but I cannot say where.' The shared moment in the English garden, in the arbour when the rain beat, and in the draughty church in the November mist, provide only the impetus to discover the infinitude of the private man. Eliot was asking for 'freedom' from desire, from the obligations of the usual 'action', from all 'outer compulsion', in order to live by 'a grace of sense'.

It is impossible as yet to be sure if Emily Hale understood this challenge, and, if so, how she met it. My guess is that she was exalted in the way that Emerson's listeners were intoxicated by his offer of spiritual power. One of her pupils at Smith College reported that she read aloud an advance typescript of *East Coker* 'as if it were a love letter from God'. I imagine that, given Eliot's marital tie, she tried to make the most of a unique friendship. She gave a copy of *East Coker* to a pupil, inscribing it 'From Emily Hale, a friend of T. S. Eliot'. Some years later she retrieved the copy when she was going to meet Eliot, and returned it with a further inscription: 'From T. S. Eliot, a friend of Emily Hale.' She was, understandably, not quite content with beautiful friendship, and hoped, even expected, that they might one day marry.

The Word, Eliot says, is most attacked by 'voices of temptation'. These were, the draft shows, a 'circling Fury' (derived from Vivienne) and a 'sweet' temptation (derived from Emily, in her marriageable aspect). To have yoked these together may seem as reductive as the note to *The Waste Land* which asserts that 'all the women are one woman'. But here, I think, he owns to fear. To succumb to sweetness as he had once succumbed to Vivienne— now the 'crying shadow in the funeral dance'—would distract the poet from his duty to approach the Word.

So Eliot wove unrelated strands of his existence together 'in an emotional whole', he told Anne Ridler. The fear of Vivienne, the love of Emily, the aims of art, and the endless reach of the religious life were brought together and cohere within the formal structure of the *Quartet*. Outside his poetry, the strands remained disparate, which is why we get such varied and sometimes conflicting reports of Eliot's behaviour: humorous, pious, domestic, distant. Only through the poetry do we see the whole man, for whom the important ties were those that served religious emotion by generating some feeling—it might be horror, it might be ardour—strong enough, extreme enough, to open him to 'vibrations beyond the range of ordinary men'.

Eliot's fascination for the extremities of the religious life came to him early, in his poems of 1914–15. 'The Burnt Dancer' (unpublished) and 'The Death of St Narcissus' show the origin of the refining fire of *Four Quartets* in which you 'move in measure, like a dancer.' In 1914, noticing a moth dance round a candle, Eliot had defined a martyr's state of daring, almost reckless surrender to a dazzling energy. A fragile mortal creature, unable to absorb a flame of such intensity, will burn itself out, and the young poet had watched the inevitable with pity and terror. In 1935 Eliot revived the state of mind implied by burning and dancing, but now the dance is less abandoned, more like the precise, controlled movements of classical ballet (of which Eliot had become a patron). The discipline of dance is like the discipline of the religious life as Eliot began to understand it through the extreme demand of St John of the Cross:

> In order to arrive at what you are not
> You must go through the way in which you are not.

St John of the Cross revealed the way down. A few months after Emily Hale's long-term departure for America on the outbreak of war, Eliot kicked away from the attachments of earth in order to find sublimity in some more enduring form. The way up was now closed to him, but its memory was to remain 'always' as a high point of attainment. For it realized the uncompromising biographical premiss that Eliot had framed in 1910, that such a moment is the essence of existence. Emily Dickinson has the same premiss when she says:

> . . . I weigh
> The time 'twill be till six o'clock

> I have so much to do—
> And yet—Existence—some way back—
> Stopped—struck—my ticking—through—

A draft of *Burnt Norton*, so far unknown, ends in this way with a multitude of blanks which inject into language the silence of revelation when language fails. In this draft the final emphasis falls not on 'waste time', but on the divine light,* in repeated flashes that pulsate beyond the poem.

Is there life after vision? What does one do with the leaden stretches of the life-span before and after?

Eliot began to explore different forms of life, with their patterns of repetition and possibilities for progress. There is the placid rural existence based on seasonal recurrence. There is the danger-filled life of New England fishermen, who routinely confront death on their rocky coast. There is, finally, the disciplined life of a religious community, which combines repetition of ritual and striving of the soul. But cutting through all these, and never to be forgotten, is the visionary experience at the still point of the turning world.

Eliot knew that he could not hope to repeat that spontaneous intuition, but could hope to retrieve its import through the Word. Contaminated by sin, as he felt, in the four years between the first and second *Quartets*, he had now to begin a long ordeal of self-transformation to make himself worthy of the Word. Beginning— this word reverberates through *East Coker*—once more from the bedrock of temporal existence, he set out to find the pattern of the perfect life.

The model for this life was with Eliot from earliest childhood in his mother's poems, and in the dauntless image of the Pilgrim Fathers, cherished by his family. (Charlotte Eliot gave a lecture on 'The Romantic History of the Pilgrim Fathers' to ten schools, and was a charter member and eventually president of the Missouri Society of the Colonial Dames of America.) Eliot's last step at the

---

* Eliot sent this draft to Frank Morley in New York, and it is now in the Houghton Library. The other extant draft, which Eliot gave to John Hayward, is cited by Helen Gardner, but she does not mention that, following the well-known final lines, are two further lines consisting of two words: 'Light' followed by a space is succeeded by 'Gone' indented on another new line. 'Gone' is added in pencil, as though it were an afterthought. Both lines are cancelled. King's College Library, Cambridge, England.

end of the whole sequence was to discover that the models of childhood are inescapable; his life had been destined to take the frontiering pattern of family history that had led to his birth on 'the longest river':*

> And the end of all our exploring
> Will be to arrive where we started
> And know the place for the first time.

The New World voyage takes off at the end of *East Coker*. Eliot rehearsed it back in 1930, where a pilgrim approaches the New England shore after the long ordeal of the sea. *Marina* had described the 'Bowsprit cracked with ice', the weak rigging, the rotten canvas, the leak, and the seams that needed 'caulking' in the same detail as Bradford's history of the voyage of the Pilgrim Fathers, written between 1630 and 1650: '. . . the shipe was shroudly shaken, and her upper works made very leakie; and one of the maine beames in the midd ships was bowed and craked, which put them in some fear that the shipe could not be able to performe the voiage.' Some wished to return, but others heartened them: 'And as for the decks and uper workes they would calke them as well as they could. . . . So they commited them selves to the will of God, and resolved to proseede.' For they were convinced, as another early historian, Edward Johnson, put it, that they were destined for 'the place where the Lord will create a new Heaven, and a new Earth in, new Churches, and a new Common-wealth together'. So Eliot's dream-voyage points towards a new life. East Coker is the point of departure, and it is there that the poet re-enacts the about-face which gained its energy from rejection, the annihilating force of a condemnation of the comfort-able Old World. His journey towards perfection takes its initiating impulse from a rejection of the earthly life and its oblivious pleasures. East Coker is the village in Somerset from which Andrew Eliot set out. His voyage pushes off from merrymakers who dance in their communal ring from time immemorial. Eliot's condemnation of them to 'Dung and death' repeats his 1930 condemnations: Death to those 'who suffer the ecstasy of the

* The immediate model was Eliot's grandfather, William Greenleaf Eliot, who settled on the Mississippi, then the frontier, in 1834, in order to found the Unitarian Church in St Louis. His image dominated the family, and Charlotte Eliot wrote his biography. See *Eliot's Early Years*, ch. 1.

animals', and Death to vanity in bright clothes, and Death to pigs
'who sit in the sty of contentment'. (Was this the holy Word,
Hawthorne might have asked, or did the dark ancestral shade of
Salem hover over Eliot's lips?)

It is from the joining of men and women that Eliot recoils most
strongly. He hastens couples to 'death' with a finality that suggests
Eliot's own abortive marriage: the one dead end in his life. The year
he visited East Coker, 1937, just preceded the final drama of his
marriage. The energy of the poem comes from acute personal
reminiscence, that tests and validates the abstract terms of the
poem's surface. John Hayward, the first to read a draft in February
1940, found it poignantly self-revealing. Much of what is obscure in
East Coker does become clear in terms of the facts of Eliot's life: the
conflict between recoil from marriage, and the longing provoked
by Emily Hale's departure in the autumn of 1939, shortly before
Eliot wrote the poem. Its cryptic generalization about 'disturbance' is fuelled by pangs of love, rejected, unwanted, but forcing
their way to the surface. As in the youthful 'Love Song of Saint
Sebastian', Eliot magnifies sexual turmoil as the dissolution of the
whole universe into an original chaos of freezing heat likened, in a
letter of 1935, to the embraces of the Devil. The youthful would-be
'saint' rejects his sexual need; the ageing poet—exaggerating his
age—deprecates 'the disturbance of the spring'.

Eliot's sustained fear of love—if one belonged to another, one
might become a 'creature' of 'summer heat'—finds its precise
parallel outside English tradition in the New England figure of
Goodman Brown, who discovers sin in a dark wood. There he
stands with his bride 'beneath the canopy of fire', menaced by
Boston townsmen who would draw him into devilish enchant-
ments. At the last moment, Brown seems to save himself by a recoil
from his fellow-townsmen, but his life and his wife's are blighted
ever after by the unrelenting sense of sin.

The New World journey from East Coker takes the lone
voyager away from the community of couples destined solely for
death. The radical spirit of the American lurks, invisible but
dominant, on the edge of the English scene. *East Coker* is a poem
about family origins that links the American progenitor with his
English roots: a way for Eliot to resolve his own dual allegiance.

In August 1937 he went to stay with Sir Matthew Nathan at a
manor house in West Coker in Somerset, and from there explored

his family village. The poem retraces his approach that late summer day, looking down the lane in the haze of heat. The dahlias sleep. And then, as he hears a faint pipe, the present dissolves in a dream of the past: ancient ancestors with their clumsy, loam-clogged feet as they dance in a ring. Eliot will not 'keep time'. He maintains a spectatorial distance that is not only distance in time, but a refusal of the rounds of temporal life. What alerts him is the dawn wind that beckons the emigrant to the New World. At this point Eliot joins in.

'I am here', he says suddenly. 'In my beginning.'

Early in 1939 Eliot searched out his beginnings in the *Sketch of the Eliot Family* in the British Museum. There was, he discovered, an earlier phase of the family in Devon, where they had been respectable squires in the fourteenth and fifteenth centuries. One had been a knight of the shire for Devon in about 1430. In the poem, though, Eliot chose to ignore this and concentrate on the two centuries when the family lived at East Coker. He identified himself with the grave Tudor moralist, Sir Thomas Elyot, grandson of Simon Elyot of East Coker, and Andrew, the cordwainer who left East Coker in 1669. Bold in their piety, both fulfilled the family motto, *tace aut face*, act or be silent.

It was Eliot's view that the family fortunes had declined from about 1914. In the mid-nineteenth century, William Greenleaf Eliot had been a financial genius, but in the 1930s and 1940s his grandchildren, Eliot's brother and unmarried sisters, lived in modest apartments by comparison with the large, rather grand house that their father had built in 1896 at Gloucester, Cape Ann. Eliot never returned to that house after 1915—the family must have lost it—but he said that he had it in mind when he described the long-deserted house, left to the field mouse, at East Coker.

As the New World journey broke the pattern of generations, so Eliot broke with family expectations in 1915 to take a lone course—the course that would ultimately revive family distinction as well as its boldest tradition of moral or spiritual frontiering. Eliot was past fifty when he launched a new course in *East Coker*. 'Old men ought to be explorers', he said, and though, in a sense, he was making an interior journey all his life, the course he set himself in 1940 was more dangerous and demanding than anything he had done before.

Despite previous efforts to change—marriage in 1915, conversion in 1927, the change of nationality, the vow of celibacy in 1928, and the separation from his wife—Eliot seems to have felt early in 1940 that the true inward change had yet to begin. It had, in fact, already begun with the declaration of war, which broke a pattern of existence which he had accepted from 1933 to 1939: the regular spring or summer reunions with Emily Hale. The upheaval that followed her departure in September 1939 was the signal for a new and fiercer discipline of asceticism.

In this discipline Eliot was consciously following others in earlier centuries whom, he adds modestly, one cannot hope to emulate. Its actuality was still as untested as the 'vast waters' and infinitely remote farther shore must have seemed to those who ventured to colonize America. The English houses vanish, and in their place the sea stretches out. The world becomes stranger as the explorer passes the frontiers of the most demanding form of the religious life. Holding to the identity of explorer, he is not sure of his fate—it may be death on the hidden rocks, as others before him went down—but he is determined to break the mould of the empty life, to let its scenes recede, and to hear its twitter fade. He will be alone: this much he knows. So he goes forward into 'the dark' to be remade: 'O dark dark dark.' Cut off from the light (the known world, the senses) he enters the mysterious dark night of the soul.

St John of the Cross speaks of the 'fortunate night' in which there is no light but 'that which burned in my heart'. It guides him 'more surely than the light of noon'. Samson, the other model, also waits in blind darkness 'amid the blaze of noon'. Such was to be Eliot's future life in the forties and fifties, as he moved through the blaze of publicity that came with fame. In the central sections of the first two *Quartets*, he distinguishes one sort of darkness from another. There is the darkness of the tube trains, where oblivious commuters shuttle to no purpose along the metalled rails of their lives; but descending lower, into the night of the soul, there is a different darkness: a conscious stripping of identity's props, knowledge and emotions, and, most risky, of identity itself. The idea is that if divinity is unutterably other, remote, and hidden beneath a cloud of unknowing, it is essential to strip oneself of everything one knows in order to encounter it. Like all asceticism, its aim is to liberate the divine image in man, hidden under layers of unlikeness.

Eliot said that this dark night was analogous to 'the drought' which is an essential stage in the progress of a mystic. This stage drew Eliot, and throughout his career he explored it in a variety of scenes: the urban waste, the desert, the jagged stair, the disturbing journey of the magi, the grim voyage, and here Samson's period of abasement—betrayed by his wife, a prisoner of the Philistines—on his way to becoming God's agent. Eliot follows Milton in his focus on the period of waiting in darkness that was, for Eliot, so clearly the route to the new life that in his poetry (where there is little attainment) it comes to be the religious life itself.

All these physical and psychic ordeals demonstrate a single condition, a state of trial with its strains of terror, emptiness, and patient endurance. The state is dramatized with increasing subtlety and maturity until, in *East Coker*, Eliot is able to speak the riddling language of St John of the Cross which contains the secret of transformation:

> In order to arrive at what you do not know
>   You must go by a way which is the way of ignorance.
> In order to possess what you do not possess
>   You must go by the way of dispossession.
> In order to arrive at what you are not
>   You must go through the way in which you are not.*

This method abjures soul-searching—no clamouring self-hatred—for a quiet nonentity: 'where you are is where you are not.'

Thomas Merton has described St John of the Cross as the 'most hidden of saints', and 'the patron of those who have a vocation that is thought, by others, to be spectacular, but which, in reality, is lowly, difficult, and obscure. He is the patron . . . and the Master of those whom God had led into the uninteresting wilderness of contemplative prayer'. Uninteresting? The word defies us to understand this neutral state far removed from the spurious status and possible charlatanism of overt holiness.

---

* When Eliot uses the words of St John of the Cross they are not twisted as are many other allusions in Eliot's earlier poetry. The words come from *The Ascent of Mount Carmel*, I. xiii, in the translation of E. Allison Peers which was in Eliot's library:

> In order to arrive at that which thou knowest not,
> Thou must go by a way that thou knowest not.
> In order to arrive at that which thou possessest not,
> Thou must go by a way that thou possessest not.
> In order to arrive at that which thou art not,
> Thou must go through that which thou art not.

Accordingly, Eliot set himself to negate the senses and all worldly notions of success in order to become a vacuum for grace to fill. The *via negativa* demands a new and more extreme surrender, as Eliot phrased it, 'Inoperancy of the world of spirit'. The saint's chart of the narrow way to perfection is marked with the words: 'Nothing—nothing—nothing—nothing.' To do nothing is not a passive state, explained Father Bede Frost in *St John of the Cross* which was reviewed in the *Criterion* in April 1938, 'it is the highest activity of which the soul is capable, the deliberate and sustained effort of the soul to suffer, in the sense of allow, all that God may will to effect in it'. *East Coker* records Eliot's attempt to put this into practice:

> I said to my soul, be still, and let the dark come upon you
> Which shall be the darkness of God.

In the earlier years Eliot had imagined drastic attempts at transformation through violent death in his early 'Saint Sebastian', and in the many death fragments of *The Waste Land* manuscript. The way down of the *Quartets* is a more gradual and delicate moral process. Its main challenge is patient 'waiting'. The Catholic mystics stress the length of the process: usually it takes years. *The Cloud of Unknowing* insists that the process must not be forced: no abuse of the body to induce a glow, no staring eyes, no humble bleats, if you please. The Rule of the Reformed Carmelites, which St John of the Cross joined, was severe but not fanatical. The saint warned monks and nuns not to perform any penance because it gave them satisfaction. This would be 'animal penance', and would gain them nothing by its mechanical extravagance. The ascetic stunts favoured by the deluded 'saints' in Eliot's student poems would not do by these exacting standards. Nor, too, the strained philosophic vigils in Paris in 1911. In 1940 Eliot preaches an opposite course: 'Wait without thought, for you are not ready for thought', repeating the fourteenth-century dictum that interior work proceeds through lack of knowing, patience and love.

The discipline does include love. Eliot has not forgotten the laughter at Burnt Norton, but is now determined to rid himself of 'Undisciplined squads of emotion'. He must retrain love to serve his solitary search for perfection. 'The Lover', he jotted in his notes, is 'ill of love', so ill that an operation is necessary. Eliot told Anne Ridler that the operation was 'the heart of the matter'. It's a strange heart, bleak and rather cruel compared with the compassion of the saints. The scene switches from a patient under ether 'conscious of nothing' to a patient awake to surgery. The surgeon with 'bleeding hands' (Christ) plies his steel knife to the patient's 'distempered part'. Eliot would have us witness the treatment in slow motion: the agonizing freeze of the fevered senses.

'I faint with heat', Eliot's manuscript notes explain, '—must be frozen in the lonely North.'

The patient quakes as the 'chill ascends from feet to knees'. The fever 'sings'—it issues in poetry—as it is extinguished. At length, an ice-cap 'reigns' over destructive fire. Triumphant, the now 'frigid' lover shows off the briars of his punishment. The briars hint a parallel with Christ's crown of thorns, but the claim seems untenable. The insistence on blood and pain is self-consciously dramatic, like the agonies in Eliot's early 'saint' poems.

Here in the midst of the measured regimen of the mystics, Eliot's New England rigour reasserts itself in its severest form. He admitted that the exercise was 'very un-English' and, when George Every called it 'Jansenist', he seized the label. Jansenism was a movement in seventeenth-century France which seems interchangeable with Puritanism in its insistence on the degraded and helpless state of man. Eliot argued that in certain men of intense penetrating power, there is 'a Jansenism of the individual biography'.

While Eliot explored these ordeals of the inner life, he continued to conduct an outer life of impeccable conformity as he shuttled to the office on the Underground in his bowler hat. Perhaps this was his own form of uninteresting neutrality. William Force Stead pictured him at this time: his hair, still dark, was parted on one side and sleeked down, perhaps with a dab of brilliantine. His expression behind his spectacles was earnest, a little pensive or wistful, with a hint of humour at the corners of the mouth. He continued to play the Old Buffer, particularly with Virginia Woolf who could be relied on to see through the mask. On 16 February 1940 she saw the 'great yellow bronze mask all draped upon an iron framework. An inhibited, nerve drawn; dropped face—as if hung on a scaffold of heavy private brooding.'

At the furthest extremity of the inner life was 'a lifetime burning in every moment'. Such private extremity in 1940 matched public extremity at the time of the Blitz. Eliot offered to those undergoing the war an acceptance of a process of suffering. He wrote on 8 February 1940: 'We can have very little hope of contributing to any immediate social change; and we are more disposed to see our hope in modest and local beginnings, than in transforming the whole world at once.... We must keep alive aspirations which can remain valid throughout the longest and darkest period of universal calamity and degradation.' *East Coker*, with its long view of history and deeply-felt sense of place gave assurance that the age-old routines of the English village would survive the disasters of the present. For all its rigour, *East Coker* is the most optimistic of the *Quartets*. Helen Gardner recalled the extraordinary impact of this poem at the darkest moment of the war. Published as a supplement to the *New English Weekly*'s Easter number (21 March 1940) it had to be reprinted in May and June, and within a year sold nearly 12,000 copies.

At this time the thirties poets—the 'Pylon Boys' as the Faber poets were called—declined in public favour. Maynard Keynes, writing to the *New Statesman and Nation* in October 1939, noted that the intelligentsia of the Left had been loudest in demanding that the Nazis be resisted, but 'scarcely four weeks have passed before they remember that they are pacifists and write defeatist letters to your columns, leaving the defence of freedom to Colonel Blimp and the Old School Tie'. John Hayward reported with his usual acidity that the poet George Barker was moving heaven to be sent to Japan. With the disappearance of other writers (Auden and Isherwood to America; MacNeice to Ireland), the recent death of Yeats, and the success of *East Coker*, Eliot became from this time pre-eminent in England.

As he completed the poem, he told John Hayward that he spent the weekend playing chess, eating large meals, and reading the detective novels of Peter Cheyney. How does this Eliot fit the tormented penitent that Virginia Woolf glimpsed at the time he was writing *East Coker*? I don't think that it was a blind: the two apparently antithetical sides, the domestic cat of regular habits, and the pioneer on the frontiers of consciousness, were inter-dependent. The two sides worked together most effectively in the special circumstances of the war, when there was less interference with their balance: fewer office demands and no social ones. As an air-raid warden, he had to visit houses in his area and to talk to people about stirrup pumps and incendiary bombs, and he spent one or two nights a week fire-watching, but he saw almost nothing of strenuous intellectuals. The Woolfs were more often marooned in Rodmell, and stayed there permanently after their home in Mecklenburgh Square was bombed later in 1940. The Hayward circle had broken up. Frank Morley was working at Harcourt Brace in New York. John Hayward himself was evacuated from Bina Gardens by Lord Rothschild, and carried off as his guest to Merton Hall, Cambridge. It is clear from Hayward's bulletins to Morley that, for a while, Eliot kept Hayward's feelers at bay with lengthy reports of air-raid practice in the basement of Russell Square and comic accounts of his experiences in the black-out. Hayward had to try hard to squeeze a drop of juice out of him. William Force Stead said that Eliot's address in 1940 was still something of a secret: 'I believe', he adds, 'he is an introvert living mostly in himself and only now and then seeking distraction.'

Eliot's two greatest poems, *The Waste Land* and the *Quartets*, seem to speak directly to their times, yet both draw on private, sometimes strange experience, to generalize for all time. In *East Coker*, a strange, private turmoil is reflected in world war, reflected in turn in cosmic disorder. Eliot takes these Transcendentalist leaps from one order of existence to another to the outermost reaches of the universe, but then, lapsing into prosaic terms, admits that this exercise has its origin in the pangs of love. His literary advisers, Hayward and Faber, as well as later critics, missed the comic point when they deplored the lapse from high style. The bathos was deliberate: 'That was a way of putting it—not very satisfactory.' Poetry or philosophy is undercut as an absurd elaboration of exact private truth. The blunt truth is the struggle in middle age to cope with disturbing emotions, and at the same time to break the deadening round of habit.

Eliot found middle age to be a time of choices, not the retrievable choices of youth, but those that risk the soul. The worst danger is to avoid choice, to lapse into 'autumnal serenity', to cover yourself 'in forgetful snow', the death-in-life that Eliot had always feared: in the round of Boston tea-parties of 'Prufrock', in the London work-routines of *The Waste Land*, and now in the tube trains of *East Coker*, which carry eminent men of letters, merchants, civil servants, chairmen of many committees, directors, and readers of the *Stock Exchange Gazette* to Hampstead, Putney, and Ludgate. Eliot was one of these directors, on his way to

Hampstead (to bath at the Fabers, since his landlady could provide
only one jug of water). In his capacity as director, he was the heir of
those old English Eliots who went round and round in a ring. In
East Coker he rebels not only against the social round, but against
all pointless recurrence: the recurrent life-spans of passing generations, and the repeated destructions in history.

In 1934 he laments our imprisonment in time's round:

> O perpetual revolution of configured stars,
> O perpetual recurrence of determined seasons,
> O world of spring and autumn, birth and dying!
> The endless cycle . . .

Nothing lasts as this wheel turns. The perpetually moving circum-
ference of the wheel is the temporal order. Theoretically, there
would be a still point at the centre of the hub that would represent
an eternal stillness at the heart of churning existence—if only one
could glimpse it, as Eliot did for one moment at Burnt Norton. For
one man, at a particular point in time, time itself may be
conquered. Thomas à Becket, through an act in time—his martyrdom on 29 December 1170—is able to transcend time, and reach
the stillness of eternity. *Murder in the Cathedral* and *Burnt Norton*
confirm the existence of the spiritual order, that 'the light is still /
At the still point of the turning world'.

To reach, not just glimpse, that still point demands a transformed life. When Harry abandons his family, with its fixed habits
and plans, he is liberated from the human wheel. So, too, is the
pilgrim who abandons East Coker, like the pilgrims of the
seventeenth century who left what they saw as Babylon for a New
Jerusalem, 'a city on a hill',* a holy life. Mere physical existence in
Eliot's opening line, 'In my beginning is my end', finds its alternative in an ideal pattern of existence that leads to the final
triumphant claim to eternal life: 'In my end is my beginning.'

Each person must apply the formula for transformation to his
own experience. So Eliot translates Dante's transforming stairway
into his own life, through the granite seascape of Cape Ann which
bursts upon the penitent at the end of *Ash Wednesday*. Again, in
East Coker, the formula comes to life as St John of the Cross gives

---

* The phrase from Matt. 5: 14 gained its particular importance in America from a
sermon given by John Winthrop, leader of the Great Migration, on the flagship the
Arbella, in 1630. Eliot's ancestor, Isaac Stearns, sailed in that year.

way to the American progenitor who had the nerve to make the crossing. Eliot must follow, not of course in actuality (though he does draw on sailing memories), but in spirit. This will be the trial of the next *Quartet*. He must renew the ancestral state of mind: venturesomeness ('Home is where one starts from') and more, a willing, almost reckless self-exposure to the unknown.

Eliot switches back and forth from English to American perspectives. *Four Quartets* is thought of as an English work with some reference to America, but the reverse may be true. The very notion of an Old World implies a New-World perspective from which 'the old world may be seen, made explicit'. The sequence of poems, as it evolved early in 1940 when it was to conclude with the third *Quartet*, had at this point a plot that was essentially American: a recoil from civilization to expose oneself to the wilderness, in this case the sea. The 'three quatuors' would move from the civilized enclosures of the English garden with its box hedge, straight walk, and concrete pool, to the wild ocean; from the predictable routines of the small English village to encounter

> Through the dark cold and empty desolation,
> The wave cry, the wind cry, the vast waters
> Of the petrel and the porpoise.

The waterway beckons the American—Ishmael, Huck Finn, Arthur Gordon Pym—as a mysterious and terrible power. Eliot's sea is strewn with treacherous rocks and drowned men; his Mississippi in spring flood carries its usual 'cargo' of negro bodies and chicken coops. This nature is not English. It is not the nurse, the guide, the guardian. It is alien to man; he cannot interfuse with its moods. He might pit himself against it, like Ahab or the Gloucester fishermen, or he might beat obedient to its control. Poetry must explore the frontiers of the spirit, Eliot wrote on 27 April 1939, but 'these frontiers are not the surveys of geographical explorers conquered once for all and settled'. He imagines rather a perpetual frontier, a perpetual mystery on the borders of the known world.

The end of such a voyage is a divine call. *Marina* sketched a complete scenario for a task which the *Quartets* undertake only in part. For they show with admirable honesty that, in practice, the voyager can't make it or not in the same way. Too flawed now for the planned approach to grace, the voyager can hope only for a haven, an orderly life of prayer and observance. In the course of writing *East Coker* Eliot changed plan. It was part of the exercise in humility to put off hope of attainment to a fourth poem, and so to prolong the trial by water with a further trial by fire.*

If in 1940–1 Eliot was unfit as yet for grace, he could still hold to love. In the scenario of 1930 the battered old voyager with lips parted in hope homes to the shore where a familiar woman awaits him. In 1940, distanced from the beloved woman, Eliot defines love as an emotion that is truest when here or there do not matter. Love survives with its promise of a further 'intensity'. It is at once religious and personal, a strange love-letter saying in public what Eliot possibly could not say in private. It is love cherished like a vision across the sea, to be reached by a most gallant venture. This dream stirred Eliot more than the actual presence of Emily Hale.

Separation and chastity: these were the conditions of continued love as Eliot jotted pencil notes for the conclusion:

> Alone—the ice cap
> Separated from the surfaces of human beings
> To be reunited in the communion

The first draft set it out clearly: one must 'be separated' for 'a further union, a deeper communion'.

Where does one's beginning start? Is the beginning somewhere along the line of forebears, or is one shaped by some scene of childhood? In December 1940 Eliot turned to personal memories, his beginnings in St Louis, where the rhythm of the Mississippi beats inside him in the nursery bedroom, in the backyard where he plays, and in the gaslit nights of the early 1890s. The Mississippi, he said, 'made a deeper impression upon me than any other part of the world'. He remembered it as 'a treacherous and capricious dictator' which in flood 'may obliterate the low Illinois shore to a horizon of water, while in its bed it runs with a speed such that no man or beast can survive in it. At such times, it carried down

---

* Eliot told Hayward that he began at this point to see four poems on the basis of four elements. This is a late, and I think, superficial organizing idea. Eliot wrote to Professor William Matchett on 19 Jan. 1949: 'Certainly by the time that poem [*East Coker*] was finished I envisaged the whole work as having four parts which gradually began to assume, perhaps only for convenience sake, a relation to the four seasons and the four elements.'

human bodies, cattle and houses. At least twice, at St Louis, the western and eastern shores have been separated by the fall of bridges'. A native does not merely see the river, he experiences it: he accepts the river god as his god.

In the third *Quartet*, Eliot took up the challenge of auto-biography: to make sense of one's life. This was his climactic effort to fuse past and future in a single pattern. To do this, he must once more sink back into the past to extract his defining scenes: the childhood on the longest river; the 10-year-old peering into a rockpool on Cape Ann; the youth sailing his precarious course through the granite teeth of the rocks. There, far off in the past, were the crucial intuitions of the divine nature: the power and terror of the Mississippi in flood, an implacable destroyer, a 'strong brown god', and the sea with its 'Many gods and many voices'.

A group of three rocks called the Dry Salvages was the last landmark when the young Eliot had sailed from Cape Ann to Maine. Four-and-a-half miles offshore from Rockport, the farthest mainland of Massachusetts projecting out into the Atlantic, the Salvages consist of two great ledges. The Big Salvage is always out of water but the Dry Salvages are hidden at high tide. The name, it is said, derived from the fact that the dangerous, partly hidden rocks reminded settlers of the red men, the 'savages'. The ledges, which have been the scene of many shipwrecks, extend far under water; big seas break over them, and only seamen who know the channels can make the passage safely. In a fog, Eliot and his class-mate Harold Peters would hear the 'groaner', a whistling buoy east of Thatcher's Island, scene of a famous shipwreck in the seven-teenth century. Once, in a nineteen-foot knockabout, Eliot and Peters rounded Mount Desert Rock in a fog and heavy sea. They took refuge on Duck Island, and after a rough night and with a gale still blowing, made it to the little harbour at Somesville, Maine. The log-book showed a sketch of Eliot unmooring in the wind with the caption: 'Heroic work by the swab.'

This forbidding sea with its hidden rocks, its 'sea howl', its warning foghorn, and multitudes of drowned fishermen, opens up the farthest horizon of the *Quartets*. The sailor, exposed to a force beyond human control and a time beyond history, feels 'the ground swell, that is and was from the beginning'. The sea is in touch with its genesis, and to be adrift there is like being moved on the face of creation.

At first Eliot planned a 'sea picture' only, then approached the sea by way of the river. The river is tamed to some extent by human history, its commerce and bridges. The sea is untamed, unchanged, eternal. At the land's edge the sea (endless time) and the land (historical time) encroach upon each other. The sea's salt is on the briar rose; rocks, the farthest point of land, jut out to sea. These rocks mark the course of the poet who, from his place in time's scheme, sets out on the timeless sea.

Eliot's own experience at the edge of time—as sailor, poet, or pilgrim—provides the live matter for generalization. A poem about time and how to conquer time appears, to many readers, philosophical but Eliot was not, he insisted, a philosopher. He was not concerned with abstract thought but with states of feeling. He once said, 'I suspect that what is often held to be a capacity for abstract thought, in a poet, is a capacity for abstract feeling—something much more properly the poet's business.' *Four Quartets* gives to such feelings a sequential order that would hold good at any time, in any place, for those who demand more of themselves than a routine life. Illumination is followed by the darkness of humility, which is followed, in turn, by an almost reckless daring, and finally by a resolute calm. Such feelings are too rare for conventional statement. They are explored through four landscapes, each of which provides only a starting-point for the complex interior landscape of each stage of the soul's progress. Each is at the edge, what Eliot calls the 'point of intersection of the timeless'. And although he says that to be there is 'an occupation for the saint' and not, he adds modestly, for 'most of us', in fact this is exactly where the poem proves Eliot to be as he discerns an ideal order in the turbulent feelings of the private life.

It is not before the world but out of sight 'between the rocks' that a convert must test the authenticity and reach of his faith. And farther out, in the lap of creation, where there is nothing else—no personal or intellectual distraction—is some naked confrontation of which Eliot can speak only indirectly. His venture is always to confront 'reality', his word for whatever lies beyond the 'Unreal City'. He believes that 'reality' exists—it comes to him in the silence that obliterates the twittering world—but he is never sure if he can meet it. Eliot despised a watered-down Christianity of sweet promises. He looked to the spring of 'Christ the tiger' or the

'And the deep lane insists on the direction / Into the village'. Eliot's
photograph (1937) of the road from West Coker to East Coker, Somerset.

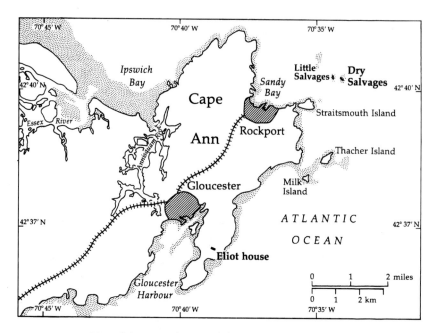

Map of the Dry Salvages in relation to Cape Ann, Mass.

'The granite teeth' of the Dry Salvages offshore from Cape Ann.

Little Gidding, Huntingdonshire: 'You are here to kneel where prayer has been valid'.

Eliot and Emily Hale in Vermont, 1946. He came to see her perform in Noel Coward's *Blithe Spirit*.

havoc of the sea. If 'reality' ever came it would possess him with annihilating power.

Eliot first rehearsed this voyage in a long narrative which Pound cut in its entirety from *The Waste Land* manuscript. The hardy Gloucester fishermen who sail through winter seas to the Grand Banks were Eliot's boyhood heroes, and their journey, terrible as it is, does turn its back on sterile life in the urban waste. Eliot did, at once stage, counter London, the 'Unreal City', with the venturing nerve of his native tradition. The draft was like a scene from Melville or, more likely, Poe's 'Narrative of Arthur Gordon Pym' in its visionary horrors and approach to the ice. This native strain remained part of Eliot in all the strange journeys in his poetry that find a final expression in *The Dry Salvages*.

In 1921 he foresaw disaster: the ship strikes an iceberg, and goes down. Can this be God's will? 'And if Another knows, I know I know not'. In 1940–1 a voyager again braves the sea conscious of the menace to all who venture from their natural habitat. He is in a 'drifting boat', at the mercy of winds and currents, but yet there is a vein of optimism. The urge to 'Fare forward' echoes Whitman and, through him, Columbus, voyagers with inextinguishable visions in their heads. 'Sail forth', urges Whitman, 'bound where mariner has not yet dared to go.' The daring in *The Dry Salvages* recovers the heady recklessness of Whitman's pioneer: 'And we will risk the ship, ourselves and all' seeking 'You, strew'd with the wrecks of skeletons, that, living, never reach'd you.' Eliot, too, has seen the bone on the beach. Stretched on the far-flung mesh of the sestine,* to which he clings as he moves on, he takes in the terror of an ocean littered with the wrecks of those who were not strong enough to survive the alien element.

Going to sea is itself an act of faith. The sailor drifts in a state of unattached devotion when, suddenly, he hears a bell that warns of death and judgement. Appalled by the destruction and 'silent withering' of all life, accompanied by 'the soundless wailing', he asks the overwhelming question: 'Where is there an end of it'? There is no bitterness at this point, only surrender to a reality he cannot fathom. The repeated 'There is no end of it' finds an answer in what appears almost as an afterthought: there is no point to

---

* The sestine or sestina (as in *The Dry Salvages*: II) is 'a poem of six six-line stanzas, in which the line-endings of the first stanza are repeated, but in a different order, in the other five' (*OED*).

existence except, he adds, the divine spirit that sustained the life of Christ. Death no longer appals, and Eliot sinks into massive repose, content now to lie near his ancestors in St Michael's Church at East Coker.

The quiet end is taken by some to be a poetic failure. But the greatness of Eliot's conception lies precisely in the integrity with which he backs down from dreams of attainment in favour of modest expectations—modest, in view of the glimpse of divine light at Burnt Norton, the pulsing call in *Marina*, and, going back, the 'Silence' in the Boston street. Progress will not, in his case, follow the perfect sequence. After the third repeated effort, he must acknowledge his mere human status and his mortality. He must return to the once-despised earth, and nourish the soil. He is now convinced that earthly life can be 'significant' even if not inspired with visionary light. The final notes of the third *Quartet* play out his acceptance of life on these restricted terms, an acceptance hard won, and itself a measure of moral progress. He is not, after all, one of the saints. This very recognition is an advance in the difficult exercise in humility.

The Waste Land concludes with a dramatic progression into the mountains. There are no such peaks of attainment in *Four Quartets*, no thunderous message. Eliot owns that for him, as for other people, the most to be looked for is the odd hint or guess that comes in rare 'unattended' moments when he drifts into the interface between time and the timeless. Part of the exercise in humility was not to play up, or even expect, progression. Eliot was bent on accuracy, not drama. The later *Quartets* are a corrective to the self-absorbed heroics of Harry when he exits to follow the bright angels. What drama remains lies in a renunciation so subtle, that it seems, even to astute readers, to fall flat. Such readers do not see that drama is a consolation that Eliot has refused. It is braver, and certainly more realistic, to face one's sheer ordinariness, to expect no divine call, to write (as Hopkins put it) letters to 'dearest him that lives alas! away', and still to go on trying to perfect existence. This is what Eliot now meant by 'action'. The desperate valour of the voyager gives way to unseen action that might go on in the most obscure of lives.

So it was that Eliot finally renounced an ambition which, in early years, sent Narcissus out of town to avoid the common press of thighs and knees in order to become 'a dancer to God'; sent the pilgrim of *The Waste Land* to the far-off mountains to surrender to divine control; and sent the 'turning' convert of *Ash Wednesday* into the desert to cry 'unto Thee'. The impulse to turn from a contemptible society was reversed in the winter of 1940/1, when Eliot came to concede an interdebtedness with his kind without which he must forfeit the very religious hopes that, for so long, had seemed to set him apart. The terror and isolation of the sea turned him back, full circle, to the time-bound land he had left, to 'know the place for the first time'. It is there, not at the extremity of the sea's jaws, that he must live and act, and find matter for future poems and plays.

This was not a retreat, but a new challenge. He had to find a way to use what he knew of the perfect life of the spiritual élite to improve the life of ordinary people. The injunctions he offers— 'Prayer, observance, discipline, thought and action'—are not as mysteriously thrilling as '*Datta, Dayadhvam, Damyata*', but like the Ten Commandments, they have the advantage of being plain and attainable.

Strangely, love is not included. At this time, Eliot did not think of love in the daily terms of 'trying'. But it was logical that sooner or later he would come to this, once he had accomplished what had, for him, priority: atonement, and through that, liberation from the past.

The Dry Salvages is about the frontiers of action where a significant life is made. There are two struggles, first with the ghosts of the past, then with the ghosts of the future. Memories, expectations: these impede the new life, and must be dissolved in the timeless pattern of spiritual autobiography.

The memory of Burnt Norton, which might have led another man into 'affection' and the 'security' of family bonds, came to be for Eliot the basis of a quite different life which seems always to have hovered on his horizon. He must act on the urge to switch from one biographical plot to another, as Harry, his portent, had switched to the plot of salvation. Leave father and mother and follow me, Christ said. Eliot had planned at one point to explore the 'meaning of "mother" & "father"', but abandoned this, retaining an invocation to the Virgin. Looking back to Burnt Norton, he now decides: 'We had the experience but missed the meaning.' It had been an alert. The miraculous light, the children's voices (like the children's voices that brought on the conversion of St Augustine), the clang of the bell: all signs point one way.

Looking back on his life, Eliot discounts the usual plot. The past, he says categorically, is not mere 'sequence' or even 'development', and to see it in this way would be as bogus as to spell out a life from palms, tea-leaves, entrails , or psycho-analysis. Character composed by such routines, said Eliot (thinking of Freud), 'has all the defects of the synthetic substitute; its actions are tediously predictable; it is always unconvincing, and usually false'. For the significant life is an imaginative act. A man like Eliot becomes significant precisely because he conceives a shape to his life which he defines repeatedly through the visionary moments which formed the dominant figure in the carpet of his existence.* These transforming moments were invitations to a new life, but they lay 'unattended' beneath the trivia of external action, as Eliot put it explicitly: '. . . our own past is covered by the currents of action.' In a draft he uncovers the essential moments of his own history: the vigils in Paris in 1911, and the emotional quickening that came to him as a young man as he sailed off the coast of Cape Ann:

> Remember rather the essential moments
>   That were the times of birth and death and change
>   The agony and the solitary vigil.
> Remember also fear, loathing and hate,
>
>   .   .   .   .
>
> The fresh new season's rope, the smell of varnish
>   On the clean oar, the drying of the sails,
>   Such things seem of least and most importance.
> So, as you circumscribe this dreary round,
>   Shall your life pass from you . . .

It seems to have been harder to integrate the 'moments of agony' that were as lasting as the moments of happiness. In his notes he jotted: 'problem of permanence of past pain.' He cannot, and must not, forget 'the ragged rock in the restless waters', torment like Vivienne's, not visible, but there. On a calm day the rock appears merely a monument to past danger; in rougher weather there is the sense of sin brought on him by a woman; but in the 'sudden fury'

---

* Eliot said after completing *The Dry Salvages*: 'We look in a poet as well as in a novelist, for what Henry James called the Figure in the Carpet.' 'Rudyard Kipling' *A Choice of Kipling's Verse* (London: Faber, 1941), 15.

all the menace of the past returns, the old horrors, Harry haunted by Furies, and the 'circling fury' in a draft of *Burnt Norton*. Eliot's own life goes on like the longest river, bearing its carrion away, the remains of things done to others' harm: this moral burden will be there always.

From the past he turns to a future that is blighted by this past, and touched by nostalgic regret for the fragile sensations of love that must wither with time: the faded songs, 'Ecstasy' and 'May Morning' that Emily Hale had sung in 1913 in a Boston drawing-room where the young Eliot had sat applauding with his Hinckley cousins. Love will become a wistful memory, like a spray of lavender pressed in a book yellowing with time. This future he foresaw even before he experienced love, and from the start it gave him a detachment that is not to be confused with cool worldliness. It is an absolute detachment from time itself. It is partly this, I think, that drew him so early to the saints.

Eliot resolves to look to the future with 'an equal mind', an idea that he derived first from the *Bhagavad-gita*, which he read and annotated at Harvard. He learnt disinterestedness from the Indian scriptures, not to be concerned with the fruits of action. In the third *Quartet*, he points to a battle scene where the god, Krishna, justifies the killing of kin to Arjuna, who shrinks from it. Krishna urges Arjuna, as a member of the ruling, warrior class, to fulfil his *dharma*, to play out his appointed role in a cosmic drama, and says that slayer and slain cannot comprehend the Lord's will. But given a modern, civilian context of the battlefield of life, and without the concomitant Indian faith in reincarnation, how can the command to fare forward regardless of the destruction of others be 'right action'?

At this time Eliot refused to concern himself about Vivienne during the bombardment of London. His practical friend, Mary Trevelyan, ventured to suggest that he move her to a place of safety. Though Eliot himself had now settled outside London, he replied that, in his wife's case, he had no authority to contravene court orders.

Eliot's characteristic form of action turns away to inward suffering, as one draft shows: 'And Atonement makes action possible.' He must still fare forward, but as a flawed man, one of those who try but who may well not succeed. He belongs with those who have no definite vocation, and who still risk the journey into timelessness. The risk is to relinquish one's self in the vain hope of transformation. That way lies mental wreckage, to be washed up like the bone on the beach. The only hope is not to hope at all, which is to surrender all sense of personal future to those, in generations to come, who will make the same effort at perfection. He sees his future always in suspension between the flawed and the perfect life, like a traveller who has left one shore and has not reached the other, moving uncertain through the space of his lifespan.

In October 1940 Eliot had moved out of London to become a paying guest of Hope Mirrlees, her mother, and aunt in their house at the top of a steep hill in Shamley Green, near Guildford in Surrey. After the bachelor quarters of the last six years, as Leonard Woolf put it, 'surrounded by curates', he was now surrounded by women. The household was filled with evacuees from Wandsworth and Barking, between eighteen and twenty-two women and children, with a few husbands on Saturday nights. In the cosy, over-heated atmosphere of the 'Shambles', Eliot enjoyed his position as prize domestic pet amongst the old ladies who cherished numerous cats and dogs. Someone in the house called Cocky believed they would meet up with pets in the next world. I suspect he relished the comic discrepancy between his venturesome inner life and the upholstered setting where conversation centred on the importance of the vet (who was constantly needed for the over-fed dogs), and the nightly ventures of the Field Marshal (Margaret Behrens) who had to go out after her peke who took to chasing rabbits by moonlight. The only other male about was a gardener who was afraid of mice and a writer of letters of condolence to the royal family (he used the acknowledgements as testimonials). Eliot's letters from the Shambles have his characteristic humorous note of content in soothing female company. Enid Faber noticed that he took on a comfortable look, like that of a practical cat, by which she concluded that life at the Shambles must suit him. It was, he told Virginia Woolf, the healthiest life in years.

This was the improbable setting in which Eliot dreamed up his most daring imaginative enterprise. The writing of *The Dry Salvages* was interrupted by weekly forays to a bombed London. He usually went up on Tuesdays or Wednesdays (driven by Sir Philip Gibbs), got through a few brief duties, and stayed over with the Fabers, who had a reinforced basement shelter. On Thursdays he returned to the country with his correspondence and manuscripts, and settled again to write. In the winter of 1940/1 he saw almost no one, and was free as never before to give his prime energy to poetry. He was always able to write plays intermittently, but for poetry he needed sustained concentration.

Eliot's most elusive self who disappears across the horizon of *The Dry Salvages* is not, he says, the same person who disembarks. The cosy Eliot of Shamley Green and the public Eliot of the many masks is superfluous to this hidden man, not to be known outside his work, and even there vanishing into silence. Faceless, he relaxes from all the masks of manners—of, say, obligatory grief at parting—to 'the sleepy rhythm' of the poem itself as it wells in the mind. He is inchoate, carried along, always in the making. The passage, the poem itself, represents Eliot's homelessness in the Kensington period and during the war years. It is impossible to fix him through his past, or even through the saintly life of his ideal future. He is kin only to those who experience the fading of personal emotion, and fear defeat *en route* to the perfect life.

Eliot lacked the assurance of his puritan fathers that the promised land lay ahead. Writing at a critical stage of the second world war, he was more conscious of the likelihood of defeat. Each week he went up to a London that was partially destroyed, its continued existence more threatened than at any time in its history. At the very time that Eliot came to take action, to make the imaginative crossing to the New World, he found that his allegiance to the old world had taken too deep a root. So his way forward, his progress in the new life, turned out to be the way back. He jotted in his notes: 'To get beyond time & at the same time deeper into time.' He must now reconcile himself to a continual suspension in time, on the verge of 'hints and guesses'.

To keep the verge open is to retain the native posture of the American: the openness of mind implied in the persistent 'Fare forward, voyagers'. He is urged on by a disembodied voice, like the alien pulse that beats in the arm of the voyager in *Marina*. This voice warns him to think of the lives of others. Future action must lie in his power to affect other lives, especially lives to come. The voice descants in the rigging, like the eerie quickening of the strings in the finale of Beethoven's A minor quartet, composed when he was deaf and which, Eliot said, had a sort of heavenly

gaiety. The voice descants 'not to the ear' but to the spirit.
It speaks 'not in any language', as Eliot himself wished to
get *'beyond poetry*, as Beethoven, in his later works, strove to
get *beyond music'*. Out at sea, at the furthest verge of time,
there is a renewed intimation of immortality that was to bring
him, in the final *Quartet*, into unison with the timeless poets of
the past.

Eliot now set himself to imagine the 'unimaginable'. The last
Quartet reaches for a sublimity that Eliot knew to be beyond him,
beyond everyone. God has said: 'Thou canst not see my face, for
there shall no man see me, and live.' Christ and the saints have
faces. This unimaginable divinity is more remote, the unnamable
creator. Eliot said that the poetry of the Bible (at its height in
Psalms and Isaiah) was secondary to religious experience. The
Bible must not be read as literature but as an experience of the
Word. The problem for the religious poet, Eliot went on, is that he
is dependent on the experience but cannot command it. He can
speak the Word only if the divine spark enters him.
    This would be the ideal conclusion to spiritual autobiography:
a simultaneous ascent and descent of the ladder to heaven. The
design was there from the start in the figure of the ten stairs
from St John of the Cross that appears in *Burnt Norton*. In the
middle two *Quartets*, Eliot had duly performed his descent into
the dark night of humility. Now, he set before himself the
possibility of ascent, but it would depend upon the yield of his
own life.
    Eliot had created a framework into which God-given life might
be breathed. That breath had flitted through the garden at Burnt
Norton. Then, between the first and second *Quartets*, came what in
Eliot's eyes (though not in any public view), was the prime sin of
his life, and hope of beatitude was put aside for a Thibet of
penitence. His solution to sin was to recall the design of a life in
which abasement was essential to the holy scheme of recovery: the
pattern given in Exodus, and repeated in the lives of prophets,
Christ, and the Christian saints and mystics. One reason why he
turned from the theatre back to poetry may have been the need to
explore the design of spiritual autobiography three more times, in
order to wring from his life that classic pattern.

This life, in past centuries or in the present of 1941-2, always has a single aim: to recover the divine. It might well not happen at once, or in the space of *Four Quartets*, but it was to happen at some stage in the future, even if that event lay beyond life itself. That consummation Eliot forecast from the 'Shantih', the peace which passeth understanding, echoing on after *The Waste Land*. It 'haunts us like the prayers of childhood'.

A muted longing for renewal breathes through the opening of the last *Quartet*. If only it would come now. He imagines how it would be: how the sun would flame the ice of his body. For Eliot it was late middle age; the senses had been frozen; and as he looked now to the winter of his being, he wondered if the divine fire that seemed so remote would ever quicken him.

The individual struggle goes in tandem with the set pattern of spiritual autobiography. The voices of tradition, of St John of the Cross, Milton's Samson, and the English mystics of the fourteenth century all confirm its accuracy. The tension between individual tumult and the discipline of set form, predictable in the religious life, is found also in the classic arts, and in the sphere of the arts was demonstrated for Eliot's generation most stunningly by the Russian Ballet. The abandon of Nijinsky's famous leap in *Le Spectre de la rose*—Nijinsky said that he would simply forget to come down—was contained within the strict decorum of the classical positions. Eliot had this particular ballet in mind as he wrote the last *Quartet*. On 10 December 1941, when Hitler was at the gates of Moscow, Eliot wrote to *The Times* to urge that the Ballet be invited for a season in London.

The danger of an additional *Quartet*, Eliot realized, was that the repeated formula might come to dominate the individual effort, which might then fail to hold its own. By the end of the third *Quartet* the formula and the poet were pulling in harmony, set for unambitious but continuous action. In the fourth *Quartet*, he took an enormous risk. Poised over the turning rim of the wheel, he now made for the hub, the still point. This was his Nijinsky leap. Could he achieve that sustained height, or must he fall back into the repeated round of purgation? An honest reading of the scale of perfection would indicate his present state: would it be purgatory or beatitude?

Eliot's initial notes, as well as his first typescript of July 1941, suggest that his first impulse was to look to beatitude. The dumb spirit, he imagines, would stir. The high points of his past are answered by a burst of light from the rising sun.

The initiating scene is this flaming light, and a pilgrim kneeling in a secluded church, the site of a devout community in the seventeenth century. Little Gidding is the only one of the four places that had no autobiographical association, nor is it mentioned in Eliot's plan. It could have been, he admits, any of a number of holy places. This was simply the most convenient, 'Now and in England'. There, deliberately, he placed himself in his imagination, in the icy brilliance of the winter light, in prayer. 'And let my cry come unto Thee' had been the last prayer of *Ash Wednesday*. Would the divine spirit descend 'now' in a place where 'prayer has been valid'?

Eliot had to find a place to come to rest, and it had to answer certain needs. He wished to reaffirm the devotional life as practised long ago at Little Gidding where two brothers and a sister, Nicholas, John, and Susanna Ferrar, developed a unique blend of the domestic and monastic. Eliot would have been attracted by the venturesomeness of this group (of about forty people) who had gone off into a lonely area of Huntingdonshire to found their own way of life which conformed, at the same time, to the strict rules of their faith. It may be the closest phenomenon in Anglican history to the American Puritan impulse to go into the wilderness to found a 'city on a hill'.*

The word 'now' is crucial to *Little Gidding*. Now—when Eliot planned the poem some time in the first half of 1941—was the Blitz. On 10 May 1941, 3,000 civilians were killed or injured in one air-raid. The rest of Europe had fallen to Hitler, and England was in imminent danger of invasion. Little Gidding was particularly appropriate to this time of stress because it, too, had suffered damage in time of war, and survived it. After the community gave refuge to Charles I, Cromwell's soldiers ransacked the church in the winter of 1646.† They ripped out the organ and the pulpit, which they burnt outside, and threw the font, lectern, and

---

* The phrase appears in a *Criterion* review of Oct. 1938. Bernard Blackstone reviewed A. L. Maycock's *Nicholas Ferrar of Little Gidding*, 154-7. Little Gidding appears again in the *Criterion* in Jan. 1939 when Charles Smyth reviewed Blackstone's edition of *The Ferrar Papers*, 366-71 (he notes that Ferrar was called 'a saint of the Church of England').

† The church was rebuilt in the eighteenth century, and added to in the nineteenth.

engravings into a nearby pond. Nicholas, the deacon, had died in 1637, but John and Susanna sustained their pattern of life until 1657 when both died.

The other attraction of Little Gidding was that, like Burnt Norton, it is one of England's hidden places. Hard to find, down an obscure track, the civilized beauty and order of Burnt Norton is hidden from the world. So, too, the minute, perfect church at Little Gidding is buried in the still sparsely-populated rolling country-side between Huntingdon and Oundle. As you approach it down a 'rough road', on the left is the site of a medieval village which was deserted after the Black Death in the fourteenth century. When Nicholas Ferrar arrived there in 1625, the local manor house and medieval church were derelict, and for the next five years he and his family restored them. They are there, intact, 'when you leave the rough road / And turn behind the pig-sty'. Like the garden at Burnt Norton, it is still exactly as Eliot described it. For him it is in the secret places that meaning 'breaks'.

In the actual sequence of Eliot's visits to the four sites of the poems, Little Gidding followed Burnt Norton. Imaginatively the two are linked: the evanescent light and the rising sun; the evanescent rose of human love and the everlasting rose of divine love. The nostalgia for 'the passage which we did not take / Towards the door we never opened' recalls the poet's lingering thought of La Figlia, 'how they should have been together'. There is, again, a slight, lingering stir of the maytime-playtime of the senses in the first draft of *Little Gidding* as Eliot goes back to the actual May of his only visit to the place in 1936. The first typescript recalls the 'voluptuary sweetness' of that May, the 'playtime' of the wakened senses which gives 'human joy' but no 'greater rapture'. When Hayward questioned 'playtime' Eliot said that he was referring back to the rose-garden of *Burnt Norton* and the children in the apple-tree of 'New Hampshire'. The web of private cross-reference also links the voluptuary sweetness with the 'sweet disconsolate chimera' that lingered in the mind at the end of a draft of *Burnt Norton*. Later that year Eliot crossed to America and Emily Hale, and after that reunion came the final stage of Vivienne's tragedy.

The years in which he visited the scenes of *Four Quartets* — Burnt Norton in September 1934, Little Gidding in the spring of 1936, the crossing to New England later in 1936 and, finally, East

Coker in 1937—were years of upheaval, torn between nostalgia for unfulfilled love and the fury of tormented conscience. At the core of *Four Quartets* are the compacted memories of four years during which Eliot's new life was taking a decisive shape. The *Quartets* gestated in Eliot's mind for about as long as *The Waste Land*: seven years in all. While *The Waste Land* grew out of a rag-bag of fragments that, for some years, had no focus, *Four Quartets* grew in concentric layers around the core of personal memories which continued to nourish the poems from well below the surface.

In 1940–1 the core was overlaid with the freezing asceticism of Eliot's chosen way. The remembered ecstasy in the rose-garden and the remembered maytime of the senses were subdued to the dark night of the soul. This was the substantial central layer of *Four Quartets*: the body's punishment, the soul's trial, its progress, and (a still-remote possibility) its reward.

The final layer, no more than an outer casing, is the public point of reference: the war. The fire of bombs comes, in turn, to overlay the ice. Ideally, there would have been a divine fire. Instead, Eliot settles for what is more common, a punitive fire. Fire-watching during the air-raids, Eliot saw 'the dark dove with flickering tongue'. The bomber brings home once again the intolerable question of the waste of life, a question repeated in each *Quartet*: in the rose of love that turned to dust; in the family that flourished, fell, and lay buried in earth; in the black bodies brought down by the flooding water of the Mississippi. The elements that sustain us also destroy us. The fourth *Quartet* speaks of the victims of the fire of war who, too, might ask 'Where is there an end of it'?

Superimposed upon the bomber is the dove of the holy spirit. The refining fire—pain that is God-given and, as such, accepted—may redeem what Eliot called (in his outline) the 'daemonic' fire of war. To this pain he was drawn by temperament as much as by identification with his adopted country in time of trial. When Forster reread *Little Gidding* his enthusiasm was tempered by his dislike of Eliot's 'homage to pain': 'What animal except the human could have excogitated it? Of course there's pain on and off through each individual's life. . . . You can't shirk it and so on. But why should it be endorsed by the schoolmaster and sanctified by the priest until the fire and the rose are one when so much of it is caused by disease and bullies? It is here that Eliot becomes unsatisfactory as a seer.'

There are times in the final *Quartet* when Eliot reaches for a loftiness that cuts him off from the impact of human suffering. He told the Greek poet, George Seferis, that in a shelter, 'I would feel the need to get out as quickly as possible, to escape all those faces gathered there, to escape all that humanity'.

To Eliot war, as a historical event, was peripheral to its private moral meaning, as the first world war had been peripheral to the private waste land. London bridge 'falling down falling down falling down' was a token of personal collapse on Eliot's return to London in January 1922 from his breakdown in Lausanne, and only tangentially Bertrand Russell's wartime hallucination when he had seen the jammed troop trains of the doomed depart from Waterloo. In the same way, for Eliot, the historical event of the Blitz was, in Emersonian terms, a token of his being and becoming. He saw in the bombs the curative possibilities of purgatorial fire, and wrote in the manuscript:

> Fire without and fire within
> ~~Expel~~
> Purge the unidentified sin . . .

He remembered how, in the aftermath of air-raids, the accumulated debris would be suspended in the London air for hours, and then would slowly descend, covering one in a fine, white ash. This was the fire 'without'. But the fire 'within' would outlast the war, a sign that he was chosen, if not for bliss, at least for endurance. Eliot's ARP* duties, watching 'firecrackers' from a rooftop in South Kensington (a fairly safe post between the bombing points of Earl's Court and the Museums) provided a perfect apocalyptic setting for the culminating scene of the *Quartets*. He gazed down on a London, much of which had turned into smouldering heaps of rubble. After a raid there would be an eerie silence. There was no traffic, since most of the streets were blocked by fallen buildings, and hardly any pedestrians, only a pall of smoke and everywhere an acrid smell of burning. Eliot was animated, not harrowed, by this horrific scene as he chatted to other fire-watchers, mostly retired Indian majors.

***

* Air-Raid Precautions.

I have said that the feat of Eliot's greatest poetry was to convert urban reality into nightmare, hallucination, vision. Here was the vision ready-made. From the charred and smoking ruins a shade rises, a 'familiar compound ghost', who speaks from beyond time in Eliot's own voice. This is the poet's climactic encounter with his other self: a ghost of the immortals who bears a promise of immortality to the still-living Eliot.

Self-judgement turns on the ghost's prophecy. In the first version the ghost brings a promise of the 'eternal': 'it is here.' It is the logical outcome of secret experience, the youthful vigils and voyages, the 'fear, loathing and hate' he had known through Vivienne, and the heady escape to the South of France with the Pounds in 1919 ('The walls of Poitiers, and the Anjou wine'). These he rehearses for the last time: the formative times 'of birth and death and change'. Forget the modish theories, the ghost tells him, and the modish language that sustained them. Modernism is already fading, the fate of all literary fashions. Compounded with the ghost, Eliot watches his life pass in sequence, all he loved and all he hated, strained for the essential moments that will link him with generations gone and generations to come. 'After many seas and after many lands', he watches his individual past dissolve into the mists of time. He must now draw nearer to the 'dead and the unborn', and detach himself from present people, 'the voices and the faces that were most near'.

It is specifically 'autumn' in the first draft. It was autumn in Eliot's first imagined parting with Emily Hale to go abroad; and autumn here, he told Hayward, was 'to throw back to Figlia che piange' (just as the chatter of unborn children at Burnt Norton was meant to throw back to the dream children of 'New Hampshire'). This wartime autumn he must again resign 'the last love on earth'. It is a test of his strength of purpose. Can be relinquish her memory as the young Eliot had struggled to do in 1912:

> She turned away, but with the autumn weather
> Compelled my imagination many days.

It is his private trial to repeat this scene, resigning love again and yet again, till it becomes the emblematic gesture of his journey. The youth who broke with the dismayed girl had been destined to join the company of the timeless even before Eliot's departure for Europe in 1914.

This is all he can do, the ghost assures him in 1941. 'The rest is grace'. With this resonant promise, the sound of an explosion wakes the poet to the present: 'At which I started: and the sun had risen.' The sun may confer the longed-for radiance; it also signals a return to time.

Eliot's adviser, John Hayward, said oddly little when he read this ambitious piece in the summer of 1941. He said it was 'all right', as were parts I and V. There were limitations to Hayward. He was a stickler for language, and certainly, in many places, helped Eliot towards accuracy of statement. But, like Pound, he was obtuse to Eliot's more veiled reference to religious experience. He did not remotely understand what was meant by the revelation of 'Zero summer'. Too clever by half, he thought it had something to do with the absolute zero of physics. Nor did he grasp the import of 'silence'. Hayward's failure to respond to the ghost's visitation convinced Eliot that its call was too fragile to survive communication. He took the failure upon himself, and put the poem aside for a year. Then he struck through the passage in heavy pencil. He said later that it 'cost me far more time and trouble and vexation than any passage of the same length that I have ever written.'

Some time between the summer of 1941 and the summer of 1942, Eliot decided that greatness would come not through sublimity, as he had hoped, but through a brutal honesty as he aged. Eliot was still consciously aiming at his highest reach as a poet, still walking shoulder to shoulder with the compound ghost of the immortals, Yeats, Shelley, and above all Dante whose verse form he still adopts, all the poets who wrote words that won't decay. But in the drastic revision that Eliot undertook in August–September 1942, it was as though he recognized that he could not touch the ultimate heights of the *Paradiso*, and so settled instead for other Dantean achievements, the sense of sin and the piercing clarity.

Eliot used sin, as Yeats used the foul rag and bone shop of the heart, to spur new poetry in a rough draft for the ghost's revised speech:

> . . . old rooted sin puts forth again
> Even in exhausted soil, after many seasons,
> When the starved unflowering growth shows still more foul . . .

Eliot pulls out the same ugly emotions as Yeats, the lust, the rage, the remorse,* but in Yeats the compunction is short-lived: he is the wild, wicked old man. Eliot's compunction will go on. For Yeats the fire refines art; for Eliot it is the remedy for sin. The absence of any real affinity with Yeats is clear in Eliot's familiar solution when he redrafts the speech in prose: 'there is only the one remedy, pain for pain, in that purgative fire which you must will . . .'.

He now began to cultivate the 'rending pain' of recall, of 'motives late revealed' and 'things ill done and done to others' harm' in all assurance of virtue. He explained this carefully to Hayward on 7 September 1942: 'I mean not simply something not questioned but something consciously approved.' He had told Hayward that he intended to inject 'some acute personal reminiscence', and the emotional impact of the ghost's revised speech came from Eliot's exposure of his sense of guilt, obviously about Vivienne. The approval of his contemporaries now served only to deepen that guilt: 'fools' approval stings.'

It took a grim moral courage to let go the visionary moments of his early life, with their latent promise, and let judgement fall, with the utmost severity, on what he must have wished to forget. But the reward of this public self-laceration was what is probably the strongest passage of poetry that he ever wrote, as he turned away from the plot of attainment to his habitat of pain.

Eliot intended some sharpening of personal poignancy in the revised version, but in fact both versions are personal in different ways. The first is more autobiographical; the second more confessional. The first distils the shape of a life that will call the poet out of himself into eternity. The second takes a hard look, savage in its honesty, at the residual flaws that he will share with other ageing men: the cold craving of the senses for what they can no longer enjoy, and the stale sneers that fail to amuse. The first version singles Eliot out, the heir to the immortals. The second version thrusts him back in place as ordinary stained creature. And

---

* Eliot alludes to lines from 'Vacillation', which he had quoted in *After Strange Gods*:

> Things said or done long years ago,
> Or things I did not do or say
> But thought that I might say or do,
> Weigh me down, and not a day
> But something is recalled,
> My conscience or my vanity appalled.

yet it points the stains with such unerring brilliance that, in another way, it, too, breaks through the veils of existence, exchanging introspective clarity for a lost visionary power.

Eliot did more drafts of *Little Gidding* than of any other *Quartet*. The first three *Quartets* he wrote quickly and with ease; the last took eighteen drafts in all (if we count working carbons as well as top copies). Why was it so immense and prolonged a struggle? Of course, *Little Gidding* had to be the summation of the preceding poems, and, as such, of Eliot's whole career. But I have wondered if there was not another reason. Could he have been waiting for some yield from his life that did not, in the end, come? In disclaiming the life of a saint, Eliot was performing an act of humility essential to the life of a saint. He would wipe out pride and spiritual ambition—and yet, could he have embarked on a series of religious ordeals without some sort of ambition or, as we may prefer to call it, need or hope?

The survival of the many drafts makes it possible to see the evolution of *Little Gidding* as the logic of its emotions changed. There were three main layers of composition: a brief handwritten outline, the first complete typescript of July 1941, and the revised poem of August–September 1942. The initial outline set out the sequence of the transfigured life in four stages, each with some intimation of immortality. The first two stages would be Eliot's own: a wintry state shot through with heavenly light, which must supersede the natural play of the senses, and then a stage of destruction by 'daemonic fire' ('The Inferno'). Following this, the plan looks forward to detachment from human ties, and then, finally, all life would be absorbed into a 'central fire'. It concludes with an Invocation to the Holy Spirit.

Central to this plan is the deliberate exercise in detachment: 'They vanish, the individuals, and our feeling for them sinks into the flame which refines.' There is nothing, initially, about communal feeling: that came later. The underlying wish is for emotional withdrawal. This risky action, I imagine, is what Eliot undertook in 1941–2, and I shall argue that here is the clue to his problem with the last stage of the *Quartets*, essentially the difficulty in reaching that divine fire.

It was through detachment that Eliot would follow the mystics into their state of grace. For this reason he clung to detachment throughout the period of revision—the passage remains unchanged from the first to final draft—despite just criticism from Hayward that his idea was 'uncompromising' and 'rather laboured'. Hayward was not the first of Eliot's friends made uneasy by his assumption that the divine is to be found through withdrawal from human ties. There had been a dismayed response to his epigraph to *Sweeney Agonistes* to this effect, taken from St John of the Cross. Unquestionably, the precedent for Eliot's detachment is there in monastic tradition, while *The Cloud of Unknowing* urges a pupil to 'forget all created things . . . so that your thought and longing do not turn or reach out to them'. So, too, the *Imitation of Christ*: 'See that you are inwardly free and purified, unattached to any created thing.' You must find the grace to send others 'right away and then when you are left alone, be joined to God alone'. Eliot naturally set his sights lower. For him the end of detachment is only 'the purification of the motive'. In personal terms, he could justify his severance from Vivienne only by a purer motive than attachment to another woman.

Eliot's curt exposition of detachment is curiously flat, because it is not less lofty than the mystics', but it has a different quality of feeling. The mystics show concurrent love for fellow beings, which is a convincing sign of their state of grace; Eliot's detachment is more rigid. He seems oblivious (as Harry) to the effect that detachment, even of the purest kind, will have on other people. The poetry of 'Love' came late in the evolution of *Little Gidding*, only in September 1942, in the very last stage of revision, when a penitent approaches the 'unfamiliar Name' through the fires purgatory.

In the planned sequence, detachment immediately precedes the coming of 'Love', but in the first draft this is where the poem broke down. In a first, scrawled manuscript, part IV began at a high point with the poet's speaking in 'tongues' of the 'culmination of desire' and 'hope' in the approach to the cross in a way that recalls an unpublished poem of 1911, 'The Little Passion', where the lines of street-lights lead towards a cross. Then, in the second stanza, comes the collapse of confidence as Eliot reviews life from baptism to death, and finds sin in place of grace. The 'sign that brands' is straight out of *The Scarlet Letter*: a dire, puritanical vision of pervasive sin from which there is no escape. He speaks dully of a gambler who has lost the game of salvation.* This man staked all for heaven, but will moulder in the grave, like the despised revellers at East Coker.

Here was a serious failure. The feeling was dead. Eliot was simply not possessed by the central fire of his plan. As he could not meet the demands of transfiguration, he deflects poetic energy into heavy denunciations of '*Unprofitable Sin*' and '*Sundry Pleasures*'. John Hayward, after reading this in late July 1941, told Eliot candidly on 1 August that it did not fit the rest of the poem. It was 'obfuscating', he said. The sad fact was that the 'eternal' promised by the ghost was not, after all, at hand.

Eliot's immediate diagnosis was that the flaw (in part IV) lay with the ghost's prophecy (in part II). That would have to change. To presume to name Love as the outcome of the process, he had to climb down, and, once more, try to purify his poetic instrument with self-laceration. This would fit the stanza that he retained from part IV, where redemption comes 'from fire by fire'. It did have to be the old stand-by, pain—not vision—that would bring the poem to life.

There is a way of suffering, Eliot argued, that has in it 'already a kind of presence of the supernatural and of the superhuman'. Because the sufferer 'cannot adjust himself to the actual world he has to reject it in favour of Heaven and Hell, or because he has the perception of Heaven and Hell he rejects the present world'. This explanation helps us understand his position, but it falls short of the sublime pain to which part IV aspired, and which St Bernard has described with confident acumen. A burning compunction can be a mystical grace, he says,

which consumes but does not affect. It burns sweetly, it produces a delightful desolation. It acts at the same time as fire upon our vices and as ointment upon our souls. ... When you experience this power which totally changes you, and the love which sets you on fire, understand that the Lord is present in your heart. (Sermon in 1053)

Despite Eliot's problems with parts II and IV, much of the first draft does show the poem's final greatness, and much of the final

---

* In the first typescript the gambler is depersonalized by the barren language of financial transaction: 'debt', 'deficit', 'stocks', 'dues'. Cf. Phlebas the Phoenician (in *The Waste Land*: IV) who forgot 'the profit and loss' as his mercantile identity was washed away in a baptismal death to the world.

draft was already there in July 1941. What makes this first draft so interesting is the evidence of an underlying schema that was loftier, potentially, than the final one, and which might have provided a heaven-sent climax to Eliot's earlier work, but which he could not (for reasons we can only guess) fulfil.

I have wondered whether, had Eliot delayed longer, his experience could have caught up with his initial conception, and if so whether *Little Gidding* could have succeeded equally well as a rather different finale. But he was impatient to finish. With other jobs in the offing, he allowed far less than his usual yearly space between *Quartets*. The third *Quartet* was published in February 1941, and by June he had a rough preliminary draft for the fourth. After his bout of revision a year later, he told Hayward in September 1942 that 'to spend much more time over this poem might be dangerous. After a time one loses the original feeling of the impulse, and then it is no longer safe to alter. It is time to close the chapter.'

The introspective mind of the last *Quartet* remains, as always, the votary of 'Solidad' (solitude) waiting, a trifle less patiently, for the incursion of divine fire. Behind this act of attention, a community comes into focus. During the long wait it is a prop, and if the worst—spiritual defeat—should happen it would be a haven, as once the community at Little Gidding gave refuge to Charles I, a 'broken king' at night, after his crushing defeat at the battle of Naseby.

People who lived through the Battle of Britain remark on the extraordinary fellow-feeling and good-humoured resilience during the shared danger. It was under these unique conditions that Eliot was making an effort, through *Little Gidding*, to feel his way into that sense of community. Although he judged the English as 'not wholly commendable', and although, too, they were of 'no immediate kin', he could identify with their endurance and indomitability in the face of defeat. When Allen Tate invited Eliot to Princeton, he replied in March 1943 that he could not leave London during the war.

Three scenes of this time show him feeling his way into the English community—not the intellectual élite who had always welcomed him, but groups of ordinary people. There were the chats with retired Indian majors through the long night hours at the Post. There was his life amongst the women at the Shambles where he absorbed the English tone of affectionate humour, the domestic flair for comic drama as a kind of resourcefulness. One day in September 1942 old Mrs Mirrlees got herself locked in the bathroom: the lock was jammed. The whole of the population of the Wood congregated outside the door as Eliot—the only other male was presumably the ancient gardener—climbed up a ladder. When the rescuer reached the window he found Mrs Mirrlees placidly reading a thriller. Anyway, he could do nothing that way. Holmes and Watson, he thought, would have put their shoulders to the door and burst through, but Eliot and the gardener only got sore shoulders. The gardener tried a crowbar in vain, the dogs barked, and everyone implored everyone else to keep cool. Finally, a servant shook the door, and it opened.

The third scene was on a train in August 1941, when Eliot took on the character of the lovable English eccentric as he read over the first typescript of *Little Gidding*:

... re-reading the poem in the train yesterday (with a Three Nuns Vicar peeping over my shoulder: I wonder what he made of it, together with the Giant Umbrella and a volume of Kipling—he probably thought I was what is now euphemistically called an Anglo Indian) ...

At this time he was putting together a selection of Kipling's verse. It was through Kipling, the insider who was also an outsider, that he found his position in relation to England. Kipling, Eliot said in his Introduction, had 'a universal foreignness', and yet could see more clearly because he was 'alien'. He had also 'a sense of the antiquity of England, of the number of generations and peoples who have laboured the soil and been buried beneath it, and of the contemporaneity of the past.'*

Records of the past tend to follow the lines of victory. Eliot counters this with a record of historical figures in their times of defeat. His drafts cite Richard III (defeated on Bosworth Field in 1485)† and the Duke of Wellington, not as the victor of Waterloo but as the unpopular politician in 1831, when a mob, believing him

---

* How curiously Eliot's Kipling and *East Coker* merge. Eliot was thinking in particular of *Puck of Pook's Hill*, *Rewards and Fairies*, 'The Wish House', and 'The Friendly Brook'.

† 'Richard seems an odd companion for Charles I', Helen Gardner comments (*The Composition of the Four Quartets*, 209), and explains that they were brought together by Mr George Every in a play about King Charles's visit to Little Gidding, which Eliot read in 1936.

the major opponent of the Reform Bill, broke his windows. In each case, Eliot extracts a pure moral emblem from its murky historical context. The courage to go on in the face of defeat had its public meaning at a time when England stood alone against Hitler, but Eliot's odd persistence in wearing a white rose in his lapel on the anniversary of Bosworth, for years after the war, suggests that for him the private sense of defeat was pre-eminent. When Eliot sees history as a pattern of 'timeless moments', he extracts arbitrarily certain scenes that bear on the peculiar history of his own soul. He implies that the private individual may create the past, as Emerson put it: 'it is part of the business of the critic to preserve tradition— where a good tradition exists . . . but this is eminently to see it *not* as consecrated by time but to see it beyond time.' This idea is reinforced by Hegel's *Philosophy of History* which Eliot owned and marked as a student. Hegel saw history as a manifestation of the Spirit which is eternally present: 'Spirit is immortal; with it there is no past, no future, but an essential *now*.' For Eliot it is the spirit in the face of defeat that is 'now and England'.

As he wrote the wartime *Quartets*, Eliot began to take on the aura of fame that remained for the rest of his life. He was from then on a man in constant public demand, broadcasting and lecturing abroad for the British Council, as well as talking on Shakespeare (in autumn 1941, in Bristol), on 'The Music of Poetry' (in February 1942, in Glasgow), and on 'The Classics and the Man of Letters' (in April 1942, to the Classical Association). Eliot told Martin Browne that all this public activity was a 'drug' as opposed to the 'solitary toil' of *Little Gidding* which 'often seems so pointless'. He was invited to Iceland in the autumn of 1941 (though the engagement was cancelled due to illness), and to Sweden in the spring of 1942. At a time when semi-official relations with Sweden were being established, he flew to Stockholm with Bishop Bell for five weeks. Bell made contact with two Germans, Hans Schönfeld and Dietrich Bonhoeffer, representatives of an organized opposition to Hitler who wished to make contact with the British Government. Bishop Bell duly contacted Anthony Eden, the Foreign Secretary, on their return, but the Foreign Office failed to respond to this initiative.

Eliot had hoped to revise *Little Gidding* in the winter of 1941/2, but had to put it off to the following August, when he reworked the ghost's prophecy and the defective part IV. He sent the final poem to John Hayward on 2 September. The success of the 1942 version lies in Eliot's acceptance of the fact that he would not himself receive the divine spirit. He would not fudge this with a verbal 'smoke-screen'. He had, at least in theory, the dove's descent. And, in theory, he names God as 'Love'. He did try, at this last stage, to infuse feeling by reverting to the emotion of *Burnt Norton* ('Who heaped the brittle roseleaves? Love.') but his final revision turns from this fragile, inspirational love to love born of torment as he puts on the 'intolerable shirt of flame'.

The poem still lacked something, some note of attainment, of sublimity and tenderness, and Eliot's last additions were the voices of two fourteenth-century mystics: Dame Julian of Norwich's *Revelations of Divine Love*, and the 'Calling' of the anonymous writer of *The Cloud of Unknowing* which draws Love into him. The compassionate woman and the learned man represented, to Eliot, 'the two mystical extremes'.

Except for the voices of the mystics and the opening flash, when the sun flamed the ice, the final *Quartet* became wholly purgatorial. This balance between ephemeral intimation and ongoing endurance was Eliot's accurate judgement of his own condition as index of a general human condition. The conclusion, in one sense, remains provisional. Spiritual autobiography is always in the making. *Little Gidding*, like all Eliot's poems, resonates into a future beyond the poem which is ours as much as the poet's. This may be less triumphant than his initial plan, but its advantage is to make the poem more moving to those of us whose lives are imperfect, and who can make no claim to beatitude.

Little Gidding recounts 'the end of the journey': 'end', 'purpose', 'fulfilment' are the words in the air. The 'end' is to come to rest in theological orthodoxy. It does not matter, though, if we do not share Eliot's precise belief, since the greatness of the work has been the authenticity of the search.* Eliot does not state truth. He

---

* In Eliot's 1929 essay on Dante he said that 'there is a difference ... between philosophical *belief* and poetic *assent*' (*Selected Essays*, 218). In Dec. 1932, in an unpublished address in King's Chapel in Boston, he reminded his audience that it was not necessary to believe what Dante believed in order to enjoy the poetry, although to enjoy it fully one ought to understand what he believed. Eliot repeated this idea yet again in 1945, in Paris, in another unpublished lecture. Lucretius and Dante, he said, do not try to persuade readers of their beliefs but to convey what it feels like to hold

simply points towards it by arriving at places where truth is manifest.

Another 'end' is to sum up a pattern of experience in the preceding *Quartets*, which is inherent also in Eliot's life. In his early poetry, he had perceived the move from divine reality back into ordinary life as a jolt across a vast gap, because, in early years, he had seen ordinary life as corrupt, in opposition to the life of the spirit. One triumph of *Little Gidding* was to close this gap. After the air-raid the two worlds of time and timelessness seem alike, and the poet treads between them with an 'ease' that 'is cause of wonder'.

The implied question—it may go back to the overwhelming question that Prufrock was too locked in time to frame—is how to rescue ordinary life from its worthless banality. The answer is now quite simple: to pare away the agitations of the present—the tug of the senses, the modish sneers, and all the nonsense of fame—and hold fast to a lasting judgement, like the Word in the desert. The very appearance of Eliot's ghost in the Cromwell Road, speaking in his own prophetic voice, demonstrates the incursion of the timeless into time—if we have the wit to see it.

In *Little Gidding*, Eliot is doing it all for us: in each part, the eternal pierces the familiar façades of ordinary life. It is behind the pigsty in the English countryside, it is on the ash-strewn London pavement, and it is in the silence between the waves, a permanent presence as Eliot knew it, already, as a child on the Cape Ann shore. Given this awareness, an ordinary life can be transfigured. This is the 'end' of *Little Gidding* and of *Four Quartets* as a whole: nothing less than to recreate our existence.

Eliot recreates an actual place, Little Gidding, as a model of the transfigured life, much as his ancestors dreamt of a godly society that would be a model to all the world. Little Gidding itself is subsidiary to the icy fire which Eliot projects upon the memory of his visit on a 'really lovely day' at the end of May, the only good day in the spring of 1936, he wrote to Mrs Perkins in Boston.

Little Gidding was just one instance of a way of life that could absorb the timeless. It projected from past to future the shape of a life that might be a perfect vessel for the divine spirit to fill. As the

certain beliefs ('*Le Rôle social des poètes*'. An English translation is part of the Hayward Bequest in King's College, Cambridge).

ritual of the devotional life was to be Eliot's valid alternative to a lifetime burning in every moment, so the rhythmic words of poetry must be an alternative to God's burning Word. A classic language, precise, ordered, wide to both old and new, receptive to subtleties of thought and feeling, might become (like the life) a perfected vessel for timeless content.

In an unpublished lecture in 1937, Eliot spoke of a pattern of emotion in which a man acts beyond character, according to a hidden and mysterious order. *Four Quartets* follows emotions beyond those we ordinarily know as human, though we may have hints and guesses. The drafts show the personal source of these emotions; the revisions Eliot's control of personal matter, allowing just enough to enliven the poem with the urgency of private struggle, yet subduing it to the ideal pattern. Deliberately, he allowed his own life to fall away so that it is the perfect life that remains before us.

In the course of this experiment, three forms of life are super-imposed one upon another. First, there is the parallel: the repeti-tion of lives that have gone before, and the ritual repetition of the observant life. This coexists with the aspiring line of progressive development: this would fit the linear form of the converted life which leads through the ordeals of the wilderness to a vision of the promised land, the grail, or the Celestial City. Eliot's journey, though, ends where it began. Its final form is circular. After the effort at transformation, he realizes that he has become what was always implicit in his origins. In so far as he has been true to his child's sense of being, he has not changed. The wheel which seemed to suggest the dull repetition of meaningless existence fades into the circle, a singleness of being, self-contained, complete, as he returns at the last to his American childhood to recover simplicity and innocence. This biographical circle is intact also from the opposite angle: Eliot's 'way back' to England completes the 'way forward' of Andrew Eliot to the New World. Eliot planned that his life should end, even more neatly than his poem, in the ancestral earth of East Coker where his ashes do, in fact, now lie. The parallel, line, and circle compose an abstract design, but one distilled from actual life.

To read *Four Quartets* accurately is not to dwell on its separate parts, but to experience a cumulative effect, like a great piece of music. As in music, there is a set form: each *Quartet* begins with an actual experience in Eliot's life; at the centre of each is some action, say, a journey; at the end of each some struggle with language that parallels the effort at the perfect life. Yet, cumulatively, the *Quartets* convey a profounder unity than the repetition of set form. This is the ultra-human pattern to which he wished to give the accuracy of a formula. The successive poems tell the story of Eliot's gradual discovery of this formula, starting—like a scientist— from a flash of intuition. With painstaking care, he goes on to test intuition against experience: the experience of his own life, and the experience of others in other ages. The essential intuition was there in childhood, not looked for but (as a first draft put it) 'heard, half-heard, in the silence / Of distant lands and seas'.* Exploration takes him back to this past to repossess the intuition, and behind it the dead, his mother and, stretching back in turn behind her, the line of ancestors who strove to purify their lives:

> We are born with the dead;
> See, they return, and bring us with them.

Exploration depends on the talent to '*see*'—to detect conduct— which implies intuition of another kind. It was Eliot's habit to pounce on the emotional vibrations of moral crisis: 'the horror! the horror!' of the dying Kurtz in the Congo, or his own 'ragged rock' of guilt. Eliot did not dwell on moral crisis for its own sake: he extracts the permanent import swiftly, almost ruthlessly, shedding his life like a husk.

To '*see*' is to have a sure sense for the telling words of others. Exploration, to some extent, meant books, the records of the past, and the swoop of selection from the morass of worthless detail. This kind of exploration began for Eliot at Harvard when he ransacked books on ways to transcend the banalities of daily life. *Four Quartets* is rooted in this period, not only in the early purgatorial extravagances of 'The Burnt Dancer', and in the *Gita* and *Mysticism*, but also in a more obscure source, a book called *Truth and Reality* by John Elof Boodin which Eliot marked heavily

---

* This was the original conclusion. When the phrase 'distant lands and seas' was changed to 'between two waves of the sea', literal-minded John Hayward queried if there could be 'silence' between waves. Eliot then exchanged this important word for the less dramatic 'stillness'.

some time between 1911 and 1914. One marked passage suggests an ambitious unity of design that Eliot eventually fulfilled in *Four Quartets*: 'the realization of a whole of our inner life or the unitary self; the realization of a whole of the outer world, or the systematic unity of nature; and the realization of a whole in our fellow world, or the systematic unity of history.' *Truth and Reality* goes on to urge a still more comprehensive unity 'namely, the complete synthesis of all experience or the absolute.'

When Edith Sitwell wanted to select one of the *Quartets* for an anthology, she wrote to Eliot: 'I am now tearing myself to pieces about which of the *Quartets* I am going to ask for (the moment I choose one, I want the others too . . .).'* Although the poems were published separately—the last also on its own in October 1942— they are, as Sitwell felt, a unit. The complete sequence was published first in America on 11 May 1943, and eighteen months later in England. Eliot said that the poems got better as they went along: 'the fourth is the best of all.' In an interview, he told Helen Gardner that of all his poems *Little Gidding* best stood the test of saying exactly what it meant. And, as she said, this satisfaction was unparalleled in Eliot's comments on his own work. 'The *Four Quartets*: I rest on those', Eliot continued to state in his last important interview in 1959, and said the same in conversation: 'I stand or fall on them.'

In Eliot's early years a gap yawned between body and soul, between the wasted land and the white towers of Wren's churches. His polar oppositions seemed irreconcilable as the poetry rocked from scene to scene. In *Four Quartets* the opposition of time and eternity is resolved as he found points of intersection in art, the life of Christ, and the church.

On 28 March 1931 he had written to Stephen Spender:

I have the A minor Quartet [of Beethoven] on the gramophone, and I find it quite inexhaustible to study. There is a sort of heavenly or at least more than human gaiety about some of his later things which one imagines might come to oneself as the fruit of reconciliation and relief after immense suffering; I should like to get something of that into verse before I die.

In his youth Eliot had dared to hope for heavenly bliss ('your heart would have responded / Gaily . . . beating obedient / To

* She chose *Burnt Norton*.

controlling hands'), but in maturity had to content himself with reconciliation and relief. In the final lines of *Four Quartets* he reaches towards—though cannot himself attain—reconciliation of pain and divine love. The fire and the rose are one. Here the 'unimaginable' is stated: the coexistence of opposite, God-given sensations. Eliot dared to formulate this longed-for 'reality' of feeling that, some day, it might once more call out a perfect life—not necessarily his own. The true artist, he quoted, 'knows that he is but the vessel of an emotion whence others, not he, must drink'.

The last lines are a finale not only to *Four Quartets* but to Eliot's poetry as a whole, which seeks repeatedly to formulate a pattern that would give meaning to our ephemeral existence, and to reconcile that existence with whatever lies beyond our compass. For it is the function of art, he said, to give us some perception of an order in life by imposing an order upon it.

This order, though, remains a mere formula unless it touches the life of the reader. Mary Lee Settle, an American novelist who did war-service in London, recalled the impact of *Four Quartets* when there really was 'dust in the air' and the ruined rows of houses stood like empty husks, their wallpaper stained with rain. At a time when people queued for rations and suffered loss and privation, Eliot 'had somehow refined what he had to tell us, beyond the banality of disappointment and hopelessness, into a promise like steel'. That first generation of readers responded to a promise of recovery made with 'a miraculous effrontery of spirit' in the face of years of wrong. He became, she remembered, 'our lay priest'.

For other readers, at other times, *Four Quartets* makes its mark when we come alive to feeling 'which we can only detect . . . out of the corner of the eye and can never completely focus. . . . At such moments, we touch the border of those feelings which only music can express.' The rhythm and order of the artist bring us to a condition of 'stillness and reconciliation', and then, Eliot adds, must 'leave us as Virgil left Dante to proceed towards a region where that guide can avail us no farther'.

Eliot did himself enter some new region after the autumn air-raid, presumably in 1940 when London was bombed every night from 7 September to 2 November. '. . . It *was* autumn', he told Hayward on 5 August 1941. In that eerie silence, the still-living poet met the compound ghost of the immortals whom, it was now clear, he would join. Together they patrolled the ruined streets in defeat and purgatory beyond Eliot's own time. So he passed the border of personal trial towards a transcendent calm that he shared with a wise woman, Juliana of Norwich, in another, distant century of disaster:

> And all shall be well and
> All manner of thing shall be well.

4. *Lady of Silences*

In the years following *Four Quartets* the growing eminence of Eliot's public character seems to obscure the private man. The more visible he became, the more invisible the self that sought what he called 'reality'. The next chapter will follow Eliot's public career, but this one will explore what is harder to know, the elusive private life without which the public life would appear rather hollow. From the thirties to the fifties, Eliot's private life was centred on Emily Hale, who was also the strongest personal influence on his work. The more that is known about Eliot's relation to her, the stranger and more complex he appears.

Evidence for this story is not complete nor, very likely, ever will be. It has remained the secret of Eliot's life because Emily Hale, in her devotion to him, played out the role he assigned: a 'Lady of silences'. Eliot wrote more than a thousand letters to her, far more than to any other person, an average of between one a week and one a fortnight over the thirty years of their attachment. But, according to some arrangement, the letters were to be sequestered for fifty years after the death of the survivor. The other long-term ban was on letters to John Hayward (containing acid remarks about contemporaries). These were to be inaccessible until 2000, while the letters to Emily Hale were formally sealed until 12 October 2019.

More discouraging, in the longer view, is that Emily Hale's letters to Eliot are missing. She wished them to be read after her death, and at some stage Eliot thought of leaving them to the Bodleian Library. But when she made enquiries, of Eliot himself in 1963 and of the library in 1965, she drew a blank. She concluded that Eliot had destroyed her letters, and she told herself that he did it 'to protect me'. Peter du Sautoy, Eliot's fellow-director at Faber, recalled that, in 1963, Eliot gave him a fairly large, old-fashioned metal cash-box with gilt embellishments. It contained a good many letters, tightly packed, which, he said, he had long meant to destroy. Mr du Sautoy duly burnt them, at Eliot's request, without looking at them. It is likely that these were the Hale letters.

Luckily, a letter of 1947 to a close friend, Lorraine Havens, has survived, and also a good batch of letters to Willard Thorp, written between 1957 and 1969 (mostly to do with her bequest of Eliot's letters to Princeton). These do give some idea of her relation to Eliot from her point of view. They are the letters of a woman of distinction: not a writer—she was more articulate orally than on paper—but something of a heroine. She reminds me of the heroines of Anita Brookner, single women with a passionate depth of feeling contained by absolute standards of conduct. That combination of passion and decorum is their tragedy, for they are out of line with the facile world in which they live.

Without her letters to Eliot, and perhaps even with them, the whole truth can never be known, for there is no end to the nuances of a relationship. Yet there is a story to be told, a Jamesian story of old Boston, of high-minded people, caught in their own web of intricate moral complexity. The foil for this hidden love is Eliot's public friendship from 1938 to 1956 with Mary Trevelyan, his escort at parties, the theatre, and, most often, church. Her story is part of the next chapter. Suffice it to say now that the tone of the friendship with Mary Trevelyan was as different as national character, conducted with candour rather than intimacy, with jollity, and, on her part, tolerant good sense. She had the English relish for the comic drama of ordinary life, which may have helped Eliot find a voice for the kind of comedies he now tried to write, and she had an organizational energy which was sometimes too intrusive. Though he saw more of Mary than he ever saw of Emily Hale, she was for him less significant. In the forties and fifties, his distance from all friends, even the fearless Mary, was so firmly governed by what he called 'rules', that he seems harder to know in this period than any other. The other obscure period is 1911–14, the graduate years at Harvard which, it turns out, were a time of fevered upheaval. It now appears that in the late forties he had another upheaval, for on 27 April 1949 he told Mary that he had experienced, some time before, a sort of psychological change of life.

The change began with a phone call from Maurice Haigh-Wood on the morning of 23 January 1947, to say that Vivienne (aged 58) had died suddenly of heart failure in the night. John Hayward took the call, and it was he who broke the news.

'Oh God! Oh God!' Eliot said, and buried his face in his hands. He was shocked by the death, but also by its consequences. For now, unexpectedly, he was free to marry Emily Hale, which, for the last fifteen years, she and his family had believed was what he most wanted. Yet at once he realized that he had no emotions or desires to share. This, he later told Mary, was his tragedy. 'I have met myself as a middle-aged man', says the hero of *The Cocktail Party* when he discovers, after his wife departs, that he has lost his wish to marry the devoted Celia. The worst moment, he adds, is when you feel that you have lost the desire for all that was most desirable.

In 1950 he told Mary Trevelyan that it now seemed to him impossible to share his life with anyone. This was a reply to a letter in which, for the second time, Mary proposed to him. It seemed to him that his life was effectively over: the rest would simply mark time.

The ending of crucial relationships with women, in the late forties and early fifties, is a suggestive counterpoint to some decline in emotional vitality in Eliot's lectures and plays. He was always drawn to women of great vitality who, in different ways, energized his writing. The death of Vivienne meant the loss of his focus of torment. His rejection of Emily Hale finally broke the dream that had given the rare moments of radiance to his poetry. So Eliot lost at once the two women who had stirred his greatest work. Instead, they preyed on his conscience.

In the crises of their marriage, Vivienne used to declare herself unfit to live. Eliot would then promise anything, and she would dissolve into floods of tears. He described these scenes to Mary Trevelyan who was *not* particularly fascinated. She was a bracing person who did not encourage self-pity. Her diary (part of an unpublished memoir of her friendship with Eliot) passes over these confidences a little briskly.

Eliot had never quite believed in Vivienne's threats of death, and had feared more the nakedness of her emotional demand. No woman in his family, daughters of genteel New England, would have behaved with such degrading abandon. Eliot never visited Vivienne in the asylum, not, I imagine, out of callousness, but because he must have feared the compelling power of her strong Welsh shriek. The fact that he had not been able to love her would have been, in any case, a denial of her cries for help. Poor Vivienne with her urgent self-absorption had not been, in the long term, lovable, her behaviour based more and more on wild and often offensive misjudgements. In the view of those who saw Eliot and his wife together, he had shown amazing endurance.

All this time, his nostalgia for Emily Hale had been mainly for a dream in which he retained a capacity for love, as a purity of feeling, rooted in recovered innocence. He had been sustained by this dream, yet the fact remained that, throughout the marriage to Vivienne, he had cared for someone else. Because, during the early forties, he had disciplined this feeling by asceticism, he had still hoped to redeem himself by extravagant rectitude. Vivienne's death exploded this scheme.

Eliot told E. W. F. Tomlin (a writer on philosophy who had contributed reviews to the *Criterion*) that feelings of guilt and horror haunted him daily. 'I can never forget anything', he said. 'The horror! the horror!' of all those years of waste land came back, draining hopes of salvation. In Eliot's new play *The Cocktail Party* (drafted in 1948), an estranged wife, Lavinia, returns to repossess her husband, Edward, in the worst way. For she confers on him a character he dreads, that of an unreal man, incapable of feeling. This is the 'death of the spirit' which, in the original acted version, Edward declares is even worse than fear of madness: a solitary mental prison from which there is no escape. That this should be a permanent condition is Eliot's definition of hell:

> What is hell? Hell is oneself,
> Hell is alone, the other figures
> Merely projections.

In this scene, the husband calls his wife the 'angel of destruction'. At her touch, he tells her, there is nothing but ruin:

> O God, what have I done? . . .
> Must I become after all what you would make me?

In *The Cocktail Party*, Eliot transmutes the power-play of his marriage—which partner's image of the other will prevail?—into a fictitious comedy which resolves their impasse. Lavinia, a sharp-tongued woman, is too efficient and unspectacular to derive much from Vivienne, and yet there is the odd line that recalls her power, as when Edward speaks of

> The whole oppression, the unreality
> Of the role she had always imposed upon me
> With the obstinate, unconscious, sub-human strength
> That some women have.

'I cannot live with her', he goes on, but also 'cannot live without her.' She has made him incapable of any existence of his own. There is an awakening to psychological horror here, as though Poe's Roderick Usher were to analyse the lifelessness that descends upon him once his frenzied twin, the Lady Madeleine, is buried, for she represents the vital half of his mind. Ghoulishly, she continues to exist in the vaults of the subconscious, and within a few days returns to haunt and destroy the dwindling life of Usher.

In a strange way Vivienne's wild cries that she could not live and Eliot's macabre fantasies of the death of women were complementary, and came true in her premature end. She was the dark mirror of her husband's imagination, for she held up to him her unforgettable degradation. During those frightful nights with Vivienne, he had only to see the 'face that sweats with tears' to realize the torments of hell. Though his experiences with her had validated the poetry of 1915–26, he had feared that she would contaminate his soul, and possess it wholly. For Eliot felt his primal self to be pure—a purity he associated in his poetry with radiant memories of childhood, the New England shore, and Emily Hale. The great effort of his mature years had been to shake off degradation (and Vivienne with it) so as to recover, through the vigilant practice of virtue and prayer, a pristine beatitude. In *Four Quartets* he had ventured to look towards blessedness, but here was denial. Was he to live out his life locked to the shade of Vivienne, the memory of her physical prison the mirror of his mental prison, her denial the mirror of his? Was his guilty soul to be forever irredeemable? It was natural for Eliot to take extreme measures. Christopher Sykes said that he thought of retiring into complete seclusion, but was dissuaded by John Hayward. Mary Trevelyan came to believe that, following Vivienne's death, he committed himself to ten years of penitence.

Eliot said that he felt more disintegrated now than if Vivienne had died fifteen years earlier. There was now less resistance, he added by way of explanation. In 1947 he was 58, and showed signs of ageing. In America that spring he was seen to be gaunt, pallid, 'and tensely withdrawn from anything reminiscent of the flesh'; in July, on his return to England, he had two operations for a hernia; in October he had most of his remaining teeth extracted. An ebb might seem reasonable, and yet we cannot forget that Eliot assumed the mask of age all his life. Like Lambert Strether, in *The Ambassadors*, he sometimes played up age to avoid the demands of living. As always, the truth is as subtle as James's fiction: motives lurk behind motives in the recess of conscience. And nowhere is Eliot more mysterious than in his shifting relations to women. If he gave the impression of a remorseful man, one who seemed to an old crony, Sir Herbert Read, to have 'some secret sorrow or guilt', it was possibly not so much guilt for his wife as for Emily Hale. This, he eventually told Mary Trevelyan, was the deepest cause of his disturbance.

The stories of Vivienne and Emily must be seen together, the extreme counterpoints, like hell and heaven, of Eliot's creative life. When he told Mary Trevelyan that he would have been less upset if Vivienne had died in 1932, he did not, as yet, reveal to her his tie with Emily Hale. Fifteen years earlier, when he had left Vivienne, Emily had been the counter-dream in the ascendant. His feeling for her, idealized as the sublime Lady, had, as his poems show, an imaginative vitality that offered a renewed alternative to the hideous marriage, some human lifeline that upheld the new life of the spirit. If Vivienne had died then (as she had often threatened), could the new life have taken the form of marriage to Emily? On one level he believed, until Vivienne's death, that this is what he wanted. And yet, his work invariably tells us more than what he declares in person. The profounder introspection of *The Family Reunion*, which follows Eliot's situation so closely, suggests that there was in 1934-8 a shift in which potential love was subdued by a state of possession or sin. It suggests that even if Eliot, like Harry, were legally free, he would still not marry the waiting woman but would choose, rather, to pursue the solitary ordeals of penitence. In a curious way, his work foretold the events of his life.

In the winter of 1940/1, Eliot spoke of the 'emotionless' years of living among the breakage of what was most reliable, and therefore fittest for renunciation. This was the frozen state he cultivated in *Four Quartets*, his extreme remedy for sin, modelled on the asceticism of the saints. The result of the subjugation of the body was not an access of divine love but 'failing powers'. He was like a boat drifting towards mortality with a slow leakage. It is not surprising that, when he was free to marry, he found no desire. The anticlimax, after so many years of waiting, seemed to him a catastrophe.

Emily Hale never claimed, like Vivienne, to have been Eliot's muse. She was concerned more with the man than the poet: the Eliot of their family circles. Of the latent monk, and of the heights of a destiny that would exclude any close human contact until it was fulfilled, she saw, perhaps, not enough. With her, the comfortable family aspect of Eliot would have been to the fore, as during the weekends in Campden in the thirties when Eliot had shared a family feeling that he found soothing after years of exile.

Eliot's light verse to Emily Hale, with its details of country walks and visits to Faber, shows the playful ease and suddenly erupting humour of his verse for children. Eliot figures as the cowardly grown-up child, town-bred, who is a great nuisance on country walks because he fears the prongs of a bull lurking behind every tree. Emily Hale is the admirably composed companion, in her tweeds and brogues, who puts up with all the fuss. Eliot appears also as a low-class Cockney cat, an office cat called Morgan, who tries once again to put paw to paper to extol Miss 'Ile on her birthday: 'Now you jist try your paw—let it come from the 'art—'.

Where Emily saw Eliot in terms of this playful compatibility, Eliot saw her also as the material of religious poetry. And when his poetic searching of the soul came to an end, so too did his interest in her. In the last *Quartet*, as Eliot spelt out the end of the search in a new commitment to a Christian community, he spelt out too a new 'detachment' from individual ties. Although he pictured his psychological change as a sudden event of the late forties, his poetry suggests a more gradual and inexorable progress (as in the case of conversion) to the fixed position. This is not to imply that the course of the relationship with Emily Hale was consciously thought out, but simply that, beneath the family ease, there was a radical difference of attitude, the result of Eliot's peculiar sense of destiny as a writer. Eliot imagines in *The Cocktail Party* that a rejected woman might take off on a spiritual venture of her own, but if this was a covert fantasy for Emily Hale it was not an appropriate scenario. As a Unitarian, she was not given to the extremities of the religious life. She wanted marriage, not immolation. Marriage, she said, would have been 'so perfect a solution' to many years of waiting.

For such a long relationship, there were relatively few actual meetings. Most of the time the Atlantic divided them. It was an attachment nourished on letters, where correspondents create each other by creating images of each other. For Emily Hale, the personal letter was a form that gave her pleasure: her surviving letters have the confident warmth and play of tone—affection, irony, honesty, restraint—of a woman who is adept at friendship. For Eliot, the letter was his least distinctive mode. He wrote hundreds of reserved letters; one might say that he was adept at the reserved letter: the kindly let-down to would-be poets, the business letter, the distant letter, the droning letter, the bread-and-butter letter of thanks, above all the letter of excuse with a profusion of elaborate detail that carried politeness, sometimes, to the verge of insult. Eliot's lively letters to select friends—to Pound, Virginia Woolf, John Hayward—are witty, not intimate. There were times of stress when he did confide in Virginia Woolf, but always orally; he was cautious about committing himself in the overtly personal form of the letter. It is possible that his letters to Emily Hale will give no more than further details of a relationship that might be discerned in the works now open before us. There is one clue to the contents of the Eliot–Hale letters. I know what is *not* there, an explicit explanation of Eliot's position, for this was part of Emily Hale's sense of loss at the time of his death. Not to explain would have been entirely in character: he avoided confrontation. But there are implicit explanations in his poetry, so subtle and introspective that it is hard to imagine that actual letters could surpass them. If Emily read *East Coker* as 'a love-letter from God', may there not have been other such communications buried in the published works in which Eliot allowed himself, under the effective cover of poetic license, to explore a profounder and more changeable understanding of what love meant to him than he would have permitted himself in any personal form of discourse? We might, then, read back from the work to the life to find, as Emily Hale found rereading *The Cocktail Party*, 'many a passage which *could* have hidden meaning for me and for him.'

So long a bond is not a mere sequence of biographical facts.

There remains the search for meaning: what the relationship meant to Eliot as the material of art, and what it meant to Emily who would have read his poems and plays in the light of their attachment. What the 'catastrophe' of 1947 will make clear is that, over the course of many years, they developed divergent views of the exact nature of their tie. We recall Eliot's letter to Martin Browne about a hero who takes refuge from natural love in an 'ambiguous' relation. To understand the shifting subtleties of Eliot's view it is necessary to go back, briefly, to its origins.

Miss Hale had the gift, her pupils said, for bringing out the gifts of others. She had the strength that comes from imaginative generosity not, like Eliot's, from the will. As she became the presiding 'Lady' of Eliot's poetry, he would lay down will and pride before what he pictured as the purest altruism. This Lady is continuous with a lady in a white gown in Eliot's fevered unpublished poem of 1914, 'The Love Song of Saint Sebastian'. Here, a man lashes himself at the foot of a lady's stair, and then, bespattered in the blood of penitence, is permitted to ascend and die between her breasts. Her function is to disinfect the spirit of its contaminating desires. Whether she is drawn from Emily Hale or anyone else does not matter, for she has no real existence except as a projection of the poet's fantasy. In retrospect, Eliot said that in the youthful experience of love 'we do not so much see the person as infer the existence of some outside object which sets in motion these new and delightful feelings in which we are absorbed'.

It was only when Eliot was distanced by the Atlantic from Emily Hale and cut off irrevocably, as it then seemed, by his rash marriage, that she took on a durable imaginative importance. In the depths of his waste, she visited his memory as a lost dream of love untarnished. And then, suddenly, the memory itself showed a remarkable power. A healing surge of fertile feeling came back with 'Memory and desire' to induce in the speaker of *The Waste Land* a revelation which blots out sense ('my eyes failed') and language ('I could not / Speak') as he grasps a timeless 'silence'. To this he holds ('I remember / The hyacinth garden'), as to a lifeline, in the claustrophobic marital chamber while the wife's desperate words beat against him.

What Eliot needed was not love in the usual sense, passion or care, but love's transforming power, the idea of a momentous drama, partly on the model of Dante and Beatrice, partly a subtle

Jamesian drama of buried sensibilities. How is it possible that James seems almost to create Eliot, to forecast him? James imagined a sensibility so highly developed that it did not as yet exist, but might conceivably exist, might evolve, particularly in the high-minded context of the refined New England in which both writers spent their formative years. In James's *Notebooks*, on 5 February 1895, he set out a 'little formula' for a strange love story that is uncannily like the fancy evolving in Eliot's work between 1927 and 1930:

... the man of genius who, in some accursed hour of his youth, has bartered away the fondest vision of that youth and lives ever afterwards in the shadow of the bitterness of the regret. ... The fancy of his *recovering* a little of the lost joy, of the Dead Self, in his intercourse with some person, some woman, who knows what that self was, in whom it still lives a little. This intercourse is his real life.... *She is his Dead Self: he is alive in her and dead in himself*.

The 1927 essay on Shakespeare, with its passionate personal resonance, was Eliot's first covert confession of his dream. The second begins more directly: 'Lady, ...' In this poem, called appropriately 'Salutation', and written later in 1927, after Eliot's conversion, the first tentative impulse to convert memory and desire into holiness has become a definite programme, the woman a visible figure with an assigned role. She is to be a 'Lady of silences' who presides over a dead self, guardian of its demise. The frail memory of love—'Rose of memory'—supports the end of a tormented life with a promise of paradise. There is this consolation in the very existence of the Lady, for the bare bones of the lost self still live through her watchful fidelity.

The poem concludes with a renewal of visionary power as the poet looks to a promised land which is his rightful inheritance. God speaks to him as to Moses: 'This is the land.' A poem that begins with a Lady and ends with the voice of God is the formula for the central imaginative drama of Eliot's mature years. In this, the woman is to be the initiating influence and prime listener.

'Salutation' is startlingly intimate, all the more so for the fact that it is proclaimed in public. It is always a woman who is the recipient, or potential recipient, of poetic confession, which makes women matter to Eliot in quite a different way from their appearance as Laforgian butts of ironic dismissal, or as targets of a sense of sin. Although Eliot does dismiss some women as animals and pity others as victims of male lust, he had also an appreciation of a woman's intelligent receptivity. In 1927 Emily Hale was not important to Eliot as a person, but as an ear for his confession. The poetic confession, with its savage, spectacular drama of three pure-white leopards who devour the penitent's flesh, was the imaginative complement to formal confession at church which Eliot began early in 1928. The Lady's purity makes her a modern avatar of the Virgin; as sequels to 'Salutation' followed, she is, increasingly, the object of worship.

'Salutation' was originally written on its own, then became the second part of the long sequence, *Ash Wednesday*. The rearranged order shifts the focus from the merciful Lady to the agonies of the penitent man. His ordeals of self-confrontation and fearful solitude are succeeded by a final ordeal: the temptation to erotic love. Looking out on the past, through the window of memory 'bellied like the fig's fruit', he recalls a woman's sweet brown hair in an enchanted 'maytime', but he must hold back from its distracting appeal. The music of the flute must play, not to the senses but to the spirit, ditties of no tone, while the 'silent' woman bends her head in assent. It is a sign of grace, a token of the Word to come, 'unheard, unspoken'. Life is no longer the painful and seemingly pointless round of the 'prickly pear', the hollow existence of the mid-twenties; now the centre of all existence is 'the silent Word'. Though moments of doubt remain, the veiled woman continues to preside together with distant ghosts of the New England past until the fountain of the spirit shoots up and the renewing waters flow.

The initial impulse for a long poem, with its protracted and recurring effort of renewal, is an encounter with a nameless, faceless, and silent woman. The impulse recurs with the *Quartets*, and goes back to Prufrock's need to confess to a woman—not love, but vision and madness (in the manuscript called, appropriately, 'Prufrock Among the Women'). The confessional content of these encounters with women is a brooding sense of fate: a man whose life marks time for some overwhelming experience, something rare and strange, possibly horrible and devouring. In the view of society women, who come and go, this private conviction must seem absurd, and Prufrock finds no woman in the Boston of 1911 in whom he can confide. But between 'Prufrock' and 'Gerontion', written in 1919, Eliot came to know, trust—and leave Emily Hale.

In 'Gerontion', a silent listener is there, addressed only as 'you', to hear his rapid, low-voiced confession: 'I would meet you upon this honestly. / I that was near your heart was removed therefrom . . . / I have lost my passion.'

Passion, he explains, has dissolved in fear. It has also been 'adulterated', possibly because the man has abused his emotions—denied them, succumbed to the impulse of dull lust—and possibly also because he has become the victim of adultery, like Eliot himself who had learnt of his wife's adultery with his former teacher and benefactor, Bertrand Russell. In 1919 Eliot mourned a youthful capacity for love which had atrophied in a pervasive sense of corruption.

Willard Thorp, the husband of Emily Hale's lifelong friend, Margaret Thorp, suggested that 'you' is a woman with whom the speaker had known some moments of passion and beauty. She has urged him to relive these moments, at least in memory, as an antidote to his barren existence, but he would be honest with her: he has lost the acuteness of his senses. 'How should I use them for your closer contact?'

The torment of the lost and unfulfilled moment of experience is part of the larger drama of this speaker: the loss of a directed life, signalled by a youthful premonition of 'Christ the tiger'. The rhythms of his voice carry an echo of the death speech in *The Changeling* of one who succumbed to a wanton, evil creature, and so fell 'Beneath the stars' to light on a baser object of desire. The ruined, dying lover says to the lost legitimate mate: 'I that am of your blood was taken from you / For your better health . . . / Let the common sewer take it from distinction'.

The 'merds' and decay of a ruined civilization is the outward sign of this core of confessional intimacy. It is not disillusion that rivets the reader so much as the dramatic irruption of astonishing candour through the crust of historical generalization. The private experience prompts a general conclusion: the image of a waste land. This is the counter to a promised land, a loss of prophetic vision which was to be renewed, years later, by the Lady.

Emily Hale did not disrupt Eliot's dream; if anything, she confirmed it. Her dark hair was drawn back in a coil from a long, fine face that appeared immobile until her decorum was belied by a glint of humour. Her manners had the impeccability of Boston. She was formal even in the way she moved, straight, controlled;

then her eyes would crinkle and she would be mischievous. Like Eliot, she had self-discipline but her formality would relent with intimates: for these, as Barbara Gates Burwell put it, her feeling was 'magnanimous', and she had lifelong attachments. Though she had lived on harder terms than women of their background, earning her living, she had aged well.

What was it about her that made it possible for Eliot to pursue his dream? Could it be that, in their youth, Eliot had dared to convey to Emily Hale his then active and disturbing sense of rarefied destiny, so that, at that time of upheaval, she had entered into his private dream as no one else ever could? This would explain why, over so many years, he retained a special bond, and why he remained loyal to her quite outside any question of marriage. My guess is that she had somehow managed to convey to him that she understood and honoured his glimpse of the infinite, a 'thing' strange to others, and nameless, but corresponding to what he called 'reality'. In the intervening years of exile in the 'Unreal City', Eliot came to believe that she alone might re-confer 'reality' through some innate grace of her nature. She was to be the guardian of his promise in the 'new years' ahead.

Marina, written in the summer that Emily Hale came to England, is about the rediscovery of a woman long-lost and dearly loved. She evokes in a man a tender, almost tremulous longing, comfort, and hope. It is as though a bolt is shot back, and a lost feeling stirs, not romantic love, but a family feeling that brings him back to his primal self. So grace comes to Eliot in a more human form, no longer veiled, but close as family. The recognition of kinship brings a joy that will outlast the pulsing moment of approach.

This woman is identified with New England, to which Emily Hale was about to return. The New England shore is, once again, the promised land, to be attained after a long and perilous journey. On that farther shore, and part of its divine call, the beloved woman will await the battered traveller. Like 'Cape Ann', written on the eve of Emily's departure from England in December 1935, Eliot's mind follows her back to scenes of his youth where, more than twenty years before, he had watched birds, and that now-remote memory provides the focus for the quickening of a more immediate emotion: 'O quick, quick, quick . . . Sweet sweet sweet.' In the final part of *Ash Wednesday*, in *Marina*, and in 'Cape Ann'

Eliot was projecting himself over the heads of his associates in London into the waiting life that came to him as a far-off reverberation from the depths of the past that was, at the same time, the mystical other world that might have flourished for him, had he not abandoned it for art and fame. 'Death' he now says to all that, to the lust and vanity of the worldly life.

The source of this reverberation lies far back in their youth, in an unpublished poem, 'Hidden under the heron's wing', which Eliot wrote at the time when he was first drawn to Emily Hale. It follows a desperate piece, 'Do I know what I feel?' about a man who senses, but fails to grasp, some overwhelming intuition just beyond his range. 'Hidden' is a hopeful counterpoise, about a whisper from the stars that comes with the approach of a girl as she walks lightly across the grass, her slender arms dividing the evening mist. The beloved brings this whisper of hidden revelation, hidden under the heron's wing or enclosed in lotus-buds before daybreak. At this time Eliot was studying Indian philosophy, which makes frequent reference to a thousand-petalled lotus that enfolds enlightenment, a pristine life force or spiritual awakening. It is associated in the *Kama Shastras* with the most desirable of women, the lotus-lady or *padmini*. Though, usually, Eliot tended to separate body and soul, he derived from Eastern thought the image of a woman where such a distinction is not made. The traditional connotations of the lotus-lady range from sensual to spiritual.

The meeting with Emily Hale in 1930 revived this promise. 'Difficulties of a Statesman' (1931) harks back to the early love poem, with its recall of a vital intimation concealed in the breast of a dove: 'O hidden'. The memory rises like a loud call to a public figure to 'RESIGN' the sterile performance of his life in order to recover that fertile spurt of 'hidden' emotion. Its recovery is to serve a high purpose: to quicken the spiritual power that could give birth to a 'cry', and by virtue of that, to a new kind of leader.

The love scene in 'Hidden' had the tenacity of Eliot's feeling for Emily Hale: its details recur not only in 'Difficulties of a Statesman' but yet again in *Burnt Norton*. The lotus that once sang, at break of day, to the young lover in Boston, now unfolds its hidden vision: 'And the lotos rose, quietly, quietly . . .'.

In the end this is all that Eliot wanted from Emily Hale. Human love remains only in so far as it recalls that vision. There is a startling single-mindedness about this reach for ultra-human bliss, reminiscent of Abelard and St Augustine, men who were capable of passionate devotion yet were avid for purity. For such men, purity was the counter to the human love that they came to perceive as temptation. This state of mind, alien to this century, is what makes Eliot the most elusive of poets. Christianity has recognized the danger of religious emotion, the temptation to pride, by attempting to guard it with the virtue of humility, but the ultimate danger is that humility should coexist with pride and even mask it. Hawthorne explored this state of mind in the figure of the Puritan minister, Dimmesdale, who acknowledges himself to be a sinner both in private and finally in public, but sins more than he knows in the self-centred extravagance of his humility and in his denial of the human heart, the natural bond with Hester Prynne that is the consequence of passion. Defused passion does not necessarily exonerate Eliot from the emotional bond that, by 1935, had been established. How could the woman who had shared the heart of light come to be distanced from its import for the life ahead? It is easy to justify a solitary religious position in the case of monks and nuns who have incurred no other obligation; less easy where the solitary path cuts through human obligation. It has then to be self-serving, and the denial of other obligation implies a belief in the exclusiveness of the soul's superior instants. This state of mind is heroic, that is, not wholly moral, though often clothed in rectitude.

Through the six years from 1928 to 1934, Eliot's celibate course was challenged by the alternative that Emily presented, the possibility that grace could come through natural love, and, as she awaited a sign, he had to balance the evanescent charms of this way against the solider gains of renewed asceticism. Virginia Woolf, who knew nothing of Emily Hale for another year did, on 21 November 1934, discern Eliot's divided state with brilliant acumen:

Tom's head [she wrote in her diary] is very remarkable; such a conflict; so many forces have smashed against him: the wild eye still; but all rocky, yellow, riven, & constricted. Sits very solid—large shoulders—in his chair, & talks easily but with authority. Is a great man, in a way, now: self-confident, didactic. But to me, still, a dear old ass; I mean I cant be frozen off with this divine authority any longer.

Virginia Woolf was too rational, too secular, too confident herself to submit to Eliot's divine authority, but, inevitably, Emily could not but put his need before her own, and so, in the winter of 1934/5, while Eliot composed his drama about the making of a saint, she was 'frozen off'. Something happened or, more likely, did *not* happen, so that, on 30 January she wrote to President Jaqua to ask if she might return to Scripps, her characteristic clarity clouded by cryptic words of dismay: '... The future holds no answer to the problem of the moment, and the question between East and West was indeed one of their never meeting as Mr. Kipling said long ago. But I am doing what seems to me the best thing now, and that is all any of us *can* do, I suppose.' But she had held on too long; Jaqua had given her post away. In her reply from Florence on 12 March she explained the delay: there had been 'problems' to settle.

By Easter she had returned from Italy to Chipping Campden, and Eliot came at once to visit. It would have been soon after that he wrote *Burnt Norton* which summed up his new position: it was impossible, for the time being, to recover the actuality of love. Though it was the essential matter of the past that must shape the future, it was at present fading with the fading light of the election in the rose-garden. He must 'Descend lower . . . / Into the world of perpetual solitude'. He must purify the soul, alone, before he might recover a transfigured love. But the moment in the garden, remembered in 1935, would remain the guiding light of future trials: 'Quick now, here, now, always—'.

'Always', like the ring, was a guarantee that some bond would endure, though commitment was indefinitely postponed. There was no knowing how long the way down would take. *Burnt Norton* initiated a phase of waiting that lasted through the years that Eliot composed the *Quartets*. Seven years later the finale to the whole sequence repeats, in *Little Gidding*, the memory of their visit to Burnt Norton: 'Quick now, here, now, always—.' In the course of this long exploration, nothing topped that rapture nor changed Eliot's recollection of it as the height of experience.

Since Emily Hale had now no post for the fall of 1935, she stayed on in England to the end of the year. There must have been meetings for which there is (as yet) no record, but they were certainly together at Chipping Campden just before Easter, again in May, and once more in the latter half of July. On 25 July the Morleys picked up Eliot at Chipping Campden to take him for ten days to Wales. 'Usk', which resulted from that journey, was printed privately in October 1935 together with 'Cape Ann'. Emily had a copy for Christmas, signed 'Tom',* and she kept the gift until Eliot's second marriage in 1957.

The last notable event of 1935 was on 26 November when, at Eliot's insistence, Virginia Woolf invited Emily with Eliot to tea. Virginia Woolf, who was hard pressed with visitors, gave her scant attention, writing her off as a prim Bostonian. On this occasion Emily showed more acuteness. She wrote the following account to Ruth George:

> 19, Rosary Gardens,
> South Kensington, S.W.7.
> December 6, 1935.

Dearest Ruth,

Your letter of late October was such a joy, comfort and privilege to receive, that by the measure of my gratitude and love to and for you, you should have been swamped with my answers ever since. . . .

As to coming out to see you, Ruth, how I wish I could. We sail for Boston the Friday of next week, arriving just before the Christmas week. I shall be with my old friend Miss Ware with whom I lived in Boston before, but how long I shall stay there I do not know. All my energies must be devoted to finding some sort of position for the coming year. Of course I feel I cannot return to Scripps, unless Dr Jaqua makes the first move and even if he did, I do not know that I could be confident of my future standing at the college. I grieve more over this forced severing of a possible return, than over the actual mess of last year. Should I find I had the money to come out, I should, on the pretext of seeing to my things, and I should come to you, dear Ruth, and ask for the unfulfilled visit to the Ranch also.

I can think of no Christmas greeting more to your taste, than for me to try inadequately to tell you of my taking tea with Virginia Woolf and Mr Woolf, last week Tuesday. Of course this was done in the company of Tom Eliot, who is one of a closer circle of friends, admitted to their life. They live in the upper floors of their press, the Hogarth, and in ample tree shaded Tavistock Square. We mounted one flight of stairs to the narrow door locked, till opened by a neatly dressed charwoman who led us up another flight, narrow and steep, at the top of which we removed our wraps. Taking breath, we ascended yet again, to the small, low-

---

* This was rare. Nearly always he signed his books 'T. S. Eliot'. Emily Hale too signed letters, even to a close friend, with her full name.

ceilinged dining-room, where our hosts had preceded us, with the other guest, young Stephen Spender. In the soft light of a small lamp on the square tea table, Mrs Woolf rose to greet me, and I thought of you even then, as I faced a very tall slender woman, dressed in a dark non-descript dress, over which was worn a short dark velvet coat. The simple dark clothes set off to advantage the small head carrying a wealth of greying hair, thick, but soft, which she wears simply off the forehead, and massed in a great Rossetti like coil at the nape of the very long slender neck. A narrow dark ribbon binds the hair accentuating the pre-raphaelite impression. The features are delicately modelled, if claiming no regularity of beauty, and although the face is lacking in mobility, as we think of the term, there appeared to me a sense of the mind's attentiveness and color, (if I may so put it) traceable under the mask-like expression, mask-like except for the eyes, which register the reaction of each moment. A strong impression of cool detachment constantly contradicts itself by an equally strong impression of highly charged concentration. Her manner is not one to place people at ease, quite frankly speaking, though with Tom Eliot and Spender she was simple, friendly and responsive in an almost girlish way. I sat opposite her at the tea-table, an excellent place in which to listen (yes, listen, not chatter, Ruth) and to observe. Mr Woolf was at my right, as thin as she, but much less tall; the face is almost emaciated, the features very aquiline but not necessarily Hebraic, the expression warmer than hers, especially the eyes which to me revealed a number of qualities, as patience, weariness and isolation. He carries on his shoulder, not an atlas world of care, but a tiny marmoset, who lives on this human hill crest, all day long, peering out at one, first from one side, then the other; this tiny furry ball has a long tail which hangs down his master's neck almost like a short queue, slightly confusing at first. I found myself getting on very well with Mr Woolf, who consciously or not puts one soon at ease. After an introductory theme of marmoset and affectionate spaniel Sally, who was at our feet, he took up a more serious note of conversation, asking thoughtful questions about America, question[s] almost naive, like an inquiry 'whether the American Indian mingled in our good society'. For the most part, the conversation was upon topics and personalities, known to the other four, Stephen Spender being very much at home with his hosts also, and by his very boyish open eyed, gentle manner, affording an interesting contrast to the profundity of his remarks. Tea was simple, but abundant, a comb of honey from the Woolfs' country place, receiving second place of honor with Mr. Ws. birthday cake which his very old mother never fails to send to each of her children on the anniversaries; there is a very odd assortment of furnishing in the dining room and in the larger drawing room below, whose walls are covered with decorative panels by Mrs Ws. sister, Vanessa Bell. There is a slight French flavor in this room, but I had the impression that their surroundings make little difference to either of the owners, or at best are artistic too unconventionally to be admired by the average visitor. Downstairs Mrs. W. addressed several questions directly to me, suddenly but very carefully, so to speak, as if it really mattered what you answered her, and you found yourself wanting very much to make it matter and were curiously aware of your English as you answered. She sat quite gracefully, on a small sofa at the further end from S.S. and me (I had hoped she would be next to me) and smoked languidly but in a very practised way. The impression of cool, half mocking detachment began to lessen, it became a reserve, a shyness, a husbanding of fine abilities for the moments when they must be used and tested. As one felt the atmosphere warming and jollier, an interruption unwelcome to all of us, I believe, came in the shape of two French visitors, a man connected with the Revue des Deux Mondes, and his wife. Mrs W. began in French with him, which I am told she does not like to speak although she does it well. There seemed no need for us to stay, nor promise of a return to the earlier mood of the afternoon, so we said good-by. Since then I wrote to tell Mrs W. of how much I had enjoyed her books (I had no good chance to, you can see) and referred to you as a lovely personality who admired her from far away California.

Now I must stop, although I have many other things to relate, all making it very difficult to leave London. I wear the lovely scarf you gave me, by the way. All warmest Christmas greetings to the Masts,* please, and to you dear love and wishes for a blessed New Year,

Yours,
Emily Hale

P.S. I read to Tom much of your letter and he loved it, too.

Until the outbreak of the second world war there was as frequent contact between Eliot and Emily Hale as was possible for two people who lived and worked on opposite sides of the Atlantic. She came to England every summer except 1936, when Eliot came to America. By April 1937 the Perkinses were back at Chipping Campden, and Emily Hale joined them as usual, after completing her first academic year at Smith College where she had managed to obtain a position. Eliot visited Campden in August and September. That summer she accompanied him to Edinburgh for his honorary degree. At the very last minute she discovered that a long dress was obligatory, sped out, and returned in a dress

---

* Ruth George was spending Christmas with the Mast family in Hemet, California.

splashed with a dramatic print. Eliot was delighted with her theatrical sense of colour, and teased her about her brightness at so sober a gathering. Emily herself liked to tell of being snubbed. She was admiring a private garden when Lady Drummond, looking pointedly at the floral colours of her guest's dress, said: 'I see that Miss *Hale* has brought her garden with her.'

Emily continued to teach at Smith, and would arrive in England at the close of each academic year. Over the years it became a ritual for Eliot to meet her boat train, a ritual that went on into the fifties, through his ageing years of great fame, when Mary Trevelyan noted the priority of this commitment with some surprise. Considering the amount of time Emily Hale was in England, there is an odd dearth of information about her, as if she was covered with a veil of silence. The 'Lady of silences' was not herself a silent person; she was, on the contrary, as friends remember, distinctly articulate. The silences emanate from Eliot: 'silence' as his word for an experience of unspeakable bliss and silence, it would seem, also as a practical policy, accepted by his friends and by Emily herself. She never embarrassed him by any public disclosure of their understanding.

Still, a few facts of their meetings filter through. In July 1938 Eliot was in Chipping Campden, and the same month Emily Hale may have been the woman who accompanied him to his poetry reading at a Student Christian Movement Conference at Swanwick in Derbyshire. Mary Trevelyan, who first met Eliot here, thought the woman was his wife. When in London, she used to visit Cat Morgan at Faber, where Eliot's secretary, Miss Swan, made her welcome. She was known to Faber colleagues, but clearly there was some agreement to keep her under wraps, possibly because Vivienne (until she was institutionalized in July 1938) would not have been averse to scandal. It could not have been an unforeseen danger that the two women might cross paths on their visits to Faber.

In July 1939 Emily went to a theatre workshop in an uncomfortable castle in a marvellous setting on the west coast of Scotland, where she performed in a play. On 30 August, with war imminent, John Hayward reported to Morley that Eliot was trying to embark Æmilia with her uncle and aunt on anything seaworthy sailing westward.

Some years of separation followed. Eliot completed the wartime

Quartets, and Emily Hale continued at Smith. She understood that
only by unremitting atonement could Eliot hope to transform the
furies of conscience. In 1942 Emily Hale left Smith College
abruptly, without an alternative job. Some disagreement preceded
her departure, but it was so minor that I have wondered if
something else disturbed her. Had she hoped, with the completion
of the *Quartets*, for some resolution of her own long trial of
patience? At some point she must have had to come to terms with
the fact that, so long as Vivienne lived, Eliot would not marry.

There followed a difficult time. For a short while, in 1943, she
taught at Bennett Junior College in Millbrook, New York, then
moved on to teach in high schools. She never held an academic
post again. Later in 1943 she had a temporary position at Concord
Academy in Concord, Massachusetts, and managed to stay on. At
the beginning of the new school year in 1944, the headmistress,
Miss Josephine Tucker, announced that Miss Hale had 'returned to
spend the entire year on dramatics and speech training'. This post
may not have been secure, for she put her furniture and books in
storage, and lived in one furnished room after another. In 1945 she
spoke of 'my wretched way of living in the last three years'. Her
apparent poverty continued all through her years in Concord until
the end of 1947.

Meanwhile, in London, the wartime separation from Emily
Hale brought Eliot closer to Mary Trevelyan. Through Emily he
had lived the secret life of memory that was vital to his poetry, but
he was not above finding some measure of daily comfort in the
jolly company of Mary, who mattered not a whit to his poetry but
was agreeable partly for the very reason that there was, as yet, no
basis for an emotional claim.

Mary was what the English call a good sort, reliable without
being in the least dull. She had the English blend of sturdiness and
humour, with the confident determination of women like Mary
Kingsley, whose *Travels in West Africa* she read aloud to Eliot.
Janet Adam Smith recalled how she always talked to a man and
ignored his little wife. Where Emily Hale was drawn mainly to
women, Mary liked to be with men; where Emily had the elegance
and subtle shades of the past, Mary was the type of the moment, a
woman in the uniform of the Armed Forces, hearty, back-slapping,
her very Englishness propping Eliot's commitment, at the end of
Four Quartets, to a particular destiny, 'now and in England'.

In 1945 Eliot sent Emily Hale another of those literary 'letters' that she kept to the end of her life. In *What is a Classic?* he spoke of an obligation to resign love for a higher 'destiny'. His model was Aeneas, 'the man in fate' who must abandon Dido as the gods command. Eliot, though, unlike Virgil, does not consider the woman's anguish. Aeneas justifies himself on the ground that he made no formal commitment: 'I have never held the wedding torches as a husband; I have never entered into such agreements.' Eliot's account skirts the confrontation, to dwell on the hero's burden of guilt, as though suffering were his exclusively. Later, Aeneas descends to visit the shades of the dead, and there encounters his lost love. Eliot sees her agonized withdrawal not for its own pathos but as a mere 'projection' of the hero's conscience. Aeneas, he added in 1951, felt 'a worm', and then, more warmly: such a destiny 'is a very heavy cross to bear.'

To Eliot, Dido in the Underworld is a model woman who behaves just as a man would have her behave: she does not rail; she does not say a word; just takes herself away. He finds in this dreamlike scene of parting 'a refinement of manner, springing from a delicate sensibility, . . . in that test of manners, private and public conduct between the sexes'. Parting, he goes on, must be 'civilized' in the style of Henry James. Eliot's concern for manners—his appreciation of what he calls Dido's 'snub'—belies the emotional tension of the woman's flight into the forest of shadows, 'burning' and 'fierce-eyed' as she 'tears herself away'. Aeneas, too, is not quite so refined and wormish as Eliot suggests. He is 'stunned', and 'follows at a distance with tears and pity for her as she goes'.

What is a Classic? was inspired in part by Eliot's own concern with destiny. The spiritual voyager of his poetry was a willed identity: the gods never quite distinguished him, as they did Aeneas, with explicit command, but he denied love all the same. Crucial to Eliot's dream of destiny was its burden of guilt. The fated man, he said, 'does not forgive himself—and this, significantly, in spite of the fact of which he is well aware, that all that he has done has been in compliance with destiny', with 'a greater inscrutable power'. He projects himself through a Jamesian version of this exile, whose destiny it was to be the link between two great cultures. A. Walton Litz has said that *Four Quartets* was the last poem of this century to speak to English and American alike. For

Eliot, the two peoples were not only allies in war but united in a common culture, embodied in his own family and person. His praise for the exile's 'absence of provinciality' speaks for his own ambition to carry the best of his native tradition—the venturesome moral energy of America—beyond its frontiers. That voyage back to provincial origins in *The Dry Salvages*, to the Mississippi and the New England shore, retrieves a native spirit that Eliot would implant 'now and in England'.

In March 1946 Emily Hale directed Noel Coward's *Hay Fever* at Concord Academy in aid of the American Friends' Service for European Relief. It played to packed auditoriums. In the summer she acted in *Blithe Spirit* with the Dorset Players, in Dorset, Vermont, and Eliot was in the audience. This comedy about a husband whose dead wife's spirit returns to trouble his relationship with his new wife may have provided the germ for Eliot's first comedy, *The Cocktail Party*, where a wife disappears into a sanatorium, leaving her husband to his affair with another woman, and then returns to take possession of him. According to Dorothy Elsmith, Eliot 'used to follow Emily in her summer theatrical appearances. She was a clever, excellent actress' with an animation that surprised people who knew her only as a rather conscientious and disciplined elocution teacher. There is a rare photograph of Eliot and Emily Hale together in Vermont: she, slim in her simple shirtwaist with her hands in her pockets, looks at the camera with charming grace; Eliot beside her looks oddly formal in the summer setting, in his dark suit with the usual studied stylishness of the handkerchief in his breast-pocket. Another photograph was taken in Dublin, New Hampshire, where the woman beside Eliot has been cut out of the picture. What remains looks a bit like the Vermont photo, which has been kept safely at Princeton. The New Hampshire photo, which is in one of the family albums at Harvard, could well have been cut at Eliot's wish.

That summer of 1946 Eliot's base was his brother's apartment at 84 Prescott Street, Cambridge, Mass. At the end of July he sailed back to England, taking a present of maple sugar from Emily Hale to Janet Adam Smith, who had known Eliot from the time that she started her career as literary critic in the early thirties and married

Michael Roberts, who wrote regularly for the *Criterion*. Her family knew Emily Hale quite independently through its connections with the Boston élite.

Between 1933 and 1946 Eliot's relation to Emily would have established a settled pattern of occasional meetings, fondness, and jokes all of which sustained their understanding. For Eliot, a woman who did not marry might be elevated as an object of worship. In this way he could appropriate Emily imaginatively, in Jamesian terms 'have' or 'possess' her to the point that she became no more than a projection of his will. Her inaudible presence in *Ash Wednesday*, *Marina*, and the first part of *Burnt Norton* is apprehended solely by its effect on the speaker. From the time of Eliot's conversion to the time of Vivienne's death she provided a perfect impetus for his art: an ethereal love that could be sustained, it seemed, indefinitely. To have refused to be the 'Lady' would have been to become a threat. Under the circumstances she did what she could: behaved with sense, dignity, humour, and discretion. She managed not to offend Eliot, yet not to betray her sex by complying with the types of his imagination: woman as animal; woman as nun; woman as daughter. She was rather like Bessie Alden, the straight, idealistic Bostonian in James's story, 'An International Episode': when her lordly English lover strikes Bessie as 'deficient', she aspires 'by that very reason to some finer way of liking him'.

The unexpected death of Vivienne challenged the stable bond. Eliot retreated at once from the possibility of action, asserting (like Lambert Strether) that it was too late. He told Mary Trevelyan, on 15 April 1947, that he dreaded the coming visit to America so much that it would be a relief to get started so that he could look forward to his return. He sailed on 22 April. Soon after his arrival, his brother Henry died of leukemia. He stayed with his sister Margaret at 41 Kirkland Street, Cambridge. Emily Hale was not far away in Concord where, that spring, she put on one of her most ambitious and successful productions, *Richard II*. Henry's widow, Theresa, invited Emily to her apartment, meaning with all good will to bring her together with Eliot on the assumption that they would both wish to marry. But when Eliot arrived he turned on Theresa in a white fury which she remembered to the last months of her life.

Still, sooner or later, it became necessary to make his

psychological change of life known to Emily Hale. They met privately two or three times. One meeting took place in June when Eliot went, at her instigation, to Concord Academy to give an address at its 25th anniversary Commencement. On 3 June he sat in the school hall like an aged eagle, with stooping shoulders and forward-thrusting head, but spoke with 'the wry Yankee wit; he might have been Emerson himself, except for the cosmopolite suavity'. He told the girls that he had written *The Waste Land* 'to relieve my emotions', a purely personal act. Otherwise, he appeared at his most withdrawn, applauding automatically, but looking up only with effort. A letter from Emily to Lorraine Havens recounts exactly what happened between them:

> with the Dorset Players
> Dorset. Vt.
> August 7 '47

Dearest Lorraine,

... His visit here was a sort of public nightmare of events—his only brother died soon after he arrived—and from that strain he had spent himself thro' lectures and readings plus the *three* commencements when he received honorary degrees. ... I am going to tell you, dear friend, that what I confided to you long ago of a mutual affection he and I have had for each other has come to a strange impasse whether permanent or not, I do not know. Tom's wife died last winter very suddenly. I supposed he would then feel free to marry me as I believed he always intended to do. But such proves not to be the case. We met privately two or three times to try to sift the situation as thoroughly as possible—he loves me—I believe that wholly—but apparently not in the way usual to men less gifted i.e. with complete love thro' a married relationship. I have not completely given up hope that he may yet recover from this—to me—abnormal reaction, but on the other hand I cannot allow myself to hold on to anything so delicately uncertain.

I am very much at a loose end at present, having resigned from the Academy in Concord, and given up the rented house. I want dreadfully to have some little place of my own—and be free to follow my interests as I lead them or they lead me. I have even thought of trying for dramatic work seriously since I love it so and know I can do it. I am here acting with a small summer group as I did last year—had one excellent part and another promised which has had to be given up for another production. I felt badly to do nothing for your Mary last year, I assure you. Keep in touch with me, please. I value your and Paul's friendship so very much.

Perhaps you will have a brilliant idea as to what I can do another year.*
Love to Paul and yourself in full measure—

Yours

Emily Hale.

Eliot kept his stay in New England as short as possible. He left
in mid-June (after at last getting a doctorate from Harvard). He was
shaken. He later told Mary Trevelyan that he had experienced a
catastrophe which he could not reveal because it involved another
person. Emily Hale called it a 'miscarriage': emphatic words from
such restrained people.

Eliot's evident ageing in 1947 which, it has been implied, was an
outcome of Vivienne's death, more likely followed his discovery
that he had lost his passion. After his minor operations, Eliot spent
August and September convalescing in the country. Across the
Atlantic, Emily Hale soothed herself with the luxury of three
unfurnished rooms at 9 Lexington Road, Concord. There she
arranged her own things and nursed plans for a new start in the
theatre until, in the spring of 1948, she took up another teaching
post. Meanwhile, hope of Eliot's 'recovery' faded. When he was
due to return to America to the Institute for Advanced Study at
Princeton for the fall semester of 1948, she steeled herself to his
withdrawal in a sad sentence at the end of another letter to
Lorraine Havens:

[90 Commonwealth Ave]
Boston.
September 12th 48.

Dearest Lorraine,

. . . You may well ask about me, dear friend. I . . . remained in Concord,
very happily living in a small but attractive apartment made out of one
floor of a really old house. From my so-called life of leisure I was
suddenly called to Abbot Academy, Andover . . . to fill a sudden vacancy
in speech & drama for the rest of the year, having half the week in
Andover and half the week in Concord, putting on two plays and
teaching long hours on the two [?] days I was at Andover. But it was all so
happy mutually, that Miss Hearsey, who knew me years ago when we
were girls, asked me to return permanently—which offer I could not
refuse, tho' I hesitated to give up certain indulgent ways of life I enjoyed

---

* Paul Havens was now President of Wilson College, Pennsylvania. This was a hint
that he might find her a job.

so much. But I am committed now to a very fine school I think, and best of all, the school has made over some part of a house they own into a very fine apartment—repapered, repainted, etc—into which I am moving this week, tho as there are two stories, I really have more rooms than furniture to put into them. But little by little something new will be added perhaps and I *love* having my own dear possessions about . . . me after years of absence from them. . . . T. S. Eliot comes to Princeton this winter to the Institute of Higher Education—as guest visitor—but I expect I shall see him only occasionally. Dear Lorraine—

> My love as ever to you—
>   Emily Hale.

At this very time, before Eliot left for Princeton, he was drafting *The Cocktail Party*, the work which Emily Hale selected for its 'hidden meaning'. She did not specify what it was, so that to read the play for this meaning can be done only with the utmost caution. It does yield the most subtle explanation of Eliot's new position, and at the same time remains intact as a work of art. Eliot said that a play is less personal than a poem, yet the complete cover of dramatic form actually gave him the freedom to expose, more directly than in poems, a personal crisis. It is not hard to see how he transmutes the crises of 1947—the death of Vivienne and the rejection of Emily Hale—into drama. There are obvious parallels with Lavinia, the wife who vanishes without warning, and Celia, who now expects to marry the husband, Edward. But the interest of this sort of identification is trivial. What brings the play to life is the emotional charge of Eliot's feeling working, as ever, well below the surface. At this buried level there is a word of consolation as well as rejection. It would have told Emily that it was 'too late' now for marriage but that, all the same, she had been the saving grace of his life.

For the first and last time in his career, Eliot creates in this play a woman who acts in her own right, not as a foil or prop to a man's self-realization as artist, convert, or sinner. Celia is not a statue, a bodiless Virgin, or a Lady of silences. She states her surprise at Edward's defection with brave distinctness, and is the focus for sympathy in the play. Edward is a self-confessed mediocrity beside her. It is his destiny to recognize that his mediocrity lies in his inability to love, and Celia's to discover in her slighted depth of feeling the altruism of a potential saint.

In so far as Emily Hale was the source for Celia, it was Eliot's imaginative farewell: in the course of the play, Celia's fate moves off-stage. Yet, through her, Eliot expounds, with unprecedented explicitness, a very rare form of love. Never did he create so lovable a woman, at once assured and vulnerable. In the first two acts she is lovable in the ordinary human way, yet to the talented man she is also extraordinary. Two men have loved her, the middle-aged husband with whom she has had a long affair, and the young film director, Peter Quilpe, the artist who has loved her platonically. Of the two it is Peter who has a clearer understanding of her distinction. She did not arouse the usual excitement or desire for possession, but a strange feeling, at once more intense and more tranquil. Peter speaks of 'moments in which we seemed to share some perception, / Some feeling, some indefinable experience / In which we were both unaware of ourselves'. Here Eliot explores the rarefied 'moment' that he owed to Emily Hale. Peter declares it to be his only experience of what he, like Eliot, calls 'reality'. Celia, like Emily, opens the route to reality—so long as she remains physically unattainable. Edward advises Peter against consummation. In six months, he warns, you would find that she was 'another woman' and you 'another man'. Eliot's sexual prejudice shows in this rather banal cynicism. The 'fever', Edward asserts, must eventually cool; a couple must jolt onto the sterile ground of their innate difference. This is to be expected in the humdrum marriage, which may be redeemed by goodwill, but this solution would be too mundane for Celia's gifts. It would be, Edward assures her, 'the ruin of loveliness'. Marital 'tedium' must not be the 'residue of ecstasy'.

There lies behind this, Eliot's fear that to enjoy love is to destroy it. Inhibition tortured passion until it atrophied. In *The Family Reunion*, in *Burnt Norton*, and finally in *The Cocktail Party*, Eliot speaks of love as a door. In *Burnt Norton* he can peer through the door into a rose-garden. In *The Cocktail Party* the door is shut: 'There was a door / And I could not open it. I could not touch the handle.'

When Edward seems free to marry the woman he had professed to love, he discovers that he simply doesn't want her as a wife. The confrontation of Edward and Celia in the second scene of the play seems to correspond so exactly with Emily Hale's account of her exchange with Eliot in June 1947 that the dialogue may recreate the substance of their very words.

Celia confesses to Edward that, for her, 'the dream was not enough'. She wanted more. 'And I waited, and wanted to run to tell you.'

For Edward, the loss of his wife 'only brought to light the real difficulties.' He wants to be alone to 'understand'.

Celia, puzzled, wonders if it is just panic and a wish not to make an effort, a moment of fatigue. Edward replies that it is not only that.

Celia then wonders if he is on the verge of a breakdown, but Edward doesn't feel that his reaction is treatable.*

Celia begs him to assure her that 'everything is all right between us'.

Then Edward rejects her. You are a very rare person, he tells her. 'But it was too late.' He acknowledges that he should have known that it wasn't fair to her. His line of defence is that she should have assumed that the continued existence of his wife would have prevented their marriage. 'What future had you ever thought there could be?'

Celia declares that she had abandoned the future to live in 'a private world of *ours*' in which happiness had a different meaning. 'A dream. I was happy in it till to-day.'

In the dialogue that follows Eliot implies that it was the woman who betrayed the dream when she wanted 'this world'. When she breaks the dream with her wish for marriage, the man becomes aware that, for him, the dream was an escape from a given course of existence, a mere 'make-believe' which his 'tougher self' now refutes. Eliot is speaking in Emersonian terms of the integrity of the self which, in a typescript version, he calls 'the *daimon*, the genius'. It is to this intransigent self that Emerson in 1841 had addressed his heady message of self-reliance. The claim of this self is more radical, more absorbing, potentially more excluding than in other civilizations, as de Tocqueville shrewdly observed: American individualism was such that a man might be shut up in the solitude of his own heart. Eliot used the rules of society to keep it at bay: he would not permit any social tie to invade his solitude.

---

* Mary Trevelyan immediately thought of this exchange when, on 5 June 1950, Eliot said that he didn't suppose the woman he had loved 'will *ever* understand what it was all about. She, and others no doubt, would say I ought to have seen a psychologist.' This Mary Trevelyan reports in her diary.

He could not love, he told Emily Hale, as did less gifted men. It was a claim which she was bound to accept.

Eliot's consolation for Emily is, I think, the 'hidden meaning' of Edward's words to Celia:

> If I have ever been in love—and I think that I have—
> I have never been in love with anyone but you,
> And perhaps I still am.

Emily Hale had understood this from Eliot: 'he loves me—I believe that wholly', she had told Lorraine Havens. This is further confirmed on Eliot's part in a letter to Mary Trevelyan in 1950: he said that though he did not wish to marry the woman he had loved, he believed himself to be still in love with her. As Edward confides to Peter Quilpe, he must 'do nothing', and content himself with the woman he remembers. To live through memory was, Eliot once remarked to Mary Trevelyan, '*my* way of thinking'. Peter Quilpe takes this view:

> If I can only hold to the memory
> I can bear any future.

Eliot's tribute to the rarity of Emily Hale's character comes in the first two acts, where we see Celia in her human aspect. The missionary Celia of the final act is Eliot's invention, based on Charles de Foucauld whose life, Eliot said, conveyed, 'the mysterious power of holiness'. Born to wealth and social position, Foucauld found his vocation as a missionary priest at Tamanrasset in the Hoggar Mountains of the Sahara desert. His aim, Eliot saw, 'was not primarily to convert by teaching, but to *live* the Christian life, alone among the natives'. He lived in a stone hermitage and gave medical aid to tribesmen, and then was killed suddenly in 1916 by a marauding band. Celia's tragic end is equally sudden. Her crucifixion by hostile tribes on an anthill (in the script for the first performances at the Edinburgh Festival, in 1949, her body is found decomposed and eaten away by ants) is somewhat reminiscent of the dismemberment of a woman in a lysol bath in *Sweeney Agonistes*. Celia's case is intended to suggest purgatorial trial, not to rivet the audience with sensationalism, but this was its effect on the first audiences, so that Eliot was persuaded to cut the offending lines. Eliot always wishes to jolt us with some incursion of actual

horror, actual pain, and yet the distaste of the Edinburgh audience
and of the producer, Sherek, was not unjustified. There may have
been some residue of the sadism in the second stanza of Eliot's
youthful 'Love Song of Saint Sebastian'. In both poem and play, a
woman is seen to be an ideal, and then, in both cases, her flesh is
mutilated so that nothing but memory remains. 'The Love Song of
Saint Sebastian' was written in 1914, *The Cocktail Party* in 1948–9:
these were the two dates when it would have been appropriate for
Eliot to marry Emily Hale. Both times he chose as an alternative to
physical possession her idealized image, a far more powerful form
of possession because it is godlike. If he stops creating her, she
stops existing. This is what Emily had to endure, whether she knew
it or not.

Celia's sacrifice is seen from the perspective of party-people. In
Murder in the Cathedral and *The Family Reunion*, the martyr or
penitent was centre-stage; in *The Cocktail Party* she is moved aside
as the focus settles on the faintly ridiculous accommodations of
Edward and his returned wife, Lavinia. Celia's remote fate as
missionary disturbs the couple and their guests with inklings of a
form of existence they will never understand. This was the first of
Eliot's plays to be designed for a popular West-End or Broadway
audience, whom Eliot would expect to identify with Edward and
Lavinia. The success of the play turns on whether the staging can
breathe life into Eliot's theoretic and rather forced claim that a
patched-up marriage is as worthy as Celia's heroic altruism. John
Dexter, in his 1986 production at the Phoenix in London, brought
it off by having Lavinia and Edward bathe their words in the
warmth of demonstrative gestures, and the curtain came down on
marital play. Lavinia's very visible swelling belly bore out the
fertility of marriage. Their psychiatrist, Sir Henry Harcourt-Reilly,
played with messianic vehemence by Alec McCowen, shouted 'it is
a good life' with a bang on the desk.

With less assertion than in this production, the play's low view
of marriage might well vitiate the formal claim. Geoffrey Faber,
writing to Eliot on 25 August 1949, said: 'The lines where Reilly
speaks of parents who don't understand each other and neither
understand nor are understood by their children are not true of
marriage and parenthood as I have been fortunate enough to
experience these states . . .' Eliot answered on 29 August: '. . . In the
universe of discourse in which Reilly is moving during that speech

there are two primary propositions: 1. nobody understands you but God, 2. all real love is ultimately the love of God.' This argument itself implies that marital love must be inferior to that of a person, like Celia, who lives in constant relation to God.

There is another problem, less easy to solve. In Act III Eliot moves his best character, Celia, out of sight, so that her strange story comes to us like an echo from afar. The problem is that so much more is made of the grim details of her death than of the good life that led to that death. Celia is more interesting for her character than for her death, and ideally some image of that extraordinary character should dominate the scene. This would be simple on film. On stage it would be difficult, though not impossible, to open up the drawing-room to some glimpse of the real Celia, like the glimpse of the real Odette behind the ballroom in Act III of *Swan Lake*.

The Cocktail Party is worth rescue, if only for its most memorable scene, Celia's interview with the psychiatrist or 'guardian' in Act II. At this point, Eliot drops comedy of manners for exploration of the inner life. Helen Gardner once said that in his plays Eliot was writing against the bent of his genius, which was for exploration rather than the explicitness of the theatre. It was always difficult for him to make visible—to stage—the invisible life of the spirit. It is not surprising that *Hamlet*, the play *par excellence* of the inner life, was the model to which he clung. 'I have that within which passes show' had been true for Harry as it now was for Celia. But where Harry remains mysterious to the audience, Celia does clarify her discovery of her surprising vocation. Eliot achieves this clarity by distancing himself, to some degree, from the saint in the making. Celia is not tormented by the tempters and furies of Eliot's heroes with their flawed pasts. She also has the advantage of genuine humility. She is the victim of Edward's change of heart, but has no high sense of her own drama. She has a woman's modest expectations—assuming quite ordinary needs for love, marriage, society—so that her transition, in one scene, from ordinary to extraordinary is riveting.

Celia's disappointment with Edward has led her to a sense of sin and need to atone. But, all the same, she retains her capacity for high moments of love, the memory of which will carry the saint into her new life:

For what happened is remembered like a dream
In which one is exalted by intensity of loving
In the spirit, a vibration of delight
Without desire, for desire is fulfilled
In the delight of loving.

Here Eliot sums up what I think he felt for Emily Hale: she evoked a sense of exaltation without the fret of desire. Her extraordinary gift was to make him into a person capable of the delight of loving. In this sense, she created a new being. Reilly, the authoritative voice of the play, explains that knowledge of love might be used by the saint but equally by those who must reconcile themselves to the human condition. This second course is the one that Eliot chose at the end of the *Quartets* and attempts to realize in this play. Such people

> ... may remember
> The vision they have had, but they cease to regret it,
> Maintain themselves by the common routine,
> Learn to avoid excessive expectation,
> Become tolerant of themselves and others ...

This programme is the antithesis of the solitary journeys of Eliot's earlier years, the pilgrimage into the mountains, the journey of the magi, the reckless voyages. As the dream of purity receded over Eliot's horizon, he turned to confront common life which the theatre must reflect if it is to gain the wider audience to whom he hoped to speak.

For ten more years Eliot sustained the outward pattern of his friendship with Emily Hale. Twice, in 1948 and 1952, he travelled to Andover where she taught from February 1948 until June 1957. As she predicted, she saw little of him during his stay in Princeton in 1948, when he went north to Boston three times. In June 1953 she went with Eliot, his sister Marian, and Dorothy Elsmith, to St Louis to hear him reminisce about his family in the town of his birth. When she was due to arrive in London in mid-August, Eliot cancelled an annual outing to Windsor with Mary Trevelyan in order to be free to meet the train. Both women went to Edinburgh later that month for the opening night of his next play, *The Confidential Clerk*, and took turns to visit him where he sat with his niece, Theodora, in the royal box. Theodora thought that Emily should not have come: she was 'a pale shadow of her former self'.

Though Eliot still loved Emily Hale, he preferred not to see her, and felt embarrassed and unhappy when he did. He was irritated by a man's sense of being in the wrong, and decided that they now had little in common. It was, he repeated, 'too late'. He had become fixed, however much he rebelled against this fixing. He was burnt out, a haunted man. The self-image is unmistakably Jamesian. In the *Notebooks*, James had the idea of 'some friendship or passion or bond—some affection long desired and waited for, that is formed too late?—I mean too late in life altogether . . . They but meet to part or to suffer . . . They may have been dimly conscious, in the past, of the possibility between them—been groping for each other in the darkness. It's love, it's friendship, it's mutual comprehension. . . . It's a passion that *might* have been. I seem to be coinciding simply with the idea of the married person encountering the *real* mate, etc.; but that is not what I mean.' The issue of marriage is peripheral to their waiting 'too long—till something else has happened'. What happened was 'the wasting of life'.

Meanwhile, Emily Hale went on with her work. She had a good post at the oldest girls' school in the US, where she was appreciated. One pupil, Ann Kennedy Irish, said that 'Eliot's loss was Abbot's gain. Miss Hale nurtured and expanded our love for and understanding of the theatre.' Her skill in casting resulted in admired performances, and she worked as carefully with girls in minor parts as with the stars. She also showed a sympathetic concern for the girls as individuals. When Eliot arrived at the school for an impromptu talk in 1952, the rumour flew round that he was a 'very special' friend of Miss Hale. They still corresponded, and Eliot still sent her copies of his works as they came out: 'The Three Voices of Poetry' in 1953, and in 1954 'The Cultivation of Christmas Trees'. She took comfort in their old habits, and in the fact that no other woman had meant as much. For thirty years, as Barbara Burwell put it, 'her whole life and world were bound up with Mr Eliot'.

She was, therefore, devastated by his sudden marriage to his secretary in January 1957. She gave his letters to Princeton, retired from Abbot Academy, and then collapsed. She went into the

Massachusetts General Hospital in Boston complaining of dizziness, and was investigated for a brain tumour, but the doctors found nothing. It was an emotional breakdown. Barbara Burwell remembered her coming to recuperate at Woods Hole, unsteady, leaning on a cane, and looking as though she had aged ten years. She never fully recovered, never got back her vivacity. What she retained was the inner core of conduct, a stoic centre, but she withdrew from her wider circle of contacts. Caroline Willington, a family connection, said: 'When Tom married a second time, Emily really went into seclusion. We lost track of her for many years.'

This reaction was not just to his marriage, but to the fact that Eliot now broke completely with her. Mrs Burwell remembered her mother's mention of an 'unappreciative letter from Mr Eliot'. Its substance was to rule Emily Hale out of his life: he wanted, from the on, no more to do with her. He was 'shocked and angry' (Valerie Eliot recalled) about the bequest of his letters. The breach was such that Janet Adam Smith felt, as Eliot's friend, that she should not accept an invitation from Emily Hale when she visited the States in the early sixties.

From 1957 Emily turned her attention to what she called 'my memoirs'. Silenced by Eliot's wish in her lifetime, she resolved to speak to the future. On 20 July 1957 she refers in a letter to Willard Thorp of an Introduction she had written to Eliot's letters which she was now turning over to Princeton. She read the Introduction to Professor Thorp (whom she called 'my tutor in Public Affairs') and his wife, Margaret, and it had their approval. That July, she sent to Mr Dix, Princeton's librarian, a new copy of the Introduction which, she told Thorp, 'I made even *more* personal and detailed than earlier—also I enclosed the last of T. S. E.'s letters— with the exception of one—which relates directly to the disposition of the letters in the University. I am especially glad I felt like finishing off the correspondence, because Mr Dix could read for himself T's reaction and be relieved of his own sense of having brought difficulties upon me.'

Emily Hale had now to vacate the rooms belonging to Abbot Academy. Her future was uncertain. She still hoped to pick up a half- or full-time post. Then, in October, she went to 'live' in England, in Chipping Campden. It was a return to the hallowed ground of memory, the Campden of the thirties, and it could not be the same. She appeared disturbed to locals, and did not stay

Mary Trevelyan.

Emily Hale as a teacher at Abbot Academy, Andover, Mass., in the fifties.

John Hayward.

The Elder Statesman (Paul Rogers), pursued by spectres from his past, finds forgiveness through his daughter (Anna Massey). Sept. 1958.

Eliot and his wife welcome guests to a party after the London opening of
The Elder Statesman, Sept. 1958.

long; by February 1958 she was back in Boston. In March she went to teach at Oak Grove School in Vassalboro, Maine, and after one semester, retired finally. In the last decade of her life she returned to those places—the Cotswolds, Smith College, Concord—where she had been happiest. Between September 1958 and 1963 she lived at 83 Crescent Street, Northampton, Mass., but at Smith, as in Campden, she no longer had a place. She was lonely. The faculty kept to its own circles, and she was not invited by those she would have liked. She told the Thorps, 'I miss the real exchange and stimulus of worthwhile ideas and people.' In May 1963 she moved back to Concord, and settled at 9 Church Green, a little house built during the Revolution.

That summer she had another impulse to speak to the future. In July she made a recording of Eliot's letters to her, and gave it to Princeton. As a professional speaker, she had often read Eliot's poems aloud on formal occasions or in class, and this had been her only legitimate voicing of what meant more to her than anything else. For more than thirty years she had been careful not to expose to the public her relationship with the great poet. But in the summer of '63, she did raise her voice in a new way: she put on tape a spoken memoir.

On 18 August 1963 she wrote to Willard Thorp:

... I had suddenly felt almost a revulsion against the whole story—so personal—so painful in many ways—of T. S. E. and E. H.—becoming public property in years long after we both are gone.... I haven't had the courage yet to read the good secretary's transcript, but may do so to-night to one close relative I have who knows the story. For M[argaret]'s very good suggestions—biographical data etc—personal references in poems—more later.

Emily Hale tried the spoken word, her particular *métier* because, Willard Thorp explained, she had trouble putting her memories together on paper. Obviously, she had not been entirely satisfied with the Introduction of 1957. A transcript was made from the tape, and sent to the Thorps. Margaret now suggested that her friend might pick out the personal references in Eliot's poems. On 18 August, Emily suggested that she might do still better if she were to respond spontaneously to questions from Professor Thorp. She told him that she wanted to put on tape, and then to have transcribed, 'a conversation with you—question &

answer— ... I feel that *you* can get from me the material which scholars will want fully, as much as my personal memoirs'.

A week later, on 24 August, she sent the Thorps a newly edited transcript. In her covering letter, she was now anxious to secure this document for the future, and praised the 'discreet secretary' for getting so much 'from my garbled wandering words as she did'. At the same time, she admitted, she was 'appalled at the fact as you put it—"I came through" at all in the midst of the confusion'. She was torn between a sense of public duty and reticence. She said deprecatingly that she could hardly flatter herself that the changes in the transcript made the story more valuable. She shrank from Margaret's idea that she identify personal details in Eliot's work: 'Later I shall try to write out what M. suggested—tho' there is *mighty little* of me in any poetry!'

After a holiday with a 90-year-old friend of the Perkinses in Seattle, she came to a bold decision: she would break another form of silence that, for six years, she had come to accept, and write to Eliot, who was now nearly 75, in order to secure her side of their correspondence. It is a painfully correct letter, written with brave composure:

September 12, 1963

Dear Tom,

It is difficult to break the silence which has existed between us for the last several years, but you would be the first to admit I think that the changing circumstances of our lives and increasing years necessitate that we both face certain facts and problems with courage and objectiveness.

... [Professor Thorp and Mr Dix] asked me to ask you if you cannot reconsider the time limit set by you for public access to the letters to a much shorter period than the one you have already named. I concur wholly to this request myself. ...

Closely connected to the disposition of the Princeton letters are my letters to you which long ago you planned to place in the Bodle[i]an at Oxford. The question has also been asked in Princeton if these two collections should not be under the same roof. ... It would seem to me if you are still preserving my letters, that your consent in placing them in this country would be the only correct practical solution, don't you think? And do you or I have legal claim on them?

Remembering your scrupulous attention and care in all legal aspects relating to literary material, writer's rights, etc. I am sure I can count upon you to leave specific directions in all matters regarding our past correspondence which assumes very different implications today than earlier. I think you will be aware that for me to consider my life as important because of its relationship to you—a noted world figure—is very difficult. I must as now act impersonally for the sake of the future in raising these questions, equally difficult for both of us but wholly professionally and historically correct. I do hope you will accept what is thrust upon us—shall we say—because you are you.

Further, I hope your health is better than I know it to have been lately. I learn of you from time to time from the Cambridge relatives.

In the thought of past friendship,

Emily Hale

Eliot did not reply. By November, she began to think that something had changed his mind about keeping her letters. It occurred to her that he might be ill. Another possibility was that 'he as of old—can't disturb the present, to stir up past memories and plans'.

On 26 December Willard Thorp discussed 'this strange impasse with your letters to T. S. E. His silence, after your careful (and gentle) letter of last September, is incredible, unless, as you suggest, he may not be well. As you know, under the law, the letters belong to him and he can dispose of them as he wishes. But the right to quote from them or to publish any or all of them belongs to you and your legal heirs—forever, as far as we know. One would think, therefore, that he would like to know what your wishes are in the matter . . .'

She replied on 5 January 1964: 'I have *almost* a suspicion that my letters have been destroyed!'

By February 1964 Emily Hale had dotted all the i's, as she put it, in her collection. This largest, by far, of all collections of Eliot's letters was only part of what she had. From 1927 she had amassed a vast and valuable array of typescript drafts and first editions, all sent by Eliot, most of them with personal inscriptions. This collection was equalled at the time only by that of Henry Ware Eliot in Cambridge, Mass. and John Hayward in London. Emily repeatedly refers to her collection as 'personal', whereas Hayward saw his more impersonally as an archive with himself as 'keeper'. Henry Ware Eliot made his collection as head of the family, to become part of the Eliot family collection at Harvard. These last two collections have been preserved intact, but Emily Hale, forced by the loss of her job at Smith to live in a furnished room, began to make gifts (none of these were sales). The first that I can trace is a typescript of Eliot's essay on Pascal, which she gave to Harvard in 1944. As she made her offers to Scripps, Harvard, and Princeton, she always declared that she would retain certain of Eliot's works that were, for personal reasons, precious.

There is a pattern to Emily Hale's bequests: the big gifts were made in the wake of shock: in 1948–9 following the catastrophic encounter in 1947, and in 1957 after Eliot's marriage. The bulk of the first editions went to Scripps College, in honour of Ruth George, the English teacher for whom Emily always expressed great affection. President Hard made chill responses to Emily Hale's repeated suggestion that she herself should be brought out to Scripps with the books. Hard's behaviour remained graceless, the bland indifference of a man of affairs to a middle-aged female of no importance. On 8 January 1948 she made an offer to Hard that she would repay the cost of travel to California with a reading of Eliot's poems for the College or a public audience: 'I do this sort of thing professionally', she wrote, 'and as I am not attached to any teaching staff this year, I am freer to give my own programs. I have read aloud a good bit of Eliot in all his phases . . .' The spoken word helped people, she said, to understand the poetry. Future generations would give a good deal to hear the woman Eliot had loved reading poems which she in some part inspired but, of course, to all appearance, she was nothing more than a high-school teacher. Hard replied on 23 January 1948:

Dear Miss Hale,

I appreciate the suggestion that you have made concerning the lecture-visit to the campus, and I wish that it might be possible. I ought to tell you, however, that we are pretty fully committed this year, owing to the fact that we have stretched our lecture fund resources in inviting Marjorie Nicolson . . .

Sincerely yours,
Frederick Hard, President

She did not answer 'as there seemed nothing to say.' But she remained confident and quite determined that Scripps did owe her this visit. In March she suggested that the College might find some funds in the autumn. Meanwhile, she sent a good 'public' photograph of Eliot taken before the war when he was 'looking far healthier than the poor man does now'. She also offered to send

Sweeney Agonistes: 'I call to your attention that the "Sweeney Agonistes" volume has particular significance as it was inscribed to me when Mr Eliot visited Scripps in the early 1930s.' She was disappointed by the lack of notice. There was no account of her gift in the alumnae bulletin. A friend, Mrs Volkmann, who visited Scripps library, reported that the librarian in charge had no idea where the Eliot books were. Hard's reply of 27 March ignored all this. He filled the sheet with bland comments about the weather.

In 1957 another set of packages went off to Scripps, including the typescript of *The Cocktail Party*, an early typescript of *Cats*, and an address of 1947 'On Poetry'. In the early sixties, she sent Alexander Jackson of the Houghton Library, Harvard, 'unusual personal memorabilia', including a draft of *The Family Reunion* with her own marginal comments to Eliot and their correspondence relating to the play, a postcard from Eliot dated 18 October 1955, a carbon copy of the typescript of his Shakespeare lectures of 1937, the address that Eliot gave on that frightful occasion when Vivienne intercepted him at the book fair in 1935, a broadcast, with many corrections, 'Towards a Christian Britain', and an address to the English Literary Society at University College, Dublin in 1936.

She gave six 'special' items to the Thorps, including the loosely bound first editions of 'Song for Simeon' (Nov. 1928) and *Two Poems* ('Cape Ann' and 'Usk') signed by 'Tom' at Christmas 1935. She also gave a few keepsakes to Smith College and to Miss Porter's school in Farmington.

From 1963 she heard reports from Eleanor Hinckley of Eliot's failing health, but did not know how serious this was. On 4 January 1965, he died. At once memory took control, and she was able to retrieve the Eliot of their long attachment. Her concern for future scholars took second place to her allegiance to Eliot, and by extension his wife, for whom she now felt sympathy. She was, said Mrs Burwell, always gallant. She decided that Princeton should return her memoir so that she might destroy it.

> 9 Church Green
> Concord, Mass. 01742
> 17 Jan 1965

Dear Willard,

. . . I feel that the letters alone give enough evidence of so abnormal (or is it normal) a story—and for the sake of my caring for him, as friend and a loved one—I should not underline the miscarriage, so to speak, of what seemed to be so perfect a solution to the long years of waiting for happiness.

It might *not* have been happy, or right, had the relationship been consummated, and I must always remember I was unaware of the complexities of both the situation* and his nature—or ready to believe in a side I knew so well of his nature. Be what it may, I hope you and M[argaret] can realize I shrink from the intimacy of the personal disclosure ...

Willard Thorp urged her to reconsider, but for the time being, she was firm. On 31 January she replied: '... there are other elements in life which I think equally as important as the objective literary professional point of view you both have.'

Then Mr Dix suggested, as a compromise, that she edit the more intimate details out of the text. She felt she should do this, not only for Valerie Eliot's sake, 'but from *my own* feeling for shielding the association with a man I loved, and who *I* think, did not respond as he should have to my long trust, friendship and love'.

She put off making a final decision about the memoir: 'I shall wait', she said in February 1965. Her last comment on the collection, in November, does not include a decision. In this letter an ambivalence about publicity remained: she admits to curiosity about the future's response to Eliot's letters, and tries not to regret that he had probably destroyed her own:

Nov 27th [1965]

Dear Willard,

   ... This changing of T. S. E.'s mind about my letters shows how terribly secretive he was about our 'affair' and I am more grateful than hurt—which I think I am a little that friendship through difficult years as well as love—is thus wiped out for the record. But on the whole, gratitude is uppermost as he probably meant to protect me, not himself or Valerie alone. Who can say?

How are you both?
Always affectionately
Emily H.

All happiness ended with Eliot's marriage, but she continued to live in her dauntless style. Her aunt left her some money, and she

---

* Crossed out.

used it to travel to Grand Manan Island in the Bay of Fundy, to Scandinavia, and South America. She endowed a building in a college for Blacks in North Carolina. One year before her death, in 1968 when she was 77, she played Mrs Higgins in a Concord production of *My Fair Lady*. As one watcher recalled: 'When Mrs Higgins, in her picture hat, long flounced gown and parasol made her entrance, with ease, style and aplomb, to the manner born, she took over the stage and received an ovation.'

The love story of T. S. Eliot and Emily Hale is not the usual tale of waiting: waiting until love on the man's part died; the woman faithful to her death. That is only superficially true. A stranger story lurks in Eliot's poetry, essays, and plays. In *The Cocktail Party*, when the empty-hearted husband rejects the woman he has loved, she asks him if she has been merely a passing 'distraction'. He denies this firmly. Emily Hale, too, believed that her attachment to Eliot had been as momentous for him as for her. When, after knowing her nearly fifty years, he broke with her in 1957, she did not conclude that she had been negligible. She was baffled—when Eliot died she said that a past mystery was now a future mystery—but she clung to her conviction that this 'affair' had given some public importance to her life. This, in a tone of muted sadness is convincing. Her letters are otherwise modest and restrained. She was not like the Countess Tolstoy or Alma Mahler, who basked in reflected fame: that kind of woman, distorted by the sacrifice of her own lesser talents, seems now a curiosity of history. Emily Hale's triumph is to come through the veil imposed upon her—as 'hidden', as 'Lady of silences'—wonderfully undistorted. There are, as yet, few facts, few letters, but all give out the same clear note of a woman who could sustain a balance of sense and feeling, who was willing to risk her livelihood for the sake of love, and who, when it was not to be, could pull herself together: at the end of 1935 when she returned to Boston, and again in 1947, and yet again ten years later. The breaks in her career—1934–5, 1947–8, 1957–8—coincide exactly with decisive dates in Eliot's mature years. There is, for her, a repeated pattern of demoralization, followed by spirited renewal. She managed this renewal because she had the talent to 'create' others: she did this for her actors, and she must have done it for women friends, all of whom felt themselves to be special. Above all, she did it for Eliot: how exactly, we shan't know without her letters. My guess is that, because she had known him almost always, as his family did, not as the construct of fame, she was able to rescue him, in a critical phase of his life in the early thirties, from the 'unreality' that is the condition of 'hollow men'. Years later, during another phase of hollowness, Valerie Eliot was to rescue him too, a young woman rejuvenating an old man. By then it was almost too late for creativity, so that story, for all its happiness, will tease posterity less than the more mysterious tie to Emily Hale.

This mystery, as she said herself, was buried with Eliot: the strangeness of an attachment that was, for many years, bound up with the fate of his soul. Such an attachment does not fit our categories like romantic love, and to imagine it is to risk a fiction. Some answer lurks in Eliot's poetry, a figure in a carpet, aesthetically intact yet, by virtue of repetition, inviting discernment: the reluctant lover of 'La Figlia' who prefers to construct a memorable figure of a beautiful girl, literally a statue on a pedestal, to the disturbing alternative of coming together; the wretched Gerontion, who laments that he has lost his passion, even his senses, and asks, 'How should I use them for your closer contact?' Later on, the virginal Lady of *Ash Wednesday* coexists with Eliot's vow of celibacy, which defused renewed contact with Emily Hale of any danger. It was not a role she chose, but one designed by Eliot's imagination, and played out until it was, as he said, 'too late'.

It is difficult, particularly for a woman, to set aside an impression that Eliot distorted female reality in a subjective cloud of feeling warped by fear. But so distant a judgement cannot contain the whole truth. To get even a glimmer about this 'affair' it is essential to let go our usual terms of sex, love, and friendship. As Eliot went 'beyond poetry', so his relationship with Emily Hale, closely associated with his poetry, also defies definition. Agatha and Mary in *The Family Reunion* understand that they are to be 'watchers and waiters'. It may be that the traditional passive role of waiting was subordinate to the more interesting one of watching. Emily Hale watched over Eliot's new life in the thirties and forties, or they were watchers together.

Watching meant abstaining from action until it was too late. It seems impossible to escape the unlived life of mature gentlemen in the late novels and tales of Henry James: Lambert Strether,

Spencer Brydon, and above all John Marcher, whose earlier incarnations were men like Winterbourne and Robert Acton. Marcher spends nearly his whole life marking time for a fate more remarkable than common love, for some rare and strange distinction. In maturity he recovers a relationship with a woman, May, who agrees to watch with him. Marcher convinces May that it would be worth waiting for: 'I think of it simply as *the* thing.' Eliot used exactly the same term when he spoke of the notion of some infinite 'thing'. Love wouldn't be 'it', Marcher thinks, because love isn't strange enough. And you couldn't take a lady on a tiger-hunt. 'Something or other lay in wait for him, amid the twists and turns of the months and years, like a crouching beast in the jungle.' This is what Eliot meant by 'Christ the tiger'.

So Eliot, like Marcher, refrained from love, and carried his burden of suspense quietly, giving others no glimpse of its effect on his life. He used good manners as Marcher does, as the bland cover of the hidden life: 'He hadn't disturbed people with the queerness of their having to know a haunted man. . . . This is why he had such good—though possibly such rather colourless—manners.' He was on guard not to let this lapse, yet, said James, he was quite ready none the less to be selfish, just a little, when he found a woman who would let him. His destiny was not a privilege he could invite her to share. Her privilege was to stand with him 'against the rest of the world'. Their relationship was one of lightness overlying what the woman calls 'the real truth about you', and she had 'a wonderful way of making it seem . . . the secret of her own life too'. She was in the secret of the difference between the public forms he went through and the detachment that reigned beneath them, that made of all behaviour 'a long act of dissimulation'. He wore a mask painted with an expression of social decorum, but out of the eyeholes there looked eyes with an expression that did not match. The woman, alone of all the world, met those eyes, just as Emily Hale met what she saw to be 'a man of extremes'.

As they grew old she still watched with him, the guardian of his promise, and let the association give shape and colour to her own existence. Such a course of existence requires a climax, but nothing happened. The years ebbed. The story of Emily Hale was like a trailer that Eliot towed so far behind him that it was almost out of sight, bearing his frail hope of perfection. When that hope faded in the later forties and early fifties, the trailer was detached and the story of Emily Hale put aside for a quite different story of marital fulfilment.

As a wife, Emily would have shared the publicity that came to Eliot with the Nobel Prize. As a watcher she had shared, instead, the hidden core of his new life, what was pure, passionate, creative. There must have been some exhilaration in the shared moments. Naturally she wished to be recognized, but accepted that this must wait until fifty years after her death. She did regret, she owned, that she would not be here when Eliot's letters 'burst upon the world'.

5. *Fame and Friends*

IN 1950 Eliot suggested to Mary Trevelyan that they drink to The Guardians. After his rejection of Emily Hale in 1947, this was the role that he assigned to Mary and to John Hayward, his two closest friends from the late forties to the mid-fifties. Their proven loyalty was to protect Eliot, and their social astuteness guide him, through the most public phase of his career.

At the end of the war, Eliot left the seclusion of the Shambles to settle again in London. He and John Hayward took a flat in the same block in which Henry James had lived, on the Embankment in Chelsea. Eliot attempted no great work after *Four Quartets*. He turned from the private search for salvation to public life, to the lecture platform and the popular theatre. *Four Quartets* projects the final stage of a moral cure: to enter into a sense of community. This move was not a spontaneous need but a sort of mission conducted from within the centre of what Eliot continued to see as a blighted civilization.

From 1940 (with the success of *East Coker*) until 1956 Eliot was in great demand and spoke everywhere, at universities, school prize-givings, and the London Library (where he joined a line of distinguished presidents including Carlyle, Gladstone, and Leslie Stephen). When he arrived in Princeton in 1948 the whisper 'TS... TS ... TS ...' rushed like a wind through a town agog with expectation. Eventually, in 1956, he spoke in a basketball stadium in Minnesota to 13,700, the largest crowd that has ever gathered to hear literary criticism. After he won the Nobel Prize in 1948 he was treated as a star, though his gravity and tensely withdrawn expression seemed to deprecate adulation. His silences gathered weight. He used to stand with his hands against his back, his arms akimbo. With his tall frame, now slightly stooped, he looked like a benign crane in horn-rimmed glasses. Rapt and reverent audiences listened to the slow procession of scrupulously selected words, rather toneless, but carrying the breath of godlike authority. His listeners recognized him as the real thing, not a spurious god of the media. His poetry had certified that he was one of the great souls. He had already the stamp of the timeless upon him.

The trumpets of fame are predictable, sycophantic, reductive;
the public figure locked into the expected image. It was, Eliot told
Mary Trevelyan, 'the most desperately lonely business'. At a party
in 1950, when he was asked to perform Sherlock Holmes from
memory, he began softly, as if to himself: 'at a time when Europe
was ringing with his name, and when his room was literally ankle-
deep with congratulatory telegrams, I found him a prey to the
blackest depression.' In 1950 he said that he had not known till
then what it was like to be famous: 'No-one thinks of me as a poet
any more, but as a celebrity.'

Eliot's older contemporaries had seen the man, not the
celebrity. Sir Herbert Read had witnessed moods of depression
that, on occasion, had left Read 'utterly depleted'. Compared with
this, the thinness of most of the memories of Eliot's younger
associates suggests that, in this public phase, he was at his most
inscrutable. He told Mary Trevelyan that he hid behind impenetrability. His gestures of weariness and his appointment book kept
admirers at bay. Although in the early 1950s he used to see Mary
once, twice, and sometimes even three times a week, he preserved a
fiction that minimized the relationship. She must agree, he insisted,
that, over all the years, they had met only once a fortnight. His
letters to her show that, even to a constant companion, he was
guarded and changeable. In time she learnt to read the simpler
signals—his fingers drumming on the table spelt bad weather—but
he remained after twenty years still incomprehensible. As regular
companions, in later years, he seemed to choose either proven fans
(whose devotion would have been tested over many years) or
undemanding friends like Christopher Sykes, with whom he
watched football on Saturday afternoons. Sykes, nineteen years
younger, was a writer and diplomat who joined the BBC in 1948.
From about 1941, with the deaths of Joyce and Virginia Woolf,
Eliot was no longer associating with contemporaries who were
literary equals. He was now the distinguished elder. Eliot's letters
in the later forties show that he avoided Desmond MacCarthy,
another old friend of Bloomsbury. There is bafflement in
MacCarthy's letters as Eliot complained variously of minor ills, his
servant's absence, and his unwillingness to offer poor food at his
club. There is superficial cordiality, a crumb or two of literary
criticism, and behind that the gap left by Eliot's insistent retreat.
Almost all accounts of these years sound curiously empty, as we

are regaled with the anecdotes of people who 'knew' or interviewed Eliot. The man is simply not there. Did he go dead in the late forties, as he saw himself in his relation to Emily Hale, or did the prophetic soul live on, burning, inscrutable, behind the façades? The whole truth depends on holding a balance of two almost antithetical selves. There is the man who was burnt out, and accepting fame to the further depletion of his vitality; and there is a public hermit who recognized that the time had come to take up, once more, the task foreseen in 'Coriolan'* in 1931, still uncompleted: to sound a message that could pierce the worthless chatter of the sycophantic throng. To command its attention he did need fame, yet to live as a celebrity cut him off still further from the human heart. Although he took pains to be kind and attentive, he also indulged in merciless comments on people of whom he did not approve. He had a crowing, rather mocking laugh, as if he found much amusement in the follies of the world.

If the public hangs on your lips, it is difficult not to make solemn pronouncements. This Eliot began to do. Called on too often, his platform statements had sometimes the drone of set positions. Many letters to Mary Trevelyan or to William Turner Levy, a priest in New York, suggest that sensations now tapped their beaks in vain against the hardening shell of the elder statesman of letters. Despite the barrage of anecdote, I think that as Eliot's fame grew on the permanent scale he became unknowable. His manner remained modest and genial—he could still joke and tell stories— but he was as invisible to his unknowing friends as the famous writer that James imagined in 'The Private Life', whose public images give no clue to the unapproachable life behind the shut door of the writer's study. One of Eliot's characters, Sir Claude (in *The Confidential Clerk*, 1953) speaks of 'the private door / Into the real world' of the artist. Art has 'this . . . remoteness I have always longed for'.

Eliot's work itself reveals—less often, but still intermittently—a character that never appears elsewhere, except when he allowed Emily Hale to look through the 'door' at Burnt Norton. The memoirs of his friends have tended to be brief, but Mary Trevelyan has left a sustained record, still unpublished. In 1958 she put

---

* In the late forties and early fifties Eliot listened repeatedly to Mary Trevelyan's record of Beethoven's *Coriolan* Overture.

together extracts from his two hundred and twenty-one letters to her, with extracts from the diary of their meetings and conversations which she began to keep in 1949. 'The Pope of Russell Square' is the fullest record we shall have of what it was like to be Eliot's companion during his most invisible years as a public figure. This Eliot is continuous with the Eliot of the anecdotes—mischievous, joking, generous with presents—but less guarded. Mary alone, apart from Eliot's sisters and John Hayward, saw a difficult, moody man. 'Oh dear me', 'Oh La! La!' she exclaims at intervals in her diary, '*Tiens!*'

When they met, in 1938, Mary was a brainy woman of 40, with bracing energy and a lively sense of humour. She was Warden of the Student Movement House in Russell Square (later, during the war, it moved to 103 Gower Street). She had a long, intelligent, horse face (slightly pointed towards the chin) and an attractive voice, low and throaty, with a rich nuance of tone well-adapted to her flair for comic observation. Hers was humour rather than wit: her tone was of high enjoyment, mature and tolerant. She liked people; liked foreigners. The Student Movement House was mainly for foreigners, and Eliot saw her as a mainstay for her 'waifs'. At the time they met, she was keeping a diary about the exploits and trials of her charges, which, to amuse herself in shelters during the Blitz, she turned into a book called *From the Ends of the Earth*. In the summer of 1941 she offered it to Eliot, and it was published by Faber early in 1942.

Mary was born into the professional élite, a distinguished family of churchmen, academics, writers, and diplomats. After leaving Grovely College, Boscombe, she became a scholar at the Royal College of Music, and her first posts were as organist and choir-trainer at St Barnabas in Oxford, and as a music teacher at public schools for boys, Radley and Marlborough. After travelling in Ceylon and Kashmir in 1930–1, she took up the post of Warden in 1932, when she became increasingly interested in the problems of Eastern students migrating to the West for study, and its effects on their return home.

She had a relish for record (her cousin was the eminent English historian, G. M. Trevelyan). A natural diarist, her attention turned outwards to ordinary lives: students and, later, soldiers. Her letters, too, touched on multiple lives with a swift, wide range of detail. She was an acute observer—she saw, for instance, that Eliot didn't look quite natural when dressed up because he tried too hard to be correct—but she was not attuned to subtler vibrations. It is doubtful if Eliot ever revealed to her, as he may have done to Emily Hale, the side reserved for his poetry. It is fitting that their friendship was at its height when Eliot was writing *The Cocktail Party* and *The Confidential Clerk*. The absurd play of manners, with its undercurrents of feeling—but not the strenuous or high-flown feeling of his earlier plays—was perfectly complemented by Mary's familiarity with social currents. She had the range of awareness of a born nurse of the Florence Nightingale sort, with an organizational flair based on the intelligence to grasp essential needs, and she was quick to pick up the more obvious disturbance of people in a difficult situation. This is what made her so effective with displaced students and soldiers on active service. Her memoir of Eliot shows no sign of 'frontier' intuitions; nothing of the pulsating 'silence' that Eliot had shared with Emily Hale. Their relationship was based on talk, and fairly humdrum talk: church politics; Eliot's new overcoat; whether the Rondabouts (Lady Rhondda and friend) should be invited to lunch at the Shambles—would the rations stretch to this larger party? What attracted Eliot was Mary's fearlessness: she teased him, as Virginia Woolf had done in earlier days, daring to prod the outer bulwarks of his reserve.

In July 1938 she had been asked to look after Eliot when he came to read at a Student Christian Movement conference in Swanwick, Derbyshire. He had arrived with a cold and a stiff neck, and read *The Waste Land* and 'The Hollow Men' in a harsh voice, with his head on one side. After he left, the students staged a parody of this reading—harshness and stiff neck included—and, suspecting Eliot of a sense of humour, Mary sent him a copy. He sent an amused reply, and later that year agreed to read at the Student Movement House. Crowds came: young men in corduroy trousers and floppy ties, carrying Eliot's poems under their arms and looking intense. Mary noticed that Eliot seemed 'terrified' after the reading, when he had to meet some of them.

She initiated a regular correspondence with Eliot when she was appointed to the Anvil, a religious Brains Trust which broadcast on the Home Service once a week. Mary was the sole woman amongst clergymen and theologians (she was supposed to represent 'the ordinary person') who were to answer questions sent in by the public. She submitted some of these questions to Eliot, and was undaunted by his long, heavy replies. She said that, once she was on the air, she could not recall anything he had said— thankfully, because she could not have passed it off as her own.

'What were you like as a child?' she asked Eliot at their first lunch, at Viani's in Charlotte Street, in the spring of 1941.

Eliot, who had just completed *The Dry Salvages*, began promptly: 'Born on the Mississippi . . .' When they parted, he held her hand a long time. Mary was 'amused and flattered'.

What gave Mary her sense of a special friendship was that she was permitted to witness Eliot's transformations from distant politeness to informal chatter, jokes, and eventually confidences about his family, his grandfather (the Great Man of his childhood), and the trials of his marriage. To Mary this meant intimacy; to Eliot only the exchange of masks, the formal for the informal. The switch was utterly disarming to all who found themselves favoured in this way, but the informal Eliot who was witty with male colleagues, domestic with women, and a story-telling godfather with children, loaded with expensive and carefully chosen gifts, still guarded an Eliot who, I think, remained unreachable. One of the maxims in which he delighted was 'always suspect everybody' (the maxim of 'old Foxey' in *The Old Curiosity Shop*). Life was a grander version of mystery fiction, Dickens, Poe, Conan Doyle, and Eliot a master detective, the incarnation of Holmes: aloof, solitary, trusting no one but the faithful Watson. Mary was an ideal Watson: the uninspired but worthy confidante, rather worldly in outlook, to whom could be trusted the more mundane details of a great enterprise. Mary–Dr Watson would urge him not to strain his health, would cheer and console, and above all would listen. Unfortunately, Mary Trevelyan came from the governing class and had decided opinions of her own. When, in the mid-fifties, she became critical of Eliot's degree of seclusion, the friendship came to an end.

Mary had a high-handed, even bossy manner. She dominated younger friends, but was considered a 'good pal', generous with help, kind and sensible. She always had lots of friends, like Rose Macaulay, but no romance until, at the age of 44, she found her hand in Eliot's. She says straightforwardly that she realized that she was in love with him in 1942. It was irrevocable, but controlled.

Her hearty manner gave no hint of her feelings, so that when, in 1944, she took off for the Normandy beaches in the wake of the troops, Eliot bade farewell to her as 'a Man of Action'. Mary said that she was never sure what he felt for her. He certainly enjoyed her company, and came to depend on her practical propping, but there was, I think, a warning to her in a letter of 19 December 1944 in which he talks of wishing to spend the Christmas season in a monastery. The deliberation with which he signed himself her affectionate and well-meaning friend laid down the limits of their association.

As Eliot grew older, entrance to his inner circle depended on the strictest loyalty and discretion. He put Mary Trevelyan through a test. At the beginning of 1942 he asked her to take on a disturbed poet from the East, a disciple and imitator of Eliot, who had also made a wretched marriage with an English girl. Mary, provided with funds from Eliot, was to rescue him when he set fire to his clothes, or drove into a lamp-post under the drunken impression it was his wife. When, on this last occasion, Mary collected him from a casualty ward, he lay back in the taxi with his feet up on the opposite seat, reciting yards of *The Waste Land*. This was the sort of situation where Mary excelled: she was patient and attentive to Eliot's protégé. When she phoned to make her report she could not resist telling Eliot one episode. The young poet had lain back in her office chair, his eyes closed, remarking: 'I had a fantasy last night. I dreamed that you were my mother and Mr Eliot my father.'

Eliot's laugh came back: 'I really think we might have done better than that.' Mary had passed the test as a trusty nurturer of waifs. It may well have been as needy waif that Eliot had held her hand.

Mary complemented Eliot in their main difference: he sheered away from people, while she was gregarious. She told him shrewdly that when he spoke (as he often did) of 'fear' of people, he was really avoiding disturbance. Then, too, there was Mary's Englishness. During the war, when Eliot wished to partake in the feeling of national commitment, she helped to place him more firmly 'now and in England'. The solidity of her connections would have appealed to him: G. M. Trevelyan was Master of Trinity (Cambridge); her brother-in-law Warden of Keble, and later Bishop of Oxford. Another brother, Humphrey, was in the

Indian Political Service. Eliot enjoyed introducing her to his sister
Marian as 'the Vicar's daughter': she was, indeed, the devout eldest
daughter of the Revd George Philip Trevelyan, who had built
various churches of his own High Anglican persuasion, and whose
family had been connected with St Stephen's Church in the past.
She may have epitomized, for Eliot, the Anglican tradition.
Without much spiritual imagination, she was an appropriate
companion for the less ambitious regimen Eliot had prescribed for
himself in 1941 of 'prayer, observance, discipline, thought and
action'. She was welcome to accompany him to all services.

Love does not blur her picture of Eliot. He was glum at times, at
times enraged, as unpredictable and moody as the weather. Her
tone is not unsympathetic, but humorously tolerant, using
humour in the English way to melt awkwardness. She pictures
how Eliot would sing tunelessly in a harsh low voice on the way
home after dinners: music hall songs of his youth, or Negro
Spirituals. Mostly, she makes fun of his clothes. When Bishops
came to preach at St Stephen's he wore his City clothes, and
looked uncomfortable in a stiff collar. He was still devoted to his
bowler, which was too small and, Mary thought, didn't suit him.
He used to wear a black tie on the anniversary of St Bartholomew
and a red tie for Charles, King and Martyr. Sometimes an old
overcoat (inherited from his brother, and too large) would cover
the impeccable outfits: it had misshapen pockets in which he might
have stuffed a manuscript. So Mary created a lovable eccentric,
leaving out—she duly records the omission—his wounding comments on almost everyone, and her own 'deep distress'.

Her memoir offers a unique view of Eliot, a view as impossible
for his contemporaries as for his younger devotees. His artistic
contemporaries, breaking with Victorian convention, had welcomed strangeness of all kinds. They had liked Eliot for it. The
next generation, the trusty ones, tell us that, on the contrary, Eliot
was not strange: he was unbending and considerate. Mary
Trevelyan came exactly between these two generations—she was
ten years younger than Eliot—and she preserves a useful balance.
Her intellectual and social aplomb made it possible for her to like
and admire Eliot without idolizing him. He was sufficiently at ease
with her not to disguise his rages, as he called them. Later, with
Valerie Fletcher, whom he was able to love, he became different,
wholly lovable. But to Mary he was often fussy, hypochondriacal,

self-obsessed, and capricious. She was appalled by the suddenness of his fury, and would beg him to control it for both their sakes. He would get out of her car, and slam the door. Few saw Eliot from that semi-intimate perspective. He would relax his extreme formality, take off his jacket, and even (in very hot weather) his waistcoat, and they held hands before parting for their respective vacations (always apart, against Mary's wish), but it was no more than the clasp of chums. And like old chums, they put up with their tiffs.

This looks ahead to their habits of the late forties and early fifties, but even in the early phase of their friendship Eliot gave conflicting signals. He would propose lunch, then vanish for three months. This was not initial shyness, but consistent with a curious habit of their later association. Mary said that he would 'disappear' after they had had a particularly happy time together. She came to expect it. It was as though he had to take cover from the claims and fatigues of friendship, in the same way, perhaps, that Hawthorne and Thoreau would dive into the woods if they sighted each other—a potential fellow—on the Concord horizon. If Mary Trevelyan and John Hayward were useful to Eliot, that was incidental to their love for him. For Eliot, their usefulness was the *raison d'être* for the ties. He withdrew from Mary whenever the tie exceeded its uses, delimited after 1950 by 'rules'. He told Mary that it would get on his nerves to see *anyone* more than once a fortnight. He never enquired into her own needs.

To see friendship as useful is, of course, to miss the point of friendship. The notion of friendship based on use is Emersonian, that is, the notion of a man inwardly alone, essentially independent of all ties. It is a state of mind that verges on oblivion to others. Emerson said: 'treat men and women as if they were real; perhaps they are.' With fun and cameraderie, Eliot treated Mary Trevelyan and Emily Hale as if they were real, but for him they stood for something—the 'Lady of silences', 'the Vicar's daughter'—that fed into his private and adjustable scheme of existence.

Mary became Eliot's prop at a time when he was detaching himself from Emily Hale. She had no inkling of Emily's existence until 1950, when Eliot did not tell her much more than that he had been in love with one woman all his life and could find no words to explain the nature of that love. Because Emily Hale represented for Eliot New England, the past, his youth, and visionary powers, to drop her was to feel hollow. This is what he meant, I think, by his cryptic reference, in 1949, to a psychological change of life. It was Mary Trevelyan's misfortune to have tried to engage in a closer relationship with Eliot at this very stage. In the early forties everything had seemed to point to a lifelong friendship—the frequent meetings, the ease and laughter—but a peculiar hollowness echoes through Mary's memoir which is not there in her other books. The hollowness is not from her side but, at second hand, from his: his weighty comments on Culture seem to be given out at a remove from himself; his humour is often rather forced. It sometimes took the form of a pile-up of cryptic references to possibly non-existent people who beset the great man with demands for his attention, the point being Eliot's covert plea to be left alone. He also delighted in a torrent of bogus excuses, shading into the genuine which was the dictum from the book of Possum the Wise that one only achieves something by neglecting something else.

The lurking hollowness in the memoir lies, above all, in Eliot's actual relation to Mary herself. She had so secure a sense of her identity that it never occurred to her that Eliot's remarks and letters reflect back a limited caricature of a woman as guardian. Her books show that she was not just a kindly companion to a great man, tough enough to cope with his moods; she had pluck, an adventurous resilience, and a determination of her own.

Eliot did give Mary fair warning as he warmed to her, if we read between the lines of the memoir. In 1942 he warned her of his native Calvinism, which he described as a handicap he could not overcome: this slipped, characteristically, into a cascade of light-hearted trivia. The grave, stern man could relax in a fashion, though his strangeness came out as distinctly in his relaxation as in his religion. On 29 June 1942 he sent Mary an explanation of his nature. Hedged with wild fictions, the letter at once conceals and reveals his awareness of an alternating action in his conduct: he would involve himself, and then suddenly drop people. The letter speaks in terms of committees, but what he says is true of his pattern of withdrawals from closer attachments—from Conrad Aiken, Emily Hale, and eventually John Hayward and Mary herself. The dismissal of Vivienne, though understandable in itself, was part of a pattern which is there throughout his life. Towards the women in this group, quite different as they are, he behaved in a similar way, as though some inexorable and godlike Judgement had annihilated them from the face of the earth. It was the less binding, business-colleague kind of relationship that tended to survive the years: Sir Geoffrey Faber, Sir Herbert Read, Allen Tate, Peter du Sautoy.

Pound is the one exception: despite his ridicule of Eliot's faith, his crazy, exhausting, unreadable letters in the twenties and thirties, and his broadcasts for the Fascists during the war, Eliot never forgot what he owed to him. He visited him at St Elizabeths (the Washington home for the criminally insane),* and worried over Pound's funds as, in the early London years, Pound had worried over him. In the late fifties and sixties, Eliot sent him soothing final letters in which he praises Pound's achievement and plays down his own.

From 1944 to 1948 Mary Trevelyan was mostly abroad on wartime and post-war missions. This second phase of her friendship with Eliot was a period of correspondence in which Mary shone: her letters to him from Belgium in 1944–5 show her finest hour. Eliot's replies were small beer by contrast, as he admitted. While she ploughed between shell-holes across the Normandy beaches and waded through battlefield mud that submerged her wellington boots, Eliot was wrapped up in the overheated house at Shamley Green, amidst old ladies, dogs, and cats, turning over his theories about Culture and his little worries over a choice of successor to Archbishop Temple. While Mary Trevelyan marshalled 50,000 Front Line men in and out of the relief hostel that she set up in Brussels, Eliot was asking why she had not replied to his query whether he should or should not write to *The Times* about some minor issue of church politics.

Her seventeen long letters to Eliot, describing wartime experiences in France, Belgium, and Germany, were published in 1945 (with Eliot's name omitted) as *I'll Walk Beside You*. The title came from a popular song, sung to troops nostalgic for their best girls or mothers or, as Mary recognized, apprehensive of reunions. It was Mary herself who was 'beside' these men, who listened to their

---

* Pound was incarcerated after the war, having been found mentally unfit to stand trial for treason.

stories, tended the wounded in transit, and met British prisoners of war as they were released. Her exploits in the six months from September 1944 to May 1945, as she presents them in her letters to Eliot, are an important part of their story, for they show in the most admirable light the kind of woman to whom he was drawn as he put into practice his principle of detachment but found, at the same time, some need for a woman's interest, casual company, and practical advice.

Two attitudes pervade her letters written from 21 Army Group HQ (Rear) near Brussels, where she had converted the Albert, a hotel, into a hostel for troops on forty-eight hours leave from the appalling strain of fighting on the German front. First, she thought carefully about the state of mind of the troops who, after a brief taste of what some called in her visitors' book 'heaven', had to go back to killing. Some confided to her their 'fear and horror of being turned into murderers.' One evening in the chapel Mary fell into conversation with a miner who said: 'For the last four years I have been trained to kill men, now I am killing them. I hate it and I can't get away.' Military discipline forced such men to kill women, and when the fighting stopped in the early months of 1945, not to give chocolate to famished German children: this was called 'fraternization'.

So Mary was initiated into the perverting conduct that war forces on men: they confessed to her their horror at themselves, and somehow she knew how to hearten them. She both allowed them to relieve their minds, and prevented the kind of collapse that too much sympathy could have brought on. She never allowed herself to forget for one moment that there was no way to save these men from climbing back on the lorries to go back into the nightmare of bringing another country to its knees. She was concerned that the break should give the men relief without unfitting them for their terrible task. She saw it as a 'mental rehabilitation'.

Secondly, her genuine admiration for the men pervades her letters. Where Eliot looked down at ordinary men as 'termites', she found them uncomplaining, humorous, and amazingly appreciative of her smallest acts of care. Her liking was the secret of the Albert's obvious success.

In November 1944 she obtained permission to go to an air-evacuation centre, 4 miles outside Brussels, where she tended the wounded as the first batches arrived from Arnhem. She worked in a low, whitewashed building with a cement floor covered with about 250 stretchers where the wounded lay, waiting to be taken to England. 'I have never seen such a mass of human suffering,' she wrote to Eliot, 'bad head wounds and severe lung cases.' She fed one boy who had refused to respond to the orderlies and stared at the ceiling with almost sightless eyes. Eventually, very slowly, he began to talk about his life as a bank clerk in Manchester, and by the time she saw him off, even managed a little joke. She was matter-of-fact, like a good nurse, with patients on the brink of demoralization. She could normalize men: this was her gift on which, over subsequent years, Eliot was to draw. In the meantime, he wrote to her that his blind masseuse, Mrs Millington, would have to pound his neck a lot more before he might be like other people.

Mary Trevelyan was writing an epistolary form of historical record for eventual publication—she had a book of letters in mind already in 1943—and these letters to Eliot were not personal. He read them aloud to the women (and pets) at the Shambles, before sending them on to Mary's mother in Oxford. Though Mary was not thinking of herself in these letters, her intelligent judgement and high calibre is as unmistakable to the reader as it was to Eliot. Especially in her work with ex-prisoners of war in 1945, she showed a remarkable ability not to be too dismayed by the uglier aspects of the active life. She was just sensitive enough to be effective: she would not have seen, as Eliot, 'The horror! the horror!' for to see that is to become so disheartened with human nature that it takes an exhausting effort simply to keep on.

It was precisely because Eliot was often debilitated by 'the horror' that he needed a prop like Mary Trevelyan. All the women in his life were strong, with the exception of Vivienne, and even she had a certain negative strength in the power of her macabre imagination. Eliot's mother was strong in her principles; Emily Hale was gallant; Mary, strong in her fearless management; and, finally, Valerie Eliot was to be strong in her loyalty, which would protect Eliot for a generation beyond his lifetime.

Mary thought the best thing in her life was her friendship with Eliot but she mattered to him rather little, as it turned out. Her best thing was, arguably, these six months behind the Front Line. All her best qualities were to the fore. Nursing Eliot was too minor a job for her vigorous talents, and her busy-ness came to be mildly irritating, like the guardianship of the bossy Julia in *The Cocktail Party*. 'Oh, it's YOU again, Julia', Eliot greeted her in 1949 in a chemist's in Southampton Row. After the dress rehearsal for the London opening, which Mary attended with Eliot in April 1950, he said on the drive home: 'Julia can now show compassion.' Mary herself recognized that much of the knowing, good-hearted, but rather managerial Julia 'is me'. In short, she was better with thousands of ordinary men than with one genius.

In 1947 she travelled through war-devastated countries, northern France and Greece, and then Burma, Malaya, North Borneo, and Thailand, to make the first surveys of priority needs in education for UNESCO. Eliot pictured her sailing in a sampan down the Irrawaddy to lower Burma, the intrepid woman traveller responsible for little brown men called Buz Saw and Go Bang. Their letters play out the old fantasy of the white man's (now woman's) burden, but without the old earnestness and hypocrisy. Mary reported efforts that were comic in their futility, and Eliot was not surprised to hear that the future of the East was not going according to *Christian Newsletter* plans. In *The Cocktail Party*, he put an element of Mary into Celia's intrepid mission to the East, the Mary who recounted her adventures among the wilder tribes of Burma. He even asked her for tips for his East Indian island: whether there were monkeys; whether the jungle people tied up their victims and smeared them with sticky stuff to attract insects. He complained that there was no information on these vital points in her reports.

In Celia Coplestone he conceived a character with an exceptional range, wide enough to encompass the disappointed love that derived from Emily Hale and the dauntless mission in the East that derived from Mary's letters of 1947–8. I have wondered if these adventurous letters had some innocent part in detaching him from Emily. Emily was a woman to whom Eliot owed a lot: he felt the obligation of her years of faithful love. Mary, on the other hand, had the attraction of the carefree adventurer, the independent woman, ready, even eager, to help him from her bounty of organizational energy, the heat of which was, mercifully, turned elsewhere. Eliot may have contemplated their friendship with most satisfaction in those years when Mary was being energetic thousands of miles away.

Although she was only six years younger than Emily Hale, Mary was more the efficient type of the moment, made fashionable in wartime by the square shoulders of mannish costumes in plain, dark colours. Already, in 1941, in *The Dry Salvages*, Eliot had seen the emotional ties of the past fade, like the faded song that Emily Hale had sung before the first war. 'Ecstasy' of 1913 was now replaced by 'I'll Walk Beside You', a new sort of song, associated with a new sort of woman, not the Jamesian 'lady' watching and waiting, but the tough activist, shoulder-to-shoulder with men of action. Hers was not the inward ordeal of rectitude, the moral refinement of the native New England habitat, but rather the robust candour of English friendship. Humour preserves it from heaviness but also slants the truth, so that what predominates is the style of candour rather than candour itself, and the laughter that avoids the demands and dangers of intimacy.

What Mary Trevelyan offered Eliot was this kind of joking relationship that could just touch the border of intimacy. He did tell her that he could not speak so freely to anyone else, nor permit anyone else to return such forthright comment. Once he sent her one of his rebukes by mail, and, aware that this rocket was on its way, took her out for a most companionable dinner. Mary had the nerve not to let this pass. Strong in her self-assurance, less malicious than the intellectuals of the literary market-place (John Hayward, for instance), Mary Trevelyan invited Eliot to a more benign kind of laughter, not the lethal derision of his early years, but a more relaxing exchange of anecdote, like her account of her disconcerting dance with an enormous Guardsman at the Albert. He was so silent that she wondered if it was possible to fall asleep while dancing. 'After a few rounds', she said, 'I risked a crick in the neck and looked up at him. He said with extraordinary dignity, "Excuse me, madam, I am trying not to hiccup."'

While Mary Trevelyan was coming and going, Eliot settled into his new domestic arrangement with John Hayward in February–March 1946: the shared flat overlooking the Thames on the third floor of 19 Carlyle Mansions. Hayward had proposed such an arrangement as early as 1935, but at that time Eliot had been too harassed by Vivienne's pursuit to have a settled address of his own. Hayward saw himself as Eliot's *très-loyal serviteur*. Like Mary, he was a guardian in the late forties and early fifties, though he served Eliot in a different way, as literary adviser and self-styled Keeper of the Eliot Archive. Together they saw Eliot through a difficult stage of his life in which he felt, more completely than ever before, bored with all living that had no religious meaning.

Eliot's arrangement with John Hayward was not really a home. In a sense, Eliot was homeless from 1914, with the exception of brief interludes in the thirties when he had felt 'at home' with the Bostonians in Chipping Campden. Otherwise he had simply shared houses with Vivienne, with the Revd Eric Cheetham, with the Mirrleeses, and now with Hayward, in a way that sustained his interior solitude. This solitude he did not expose even to his confessors, to whom (he told Mary) he spoke of sins the confessors would understand. He saw it as an act of consideration not to mention sins too subtle or too complicated to explain. These remained unresolved. In a furious moment when he was bent on pushing Mary into conformity with new 'rules', he asked that it be understood that he was an old man with an uneasy conscience and bad dreams. He appealed not on the grounds of genius (as to Emily Hale) but as a sinner. His moodiest moments with Mary Trevelyan were not personal; they had to do with private 'horror' which he projected, once, on a pair of American tourists dining at a nearby table while he was at the Edinburgh Festival in 1953, or, in 1951, on a down-home American sing-song in Hampstead. Suddenly, he felt that he was in a cage with wild beasts, and, going white, he burst out: 'Do you know the Song of the Reconstructed Rebel?' Then he began to sing in a loud, raucous voice, with extreme violence, until Mary got him into a taxi. That still-keen alert for 'horror', compounded by the private burden of atonement, lay behind Eliot's habits in the eleven years that he lived with John Hayward.

Despite the inexorable progress of muscular dystrophy, Hayward remained the most sociable of men: the flat was the centre of his web of bibliographical contacts that extended now across Europe and America, and a point of pilgrimage for all visitors to London who loved and collected books. The stream of visitors was continuous: as one left, the next would arrive. Hayward would be sitting in his front room, half-slewed round in his wheelchair to face his guest, dominating his world so that the dim hootings outside seemed less important. His world was dispensing judgements and letting fly his lacerating barbs, hilariously funny if you were not the victim. His hand would fumble for a small cigarette which he would somehow manage to light, 'his eyes widening as some horrid but delightful thought formed itself to be uttered'.

Hayward was a keen adviser. He was known never to say no to a request for guidance, and so the network grew larger, the immobilized figure at the hub more sought after. Eliot, with Hayward's compliance, evaded this web. The two men lived quite separate lives.

The arrangement was built around Eliot's privacy. Hayward gave him the outer structure of a normal life shared with others, and sanctioned, at the same time, the withdrawal of a solitary. It was a way of life carefully balanced on a set of habits. Eliot visited Hayward's room once a day, in the evening, for a brief talk, and on Saturday afternoons took him for a walk. Sometimes Hayward would help Eliot to entertain visitors—say Adrienne Monnier and Sylvia Beach*—at King's Road restaurants. Sometimes Eliot might accompany Hayward to the literary parties of the capital: in the fifties it would create a stir when he arrived, pushing Hayward's chair. But then again, he might do nothing. He was free to shut the door of his room. Only once, at Easter 1955, did Eliot's withdrawal make for visible strain. John and Mary decided that he was making minor ailments an excuse for staying in his room, and John went so far as to hint that he was indulging in a degree of hypochondria that might affect his reputation.

The problem, of course, was Eliot's need for privacy: the excuses, the shut door, the suddenly broken arrangements with Mary were all understandable if he had to balance out the contradictory claims of his life as public hermit. For Eliot, as for Sir Claude, the private door was an 'escape into living / Escape from a sordid world to a pure one'.

Winter and summer, Eliot went by bus at 6.30 every morning to kneel on the cold stone floor of St Stephen's Church. After early mass, he wrote in the morning, standing up at a kind of lectern, typing three or four pages of a play or lecture. At about noon he would take the giant umbrella (specially made, with a large handle)

---

* In 1919 Sylvia Beach, an American, opened a bookshop called Shakespeare and Company on the Left Bank in Paris. It became a meeting-place for expatriate writers, and in 1922 published Joyce's *Ulysses*.

and catch a bus, sitting on the top deck, to Piccadilly Circus, and
from there went by Underground to Russell Square. At night, he
usually had his meal on a tray in his bedroom though, occasionally,
he would dine with Hayward, or join him for tea on weekends. On
Saturday afternoons he would push Hayward across the bridge to
Battersea Gardens or to the gardens of the Royal Hospital. It must
have meant a certain amount of domestic responsibility to live
with a disabled man, for they employed only a daily housekeeper, a
sympathetic Frenchwoman called Mme Amory. She could not
pronounce Eliot's name, and called him '*Monsieur le Professeur*'.
When Madame was not there, Hayward must have depended on
Eliot for numerous minor jobs, for morning coffee, and letters that
had to be posted. Eliot was always punctilious about duties to the
unfortunate—Mary noted how assiduously he visited an ailing
White Russian, Tereschenko, at Wandsworth—but the essential
solitude prevailed. It was simply not 'done', Mary said, to visit
Eliot and John Hayward together, and they had few friends in
common. The exceptions were Christopher Sykes, who accompanied the Saturday walks, and increasingly, as the years passed,
Mary herself. From 1952 Mary and John began to compare notes
and commiserate when Eliot was snappish with John or evasive
with Mary. 'He can't help hurting us,' she said to John, and John
added: 'He has a streak of sadism which he fights against.'

It may seem that for Eliot to live with so ill a man as John
Hayward was an act of charity but, on balance, the benefit was in
Eliot's favour. Hayward protected him from the outside world: for
some years he took all phone calls. Like Mary, he was at the centre
of the intellectual establishment, Mary by inheritance, Hayward
by his precocious achievements as editor and 'man of letters' (as he
liked to describe himself, regretting that the phrase had come to
sound affected). Eliot, the 'resident alien' ('Metoikos' as he once
signed himself), depended on Hayward, who had a passion for
accurate English, to oversee his drafts.

During the war Hayward, like Mary, had passed the test of
loyalty. From Merton Hall, Cambridge, where he was evacuated,
he had advised Eliot, with great verbal acumen, on the three
wartime *Quartets*. Later he told Helen Gardner that, of all his
activities, his share in *Four Quartets* gave him the most satisfaction.
On 27 June 1940 he wrote from Cambridge to assure Eliot that the
Eliot Archive was with him for safe-keeping. It was at this point

that his role as literary mentor, a worthy successor to Pound, was compounded with that of 'Keeper' or 'Clerk of the Works'. As the drafts of the later *Quartets* came in, he had them bound in order. After the war he mopped up other drafts of poems, talks, and plays.

Hayward was ideally suited to serve Eliot in this dual capacity. He was always there, and he was prodigiously well-versed in English poetry. He told the poet Kathleen Raine with justifiable pride, 'I have read the whole of English poetry, *twice*'. In 1947 he was behind the National Book League's exhibition of first and early editions of English poetry, the first attempt ever to present at one time in one place the whole range of English poetry from Chaucer to the present. His illustrated catalogue was variously described as 'exemplary' and 'a permanent landmark in bibliographical scholarship'. In 1951 he organized another exhibition, *Le Livre Anglais*, at the Bibliothèque Nationale in Paris. In the postwar years he edited *The Penguin Book of English Verse* (1956), as well as Penguin selections of Donne and Herrick, and prose selections of Swift and T. S. Eliot. In 1952 he also became editor of *The Book Collector*, which he ran brilliantly as a dictator until it became the pre-eminent journal in its field. Colleagues would turn the pages of a new issue, trembling at Hayward's commentary, and powerful institutions fretted under his censure, which could be intemperate.

Hayward was committed, like Eliot, to the purity of the English language. He once took the Distillers Company to task for allowing an advertisement in which three whisky bottles were photographed standing on a volume of Scott. He urged Kathleen Raine that, as she put it, 'a poem should never appear which had not been perfected in accordance with those old rigorous standards of the language whose custodian he knew himself to be'. Eliot was only one of a large number of writers who submitted their drafts or proofs to his meticulous 'carpentry', who had to endure his frank, sometimes chastening comments, and who had to admit that he was almost always right. In 1949 Mary Trevelyan noted that Eliot's experiment of sharing a flat with Hayward was a success: 'Besides a strong personal affection, he depended greatly on John as his literary critic and seldom felt quite easy in his mind about anything he had written unless John approved.'

In the post-war period, Hayward was still mobile in his wheelchair, presiding over bookish society in London with his frightfully clever and cruel remarks. He feared nobody, said a King's College fellow. 'If there was trouble—well, let there be trouble. He rather liked a row.' Eliot shared his friend's acerbity, but their tactics were opposite. Eliot's was to withdraw, Hayward's to engage with withering satire that was terrifying on a first encounter.

Gwen Watkins, wife of the Faber poet Vernon Watkins, recalled being introduced to John Hayward as 'a witty woman'.

'*Be* witty', said Hayward shortly, through his bulbous lips.

Graham Greene remembered how he would throw back his head and draw in 'a loud long breath (his left arm waved like a tentacle of an octopus, and captured his silver cigarette case), as I asked him a direct and indiscreet question about some writer whom he did not regard with unmixed friendship. A pause and out came the atrocious anecdote.' His aim was to amuse. His friends, vastly entertained by these whiffs from the Under-world (as Virginia Woolf had called the literary market-place), forgave him the malice: it was a compensation, they said, for his disease.

Hayward's powerful head, knowing, bright eye, waving, half-paralysed left tentacle, and blubbery lips gave him the appearance of fairy-tale wickedness—a wicked godfather, said Janet Adam Smith—reinforced by his mix of banter and learning. He had a way of provoking confidences, sometimes indiscreet confessions, and he relished scandal. This may be one reason that Eliot kept some protective distance. Their friendship ran on the smooth sophisti-cated routines of the joking relationship that the Tarantula and the Elephant had established in the thirties at Bina Gardens.

Both Hayward and Eliot cultivated personae. 'I shall wear, I think, my admirable red waistcoat to your party', Hayward said to Mary Hyde. She noted how he used clothes—his cummerbunds, waistcoats, needlepoint slippers, and checked summer suit—to divert attention from his infirmity. So, too, Eliot used City neutrality to distract attention from his extreme antipathy to the paganism of the age. These were his antinomies of night and day. John, like Mary, helped to create Eliot's daily life; neither approached the Eliot of the night who slept under a large crucifix (rescued by Mary from a devastated town in Germany), and whose reconstructive mission was briefly revealed when he chose the alias of Nehemiah, the rebuilder of Jerusalem. This identity he declared on the phone to Mary during one of his stays at the London Clinic, where he wished to remain incognito.

Eliot and Hayward had also the unspoken link of covert suffering: not only the obvious suffering of Hayward's body and Eliot's penitence but the strain of protracted celibacy. Hayward was paralysed from the waist down; Eliot had willed his own freezing since 1940 when he described how the 'chill ascends from the feet to knees'. Neither was a natural celibate. Hayward's torment was that desire remained alive, and he was brave enough to express openly his attraction to women. At one party, when Caitlin Thomas (wife of Dylan) asked if he would lick the ice-cream off her arm, he said he would lick it off any part of her body but not in so public a place. Graham Greene, who shared erotica with him, said that he had a strong appreciation of physical love. Hayward's frustration is easier to understand than Eliot's denial of a physicality that was, to him, unclean. Though he felt crippled in the late forties when he made the decision not to marry Emily Hale, his renewal ten years later suggests that this was a phase, consequent perhaps on his guilt for the broken lives of two women. 'Atonement' was the watchword of this time. Taken off-guard one night by a visit from the story-writer Julia Strachey (niece of Lytton), he appeared in his dressing-gown looking, she said, weird, ghostly, Strindbergian.

Despite all that they shared, there was a huge temperamental divide between Eliot and Hayward, epitomized by their rooms. Hayward's had soft green walls, a green bookcase and bed, invitations on the mantelpiece, and a wide window where he sat, back to the room, looking out at the *comédie humaine* enacted on a single bench on the Chelsea Embankment. He often asked Kathleen Raine to pull it more into his view after she left. In contrast, Eliot chose two small dark rooms at the back of the flat, looking down into the well of the building. There he lived the introspective life of a solitary, like Jeremiah in the pit or St John of the Cross in the dark prison. There, under the crucifix, he observed strict religious rules, some given, some of his own devising. He memorized passages from the Bible, said the rosary every night, and kept the fasts. During Lent he denied himself gin, and limited his favourite game of patience to one pack. Hayward thought that behind the closed door he played innumerable games of patience. It was a convenient and suggestive alibi. His life was as emblematic

as a tale by Hawthorne: the closed door; the dark well; the game of
patience—or was it endurance of the dark night of the soul? Their
first housekeeper, a young Irishwoman who soon left to be
married, refused to believe that Eliot was a distinguished writer. It
was Hayward sitting at his desk who was 'the writing man'. Eliot,
she insisted, was 'a holy man'.

Writing of the 'neutrality' of St John of the Cross, Thomas
Merton said that, at its height, the holy life does not impose itself
on the attention of others. If Eliot was invisible it was not because
he delighted merely in the sophisticated game of masks. This is
where critics often misunderstood him, and still do. At his highest
reach, his aim was the invisibility that guards a life of devotion. He
contemplated the virtue of unremarked devotion in particular
in 1952–3 while he wrote *The Confidential Clerk*. The retired
Eggerson, a clerk entirely without charisma—some would say
entirely without interest—is a 'confidential clerk' in the sense that
he is, really, a divine agent.

In 1955 Eliot pretended to Mary Trevelyan that he would like to
change his name; he would become obscure again as Bonsir or as
Goodchild. Alternatively, he might turn out to be Badboy. And so,
behind the studied neutrality of the arbiter of the literary world,
this allegorical drama, touched with faint, Hawthornian mockery,
went on. Bonsir was another alias thought up at the London Clinic.
Eliot was inordinately happy there, Mary observed, and it
occurred to her that he was malingering. But in the inaccessible
privacy of the clinic he was dreaming up new identities. The
obscure Bonsir was the other face of Nehemiah. 'Bonsir
Nehemiah' he announced on the phone.

Eventually, in 1955, Eliot came to regard Bonsir as Mary's adoptive
nephew. The third and longest phase of their friendship began in
1949, when she returned from the East to work for London
University as its first Advisor to Overseas Students. Both her flat
in Brunswick Square and her office were a few minutes walk from
Eliot's office in Russell Square, and they began to meet more
frequently than before her departure. He used to sing snatches of
American songs: 'Say gal, I'm certainly glad to know you . . .' or
'Come on my Houseboat with me . . .' Apprehensive of strangers,
Eliot held Mary's reassuring hand all through a conversation with

the Vice-Chancellor of London University after he was given an honorary degree in 1949. In parting also, he would hold her hand for a long time, even though they were to see each other quite soon. She thought it a sign of growing attachment but, more likely, he was grasping a new lifeline after his rejection of Emily Hale.

Unlike Emily, Mary Trevelyan was always visible as Eliot's escort. Their friendship went through three distinct phases: the testing phase, the wartime and post-war correspondence, and now a long phase with Mary in pursuit and Eliot backing away but increasingly dependent on her as Guardian. His dependence gave her the illusion of control which was compounded by his unwillingness to be explicit about his feelings. Marriage, he did eventually make clear, was out of the question. Instead, he devised a relationship in which he had some of the benefits of a wife—caring, companionship, the domestic pleasure of long Sunday evenings with eggs and bacon, followed by records, at Mary's flat—yet kept himself free of obligation. Tactfully, he warded off her two proposals of marriage.

Eliot worried about the frequency of their meetings and phone-calls, and periodically tried to counteract it with his rules. But frequency crept back, and established a hundred small traditions over the years, a net of habit in which he felt comfortable. There were the casual suppers on Sundays, the drives before or after church, and the notes on Mary's car, simply to say 'Goodmorning'. Once, he leapt unexpectedly into her car as she stopped at a traffic light. Mary drove him to his appointments—soothing his nerves *en route*—or deposited him on time at the station when he left on vacations which she had planned for him. In return, he plied her with gifts, including a new car.

Mary's abundant activity complemented Eliot's arrangements with John Hayward. Together, these two practical, decisive people preserved the outer structure of Eliot's life from 1949 to the beginning of 1957. Once, when Mary suggested to John that further help was needed, John replied that there was no one else: they were Eliot's sole close friends. John welcomed Mary's co-operation. In April 1950, at a party with the Shereks, the Martin Brownes, and the Kenneth Clarks at the Savoy after the London opening of *The Cocktail Party*, John, affable in his flowered waistcoat, said to Mary: 'I look on you as part of the family.'

It was an odd family: a paralysed man with a barbed tongue, an

alert and generous spinster, and a hermit doing penance in his back
room, his health flagging as he forced himself to go through with
public duties. It was, all of it, duty, Eliot told Mary. Nothing,
certainly not the fourteenth honorary degree, gave him the
slightest pleasure. Just plain nonsense, she thought in her brisk,
slightly impervious way, but he spoke the truth.

In 1949 Mary began to record her times with him. 'I set myself
this task', she wrote, 'because I have an unreliable memory and it
seemed a waste to have so close a friendship with our greatest
living poet and not to record some of his conversation.' She wrote
immediately after seeing him. The random form of a diary,
recording week-to-week events, is counterbalanced by Mary's
fixity of focus: it is always Eliot before her eyes, once looking
pitifully old as she sees him from a distance trying to pick up his
walking-stick on Chelsea Bridge; always Eliot's voice interrupting
her when she holds the floor; and Eliot's singing, like an out-of-
tune bassoon, 'Swing Low, Sweet Chariot', on car journeys home.
Her diary looks at him consistently with the attentiveness of a
woman in love with her subject but unable to fathom him. She was
astonished by the odd furious letter, accusing her of impertinence.
Her fairly controlled explosions of exasperation ('Poets!') and her
surprise at his tendency to 'disappear' after their good times, see so
far and no further: 'he seemed to take fright and going away was his
instinctive defence.' She was so much the social being that she had
no understanding of the solitary. An oblivion to his inner life goes
hand-in-hand with her observation of his switches from a sunny
face to what she calls a refugee face. It was a refugee who met her
proposals.

Two years after Vivienne's death, Mary hoped that Eliot would
be ready to settle their relationship: she wanted to know where she
stood. Her words were plain, practical, unromantic: she called
marriage a 'working arrangement'. The moderate expectation was,
of course, the opposite of Eliot's notion of heavenly love, and it
was inconceivable for him to think of her in that way.

He replied on 27 April 1949 that the thought of sharing his life
with anyone was a nightmare. He explained this by mysterious
reference to a tragedy which Mary naturally took to mean
Vivienne but which, as Eliot was to explain a year later, meant
what had happened to him and Emily Hale. For the next year she
nursed a hope that Eliot would recover, and on 29 May 1950 she

proposed again. This time it was a case of love's blindness to Eliot's unmistakable signals of withdrawal.

'Will you be looking in this week?' Mary asked on 26 March, on their way home from church.

'Not unless it's really necessary', Eliot replied.

'It's not at all necessary', said Mary shortly, and there was a pause while he got out of the car. Then he turned, contrite.

'I *would* like to come round this week and hear some music if it is possible.' That evening he brought Mary many presents.

A week later he remarked: 'I never see ANYONE for pleasure.' Mary didn't believe it.

'You're an unusual friend', she said guardedly.

'And in the end, unsatisfactory', he warned.

Mary mistook Eliot's need to be safe from molestation as a plea for more protection. She saw the same plea in his uneasy loneliness at receptions, and in his fears of falling ill, alone, as he grew old. Once again, she offered marriage as a practical solution—to her own loneliness as well as his, she ventured to say.

This time, in his reply of 2 June, Eliot took pains to make his position clear. He was driven to expose to Mary, as to no one else, what he called the most agonizing experience of his life. Concealing only Emily Hale's name, he said that he had been in love with someone else for a great many years, and that it would be too simple to say that love had faded. It was much more than that, more than he could find words to express. He had never wanted to marry anyone but this one woman. His failure to fulfil the promise of this love was felt to be an index of the state of his soul: physical exhaustion was a sign of a profounder spiritual depletion, perhaps a sense that forgiveness had not come and might never come. He told Mary, in conclusion, that there remained a pain that gnawed at his liver, and which he expected to go on till his death.

She responded to this confession with ready sympathy. She saw Eliot not as a hermit tormented by his dream of divine love but, in her more prosaic way, as a man in a prison largely of his own making. On 5 June they had a talk which, she hoped, opened the prison a chink. She assured Eliot that what he had told her would make no difference to feelings for him which could not be killed. Poor Mary needed this relief of expression, but, rather deftly, Eliot deflected her back from the role of lover to her customary one of guardian. Again, Mary misunderstood. Still hopeful, she thought that Eliot's toast to The Guardians referred to the future guardians of their relationship.

Eliot's romantic loyalty to the memory of his bond with Emily Hale could only enhance Mary's respect. He was a man capable of a great love. In the light of this, she could understand his not wanting her, or anyone, to share his life. Did he shrink from inflicting pain on her, with the consoling half-truth that he no longer enjoyed his love's company, so that, by implication, Mary was, in present day-to-day terms, first in his life? It was reasonable for him to believe, in his depleted state in 1950, that he would never again wish to marry, and he did wish to retain Mary's friendship. He could not deprive himself of the help that supported his bouts of nerves, the jollity that cheered his gloom.

Soon after the exchange, on 23 July, Mary heard that Eliot was to give lunch to an American, Miss Emily Hale. Mary jumped to the fact that this was 'THE lady'. Eliot appeared gloomy at the prospect, and Mary was not at all cast down. He had the imaginative power to project his policies on others so that, in general, they accepted them, as Mary accepted the limitations of a demanding friendship. But there were occasional crises when his powers of projection met with resistance or dismay. Vivienne's protracted refusal to be dismissed became a nightmare; Emily Hale's confidence that he still wished to marry her, and, failing that, her continued faithfulness became an embarrassment. A man, Eliot told Mary, doesn't like to be made to feel *guilty*.

Mary's proposals must have changed the friendship. The memoir does not acknowledge this, but it does show Eliot's increasing irritability from 1950. Mary was too sturdy to take this personally and, on the face of it, their habits resumed as though nothing had happened: the dinners, the drives, and the anxious confabs about such subjects as the see of London. Eliot might say, 'you always expect the worst and you are always right'. With Mary he could be mildly indiscreet about his 'mediocre' contemporaries. Shaw was 'a mischievous child'; F. R. Leavis was 'disgruntled and sneering', resentful that when the *Criterion* was in its heyday Eliot had not supported his magazine, *Scrutiny*. Pound was perhaps 'never really sane. Oh yes, as a young man I swallowed him whole. . . . I think he has become gradually, increasingly, insane through a long period of years. He only liked *good* poets and had no compassion for, or interest in anyone else. He could never laugh at himself—nor could he be laughed at—he has always been egocentric.' He thought that the best English poet was Edwin Muir (Auden, whose greatness was undisputed, he no longer regarded as English). Day Lewis he thought mediocre, and also a mediocre adulterer. Edith Sitwell was too much of an exhibitionist, but he admired Marianne Moore: '*quite* outstanding and way above most of the men of her generation. She has invented a new idiom, hitherto unused.'

He also enjoyed mild indiscretions about the Church. He did not like the Christianity of C. S. Lewis, and the Pope, he told Mary, compared favourably with our dear Archbishop [Fisher] in being less like a headmaster. He even told her that when he made his confessions (three times a year) that there were limits to what he could say, and that he accepted lunch from his confessor as part of the penance.

Eliot seemed to find what lurked in his soul incommunicable outside poetry. Just once, on 22 January 1953, he let it out to Mary in a long fiery speech which she recorded with care:

I believe in hell, yes, I do. I live in constant fear of it myself. If there is a Heaven there must also be a Hell. But it's all *outside time* and therefore beyond our earthly comprehension. Yet I *know*, I have always known hell—it is in my bones. I don't believe this is common—perhaps I am abnormal.

A few months later, he said that his religious life was 'the *whole* of me, yet too many people think it is irrelevant'. Often their talks touched the borders of intimacy but rarely went further. Eliot would touch on Vivienne or reminisce about his childhood with elderly parents or describe his sister, Marian, whom now, in his loneliness, he felt to be his very flesh and blood. He recalled, too, his visit to London in 1911 and his time at Lloyds Bank.

Mary took him on nostalgia-drives to the *Waste Land* area of the City, past Lloyds, down King William Street, along Lower Thames Street, where in his lunch hours Eliot had visited St Magnus Martyr and watched the fishermen at the Billingsgate market, and from there they drove on to the Tower, and over Tower Bridge, with a great red sun sinking behind the cargo ships. Eliot, quoting Shelley, prowled the byways of the City. They once went to Moorgate to find Bunhill Fields, the cemetery, and they explored Islington and Canonbury. Driving to Putney, where Eliot liked to

pick out odd names on little shops, was a revival of the Eeldrop
explorations of the dingy-respectable South London suburbs of
Eliot's early years, and going back further, the *fin-de-siècle*
slumming in Paris in 1911 and in the Roxbury area of Boston in
1910. One drive took them past Crawford Mansions in Marylebone, the cage in which Eliot had lived with Vivienne, and another
to Victoria Grove, the home of the Mungojerrie and Rumpelteazer. But Eliot's favourite drive was in the purlieus of Padding-
ton, and his idea of a 'splendid exploration' in 1955 was to drive the
whole length of the Portobello Road, a world of 'fantasy'
compared with the respectable charms of Chelsea.

The equivalent treat on Saturday afternoons with John
Hayward and Christopher Sykes was to watch football games in a
winter drizzle in the Chelsea Hospital Gardens. The first time they
went it was a match between the Marylebone Dustmen and a team
from the Chelsea Municipal Maintenance with one spectator, a
melancholy old man raising his voice to chant, 'Come . . . on . . . the
. . . Maintenance!' This forlorn scene fascinated Eliot, and it
became a standard excursion.

His network of habits formed a cocoon for the invisible life that,
I imagine, stirred rather feebly between the need to atone and a
more insidious hollowness of heart which neither Mary nor John
could dispel. Mary, who saw its symptom—that there was almost
no one whom Eliot found himself able to like—was alarmed, at
times, at his air of weariness, and wary of sudden plunges into
moody darkness; but he never spoke to her about atonement. Shut
out, without really knowing why, she had moments of impatience
when she thought him evasive, even 'deceitful'. When he reasserted
his distance, she assumed it was the inexplicable aberration of a
great poet who was, at the same time, a 'silly old boy'.

Yet, for a long time, the cocoon of their habits remained, so
immediate and visible that Mary never imagined it could ever
become brittle. And for a long time Mary's cocoon did protect an
unhappy creature who had little hope of transformation. With
Mary he had not domestic happiness, but a semblance of domestic
stability. When they arrived at her flat (first in Brunswick Square,
later at 23 Embankment Gardens), Eliot would work the lift, take
in the milk, put his hat, coat, and umbrella in Mary's bedroom, and
cook supper with his sleeves rolled up. His help in the kitchen was
not altogether appreciated. Afterwards they would listen to

records: the *Coriolan* Overture; Beethoven's A minor quartet, op. 132 (which had inspired *Four Quartets*); and Eliot's favourite, the Mozart clarinet quintet ('I love the *economy* of Mozart', he said). He also enjoyed Haydn's trumpet concerto, Mozart's oboe quartet, and the slow opening crescendo of the second movement of Beethoven's seventh symphony.

They sometimes went to the theatre to see, say, Cicely Courtneidge in *Gay's the Word* in 1951, or in October 1952, Emlyn Williams as Dickens, starting off with the Veneerings and Podsnaps, and going on to Paul Dombey's death. Mary liked to be taken to dine at the Garrick Club, with its long table lit by candles and surrounded by Zoffany pictures. Otherwise they dined at the more anonymous Russell Hotel, the more expensive Écu de France, or with Margaret Rhondda and Theodora Bosanquet (who had been secretary to Henry James). Another habit was an annual visit to Windsor Castle, where they were entertained by Sir Owen Morshead, the King's Librarian.

All this time Mary saw to Eliot's comforts, advised, and worried over him. Should be take legal action over a 1952 article on his supposed homosexuality? 'After all, that does NOT happen to be my temperament', he said. How kind she was to bring him rhubarb and country eggs. The eggplant had made a nice pie. He had bought himself a new coat, exactly like the last. When he returned from his jaunts to America, he turned the pages of his appointment diary, recounting to Mary the events of every single day he had been away.

His dependence on her reached its height in the summer of 1954, when he broke his rule about separate vacations. He was taking his sister Marian to Farringford (once Tennyson's home, now a hotel) on the Isle of Wight. Uneasy about managing this alone, Eliot invited Mary (and her car) to join them. With alacrity she organized their days. She drove them to Osborne to see Queen Victoria's Durbar Hall and State Apartments, and after tea she and Eliot climbed Tennyson's Down to look at the Needles. They walked two miles, and on the way back picked wild flowers and lay on the grass on the top of the down (not too near the edge, in deference to Eliot's fear of heights). A heavy sea mist descended, so they climbed down again, and walked through the fields to Freshwater Bay and along the beach. In the evening they ate in the huge hotel dining-room, with a portrait of the Poet Laureate and early portraits of Victoria and Albert, elderly couples speaking in whispers, and Eliot with his back carefully turned to the room. After dinner, Eliot taught her 'petunia', a variety of patience, his favourite game.

Mary was happy enough to discount the odd gloom. Marian admitted to Mary that her brother could be trying, and asked her not to leave him. She and the niece, Theodora, who had become Mary's friends, suggested that she might marry Eliot, but Mary told herself that she was too sensible to nourish this hope.

The next summer, Eliot, on vacation in Sussex, again summoned Mary for a weekend before she was to drive him back to London. Again, from Mary's point of view it was idyllic. On the way home, they drove past Julian and Juliette Huxley, ex-Director-General of UNESCO and his Swiss wife, whose patent curiosity left Mary with the complacent conviction that they had 'thought the worst'.

Mary's forthrightness made her relation to Eliot special in this period of fame. Even John of the barbed tongue was Eliot's devotee, and in any case, John's domestic base depended on Eliot, as well as some part of his prestige in literary circles. Mary alone of Eliot's friends mocked the *Notes Towards the Definition of Culture*, and, in February 1950, criticized the characters in Eliot's plays, as she recalled in her diary:

I suggested that his people are mere puppets, speaking what he wants them to speak—that they don't really come alive at all—and what often puzzles me is that although, in some ways, he seems to know so much about people, in other ways he seems quite blind—perhaps because he doesn't like them. ... Tom was interested ... and put up no defence except to say 'you mustn't want to know too much about people'.

He set a standard that cut off idle or destructive curiosity, but Mary detected also a limiting self-protection in the phase following the heights of the *Quartets*. If we compare Yeats or Virginia Woolf after the high flights of their maturity, the Byzantium poems or *The Waves*, there was in both a continued willingness to expose themselves to reciprocal knowing. Virginia Woolf's friendship with Ethel Smyth may have disrupted her privacy, but it did compel a new phase of outspokenness in the cause of women. Yeats, too, became more daring as he exposed the unlovely 'lust and rage' of an old man. Both could say 'What then?', and ride the crest of a new wave as it rolled across the immortal sea: their readiness was all. Eliot, in contrast, backed away from emotional risk. His withdrawal from Emily Hale in the summer of 1947 may be the biographical marker for a new degree of self-protection at the very time that he embarked on a mission that meant endless exposure to people. Did his self-protection work against the mission? Or did his remoteness actually enhance the status of judgements that came, it seemed, from above? Emerson who walked 'on stilts' was 'patient' of his remoteness, 'inasmuch as it makes my solitude dearer & the impersonal God is shed abroad in my heart more richly & more lowly welcome for this porcupine impossibility of contact with men'.

Eliot's American predecessors, Emerson, Whitman, and Pound, had prepared the platform posture of the poet who becomes the spokesman for cultural destiny. The American scholar, said Emerson, communicates principles born out of the private life, and in making those principles prevalent looks to 'the conversion of the world'. These Americans do not write literature in the European sense of the word: their rhetoric does not terminate in aesthetic forms, but in the conversion of the reader. Whitman called for a poet who could assume the status of Judgement: 'He judges not as the judge judges but as the sun falling around a helpless thing. As he sees the farthest he has the most faith.' The greatest poet, Eliot said in 1954, may not belong to his age 'not only by being behind or ahead of his age, but being above it'. Such a poet shares the problems of his age and the language in which the problems are discussed, but 'may repudiate all the current solutions'.

Eliot saw that the war had brought the sickness of civilization to a crisis without curing it: the sickness was raging everywhere. He saw the prospect of 'centuries of barbarism' which, in an interview in 1945, he related to the coming dominance of technology. His *Notes Towards the Definition of Culture* (begun in 1943 and published in 1948) rise to 'prophetic gloom' as he elaborates on a vision of a degraded society which will destroy 'our ancient edifices to make ready the ground upon which the barbarian nomads of the future will encamp in their mechanised caravans'.

Eliot's *Notes*, speeches, and comments repudiate all conventional efforts, political, international, and educational, as well as

Christian conferences which seemed futile. He sees the core of the
problem in the corruption of language, the basis of thought, which
is in turn, the basis of integrity. This he spelt out in a speech at Aix-
en-Provence on 6 December 1947. His target was those who use
words for base purposes, for their emotional effect upon themselves or upon an audience which suffers passions but does not
think. The profoundest effect, he warned in 'The Social Function
of Poetry', is that feelings become blunted: '. . . our own ability, not
merely to express, but even to feel any but the crudest emotions,
will degenerate.' The poet was the main bastion against this abuse:
without his preservation and renovation of the language, civilization will decline.

The *Notes* warn of a decline already visible in every department
of human activity, proceeding towards, he repeats, 'a period, of
some duration, of which it is possible to say that it will have *no*
culture'. In a letter to Duncan MacCarthy, he complained of films,
popular writers, Hemingway, newspapers, and the corruption of
the language arising from the progressive reduction of sensibility
to the decadent-barbaric. 'We live in an *impossible* age,' he
lamented to Mary, 'a world of thugs.' Most days he could not bring
himself to look at the newspaper until tea-time. He spoke of
Gomorrah and of Nineveh: our cities were wicked, doomed, like
those of the Bible. He took to praying in the Underground. It
might not be good for one's prayers, he told Mary, but one's
prayers might be good for the Underground.

Eliot's contempt for his age was fanned by his private horror. At
the time he began the *Notes*, back in the middle of the war, he
explained this to Mary Trevelyan. It was 1944, the flying bombs
were active, and they were discussing fear of death. Eliot said that
there was something else which he couldn't get to the bottom of,
'disgust, horror, physical nausea, the *nightmare* of evil'. As self-
styled Master of the Heresy Hounds he hunted evil, and now and
then identified it, privately, in a particular person—surprising
targets like Roger Fry, Lytton Strachey, and Charles Williams, all
of whom had been friends in earlier years.

As the voice and embodiment of Culture, Eliot addressed
audiences ostensibly about practical measures in a period of
reconstruction, but he spoke from a point of reference beyond his
time, against the worldly life in all times. In a wireless talk in 1946
he called for 'spiritual organization'. In April 1955, when asked to

give a luncheon talk to the Conservative Union, with Anthony
Eden in the chair, on the subject of literature and politics, he
planned to stump them with the question: 'What is man, that thou
are mindful of him?' Afterwards, he told Pound that he thought
Eden had not understood the talk, nor noticed an implied criticism
of himself.

Eliot's monumental judgements and warnings slide with quiet
unobtrusiveness into his social and literary criticism and his plays.
The tactic was to get an indifferent, largely atheist audience to take
in a moral message without realizing it. Reilly, who is more like a
priest than a psychiatrist, tells his patient:

> Half of the harm that is done in this world
> Is due to people who want to feel important.
> They don't mean to do harm—but the harm does not interest them.

This appears incidental to the cure of a disrupted marriage. In the
next interview, which will elicit the vocation of a potential saint,
Celia says apologetically:

> I don't hear any voices, I have no delusions—
> Except that the world I live in seems all a delusion!

Again, the judgement slides past as if it were an afterthought, as
Eliot later dropped the same passing thought into more than
13,000 minds in the Minnesota stadium: in the course of a fairly
routine lecture on literary criticism, he remarked that the pursuit
of normality is an adjustment to a 'deranged society', instead of to
the fundamental Order of Things.

To extract the sermon from plays and criticism is to realize that,
in this period, Eliot was a man with a mission, sent to warn of
'chaos', the last days of civilization. If he was remote between 1948
and 1956, there is the possibility that he had to be alone as a voice
crying in the wilderness. Auden saw that his *Notes Towards the
Definition of Culture* was not about society in the usual English
sense of the word: 'Whig? Tory? All flesh is grass. Culture? The
grass withereth.'* Eliot was speaking not in the political or critical
terms of his time but as 'a voice in Ramah weeping, that will not be
comforted'.†

---

* In Isaiah 40: 8 the grass is contrasted with the Word which shall last forever.

† The voice is that of Rachel who foresees the vision of Isaiah: her children's
children going into exile.

The prophets speak of doom, cast down by pervasive iniquity. Their style and message—the promise of renewal conditional on extended trial—has been central to American discourse from the New England divines down to their greatest descendant, Eliot. Where Christ offers being through his incarnation, the prophet has no being. The spirit is given through the Word, through language alone. Eliot took up this mantle in the forties and fifties when, repeatedly, he craves purity of language.

'In the year that King Uzziah died', Eliot began a plaintive rhyme in which Rumpuscat feels bad inside. The bathos looks back to Prufrock, who may have a hundred visions but feels insecure at a tea-party. It both conceals and reveals the poet's real point of reference, here the scene of Isaiah's verbal purification as part of his call *c.*740 BC. Isaiah laments that he is a man of 'unclean lips' who lives in the midst of a people of 'unclean lips'. Then a seraph takes a live coal from the altar,

And he laid it upon my mouth, and said, Lo, this hath touched thy lips; and thine iniquity is taken away, and thy sin purged.
Also I heard the voice of the LORD, saying, Whom shall I send, and who will go for us? Then said I, Here am I; send me.

This emissary offers himself not as a person but a channel for a message: he is to be God's instrument. This is how Eliot's Becket defined his vocation in his Christmas sermon. And this may be the closest we can get to the mission that lies behind the studied neutrality of Eliot's appearance. The unassuming demeanour, the quiet manner, the measured, deadpan voice were designed to outlive personality.

To address a whole society, Eliot had to relinquish his richest poetic material, the private agony. At every earlier stage in his career the private character resonates through the poetry, and it does reappear unmistakably in 1958 in Eliot's final play. But in the forties and early fifties he took up a task that went against the grain of his searching genius. He relinquished the outposts of experience, sublimity and degradation. The sinner, central to the earlier plays, disappears; the saint moves to one side; and the main action sorts out a middle-class marriage of no great promise. Following this course even further in *The Confidential Clerk*, Eliot turns to business people of relentless banality.

The elect amongst them is the retired clerk, Eggerson, whose obscure good life is symbolized by the suburban garden where he grows vegetables for 'Mrs. E'. Eggerson is a believable person—he was based on a real-life clerk, a Mr McKnight who had been Eliot's first colleague at Lloyds Bank—but because Eggerson's language is locked in contented cliché, there is no chance of expressive depth. Eggerson is mentor to his successor, young Colby Simpkins, a second-rate organist who has turned businessman under the aegis of his presumed father, the financier, Sir Claude. In the course of the play it is revealed that Colby is an orphan, and is therefore free to devote himself to the organ in Eggerson's parish church, and eventually, to take orders.

Eggerson is the fixed point of secure identity in a play in which the other characters seek their true selves: the financier turns out to be a frustrated potter; his bossy, classy wife, Lady Elizabeth, turns out to be—marginally—less foolish than she at first appears; his illegitimate daughter, Lucasta, turns out to be—marginally—less flighty than the female role she adopts. Salvation for these routine types is limited to dim perceptions of the fact that they have assumed 'unreal' modes of existence. In his youth, Eliot had satirized the collector of porcelain (Mr Silvero) and the bogus medium (Madame Sosostris). As late as *Four Quartets*, he ridiculed the devotees of pentagrams, tea-leaves, and psychoanalysis, the pastimes of the lost. Now, striving for charity, Eliot acknowledges that Lady Elizabeth's woolly obsession with *The Light from the East* and Sir Claude's collection of pottery are their only possible substitutes for religion.

Art, Eliot allows, can lead us to a passionate identification with a maker of forms, the likeliest approach for the secular mind to the Maker. In Colby's rare case, art—organ music—will take him further, into religious commitment, but for Sir Claude, the prototype of worldliness, art will provide only an intermittent 'escape' from his life of 'make-believe'—though, since he is not creative, the escape is itself, he owns, only another mode of make-believe. For the women in the play there is not even this escape: their salvation, if we can call it that, lies in assent to motherhood and marriage, the family structure that provides a minimal bedrock of order for the secular life.

To hold an audience it is essential to reflect it. Yet there are times when Eliot bends over too far, when he sees us, his audience, as more vulgar, obtuse, and soulless than we in fact are. In earlier

plays, in *Sweeney Agonistes* as in *The Family Reunion*, Eliot had
subjected his audience to a brutal jolt from the social round into
horrific awakenings to unknown modes of being. *The Confidential
Clerk* kindly protects us from such useless disturbance. The elect
slide smoothly into their secret suburban rites, and have nothing to
communicate beyond obedience to a given destiny. The audience is
cheered along by heavy, now-dated farce.

Many students prefer to end their consideration of Eliot's career
with *Four Quartets*. The present consensus is that his work
declined from that point. The odds would seem to have been
against his mission to speak to a vast public and yet it succeeded,
and to a degree not diminished by the tedium of certain speeches
nor the flaws of certain plays. Eliot's achievement in this phase
cannot properly be judged in aesthetic terms, and this may be the
very secret of his mass appeal. For his pronouncements attained,
both in his lifetime and no less since his death, an authority that
has been received with awe. How this absolute and enduring
authority came to be, in so cynical a century, is still a mystery. It is
backed but not explained by mere fame. He was a figure on a
platform, a voice on the wireless, a presence that made itself felt as
a standard of judgement which looked beyond its time.

After the second world war came a second wave of cultural
despair, less fertile in its literature than the first which took its rise
in the works of Flaubert, the French Symbolists, the later Dickens,
and Conrad, and reached its crest after the first world war in *The
Waste Land*. The second wave seems more predictable. Below the
froth of its black humour is the jaded automatism of received
opinion. In 1958 Eliot spoke of the monotony of nihilism which
can't be kept up indefinitely: 'Nihilism itself becomes boredom.'
The fresh voices are those whose contempt for the times, however
deep, has not been a blanket response: the stories of Flannery
O'Connor, the poetry of Stevie Smith, the ambitious detective
novels of P. D. James are diagnostic but, like the first-wave writers,
they can project minds of moral and emotional substance through
whom some encouraging form of civilization does raise its head
out of the morass of pessimism.

Eliot's comedies are not without redeeming characters, Celia
and Colby, but they are not allowed to display their strength. They

recoil from society and business worlds into pure, private vocations: Celia joins an austere nursing order, and goes off to the wilds of the East; Colby will disappear into a dim future beyond our understanding. We are not permitted to follow them, as Sylvia Plath, say, tugs us with her into the pure trajectory of her drive into the red Eye of the morning. Eliot turns us firmly to face what his great souls reject. As he sees it, the 'indomitable spirit of mediocrity' is our destiny, and our only relief from nihilism is to make the best of a bad job. The platitudes are still implied: the poverty of our marriages, the superficiality of our social exchanges, are platitudes only dimly felt through what may seem the thickening carapace of the playwright.

Helen Gardner predicted in 1965 that Eliot's comedies would come back into fashion after a few more decades. It is true that, in time, the drawing-room manners and clichés of the late forties and early fifties will take on a period quaintness. But if there is enduring substance in these two plays, it lurks perhaps in places where Eliot slides in lines which his contemporary audience is not expected to grasp. At certain points, characters speak, beyond the audience, what Eliot called '*transparent*' words. When the psychiatrist refers to his 'sanatorium' he remarks—as though it were an aside—that it is not for ordinary people but for potential saints (a monastery or a place like Kelham where Eliot went on retreats). 'You will forget this phrase', the psychiatrist goes on to Edward Chamberlayne, the ordinary patient, 'And in forgetting it will alter the condition'. He defies the West End or Broadway audience to conceive of the transformation of saints. Nor can he himself quite follow Celia through her destiny: all he knows is that her eventual martyrdom is a triumph.

The opening of the play is even more mystifying:

> ALEX. You've missed the point completely, Julia:
> There *were* no tigers. *That* was the point.

Our task is, once again, to play Watson. Directed by the all-knowing Holmes, we must do our blundering best to solve the mystery. Julia drives this challenge home later in the first scene when she says 'There's altogether too much mystery / About this place to-day'. Eliot's first plays were all mysteries of sorts. In *Murder in the Cathedral* there is the spurious question of who is responsible for the death of the Archbishop, and in *The Family*

Reunion, the question of whether Harry killed his wife. In *The Cocktail Party* there is the mystery to which Julia refers, the strange disappearance of a woman who had invited her friends to a party. But all these mysteries are blinds (rather like the pat conclusions that Hawthorne dealt out to the despised gift-book readers of his enigmatic tales), sops to an audience incapable of divining the true mystery which is the recess of consciousness: the haunted men of the first plays; the hidden destinies of *The Cocktail Party*. These are interior mysteries, hard to stage, hard to voice (and, perhaps, like James, better suited to the more intimate medium of television than to the theatre).

'You've missed the point completely . . .' We are told this before the drama has even begun. We Watsons are bound to miss the point—unless we have read 'Gerontion', and know that the tiger is Eliot's symbol for revelation ('Came Christ the tiger'). So the fact that there *were* no tigers is the opening premiss for a new interior drama: how does one live without revelation? The lines recall Holmes's insistence on the dog in the night. 'The dog did nothing in the night-time', protests a mystified inspector. That, Holmes replies, was the point.

Eliot starts without hope that the chit-chat of the cocktail hour can accommodate the coming of Christ or the immortal hand that framed the Tyger in the forests of the night. At the very outset of his intercourse with the worldly audience of the commercial theatre, he shuns the world. As he invites our attention, his teasing obscurity shuts us out from the only mystery that really matters: the meaning of existence under clouds of unknowing.

Eliot spoke most forcefully beyond the audience of his age when, in 1944, he isolated a new menace: a provincialism not of space but of time. All the peoples of the globe can be provincials together in so far as they are preoccupied with the issues of their newspapers in a way that blocks out the timeless questions of existence. Eliot seems to be muttering to himself alone when he adds: 'Those who are not content to be provincials, can only become hermits.'

Provincialism was an issue throughout Eliot's critical prose from the time that he published 'The Three Provincialities' in 1922. For Eliot, provincialism was not simply a justification for leaving America, as it was for Henry James. 'Provinciality of point of view is a vice', he asserted as early as 1918, and repeated, 'a positive literary vice', in Dublin in 1936. Writers must 'disturb the provincialism of their particular place and time'. His models were Babbitt and P. E. More, who were 'emancipated' from the prejudices of place and time, and above all Dante, the 'least provincial' of poets. Dante's universality of content and precision of language crossed national boundaries with greater ease than any other writer. This is the rationale behind Eliot's international frame of reference. To be too nationalistic, he said at the time *The Waste Land* came out, is to become 'insupportable to posterity'.

Dante, Eliot said, was the most *'European'* of writers, and this was his own insistent image. This might appear a simple repudiation of America, but for Eliot the notion of the 'European' was not a matter of locale but a state of mind that overpassed all frontiers. It actually had a native connotation which he explained in his 1918 essay, 'In Memory of Henry James': 'It is the final perfection, the consummation of an American to become, not an Englishman, but a European—something which no born European, no person of any European nationality, can become.' The benefit of transplantation was to gain a sense of the uniformity of human nature, as well as its superficial local variations. It was also to have a horizon beyond St Louis, Boston, or London. Wherever Eliot stood, part of him was not there—he had something in reserve. His self-imposed distance from home, his detachment, took on the authority of a Modernist position, but this was not an end in itself because he was also detached in time. From that vantage point he saw a biblical plot: the recurrent destruction of a corrupt society. His private horror—'the *nightmare* of evil'—was like that of the prophets for whom, alone in their time, 'history had meaning'. His other model was Aeneas, whom he saw as the prototype of Christian pilgrim: his crossing from one culture to another had its real meaning as an act of obedience to the timeless gods. He is obedient to the destiny they impose. 'For he is, humbly, a man with a mission; and the mission is everything.'

In summing up the careers of Aeneas, Pascal, and Dante, Eliot looks back on his own: the personal import is there in unobtrusive asides. This retrospective note sounds more often and with increasing authority in later talks, where Eliot lays down his guidelines for posterity. He said that his best criticism was a by-product of his private poetry workshop. In essays on the writers who influenced him—Dante (1920, 1929, and 1950), Baudelaire

(1930), Pascal (1931), and Virgil (1944 and 1951)—as well as in more general guides—'Poetry and Drama' (1951), 'The Three Voices of Poetry' (1953), 'The Frontiers of Criticism' (1956), and 'To Criticize the Critic' (1961)—Eliot suggests how we might read and assess his work. The later criticism was dismissive of the popular theoretical doctrines of his early years: 'impersonality', 'objective correlative', and a regrettable 'dissociation of sensibility'. A hundred years on, he predicts, these phrases will survive only as curiosities of the mind of his age. The same goes for the literary tradition which he made fashionable in his time—the upgrading of the Metaphysicals and wits, the downgrading of Milton: all this, he admits, was a matter of subjective feeling. Eliot's public quibbles with Milton on rhetorical grounds obscured his indebtedness (in *Sweeney Agonistes* and *East Coker*) to the great predecessor whose dramatic account of the dark trial of the soul was unsurpassable, who could speak the Word with eloquent ease, and whose story of the beginning of all creation was on a grander scale than Eliot's more personal beginning in East Coker.

'I'm surprised we were allowed *Milton* this afternoon', Dylan Thomas said to Eliot after a poetry reading. 'I thought he was dead.' Eliot at once put the blame on Leavis, but it no longer matters. Already, a quarter-century after Eliot's death, his Who's Who of literary importance is out of date.

In 1929 Eliot wrote E. M. Forster a remarkably honest letter acknowledging the element of 'bluff' in his early critical strategies. Forster had been right, of course, in guessing that there were private motives underlying the doctrine of 'impersonality'; nor was it more true as a doctrine, though on the other hand no more false, than its opposite. In his early essays Eliot aimed for an 'icy inviolability' and strict doctrine as an antidote to the sloppy impressionism of his critical predecessors who had engaged in 'that parlour game, the Polite Essay—which consists in taking a tiny point and cutting figure-eights around it'. With biting irony and swift reversals or refinements of statement, Eliot forged a disembodied voice of one 'called to the seat of judgement'. The effect was oracular; as Trilling put it, 'not I but the wind, the spirit, uttered these words'. Eliot canonized and excommunicated at will, until he came to be called 'the Pope of Russell Square'.

How did the English come to accept Eliot as supreme critical authority? Possibly the success of his influence, and the failure of

Pound's, lay not in their message, which was similar, but in Eliot's tone, which became more English than that of the English. The turning point came in 1920, when Richard Aldington introduced Eliot to Bruce Richmond, editor of the *Times Literary Supplement* from 1902–37. Eliot said that Richmond taught him to edit out 'unseemly violence', and to write in a temperate, impartial way. The precise Englishness, though, seems to me more the style of self-deprecation with its clever deployment of 'merely': 'I merely want to say ...' I am not making any particular claims, he told his audiences in his soothing way—and so they accepted everything he said. They may even have enjoyed their bafflement. Scholars certainly relished the futile source-hunting that Eliot's notes to *The Waste Land* invited. It was only decades later that Eliot declared at Minnesota that this sort of academic exercise was a waste of time unless it was secondary to 'understanding'. He confided to Helen Gardner that hers was the only criticism of his work that he could recommend to anybody. He had a thicket of reservations about Matthiessen's book and (he repeated) the kind of criticism that goes hunting for recondite sources.

Eliot also criticized the 'lemon-squeezer' approach of close critical analysis. He thought that readers might take in a little information, but should basically be left alone with a poem. His later essays undercut the neat categories of academe. In 'Yeats' (1940) he made it clear that a poem is neither wholly personal nor wholly impersonal, but transmutes the life of the writer into art. Nor is a poem 'open' or 'closed' in the current jargon: 'The fact that a poem can mean different things to different persons ... must, however paradoxically, be reconciled with the assertion that it has an absolute and unalterable meaning.'

Eliot's early essays set the fashion for the rest of the century that elegant writing should be ironic and detached, and, partly for this reason, these essays are the most famous. It may be, though, that Eliot's later, less ironic criticism is a portent of a time yet to come, when we shall tire of irony, and welcome, instead, some fresh breath of feeling. In Eliot's later essays he repeatedly owns to feeling as the source of his ideas.

The critical generalizations of the later essays give five guidelines to his career. First, they acknowledge the personal basis of art. In 1940, explaining the superiority of Yeats's later work by 'the greater expression of personality' in it, he found it necessary to revise his early doctrine of the impersonality of art. What he now understood by 'impersonality' was that of a poet 'who, out of intense and personal experience, is able to express a general truth; retaining all the particularity of his experience, to make of it a general symbol'.* In the fifties he became even more explicit: 'A poet may believe that he is expressing only his private experience; his lines may be for him only a means of talking about himself without giving himself away; yet for his readers what he has written may come to be the expression both of their own secret feelings and of the exultation or despair of a generation.'

What begins to emerge here is a poet preoccupied with self who, as it were by accident, intersects with his age. This may be less arbitrary than Eliot implies: his scenes—from urban bedsits to the country house—appear to reflect a range of the lives of his day, but for the poet they are part of his interior landscape, emblems of vice or unreality projected from his inner world of nightmare. His art of omission protects us from the full glare of its intolerable revelation: that every scene, every person—with the exceptions of the Lady of silences and the saints in the making—is worthless *sub specie aeternitatis*, and that we, his audience, are part of the 'deranged' world of our time. That is perhaps why Eliot shuts us out. His attention to his society is laboured because it is peripheral to his attention to the self and the permanent Order of Things. As a graduate student, and for the rest of his creative life, Eliot pursued an elusive sense that he was, in the words of his Harvard dissertation, 'the adjective of some transcendental self'.

Another critical guideline is Eliot's repeated insistence on the coherent career. He spoke of the capacity of a great poet to suffuse a body of work with a significant thought, as Wordsworth did: 'there is something integral about such greatness'. The unity in variety came from this 'inner compulsion'. The sense of the unity of his own career became stronger with age as he came to value 'a consistent view of life' that comes with the 'maturing of the man

---

* Eliot expounds the same idea in 'A Note on War Poetry':

> Where is the point at which the merely individual
> Explosion breaks
>
> In the path of an action merely typical
> To create the universal, originate a symbol
> Out of the impact? This is a meeting
> On which we attend. . . .

as a whole, the development and co-ordination of his various emotions'. Eliot may have feared that posterity would divide his career, and plump for the early years, ignoring the new life and the later drama. He insists that one can grasp no one work or phase without seeing it in the whole pattern formed by the sequence of works, so that the full meaning of any one of Eliot's works is not in itself alone, but in that work in the order in which it was written.

A third guideline, perhaps the least noticed, is his declaration in 1959 that his poetry came from America. This has been ignored because of the prestige of Eliot's internationalism, and understandable ignorance of the American implications of his stance as 'European'. Only Edmund Wilson, reviewing *Poems 1909-1925*, perceived at that time that Eliot's 'real significance is less that of a prophet of European disintegration than of a poet of the American Puritan temperament'. He went on to align Eliot with Marcher, Strether, and the Hawthorne of the Notebooks. Eliot himself provides a further clue to these affinities when he finds in James and Hawthorne a distinctive sense of the past. For them, as for Eliot, the present becomes pressing just as the past dominates with its ghostly presences. Eliot wrote this in 1918: it foretells the visitations of the hyacinth girl, the ghosts of the rose-garden, the Furies, and, still to come, the guilty past of the Elder Statesman. The settings are English, but the disturbed and haunted sense of the past is, by inference, American.

In 'American Literature and the American Language' (1953), Eliot recalled the early stimulus of what a man said 'long ago or in another language' which 'corresponds' to what he wanted to say. He had found remote models safer because they could not be copied. He had looked to Laforgue for *vers libre* rather than to Whitman, and to Baudelaire for psychic decadence rather than to Poe, Baudelaire's source of inspiration. So, too, he had looked to Dante for the extremities of 'depravity's despair' and 'the beatific vision', instead of to his own Puritan heritage, or to the attractions of the Jansenism of Pascal which, as Eliot had described it, was 'morally a Puritan movement within the Church', whose 'standards of conduct were at least as severe' as the Puritanism of his own American ancestors. At the end of his life, Eliot said that he had been profoundly influenced by the style of F. H. Bradley, the English idealist philosopher on whom Eliot wrote his dissertation, yet in an obscure piece of 1924 we find that Bradley's style

corresponds, for Eliot, to that of Henry James, whose prose
pulsates with the agony of the spiritual life. Bradley believed that
what we really observe are fragments of a greater Reality: this idea,
central to Eliot's poetry, corresponds to the Transcendentalism of
Emerson, who wrote that 'fractions are worth more to me because
corresponding fractions are waiting . . . that shall be made integers
by their addition'.

Who were Eliot's true models? Was there a native tradition?
Auden once remarked that no genuine European could have made
Eliot's celebrated statement that tradition is not inherited but
acquired by great labour. It has been assumed that Eliot's acquired
tradition is to be found in the historical or literary parallels by
which he attempted to universalize private states of mind. But is
there an inherited tradition none the less, obscured by the international frame of reference? Did his American forebears, the many
New England divines, or Judge Blood who made himself con-
spicuous in the punishment of witches, leave no residue?
Hawthorne was prepared to recognize that 'strong traits of their
[Puritan] nature have intertwined themselves with mine'. The
obsessive introspection of the Revd Arthur Dimmesdale in *The
Scarlet Letter* seems to prefigure something of Eliot's temperament,
the insistent agonizing of a sinner of high spiritual gifts, gazing
absorbed into the mirror of election with its associated dangers of
pride and despair:

To the high mountain peaks of faith and sanctity he would have climbed,
had not the tendency been thwarted by the burden, whatever it might be,
of crime or anguish, beneath which it was his doom to totter. It kept him
down, on a level with the lowest; him, the man of ethereal attributes . . .

Yet it is this same secret burden that gives to the minister the
power to move others through his persuasive eloquence.

The American aspect of Eliot is still neglected, but the dominant
forms of American writing, soul history and sermon, give a curious
backing to Eliot's impenetrability. He shares with Emerson,
Thoreau, Whitman, and Dickinson a guarded mode of confession.
Unlike St Augustine or Rousseau, who draw us into intimacy,
these Americans throw the onus of introspection back into the lap
of the reader. Their confessions, like *The Waste Land*, are fragmen-
tary, and, left so deliberately incomplete, demand a reciprocal
effort. The point lies not in their content so much as in the act of

self-discovery and judgement. Its ultimate purpose is not to expose
the speaker but to create the reader. In short, it is a form of sermon:
a call to the new life.

Early on, in 'The Three Provincialities', Eliot believed that
Americans had not produced works of the calibre of the best
European writers: the measure was Shakespeare and Dante. The
high-flown allusion, developed in the quatrain poems written in
1917–19 at Pound's direction, was a strategy that placed him at
once in the international league. Yet Pound himself noted the
correspondence between sophisticated and native traditions. The
quatrain form could be said to derive from Théophile Gautier's
Emaux et Camées (1852), but it also came, Pound said, from the Bay
State Hymn Book of the colonial settlers of Massachusetts.

There is another, less obvious, motive for Eliot's use of the
prestigious parallel. He was a loner in the American tradition of
cranky loners. He wished to express feelings that were savage and
strange, like the mystical hatred that is close to madness. He was
determined to expose readers to feelings they had not experienced
before. He said that the difference between a mad and an effective
writer is that the former has feelings which are unique but cannot
be shared, and are therefore useless, while the latter discovers new
variations of feelings which can be appropriated by others. Eliot
used the classic parallel to point acceptability, to claim a semblance
of normality, though he often twisted allusions to accommodate
an inertia and horror of his own. Only very occasionally did he
discover an exact equation in another writer. This is why he was
unusually reluctant to let go, at Pound's insistence, 'The horror!
the horror!' from *Heart of Darkness* as his preferred epigraph to
The Waste Land. In such rare cases of equation he does not twist
the allusion for his usual comic effects—and this is where Eliot may
be found: with the unholy loves of St Augustine's youth ('To
Carthage then I came . . .'); with Arnaut Daniel in Dante's refining
fire, purging the sin of lust; and yearning towards the scriptures'
promise of the peace that passeth understanding. These allusions
helped to preserve Eliot's sanity as they established the legitimacy
of his message. His appeal to tradition was another master-stroke
of his early years, for under its cloak he could deviate from the
norms of feeling and, at the same time, establish states of being that
might otherwise appear too rarefied or misanthropic.

Eliot's fourth critical guideline is to confound the usual

polarization of conformist and revolutionary. The rebel, he argues, may appear the most perfect social conformist. 'When a man takes politics and social affairs seriously the difference between revolution and reaction may be by the breadth of a hair.' For Eliot, to invoke the Order of Things in the midst of twentieth-century chaos, to insist on self-discipline in the face of a permissive society, to be, in short, a Critic (in poetry no less than in speeches) was to take a revolutionary line. 'Reaction' was, to him, a necessary act of social regeneration, not the stale conservatism of the mindless reactionary. To take politics seriously was to repudiate politicians in favour of poets like Wordsworth, 'the first, in the unsettled state of affairs in his time, to annex new authority for the poet, to meddle with social affairs, and to offer a new kind of religious sentiment which it seemed the peculiar prerogative of the poet to interpret'. He saw in Wordsworth 'a profound spiritual revival' which had its social sequels in the Oxford Movement and Victorian humanism. Once again, a European writer is used in a way that 'corresponds' neatly with American tradition, the revolt against deadness in a pattern of religious revivals: in the 1740s the Great Awakening led by Jonathan Edwards; in the next century the revivals of Emerson, Thoreau, and Whitman; and in the next— the logic is inescapable— *The Waste Land*.

Eliot's final guideline, now the most popular, was his concern for language. The classic poet serves his language by leaving behind him a language more precise, subtle, and capable of expressing a new range of experience. In Eliot's best critical finales he connects this linguistic challenge with the frontiers of consciousness: the poet must make people 'see and hear more at each end [of the ordinary range] than they could ever see without his help'. He feels 'the obligation to explore, to find words for the inarticulate, to capture those feelings which people can hardly even feel because they have no words for them'. Language is always dying; its categories become reductive; its emotional terms stale. It is the poet's duty to alert us to the moments when language fails, as when Eliot points to the infinitely gentle, infinitely suffering 'thing'. The gaps in his poetry alert us to 'a fringe of indefinite extent, of feeling which we can only detect, so to speak, out of the corner of the eye and can never completely focus'. These are the 'unattended' moments at the centre of Eliot's poetry, when he invites us to look with him into the silence at the still point of the turning world.

Eliot injects silence into the early poetry with blank spaces on the page. In his later poetry, words are potentially the Word; the power to write potentially a sacred power. 'The Word in the desert', language as authoritative and durable as scripture, remained a kind of mirage of perfection. Towards this Eliot set his course in obedience to his belief in a given task. As the fifties wore on there seemed no prospect of personal reward. Denied the ultimate vision, he lived only to perpetuate its possibility for other lives.

The outer casing of this mission began to erode in the mid-fifties. Mary Trevelyan hinted to Eliot that he had hurt her and John Hayward. Eliot replied that if this were true perhaps he had better sever his connection with them. Anyone less confident than Mary would have been crushed by one of Eliot's rebukes for impertinence in September 1956, but Mary was prepared to have it out.

'I refuse', she wrote, 'to be put in the corner for something I have not done.'

'I think my stomach is a little disordered', said Eliot plaintively on the phone.

'I should think it *is*', retorted Mary and invited him to tea, thinking 'jolly d. . . of me to ask you.'

Eliot once told her that she had a terribly ingenious way of putting him in the wrong, and he didn't like it. The annoyance would last some time (because, he explained, his reactions were slow), then he would climb down bearing gifts. After one of their earlier tiffs, in October 1953, he produced a peace offering after church with a shy smile, a battered tin of Breakfast Sausage.

Their cocoon of habit was fortified by daily prayers for each other, but there was increasing friction. Mary became impatient with Eliot's fuss over his minor ailments, his pills and potions, but more likely she resented the excuses and demands that went with these complaints. Eliot was, in fact, enfeebled in the mid-fifties, his main problem being 'a lesion between the left and right compartments of his heart'. From about 1954 his heart would speed up from 80 to 120 or 140, and he would be rushed to the London Clinic for several weeks at a time. But he would go there, too, for nothing more than athlete's foot. Mary thought he worried so much about himself that he made himself iller than he was. He needed cosseting, he protested, and gave Mary the name and address of a priest to summon to his deathbed. She noted with irritation that he rather enjoyed the clinic, cut off there from all obligations, from human contact—from her. This was the nub of it: Eliot wanted to be left alone. And as a mere friend, Mary had no rights. She did persuade him that, for the sake of his sisters, for whom she was the sole source of information, she must be at least allowed details of his condition, but clearly Eliot held back. He was always afraid that she would presume too far.

Mary never quite fathomed his detachment, and never imagined the intransigence of his withdrawal. Three times, Eliot retired into the citadel of the self and shut the door: in 1932 it shut on Vivienne Eliot; in 1947 on Emily Hale; and now, in 1956, it was closing on Mary Trevelyan. When, in August, she proposed a drink one Sunday evening 'if you'd *like* to see me', Eliot replied: 'You know quite well that I *never* want to see *anybody*.' Was he too feeble, or was he forming another chrysalis, from which he might burst out, a new being?

But what was he to be? As he listened to his heart bumping and racing in the night, he feared that he was coming to his end, feared loss of creativity, even loss of mind. He was disappointed by the reception of 'The Cultivation of Christmas Trees' in 1954, the first straight poem he had published in years. 'As for poetry', he told Mary, 'well, it doesn't come.' What she saw as an 'abnormal' fear of death was perhaps a fear of death without redemption. All his adult life Eliot had waited for a sign: in the earlier years a sign of grace; latterly, perhaps, a sign of forgiveness. Then, in 1956, as he felt his strength ebb, came the unexpected offer of a young woman's love. Even more surprising was his response, a new-found vindication of his capacity to love which seemed to assuage all the years of guilt.

From 1950 through the mid-fifties, Eliot was reading the Harvard theologian, Paul Tillich, who argued that forgiveness is not wrung out of the rigours of self-punishment, self-accusation, and self-humiliation. There is no condition for forgiveness, said Tillich, except the need for it. He offered a theology based on love rather than penitence; on 'the creative abundance of the heart' rather than the solitary's withholding of the self: 'Do not greedily preserve your time and strength . . . Keep yourselves open for the creative moment which may appear in the midst of what seemed to be waste.'

There came a moment, perhaps a fearful point of illness, when Eliot must have found himself ready for forgiveness. Horror, gloom, and penitence came to an end with his discovery of the unconditional love of Valerie Fletcher.

Eliot's effortless superiority had been, in a way, his cross: it set him apart, so that to love or sympathize was not simple as for most. He could be genial, jokey, painstaking, but these had been acts of deliberation, duty not pleasure. His studied kindness had masked his detachment, his mature alternative to youthful contempt. He was torn between duty to God and duty to man. Duty to God might be to fast on a saint's day, but then, he had a cold which the fast might worsen and so prevent his performing another duty to dine, say, with the vicar. He *preferred* to do his duty to God and risk the duty to man but, being an Eliot, one's duty was to do the thing one least wanted to do. So the vacillation went on, the fasting hermit deferring, unwillingly, to the public man. And when the public tug was too prolonged, he retired to the London Clinic. Mary sensed that these retirements were not wholly a matter of health: they were a relief from adulation, from people who wished to know him because he was famous, people who were exhausting like—she could not admit it—herself.

There in the clinic, as he read theology, identities passed before him: Nehemiah, Badboy, Bonsir; or was he a neurotic depressive? Or would some other being emerge? In *The Confidential Clerk*, the hero is a man in search of identity, abjuring father, mother, and the inviting Lucasta, so that he might fulfil a devotion to God alone. Soon after Eliot completed the play, he remarked to Mary that a man who has not known his parents is fortunate, and that his own parents had seemed distant, like 'ancestors'. In 1953 Eliot was still drawn to the course of unnoticed piety. None of his prospective saints is quite as humble as this second-rate organist, Simpkins, whose very name proclaims his nonentity. To be God's instrument one must become nothing. Only from nothing could new being emerge. So, in the darkest recess of the chrysalis, Eliot shed a lifelong recoil from contact for a new feeling, perhaps at first no more than a readiness, a need to be forgiven. In his Bible, he marked the words, 'I, *even* I, *am* he that blotteth out thy transgressions for mine own sake, and will not remember thy sins.' By

January 1956 Eliot was imagining an agent of forgiveness in his last play, 'a peach of a girl' who, he said, was almost too good to be true.

Eliot often remarked to Mary Trevelyan or John Hayward that he was frightened. He was frightened of travel, phone-calls, and above all of having to talk to a woman, as once during the war, when he was left to dine alone with Jean Kennerley, the wife of a Faber director. The threat of contact was defused when a woman became a Guardian. The caring women in Eliot's late plays offer consolation as they look after a battered man: Julia practically, Monica healing his tormented conscience so as to release, at last, the comfort of natural love.

Although Eliot froze for some years, he did habour a residue of feeling that could be kindled. He was not a cold fish. There were deeply buried emotions, intact but undirected, so that, even as he aged, women found him attractive, fell in love, proposed. In *Four Quartets* he spoke of the 'unattached devotion which might pass for devotionless'. Almost all his life he seems to have waited to confer this love, and at last, when he was 68, this happened in a way that changed him completely.

6. Love: the Unfamiliar Name*

IN 1957 Eliot married his secretary, Valerie Fletcher, and was transformed on his return from their honeymoon in the South of France. The wedding was a surprise to Eliot's closest friends, John Hayward, Mary Trevelyan, and Geoffrey Faber. A letter delivered by Eliot's solicitor notified Faber that the marriage had taken place. Eliot gave advance notice only to his solicitor, Mr Higginson, and his colleague, Peter du Sautoy, who was to engage a new secretary. Eliot was 68 and Valerie Fletcher was 30. They were married at 6.15 a.m. on 10 January, not at St Stephens, where it was known that Eliot went every morning, but at St Barnabas in the Addison Road. There, Eliot discovered, Laforgue had also married an English girl in 1886.

Complete understanding of the change that took place in 1956 must remain a mirage. Falling in love is, anyway, impossible to explain. There was, Eliot said after his marriage, 'thoughts without need of speech' and 'speech without need of meaning' in the attunement of lovers who make a private world. On the other hand, it would falsify the last stage of Eliot's life simply to record, as many do, the mere fact of change. For it took place in the context of nearly a whole lifetime that now stretched behind Eliot, and although we cannot know the private world itself, we might ask how he came to replace the long-guarded world of solitude with the shared world of love. For all his secrecy, he did offer clues to the nature of such a change in his last play which he began in October–November 1955: a clearly autobiographical play about a great public figure who has become hollow at heart, and is 'saved', at the very end of his life, by the steadfast love of his daughter.

'*Do* make them human beings this time', Mary Trevelyan urged Eliot in January 1956 after he drafted the first act. She was repeating a criticism she had made in February 1950 about the human blindness that made his characters seem like puppets.

'Don't I always?' Eliot protested. 'They seem to *me* human—but perhaps I don't know much about human beings.'

---

* *Little Gidding*: IV: 'Love is the unfamiliar Name.'

'How can you?' Mary retorted. 'You dislike them so much.'

'I'm sorry for them. They seem to me pathetic.'

'You only like them at a distance', Mary persisted, 'so long as they don't come near you.'

He seemed to take this in while she played some Mozart on the gramophone. Was intimacy at this late stage possible? Looking back on his life, there had been two attitudes to women: grim contempt and reverence for an ethereal Lady. Eliot's late turn to natural love seems a new thing, but the possibility is latent, as far back as 1930, in the final line of *Marina*. A great denouncer of the hateful world, a man battered after his life's journey, finds comfort in the appearance of a woman who is his kin: 'My daughter', he greets her.

Valerie Fletcher, at the age of 14, had experienced a conversion of sorts on hearing John Gielgud's recording of 'The Journey of the Magi'. From that moment, she said, she felt that she '*had* to get to Tom, to work with him'. She came from Headingley, Leeds, the daughter of a manager of the State Assurance Company who had an interest in porcelain, the Leeds Art Collection Fund, and the Leeds Library. She was sent to a girls' public school, Queen Anne's in Caversham, Reading, a school which did not, in the forties, send its products to university. Nor did its sporting ethos invite the expression of intellectual passion that would have been appropriate to the latent talent suggested by the girl's dramatic response to Eliot's poem. When she left school, she told the headmistress that she was determined to be Eliot's secretary. In the meantime, she went to work as a librarian for six months at the Brotherton Library of the University of Leeds and, after that, as a private secretary to a novelist, Charles Morgan. Then, at the end of August 1950, aged 22, she was appointed as Eliot's personal secretary, recommended by W. Collin Brooks who, like Eliot, had joined the Burke Club, a serious Tory dining club made up of MPs and journalists, when it was formed in the late thirties.

For five and a half years 'Miss Fletcher' was self-effacing, reserved, marked only for her ability and strong sense of duty. 'I can't get to know her at all,' Eliot told Mary Trevelyan in 1955, 'she shuts up like a clam.' Once in those years she surprised him. During one of his visits to America, she dined out with an Indian protégé of Eliot's. When he heard of this, his sudden impulse to violence revealed some strong, as yet unacknowledged feeling.

All this time she was amassing a vast collection of Eliot's publications, an even better collection, it is said, than his own. She worked for a man wrapped in the mantle of fame who was, moreover, nervous of women, and would dodge into the lavatory to avoid having to walk out of the building with anyone working late at the office. She did often, he noticed, work late. Slowly, he came to recognize that this contained young woman was a disciple with the absolute dedication of an ideal heir. It was a special kind of devotion, this rare, voluntary bond between generations.

In Eliot's first draft of Act I of his new play, the daughter shows her devotion in the way that she protects her father. She is at one with the need of the public man to shy away from people who would stare, gossip, and fall upon him. Their talk is all of plans to preserve his privacy: a table in a private alcove and coffee in a private sitting-room. He has come to take her rather for granted as his protective environment. At the same time, she is aware that he depends on her in a more subtle way, for she is the only one who believes in an unknown self behind the public face. She feels that she comes nearer than anyone, nearer than Claverton himself who has lost touch with his real being. He is a man who has striven for success to conceal from himself a deeper failure. After quick success in youth, the first draft tells us, he then became, for some reason, not wholly successful; rather like Eliot, whose most recent play had been received with the politeness due to a man known to have had brilliant gifts.

Eliot had already drafted the first two acts of a new play when he became seriously ill in February 1956. A severe attack of bronchitis brought on coughing and choking, which revived his cardiac trouble. Digitalis failed to help and he was in French Hospital for five weeks. In March, when he was crawling to life again, he had to turn to his Minnesota lecture on 'The Frontiers of Criticism'. He was due to leave for America in April, and at that point, did not expect to go back to the play until September. The lecture was 'sticky': he felt, that March, that he had nothing to say. He was still like the ailing Claverton of the first act: a man whose power seems gone.

Eliot continued on the verge of existence for the next six months. On the return voyage, he took ill three days out of Southampton, and was carried off the Queen Mary on a stretcher.

Then, a week later, came the news that his sister Margaret had died suddenly and alone in her home in Cambridge, Mass. People remember Eliot looking 'stricken' and 'cadaverous'.

'How does one set about *dying*?' he asked E. W. F. Tomlin.

In September he returned early from a holiday in Switzerland. He was wheeled from the plane by a nurse, and taken back to the London Clinic with a return of tachycardia and an abscess on his hip. Mary noticed a nervous spasm of the leg which he seemed unable to control.

At this lowest point love must have come like an offer of salvation. During each period of illness Valerie Fletcher had looked after his affairs, and, imperceptibly, his dependence on Mary shifted to her as his need deepened. In Eliot's second scenario for his play 'the ELD[ER] ST[ATESMAN] begins to unburden his heart to DAUGHTER'. Valerie Fletcher's response, I would guess, fitted Eliot's scenario: '. . . instead of condemning him, as he expects, she exhibits a new protective affection. He is still further affected by her response.'

Eliot's second draft introduces a love scene between the girl and a man who, in the first draft, had been a shallow mirror image of her father, a public man in the making. In this new scene, the girl finds herself saying words of love which can 'never be retraced'. She is numbed by the momentousness of these words, and says, 'they stand for something / That has left me, is lost to me, given up forever.'

Eliot showed unexpected sensitivity to a woman's feeling: he understood the shock of abandoning her reserve, the loss of self in the surrender, the daring of that moment of lifelong commitment which is too great to absorb.

The man replies as though he, too, spoke beyond himself, taken over by a voice in his head, *her* voice: 'Is it you or I who speak?' Her words seem to come from far away, yet very near. This is the very moment of transformation. 'You are changing me', he says, 'And I am changing you.'

Eliot must have protested, at first, that a young woman shouldn't do this. 'Ah, my deare, / I cannot look on thee', as Herbert put it in his poem 'Love'. Divine love, which had sent down the punitive fire of 1940–2, now spoke in a human voice with exquisite courtesy. The poet draws back, guilty 'of dust and sinne', but this benign, sacramental love is persuasive:

You must sit downe, sayes Love, and taste my meat.
So I did sit and eat.

The ease with which Eliot took up this offer of love was unprecedented. I think it had partly to do with the easing of guilt as love opened up the possibility of complete honesty, like the daughter in his play, whose entire confidence invites the public figure to make his first genuine confession. All his life the public man had been locked in a web of fiction which he wove about himself; now, at last, he longs to break out, but fears to show himself to the woman whose idol he had become. Could her innocent love survive knowledge of things ill-done and done to others' harm?

Like Eliot himself, and like Harry in *The Family Reunion*, Lord Claverton is a man of 'morbid conscience'. Again, there has been no crime punishable by law but what both call sin. Claverton, as a young man, once ran over a dead person, and did not stop. This repeats, in a different setting, the emotional situation of Harry: guilt for an imagined part in another's death. Eliot said that he began his plays with an 'emotional situation'. Both times he transmutes into drama his own long-held guilt for his unresisting part in Vivienne's end.

There is a companion-in-guilt in *The Elder Statesman*. Gomez is the type of successful scoundrel, a comic type not drawn from life, but two aspects of his career have parallels in that of Vivienne's brother, Maurice Haigh-Wood: the fact that Maurice, too, did not resist Vivienne's committal, and that, fairly soon after, he went abroad for some years. Alternatively, this may be yet another encounter with an alter ego, for way back, in January 1918, Eliot had signed 'Enrique Gomez' to a review of *The Sense of the Past* by Henry James.* In the late fifties a resurrected Gomez epitomizes Eliot's fear that the truth, known only to a secret self or to a companion-in-guilt, would come out some day in distorted form— as exposé—as, in fact, it did in a scurrilous mid-eighties play.

The other ghost from the past is an actress who has become a talkative old woman. Years ago, Lord Claverton had been her first love, and she had sued him for breach of promise. This was settled out of court, but now, late in life, Maisie lets him know that she has

---

* An amusing note adds that 'Señor Gomez wishes to thank [an equally fictitious] Miss Anna Louise Babson of New York for revising the English version of this review.'

kept his letters. To her it was no trivial affair, and the letters will prove it. He had touched her soul, as she had touched his, and she has thought about him all her life. Maisie, too, is a comic type, a low-life caricature of a sentimental singer—her famous number was 'It's Not Too Late For You To Love Me?'—but the situation of a broken understanding does look back to Eliot's guilt over Emily Hale.

Eliot had said that a character might speak 'in unison' with the author, even call out his latent potentialities, and through Claverton, he returned to the most intractable material in his life. He had said in 1940, in a rough draft of poetry, that the past is 'a pit for us still to explore'. Advancing now to this pit, Eliot revived something of the emotional daring of *The Family Reunion* as an old man explores the depths of conscience. Its furies appear this time not as featureless phantoms of punishment but as individuals, unwelcome visitors who press him with emotional blackmail. Both see him vulgarly as a dodger: with Gomez he has evaded responsibility for his actions; with Maisie, for an emotional tie. Claverton must face each on close terms, and in so far as he does face them in mind as well as in person, their menace fades, and they become what their limited characters imply, negligible.

Claverton admits the truth of his past only in the last act, which was written after Eliot's marriage. A year later, in January 1958, having completed a draft of the play, he commented: 'I can only say that it is a very different play (and I believe a better one) for so much of it having been written during this last year, than it would have been if I had finished it before our marriage.' The changes in the play make its synopses and drafts more interesting than those of the preceding, more brittle comedies. Composed as Eliot fell in love with Valerie Fletcher, it looks towards their union.

At first, in October 1955, Eliot had only a title in mind: 'The Rest Cure.'* He told Mary that it was like going with his seven characters through a long, dark railway tunnel, and that, when they emerged, he would know them. In November–December 1955, when he drafted the first act, he did not as yet quite know the young woman. She was, at first, no more than a model of filial piety, potentially a guardian angel (Eliot's first name for her was

---

* At some point Eliot made an isolated note that nothing was wrong except a mind diseased ('Miscellaneous Essays', n.d., King's).

Angela*). In this first draft the father is waiting in a void for death, and Eliot adds in pencil to the typescript that the blankness of the walls mocked the blankness of the mind. As Eliot made his way through that dark tunnel with his characters-to-be, I think he began to hope that there might be someone who would understand his essential being, and who could be trusted to continue it beyond his lifetime. In Act II, after Claverton has endured the visitations of his contemporaries, he is shaken and bruised but, in the curtain line, hopeful of a cure—and the hope is directed to the young woman.

'But have I still time?' he asks her. 'Is it too late for me?'

Some time between Act II, drafted by 1956, and Act III, written in 1957–8, I would guess that Eliot opened his heart to Valerie Fletcher, as Claverton confesses to his daughter in the certainty of her unshakeable love. What has made the difference, he tells her, is not 'the heinousness of my misdeeds / But the fact of my confession. And to you . . . / To you, of all people.' As he exorcizes the spectres from his past, he emerges from his 'spectral existence into something like reality'. Reality, now, is not transcendental: it is human contact. It is enough to confess the truth to one person, even if it must remain concealed from the rest of the world. Then his 'soul is safe', and then 'he loves that person, and his love will save him'.

This private confession takes place through the public medium of the theatre: it must be repeated, nightly, before a large audience. In this Eliot harks back, once again, to the New England trial of the soul by public confession. At the same time, as Eliot put it in a dedicatory poem to his wife, the play represents his words to her. As Eliot's public confession to one person, it is the basis of their union, which is to be the most complete bond, as the dedication takes care to describe.

During their courtship (conducted over lunches at the Russell Hotel across the square from Faber & Faber), Eliot typed several pages of Act II in late November 1956. In this Act the actress deplores the great man's 'shabby behaviour' in private: 'he doesn't understand women', she declares. 'Any woman who trusted *him* would soon find that out.'

---

* Martin Browne said that Eliot changed it because it was too much like Lucasta Angel (in *The Confidential Clerk*).

Eliot's wife-to-be had to face his ghosts. The words of the actress tell of another bond that might outlast their lives—as, in fact, Eliot's thousand letters to Emily Hale will survive for centuries to come. The actress tells the public man that she reads his letters every night.

'Were they very passionate?' he asks uneasily.

'They were very loving', she answers. In her view 'we're still together', and Eliot added in pencil to the first draft: 'And more frightening to think that we may *always* be together.'

This emotional claim precedes the confession in Act III which stirs in the old man a saving tide of feeling, sweeping fear away. In this last play, Eliot spelt out the danger of his own later years, that feeling denied deadens the soul. His carapace had thickened; his will had hardened as the years of penitence had rolled away without apparent gain. His public masks had become so habitual that they had dried up the very sources of feeling they were designed to protect. During the early fifties Mary never quite dispelled his impenetrability, and her proposals only made him more guarded. By the mid-fifties he was failing, when he found the daring to strip the mask.

Eliot often surprised people. His reckless first marriage surprised his family. His conversion in 1927 startled his contemporaries, as his conversion to human happiness in 1957 startled a younger generation of admirers. Until at least 1953, Eliot expected to retire to an abbey. 'One day I will go there to stay, permanently', he had told William Turner Levy, a priest in New York. 'It suits me. I would have no guests then ...' Was Eliot's new marriage, after a thirty-year attempt at celibacy, the one act that broke the inexorable pattern of the religious life? Or was it the consummation of that life?

At a party on Eliot's return from honeymoon, he appeared knit together with his wife, arms and hands enfolded. He looked as though a lifetime's barriers to emotion had been dissolved. When Mrs Eliot was borne off to be introduced, Gwen Watkins sat down next to Eliot and said: 'You look as if, like Dante, you'd passed into paradise.'

'Exactly', he said, pleased. For him, paradise followed purgatory with the same logic that a new life had followed the hell of the early years.

This transformation is forecast in the first draft of the second act of 'The Rest Cure', the writing of which immediately precedes Eliot's marriage. Angela discerns that the old man is going through pangs of change from one kind of life to another. She urges him to 'burst out, become a butterfly!' The words go back to 1911 and Eliot's unpublished '2nd Debate between the Body and Soul', which dreams of a condition in which the soul might burst out ingenuous and pure. If, from 1911 to 1956, Eliot was a creature in a chrysalis, testing his power of transformation, his late marriage fitted the sustained pattern of his life.

The play, written close to the events of Eliot's life, dramatizes the self-confrontation of a man waiting for death. It is when the public figure stops performing and comes to rest in a sanatorium (as Eliot took rests in the London Clinic) that he faces his whole past. The sanatorium in *The Cocktail Party* had been a place for the transformation of an appointed martyr. Claverton's position is much humbler: his cure is not to become God's agent but to receive forgiveness which comes to him through his daughter. The complex emotional situation suggests that what happened to Eliot in 1956 was not only a simple matter of falling in love but a coming to 'rest' in a changed conception of existence in relation to God. The God of fire, the intolerable shirt of flame that Eliot put on at the end of *Four Quartets*, became a God of blessings. Love, an 'unfamiliar Name' to the Eliot of 1942, made itself known to the elder Eliot of 1957.

This final position was one that Henry James, sen., had put to Emerson. All that men value as religious progress, he said, going alone, renouncing, self-mortification, was the way *from*, not the way *to* what they seek, 'for it is only as our existence is shared, not as it is self-hood, that it is divine'. Emerson, the prophet of self-reliance, copied the admonition into his journal.

Eliot's transformation through phases of hope, courtship, secret commitment, and, finally, secure public love, is charted in the evolution of the last play from synopses, to the drafts, to the stage, to the triumphant dedication of the published work to his wife. In the third Act, written after marriage, the young woman turns out to be not as passive as she appears in the drafts of the first two Acts. She is certainly not one of the puppets of whom Mary had complained. The name, Angela, was changed to Monica, the name of the strong mother of St Augustine who urged the transforming experience of his life. Monica may not actually speak other than conventional loving words, yet a subtle actress could convey that her loyalty, put to the test, is deeper than language. She has the staunchness of Antigone upholding her aged father at Colonus. As far back as March 1938, Eliot had told Martin Browne that one way to complete Harry's career would be an *Oedipus at Colonus*. In other words, the old man who finds peace of mind in the end should succeed the middle-aged man haunted by furies. We might plot a line from the savagery of Sweeney, to the mature guilt of Harry, to the loving serenity that comes like grace to Claverton as he passes through the 'door' at the end of his life.

'I am only a beginner in the practice of loving', he says. 'Well, that is something.'

Eliot broke into love poetry in his revisions to Act I (completed on 9 February 1958) and in Act III which introduce love-duets between Monica and her fiancé Charles. Charles was now reconceived as a sensitive man who finds it difficult to express love, but tries:

> ... like the asthmatic struggling for breath,
> So the lover must struggle for words.

More rewriting and cutting went on in the new love scenes than in any other part of the play.

It was first produced at the Edinburgh Festival from 25 to 30 August 1958, with a young Anna Massey in what was only her third part as Monica. Alec McCowen as the errant son, Michael, was more riveting to the audience, when he wheeled round on his heel to flash his accusation at the old man. It must have been a weakness of that production that Martin Browne did not think much of Monica as a dramatic character: he found the accusers dramatically more interesting. This conventional response mistakes the fact that the whole play turns on the extraordinary maturity of feeling in a young woman which sheds grace on awkward men of power.

In Eliot's original version of Act III for the Edinburgh production, Monica explored the process of falling in love. It is a pity that these speeches were cut from the published play, because they manifest the woman's emotional vitality. The emotional engagement of this original scene is Eliot's first writing after his marriage. What remains of it in the published version is swamped by light social patter in the vein of his earlier comedies. In the original, Monica, I think, speaks not only for herself but 'in unison' with the Eliots in their new-found bond. 'You've no idea how long I've been in love with you', Monica confesses, 'long before the words came.' She cannot trace its beginning, for 'one's whole life has been the preparation for its advent'.

The scene also brings up the long appearance of coldness in the lover who was slower to acknowledge the bond. Here, I think, Eliot speaks through Monica to his wife words which, as he put it in his dedication, 'have a further meaning / For you and me only':

> It's very frightening, falling in love:
> So frightening, that one refuses to recognise it,
> For to recognise it is to face the terror of it.
> And the terror aroused by the sight of the belovèd
> Freezes the blood.

For a moment, the strangeness of Eliot comes back, as he approaches marital love with the old power to imagine—and fear—the unknown. This is not great poetry, but it is touching that the poet of the rarefied agonies of *Four Quartets* should now try also to articulate, in the finale, the simple common things that lovers do say to each other, that they 'belong together' and 'feel alone' in company. The man speaks in wonder of the birth of 'a new person' who is 'you and me together'. The woman, more expressive, speaks of 'the certainty of love unchanging'.

There was a cost to transformation: the loss of the guardians of the preceding phase. Neither Mary Trevelyan nor John Hayward remained part of Eliot's new life. Hayward was taken by surprise when Eliot did not return from church as usual, on the morning of 10 January. Later in the day he phoned Peter du Sautoy, and spoke rather grimly about '*il matrimonio segreto*'.*

Eliot shrank, too, from telling Mary Trevelyan. He saw her according to their normal routine—church, drives, teas—up to a week before the wedding. In August 1956, while Eliot was on holiday in Geneva and Mary in Herefordshire, he sent her a postcard almost every day for a fortnight. Then, from September, Mary noticed an increased edginess. 'My *dear* lady . . .' Eliot would

---

* Cimarosa's opera had recently been in the news.

stop her, and lapse into silence. Forms of kindness remained. When Mary was ill in mid-October, he brought her whisky through the pouring rain, and in the course of one day phoned three times. From mid-December their meetings became again more genial. He dined with Mary and her brother Humphrey Trevelyan, the Ambassador to Egypt, and his wife Peggie, who spoke of their flight during the Suez crisis.* Eliot also invited himself to tea on consecutive Sundays, and on 16 December he stayed from 3.30 to 7 p.m. talking of presents. He always gave Miss Swan a present, he said, starting years ago when she was kind to Vivienne. 'But I don't give Miss Fletcher anything', he went on (relishing the private joke). 'I don't think it suitable to give one's secretary presents.' Then he picked up *Bleak House*, a present to Mary, and read his favourite bits aloud for an hour.

On 23, 27, and 29 December Mary went to tea with Eliot, who had a cold. On the 29th he looked better. She noted with approval that there were not so many medicines as usual. The last time they met was on 2 January, when they spent two hours in their old haunt, the Russell Hotel, drinking Tio Pepe and talking of Vivienne. As they parted, Eliot held Mary's hand a moment, saying: 'As you know, I always mention you in my prayer.'

Mary was away from London from 3 to 9 January. A letter from Eliot awaited her return. It said simply that on Thursday, the 10th he was being married to Valerie Fletcher. It was not a sudden decision: they loved each other very much. He added that he had prized Mary's friendship, and would be loth to lose it.

Mary, opening this letter on the morning of the 10th, was stunned. Unbelieving, she phoned Hayward again and again.

Both naturally fell back on their manners. Mary wrote a note of good wishes to Eliot's office. 'My dear chap,' Hayward said disarmingly on Eliot's return from honeymoon, 'why didn't you tell me?' This was one of two occasions when Eliot went back to the flat to collect his belongings. Hayward felt no resentment but, as the months passed, grew bewildered at Eliot's withdrawal. 'I thought that everything was alright', he said to friends in May. Now on his own after ten years, he felt his helplessness anew. His morale never recovered.

---

* Humphrey Trevelyan was Ambassador to Egypt (1953–6). He later became Ambassador to the USSR and, in the late sixties, was made a life peer.

It is not difficult, though, to understand Eliot's need for secrecy. Hayward was a notorious gossip and Mary was bound to be put out, not only as Eliot's escort, but in view of the now-embarrassing excuse which Eliot had given, in kindness in 1950, that he did not wish to marry anyone. In that letter of 2 June 1950, he had made the revealing comment that the desire not to inflict pain can often approach very near to cowardice. This might be a more subtle explanation of Eliot's actions, as Graham Greene saw precisely when he spoke of 'the moral cowardice of the sensitive man'. More obviously, Eliot feared ridicule. To neither John nor Mary could he hope to explain the idyllic nature of his attachment. He was not just a doting old man, or avid, like Yeats, for excitement. His capacity for love was bound up with intellectual respect and deep trust. He had, thus late, made the discovery that there are different kinds of pure relationship, not only the impossible purity of sublime love but the realizable ideal of a union of mind, body, and soul.

And yet an element of strangeness does still remain. It echoes in the stupefaction of Mary Trevelyan in the last pages of her memoir: 'Have John and I known and loved the real man?' She says exactly what Emily Hale said, that after years of knowing Eliot you found, suddenly, that you did not know him. He could leave relationships and pass on. Eliot was most in his element in the act of memory. He chose as his totem the elephant* who never forgets. After his marriage, he designed a joint bookplate (beautifully executed by David Jones in black and green), an elephant's head (drawn by Eliot himself) with an upraised trunk that encircles an arrow, derived from the name Fletcher, meaning 'maker of arrows'. But the elephant could forget when he chose. He denied writing obscene verses. He denied Conrad Aiken's memory of two incidents that showed 'a streak of sadism' in his nature. He would not be pinned by others' memories. Mrs Morley, who had harboured Eliot during the summer of 1933 when he broke with Vivienne, found, when she met him some years later, that he hardly seemed to know who she was. He had a capacity, not to forget in the ordinary way, but to wipe out what did not fit the model of existence as he

---

* The elephant was a family crest. Its origin is recorded in *The Oxford Guide to Heraldry* by Thomas Woodcock and John Martin Robinson (OUP, 1988): 'the *Elephant's head proper* granted in 1492 by ... John Writhe, Garter, to the brothers Thomas and John Elyott.'

devised it. His life was one of paring down, concentration. In old age he was concentrating on the paradise of love so John Hayward, who patently had no place in paradise, was left behind.

Of course Eliot did the proper thing. He paid his contribution to the Hayward flat for another two years. After six months he issued invitations to John and Mary, but he was not going to see them alone. Intimacy, such as it had been, was over. John did once come to lunch with Robert Frost and Rosamund Lehmann, and the Eliots did once return the visit, but he felt that Eliot avoided him, and contact lapsed. In the 1963 edition of the *Collected Poems*, Eliot removed his acknowledgement to John Hayward, originally printed before *Four Quartets*.

With Mary, politeness broke down at once. When Mary had no reply to her note, she wrote to Eliot again saying in her forthright way that, despite her initial shock, her affection for him would not change. This gave quick offence. She was, Eliot replied, impertinent; Mary recoiled; and soon another long friendship came to an end. Emily, too, had her 'unappreciative' letter, terminating a tie of fifty years.

There is a curious defence of the Elder Statesman in one (later) draft of Eliot's last play, to the effect that he was compelled to 'sacrifice others' for higher ends, a sacrifice justified by the sacrifice of himself. In *The Cocktail Party*, Edward hesitates to rebuild his life on another's ruin, but the priestly psychiatrist reassures him that it's alright so long as he suffers enough in private:

> Your business is not to clear your conscience
> But to learn how to bear the burdens on your conscience.

Eliot's morality of penitence dwells on a solitary agonizing that excludes full awareness of one's effect on others. Claverton's moral agony would move us more if he did not see sin so exclusively 'in relation to the sinner'.

This is the minister, Dimmesdale, speaking as he excludes the partner of his past from the high drama of public penitence. The fact that this partner is a woman of rare distinction deepens the moral ambiguity of Dimmesdale's salvation. Eliot, though, simplifies the moral position by making the partners of Claverton's past negligible. He transcends them with ease to find solitary glory in the act of confession.

The loftiness of Eliot's moral stance can provoke extreme

reactions of adherence or resistance, but neither leads to truth. The whole truth is, of course, unattainable, but some of it lies in American tradition, in the New England trait of moral reflection, in the obsessive search for moral positions, and in the authority of the spiritual frontier. 'Explore your own higher latitudes', Thoreau urged. 'If you would learn to speak all tongues and conform to the customs of all nations, if you would travel farther than all travellers, be naturalized in all climes . . . Explore thyself.' Frontiering of this kind is a radical act. It cuts loose, and moves on. It shakes off the dust of the previous frontier. So Eliot spat out the butt-ends of past days and ways, as he moved on to higher latitudes *en route* to paradise.

'Love reciprocated is always rejuvenating', Eliot said in 1958. 'Before my marriage I was getting older. Now I feel younger at seventy than I did at sixty. . . . An experience like mine makes all the more difference because of its contrast with the past.'

All at once, he seemed to shake off a lifetime's habit of introversion. His repeated declarations of happiness broke our convention that it is not seemly to show off married bliss, a convention that coexists with the platitude that marriage palls. 'None of my books are fitted to be wedding presents', Hardy remarked to Virginia Woolf when she visited him in 1926. Hardy's pessimism had reversed the platitude of his own time, the domestic sentiment of the Victorians. In 1958 Eliot, in turn, reversed pessimism with his poem, 'To My Wife'. It breaks the formality of the usual dedication, with its public announcement of 'the leaping delight' that quickens the senses of the husband, and the blissful sleep of lovers whose bodies smell of each other. Such directness from a man, old and austere, is even more startling than Yeats's admission of his 'old man's frenzy'. The old Yeats exults in the return of vitality; the old Hardy is disturbed by 'throbbings of noontide' which shake his fragile frame; but the old Eliot tells us something more subtle and unexpected. Poets speak, usually, of the frenzy of love, of its transience and loss; Eliot tells of an experience of love that is sustained. Faithful lovers breathe in unison as they sleep, with a sense of union that will infuse all their life. By contrast, the passing affair saps feeling. Eliot's early poems describe the push-button sex of the female jaguar whose bust promises 'pneumatic bliss', and the apathetic automatism of clerk and typist who couple like 'crawling bugs'. Eliot set out such scenes shortly because they are in truth boring, mere variations of emotional sterility. The alternative had been renunciation: Prufrock's inactivity in the presence of women's arms 'braceleted and white and bare', the parting with La Figlia, and, decades later, Colby's withdrawal from the seductive Lucasta. This poetic pattern reflects Eliot's own retreat until conjugal love redeemed love itself.

In 1958 Eliot introduced his wife to the United States. In Texas he opened an exhibition of his first editions and papers, and accepted a Deputy Sheriff's badge and a ten-gallon hat which he sported amongst his relatives in Boston and at church in New York. Mrs Eliot told the reporter of the *Boston Globe* that they had enjoyed Texas, but felt most at home in Cambridge. Eliot's expression of happy pride as he held his wife's hand was unprecedented. His face split into unaccustomed smiles as he faced photographers. Jovial, joking over Prufrock's lack of love-life, he seemed to enjoy the impact of his new image. The man who, at 21, had written 'I grow old . . . I grow old . . .', now told reporters that he might take dancing lessons 'as I have not danced at all for some years'. Sure enough, when some Harvard students got up a dance at a boat-house, and sent an invitation to join them to the Master of Eliot House, John Finley, and his dinner guests, the Eliots, the I. A. Richardses, the Harry Levins, and the Archibald MacLeishes, the Eliots alone went to the boathouse while the other guests made their excuses and went home.

Throughout his life Eliot could unbend unexpectedly. He had unbent in the early twenties to Virginia Woolf, when she had dared to laugh in his white marble face. He had unbent to the nerve of the younger Mary Trevelyan when, in 1938, she had sent him a parody of his stiff-necked reading. In 1949 he had unbent to Iowa students who, by way of congratulations on the Nobel Prize, had sent him a record of 'You've Come a Long Way From St Louis'. His reply was that he took note of the line: 'But, Baby, you've still got a long way to go.'

He seems to have responded, each time, to a sense of humour. With Valerie Eliot, humour became his constant note. He began to write fan letters to Groucho Marx, and was not put out by the brash intimacy of the replies. When they exchanged photographs (Eliot put Groucho on his office mantelpiece beside Yeats and

Valéry), Groucho commented 'I had no idea you were so hand-some. Why you haven't been offered the lead in some sexy movies I can only attribute to the simplicity of the casting directors.' One letter from Groucho begins daringly:

Dear Tom:
   If this isn't your first name, I'm in a hell of a fix! But I think I read somewhere that your first name is the same as Tom Gibbons', a prizefighter who once lived in St. Paul.
   My best to you and your lovely wife, whoever she may be.

To this, Eliot replied graciously: 'My lovely wife joins me in sending you our best.' He enclosed another photograph of an oil portrait done in 1961, and adds: 'It is very good-looking and my wife thinks it is a very accurate representation of me.'

Groucho responded, in turn, with a further meditation on Eliot's name: 'The name Tom fits many things. There was once a famous Jewish actor named Thomashevsky. All male cats are named Tom—unless they have been fixed. . . . So when I call you Tom, this means you are a mixture of a heavyweight prizefighter, a male alley cat and the third President of the United States.'* He went on as one writer to another: 'I have just finished my latest opus, "Memoirs of a Mangy Lover." . . . I doubt whether it will live through the ages, but if you are in a sexy mood the night you read it, it may stimulate you beyond recognition. . . . I would be interested in reading your views on sex, so don't hesitate. Confide in me.'

Eliot, who was 75 and ailing, delayed his reply for eight months, when he wrote to invite Groucho and his wife to the Eliots' flat in London in June 1964. Groucho gave a hilarious account of their meeting to Gummo Marx:

Last night Eden and I had dinner with my celebrated pen pal, T. S. Eliot. It was a memorable evening.
   The poet met us at the door with Mrs. Eliot, a good-looking, middle-aged blonde whose eyes seemed to fill up with adoration every time she looked at her husband. He, by the way, is tall, lean and rather stooped over; but whether this is from age, illness or both, I don't know.
   At any rate, your correspondent arrived at the Eliots' fully prepared

---

* Thomas Jefferson.

for a literary evening. During the week I had read 'Murder in the
Cathedral' twice; 'The Waste Land' three times, and just in case of
conversational bottleneck, I brushed up on 'King Lear.'

Well, sir, as the cocktails were served, there was a momentary lull—the
kind that is more or less inevitable when strangers meet for the first time.
So, apropos of practically nothing (and 'not with a bang but a whimper')
I tossed in a quotation from 'The Waste Land'. That, I thought, will show
him I've read a thing or two besides my press notices from Vaudeville.

Eliot smiled faintly—as though to say he was thoroughly familiar with
his poems and didn't need me to recite them. So I took a whack at 'King
Lear' . . .

That, too, failed to bowl over the poet. He seemed more interested in
discussing 'Animal Crackers' and 'A Night at the Opera'. He quoted a
joke—one of mine—that I had long since forgotten. Now it was my turn
to smile faintly.

Groucho persisted with *King Lear*; Eliot, equally determined,
asked Groucho if he remembered the courtroom scene in *Duck
Soup*. Groucho, in turn, dismissed the subject—he had forgotten
every word—but resigned himself to the end of his literary evening.
Instead they talked about what they actually had in common, an
affection for good cigars and cats. Groucho admitted a weakness
for puns, and found that Eliot was 'an unashamed—even proud—
punster'. Groucho thought him 'a dear man and a charming
host'.

Marriage brought out a sense of fun that was always there, in the
child on a St Louis street-corner, smiling mischievously with his
nurse, Annie Dunne; in the middle-aged Eliot who had entertained
Janet Adam Smith's children with readings from *Uncle Remus*, so
much so that one or two phrases—'Jest loungin' aroun' and
worryin'—passed into their family language. There was a homey
side to Eliot: the man who had 'interfered' in Mary Trevelyan's
kitchen, who had sent a recipe, 'Mrs Runcie's Pudding', for
inclusion in the *St Louis Symphony of Cooking* in 1954, and who
now discussed cake shops, fishmongers, and greengrocers in the
Gloucester Road with Ivy Compton-Burnett in a shared taxi after a
Knightsbridge party. He liked to play the humorous domestic pet,
like one of his cats who represent, in caricature, some aspects of
Eliot himself. Macavity, the monster of depravity, vanished in this
period, but Gus the theatre cat remained, and Jennyanydots, the
domestic purrer.

'I must admit that my wife makes me take life much more easily nowadays and that I flourish under this regime', Eliot wrote in 1960, in the Harvard class of 1910's fiftieth anniversary report. He now went only three days a week to the office. His chief interests were the London Library and the revision of the Psalter. Most evenings he and his wife read aloud to each other: Boswell, Coleridge's letters, *Kim*, and poetry (not much from younger writers). Eliot praised his wife's very good mind and passionate love of poetry. He was, he told Violet Schiff, madly happy to be her husband. 'It is a wonderful thing', he wrote to Levy, 'to be happily married, and a very blessed state for those who are called to it, even at my age. I have a very beautiful and good and sensitive wife . . . —she has everything to make me happy, and I am humbly thankful.'

Eliot's earlier women, Vivienne and Emily Hale, had been transmuted into figures in a morality drama. In Conrad Aiken's view the Eliot he had known in their youth was a man who put art before life: '. . . art and love—that was the primary order, for if one could sacrifice love for art . . . one could never—could one?— sacrifice art for love—or only momentarily, and with an eye over the shoulder, the unsleeping knowledge that this, like all experience, but more than most, was the indispensible raw material of art.' Valerie Eliot was not to be transformed in this way. In the last play and the dedicatory poem, Eliot celebrates her as she was: Monica's line, 'unchanging the certainty of love' was the real-life motto of their marriage, encircling the head of the elephant on their bookplate.

By this late stage, art was, in fact, no longer an issue. The impulse to write poetry had long since faded, and *The Elder Statesman* had been conceived as the last play. A surge of vitality following the marriage did awaken the possibility of further writing. Eliot told Henry Hewes in 1958 that he planned another verse play and more poems in a new style. 'I reached the end of something with the *Four Quartets*,' he said, 'and anything new will have to be expressed in a new idiom.' This would be the love idiom of the last revisions to *The Elder Statesman*. But Eliot's health flagged again in the early sixties, and he wrote only one more scrap of verse: an extra stanza to the dedicatory poem 'To My Wife' for inclusion in the last edition of the *Collected Poems*. He went back to the thirties for the image of the rose-garden, to open that door to love which, with

Emily Hale, 'we never opened'.* In *Burnt Norton* the speaker is dismissed from the garden: 'Go go go . . .'. All he has is a glimpse of a paradise never to be possessed. But now, in 1963, Eliot took possession of this garden:

> No peevish winter wind shall chill
> No sullen tropic sun shall wither
> The roses in the rose-garden which is ours and ours only . . .

In the autumn of 1964 Eliot wrote to Cyril Connolly to thank him for a kindly review: 'You were the first sympathetic reader and critic to call attention to the unusual fact that I had at last written a poem of love and happiness. It would almost seem that some readers were shocked that I should be happy.' Neither advancing age nor the months of tedium in the West Indies which doctors prescribed each winter, could dim his joy. It was, I think, more than love. He had discovered what Melville called the 'one insular Tahiti in the soul of man'.

He said: 'This last part of my life is the best, in excess of anything I could have deserved.'

Mary Trevelyan noticed that this marriage took place exactly ten years, to the month, after Vivienne's death, as though a set period of penitence had come to an end. Whether this is true or not, Eliot did fit his life to a pattern. This he pursued from the time, at Harvard, that he was struck by martyrdom and sainthood. A life that would pass through the ordeals of the waste and penitence towards the ultimate attainment of love absorbed Eliot until his last eight years. It called out his greatest poetry of search, which found its summation in *Four Quartets*. Eliot made Emily Hale the guardian spirit of this search for divine communion, but as their relation changed with Vivienne's death and Emily's wish to marry, the possibility of that communion faded. Suffering and celibacy so protracted became, I would guess, not so much a pursuit as a habit of obedience and self-discipline. There is a certain hollowness to

---

* *Burnt Norton*: I (1935):

> Footfalls echo in the memory
> Down the passage which we did not take
> Towards the door we never opened
> Into the rose-garden.

the Eliot of the early fifties, as though the author of the great poems simply wasn't there. In *The Cocktail Party*, Edward suffers from 'a loss of personality'. Then, in 1956, there appeared the possibility of a different pattern of redemption: not through the heights of divine communion—those heights of the mystics were now closed to Eliot—but through a more common solace. As Tillich describes this experience in *The New Being*, in the midst of despair there is the certainty of forgiveness, and the fire of love begins to burn. It is a breakthrough: 'it transforms everything.' The love that Eliot's wife brought him would have been a sign that he was, at last, blessed.

The more obvious benefit of the marriage was nurture. Eliot's health remained delicate. He was ill on honeymoon in February 1957, and in September had a long bout of Asian flu which lasted into October, when he caught another chill in Paris. 1958 was a better year—he travelled to America, and put on *The Elder Statesman*—but the November fogs were trying to his bronchial weakness. By the winter of 1959/60 he told Pound that he had to put most of his energy into breathing. In February 1960 he went to recuperate in Morocco, but dust from the Agadir earthquake brought on asthma. In January 1961 the Eliots took a leisurely cruise to Jamaica where they stayed at Ocho Rios until March. In 1961–2 they went to Barbados for the usual regime of swims and sunbathing. Eliot told Vernon Watkins that he found nothing to attract him to the tropical islands except the climate.

By then, Eliot had aged. He was bent over a cane, his colour ashen, his features softened and his voice weak. At the end of 1962 he collapsed after a four-day smog in early December. It was the memorably cold winter of 1962/3 (the coldest January on record since 1838) when people's bones ached from the blizzards. Instead of a projected journey to the Bahamas, Eliot spent five weeks in the Brompton Hospital under continuous oxygen. His wife never left his side, determined to be there when he came round from his coma. She fobbed off the press with a statement about bronchial trouble while she nursed him through this crisis.

In March, when he recovered, he asked Peter du Sautoy to destroy the box of letters. Eliot must have known that he was close to death, as he said of his friend Paul Elmer More in February 1937: it would be surprising if a man of so much wisdom were quite unaware of the coming of such an important event. In 1949 he had

owned to Mary Trevelyan that he was afraid of death, but now he
faced it calmly. 'Death is not oblivion', he said in 1958. 'People who
believe that are not afraid of death.'

In these last years Eliot was taking retrospective views of his
career. The most candid are in letters to Pound, now released from
St Elizabeths and back in Italy. In these letters, Eliot speaks
harshly of his sense of failure, of doubt, disgust, and despair. This
may have been as much a gesture of empathy with Pound's broken
state as an actual self-judgement. He cabled Pound on 31 October
1959 that he would never forget his great debt to him to whom all
living poets were indebted, that Pound's criticism had been
immensely helpful, and his work epochmaking. Two months later
he wrote how he envied Joyce his apparent self-confidence, and
slighted his own prose, particularly *After Strange Gods* which
expressed, he owned, his disturbed state in 1933. Nor was he
pleased with *The Use of Poetry and the Use of Criticism* except for a
few isolated paragraphs. On 29 January 1960 he went on to confess
that there was much in his life that he still could not bear to think
about for long at a time, but *The Waste Land* and the three last
Quartets did seem worthwhile. Now, it was hard to accept a
diminution of creative power, and Valerie had to work hard to
snap him out of his gloom. As late as November 1961 he still spoke
of things he wanted to do.

Eliot gave his last public lecture at the University of Leeds, in
July 1961, with an eye to posterity. In 'To Criticize the Critic', he
spoke past the predictable adulation of his present-day audience in
order to set up the judgement of the future. It is an extraordinary
exercise in detachment, for he looks back on himself, the pre-
eminent critical mind of his age, from a hundred years on. He
foresees and assents to the fading of the theories that had
captivated his time. Taking the opposite position to the doctrinal
impersonality of his early criticism, he confesses repeatedly to a
criticism based on subjective 'feeling', a kinship with certain
writers as opposed to others, 'emotional preferences' that had
given vehemence to the generalizations which, in turn, had shaped
the taste of an age.

His enduring essays, he predicted, will be on particular writers
who had fed his emotions and influenced his writing: the verbal
clarity and emotional extremities of Dante; the horror of the
seventeenth-century English dramatists (Webster, Tourneur,

Middleton, Ford); the rigorous sermons of Bishop Lancelot Andrewes; and the personality of F. H. Bradley, combining scepticism with a search for the Absolute, which gave international philosophic status to a paradox native to the New England mind (as Eliot saw it in Emerson, and as Emerson himself saw it in his aunt, Mary Moody Emerson, the purest exemplar of that strange fusion of scepticism and passionate piety). In short, Eliot's last message is to disregard the preference of his own time for his early, more aesthetic essays in favour of his mature, more 'judicial' essays. Although Eliot does 'shyly' intrude himself into the company of the foremost English poet-critics, Johnson, Coleridge, Dryden, and Arnold (in order of preference), Eliot's real claim is to go beyond criticism as he wished to go beyond poetry, to speak from on high, not words but the Word, everlasting truth.

In this talk, Eliot noted a change and narrowing of his literary tastes. The devotion to Dante remained, as ever, constant ('the comfort and amazement of my age'), but he now turned more often to Shakespeare rather than to Shakespeare's contemporaries, and to Herbert rather than to Donne. George Herbert was the subject of Eliot's last critical work, a British Council pamphlet published in 1962.

With Herbert, as with Pascal, Eliot fixed on religious personality so congenial to a present state of being that he could speak in unison with his chosen model. In 'Pascal' (1931) Eliot had described a particular 'sequence which culminates in faith', a rational scepticism transformed into religious fervour. *George Herbert* is another such exercise in spiritual autobiography, and in this sense is Eliot's last view of his life.

Eliot's portrait is of a religious poet guided in his formative years by a mother of literary tastes, piety, and exceptional gifts of mind; a man well-born, proud and snobbish, meticulous of dress and ambitious of worldly position who, in his thirties, turned aside from the world. At that point 'the pride of birth natural to Herbert was transformed into the dignity of the Servant of God'. With a powerful intellect, and by nature not meek, Herbert underwent intense spiritual struggle, unsparing self-examination and self-criticism. His poems show 'ample evidence . . . of the cost at which he acquired godliness'. There was no steady progress: he falls, he rises. Herbert avoided what Eliot tells us is the great temptation to the religious poet: to set down not what he actually feels, but what he would like to feel. It is here that Eliot is most entirely in unison with Herbert, in his scrupulous honesty about failure or limitation, and also in a proud man's struggle for humility.

Unlike his friend Donne, who drew crowds to hear the oratorical sermons at Paul's Cross, Herbert turned from the glare of fame. A close friend was Nicholas Ferrar of Little Gidding. For a time Herbert was prebend at Leighton Bromswold, 5 miles south of Little Gidding, and later took an equally modest post as Rector in the village church of Bemerton in Wiltshire. Eliot's Herbert is not a mild man in a charming pastoral retreat. Quick-tempered, given to moods of rebellion, in his poems he sets down 'the fluctuations of emotion between despair and bliss, between agitation and serenity, and the discipline of suffering which leads to peace of spirit'. Eliot's phrases could sum up his own career. Herbert was able to say, he quotes: 'And now in age I bud again.' Like Eliot, he had a happy marriage in his last years that contributed to a final picture of religious serenity. Eliot closes by quoting in full the poem 'Love' in which every line suggests a parallel with his own life:

> Love bade me welcome: yet my soul drew back,
>   Guiltie of dust and sinne.
> But quick-ey'd Love, observing me grow slack
>   From my first entrance in,
> Drew nearer to me, sweetly questioning,
>   If I lack'd any thing.
>
> A guest, I answer'd, worthy to be here:
>   Love said, You shall be he.
> I the unkinde, the ungratefull? Ah my deare,
>   I cannot look on thee.
> Love took my hand, and smiling did reply,
>   Who made the eyes but I?
>
> Truth Lord, but I have marr'd them: let my shame
>   Go where it doth deserve.
> And know you not, sayes Love, who bore the blame?
>   My deare, then I will serve.
> You must sit down, sayes Love, and taste my meat:
>   So I did sit and eat.

To a man who has known much illness there is, in this surrender, a 'convalescence of the spirit'. Such a convalescence sustained Eliot until his death on 4 January 1965. Allen Tate's account of his last visit confirms this serenity: 'The last time I saw him was in September, 1963, at his house in London. He had been seriously ill the year before and he had trouble walking. As we were leaving, he stood at the drawing-room door, leaning on two canes. I had put on my coat and I turned to wave a second good-bye. He couldn't raise his hands from the canes, but he smiled as he moved the fingers of one hand to acknowledge my gesture.'

In the last months of Eliot's life John Hayward asked after him tenderly, as if there had been no breach. He admitted how much he missed Eliot, and wished that he could see him again.

'He was—my dear—friend', Hayward said brokenly on the telephone to Helen Gardner on the day of Eliot's death.

John Hayward died later in the same year, on 17 September, aged 60, and a wit to the end. When he telephoned Kathleen Raine to say that he was not well enough to see her, she asked:

'Is there anything I can send you?'

'A wreath, I think, my dear', was his reply.

At Eliot's Westminster Abbey memorial service, the absence of John Hayward and Emily Hale, two people who were central to Eliot's mature works, went unnoticed, while the press duly recorded a great crowd of publishers, ambassadors, and family: Martha and Abigail Eliot, playmates from the New England summers of Eliot's childhood, Pound, Dr Thomas Faber who, as a child, had heard Eliot read *Cats*, and two other people from his past, Maurice Haigh-Wood and Mary Trevelyan.

In 1949 Eliot had chosen the second movement of Beethoven's seventh symphony for his funeral, rather than his favourite *Coriolan* Overture which he had feared might sound too grand. The service included also Stravinsky's setting for 'The dove descending' from *Little Gidding*; a reading by Alec Guinness from Eliot's later works; and a hymn of Herbert's, one of relief not trial:

> Thou hast granted my request,
>   Thou hast heard me;
> Thou didst note my working breast,
>   Thou hast spar'd me.

Far away, in Massachusetts, Emily Hale recorded her grief privately in a controlled letter to Margaret Thorp:

9 Church Green
Concord, Mass 01742
January 11, 1965.

Margaret my dear,

Your short note after the event of last Monday, was very welcome on Saturday. I thought naturally, a great deal of you, Willard and Bill Dix, since we four are so very intimately concerned with what is now a future—as well as a past—mystery and remarkable personal story.

I had not known until last autumn—and then not in great detail from E. H. H. [Eleanor Hinckley] how terribly ill he has been for two or three years—the old bronchial weaknesses, plus many complications, so an oxygen tent seems to have been in constant attendance, Poor Man. The family report that Valerie has been *very* remarkable in her nursing as well as other wifely duties—: her life has indeed been devoted to his wants— perhaps I could not have filled this requirement as she has done— perhaps—only perhaps—the decision to marry her was the right one.

I had gone unexpectedly from New Bedford to Woods Hole—the doctor's appointment being postponed—so that I was with Dorothy E[lsmith] who knew both T. S. E. and our relationship as intimately as anyone. I can't answer you very closely as [to] how I 'feel'—some of it has come back so vividly, it has not been easy; and having the public know *nothing* is at once a blessing and a burden . . .

I try hard to take this all dispassionately but it is a little hard . . .

Lovingly
Emily

An additional letter to Willard Thorp, on 17 January 1965, shows a growing kindness to the widow: 'I am happy I can very honestly say I am thankful she was his so devoted companion these last years. I have no feeling of anything else towards her—nor any feeling about T[om] except to *accept* it all without any bitterness or unkind thoughts.' On 20 January, in heavy snow, she attended a service for Eliot in the Memorial Church at Harvard. Harry Levin was there, also Robert Fitzgerald, and Walter Jackson Bate. She found the academic occasion 'uninspiring'.

Emily Hale continued in her poised style to act and travel, and died in Concord in 1969.

Mary Trevelyan lived on into the eighties. She was awarded an OBE in 1956, and a CBE followed in 1968. She founded the International Students House in London and, as governor, 'had little brown people to tea' as one Indian recalled. According to her nephew, Humphrey Carpenter, 'she never recovered from the shock of Eliot's marriage, and spent a great deal of the remainder of her life mulling over what had happened. Their friendship had been the centre of her life, and she was crushed by his rejection.'

Valerie Eliot still lives in the flat in Kensington, surrounded by Eliot's books and photographs. It is curious how Eliot projected Jamesian dramas on the women who loved him. Vivienne played the wild Daisy to his shocked Winterbourne. Emily played the staunch May, watching with Marcher for a spring that was not to be. Finally, Valerie Eliot had the happier task of the beneficent Alice Staverton in whose arms Spencer Brydon comes back to life, purged from his encounter with his other self in the haunted house of the past.

In Eliot's last work the spurned actress predicts that the Elder Statesman will be playing a part even in his obituary. In most of Eliot's obituaries he was, predictably, the Nobel prizeman, the international writer, the Anglican churchman, the jolly joker. But C. Day Lewis, helped by Hayward, did break through these roles to the agonized introspection of the sombre-clad son of the Puritans who stooped, lined and bowed by a sense of sin, around Russell Square. This one obituary did recognize that 'the fastidiousness, the moral taste, and the intellectual severity, which were a legacy of New England ancestors merged with the Anglo-Catholic tradition to direct his poetry ever farther in the exploration of spiritual awareness . . .'.

Some time after Eliot's arrival in England, he had acquired a photograph of Poets' Corner in Westminster Abbey, with Dryden in the foreground. On the second anniversary of Eliot's death his own plaque was placed in Poets' Corner, next to Tennyson and Browning, and at the feet of Chaucer. Reynolds Stone, a descendent of Sir Joshua Reynolds, engraved on it those lines where Eliot speaks explicitly from beyond the grave:

> And what the dead had no speech for, when living,
> They can tell you, being dead: the communication
> Of the dead is tongued with fire beyond the language of the living.

With death, the acts of a life fall into perspective, and we see its totality, its inward coherence.

'Though our outward man perish, yet the inward man is renewed day by day', read Peter du Sautoy at Eliot's memorial service. Eliot did not wish his outward man to be preserved in biography. He called, rather, for an imaginative grasp of the inner life as expressed through works of art: 'for the things which are seen are temporal; but the things which are not seen are eternal.'

'Can a lifetime represent a single motive?' Eliot asked in a pencil note in 1941.

Only in his works did he give a full account of the inner drama that dominated his life, the search for saving grace, the agonizing over harm, and the long years of patient waiting as he prepared to meet a God whose attributes were 'unimaginable'.

To Eliot the 'life of a man of genius, viewed in relation to his writing, comes to take a pattern of inevitability, and even his disabilities will seem to have stood him in good stead'. If we apply this theory to his own life, its inner coherence is obvious. If we follow, say, his relations with women, it is curious to see how they were absorbed into what seems an almost predetermined pattern. Emily Hale prompted the sublime moments; Vivienne, the sense of sin, as well as providing, throughout the first marriage, the living martyrdom. Later, sensible, efficient Mary Trevelyan served her long stint as support during the years of penitence. For her their friendship was a commitment, for Eliot quite peripheral. His passion for immortality was so commanding that it allowed him to reject each of these women with a firmness that shattered their lives.

The shape of Eliot's life is one of paring down, concentration. Much had to be discarded to make his life conform to the pattern of the pilgrim, and there is a constant tension between an idiosyncratic nature and an ideal biography. His early years turned on his acceptance of this pattern, his later years on the question of its fulfilment. Its drama lay in efforts to close the gap between nature and perfection at whatever personal cost, revelling to some degree in that cost, and inspecting his torment as the distinguishing brand of his election. To be chosen, he had to purify the very ambition that set him off. And so the moral drama of the later years, from *Murder in the Cathedral*, centres not on the earlier festering of primitive violence, epitomized by lust, but on the subtler taints of public dignitaries, epitomized by pride. Eliot always calls for judgement but, we can never forget, for divine not human judgement.

At best a life of Eliot can be but a complement to work which speaks for itself. The writer in Virgina Woolf's *The Waves* is intently aware of some future biographer dogging him. To forestall the predictable road-map from pedigree to grave, this writer speaks directly to a future reader: 'Take it. This is my life.' What he offers is an alternative to conventional biography which he calls 'a convenience, a lie.' All our stories of birth, school, marriage, and death, he argues, are not true, because lives turn on 'moments of humiliation and triumph' that happen now and then, but rarely at times of official crisis or celebration.

In Sweden in 1948 to receive the Nobel Prize, Eliot was shaving one morning when a procession of six girls, dressed (it seemed to him) in nightgowns and wearing crowns of lighted candles, marched into his room. Hastily wiping the suds from his face, he stretched an arm around the bathroom door for his overcoat which he put on over his underclothes, and then bowed to them as they sang. He shared publicity with the Harringay Rangers, a visiting hockey team composed mostly of Canadians who chewed highly scented mint gum. The celebrations of the Nobel Prize were peripheral to the moments on which his life turned, like the moment in 1926 when he fell on his knees before the *Pietà* in Rome. His first marriage was peripheral to 'the awful daring of a moment's surrender'. And his Harvard studies were peripheral to the Silence in the streets of Boston, that hour in June 1910 for which, already, he had waited, when life, he said, was justified. This vision that came to him at the age of 21 seemed to mark him for some exceptional destiny. His overriding desire was to meet this mystery.

Eliot tells us repeatedly that he was aware of feelings beyond the nameable, classifiable emotions of lives directed towards action. On 31 March 1933 he spoke of 'the deeper, unnamed feelings which form the substratum of our being, to which we rarely penetrate; for our lives are mostly a constant evasion of ourselves . . .'. Such feelings were the substance of that hidden life where words reach into silence. This might touch on the experience of the saints, though he was careful not to claim that. Yet to ignore the presence of this model, as it came to him initially through the poetry of his mother and then through his reading as a student, would be to miss a singleness of purpose to which life and art were both subordinate. With Eliot, writing was not an offshoot of the life; the life was an offshoot of writing. The work forecasts the life, even determines it, as, say, the dream of parting in 'La Figlia che Piange' forecasts Eliot's actual parting with Emily Hale, or as the drafts of the last play spell his own discovery of human love. It is not enough to see, as Henry James put it, that art *makes* life, makes importance, for with Eliot it was an exemplary pattern which made the art that made the life. So the parting at the start of his career and the love that closed it were, in a sense, dictated by the religious pattern of renunciation and blessedness.

Eliot surrendered to a form of life that would fit an ideal order which we can never directly know, but may, at moments, apprehend. At such moments he burned with the nearness of the infinite 'thing', but it slipped away, and the rude clamour of the city returned to blunt his senses. Ground down amidst the worker-termites in post-war London, he remembered 'the heart of light, the silence'. The vision was linked with desire, the memory of light on a girl's hair. Trapped in a wretched marriage, he recalled a lost capacity for feeling. There followed years of savage deadness. But feeling did come back. Protected by a vow of celibacy, Eliot called to the 'Lady of silences', a chaste and hallowed presence in his imagination. After Eliot's reunion with Emily Hale in the early thirties, the moment came once more when they visited the rose-garden at Burnt Norton. And there, at last, he grasped 'reality'. He looked right into 'the heart of light' in a beating moment. 'Quick now, here, now . . .' It was gone. This time, though, he pursued the moment to its logical conclusion, 'Love', the 'unfamiliar Name'.

In setting out the formula for this pursuit, Eliot converts life into truth. This was his aim in the year of his conversion, when he spoke of the poet's gigantic attempt to 'metamorphose' private failures and disappointments into something universal and imper-sonal. Eliot's achievement was to redefine the exemplary life in the uncongenial conditions of the twentieth century, aware all the while that its marking points—moments of light and horror—were not the markers of his own life only, but those of many genera-tions, past and future.

Eliot was only superficially a man of his time. His affinities were with the spokesmen for the exemplary life in other centuries, the Catholic mystics of the middle ages and the American Puritans of the seventeenth century. He said in 1954 that he combined 'a Catholic cast of mind, a Calvinistic heritage, and a Puritanical temperament'. This was not the cultural despair, the dead-end alienation of Modernity, but the purposeful withdrawal of one who passed through his age as a hermit, refusing its debasement. He accepted the solitude of a man of 'destiny', and for much of his life put love aside as a distraction. Denouncing the chaos of his century, he pointed to a vision that he was not himself to enjoy.

His move from America to Europe gave him a peculiar detachment from all environment, a universal foreignness which was the obverse to strong feeling for certain locales like Gloucester, Massachusetts. He remained somehow alien to Englishmen and the Anglican Church, from everything with which he identified himself. He devised an anti-self not, like Yeats, to extend the self, but to guard it: his jokey good fellowship was a cover for the solitary; his mild gentlemanliness a cover for the extremist; his impersonality a cover for confession; his acquired European tradition a cover for native roots. Eliot cut from the draft of his last play two telling lines on the exile who must exchange

> The loneliness of home among foreign strange people
> For the loneliness of home which is only memories.

His youth was interred in another land, its shadow moving with the shades behind the grey rocks of the New England shore. Hope Mirrlees perceived something of this when she said categorically: 'He wasn't a bit like an Englishman', though he could feel 'most violently English' as when he sported his white rose on the anniversaries of the death of Richard III. 'I once said to him: "You know there is this indestructible American strain in you." And he was pleased. He said: "Oh yes, there is. I'm glad you realized it. There is."'

In his last years, he stressed his origins, and declared that his poetry, in its sources, its emotional springs, came from America and its past—not a specific past. His new life was rooted in the New World idea, in its invitation to formulate new modes of life. He revived two main modes which fused in his poetry. One was the pattern of spiritual pioneering, when Eliot said 'fare forward, voyagers', a continuation of Whitman's voyaging 'With questionings . . . / *Wherefore unsatisfied soul?* and *Whither O mocking life?*' The other mode of life was the set formula laid down in seventeenth-century New England. Eliot once said that he felt at home in America as it had been before about 1830. What that date

meant to Eliot must be a guess. It was soon after that Eliot's
grandfather left Boston for the frontier. It was also then that the
civilized élite of the Eastern seaboard lost its power in the bitter
election of 1828, when John Quincy Adams fell before the rude,
uncultivated Andrew Jackson.* Was Eliot still resisting the impact
of Jacksonian democracy—more Western, more individualistic—a
hundred years on? Or was it some more subtle change: the fading
of the last traces of Calvinist piety before the cheery optimism of a
new age of self-reliance? For Emerson, the very advocate of self-
reliance, that old demanding piety remained a lingering force
through his memory of his Calvinist aunt: 'What a debt is ours to
that old religion which, in the childhood most of us, still dwelt like
a sabbath morning in the country of New England, teaching
privation, self-denial and sorrow!'

What distinguished the New England Puritans from their
English brethren was their unique demand, in the words of
Increase Mather, 'That persons should make a Relation of the
work of Gods Spirit upon their hearts'. Eliot set down such a
'Relation' from 'The Hollow Men' to the confession of the Elder
Statesman. In the seventeenth century, public confession had been
compelled by a church which saw itself as the farthest outpost of
ecclesiastical holiness. It was quite beyond the requirements of
entry into the mild Anglican church of which Eliot actually had
little immediate knowledge at the time of his conversion. It was
conversion itself that drew him, for, through that experience, he
revived the strenuousness of the New England divines for whom it
was not enough to profess faith. For Eliot too it was not enough to
repeat 'For Thine is the Kingdom'. Those words must pierce the
convert, must annihilate his rotten self. Whimpering, he must
submit to the terror of God's hand. In New England, each person
who would join the exclusive company of visible saints must
experience and declare saving grace. Grace, though, must come
unsought to a soul wrestling with sin as Eliot wrestled with the
devil of the stairs.

Eliot was an expert on election. Like the divines, his ancestors,
no one knew better the stages and signs of salvation, but he had
limited spiritual gifts. He had diagnostic self-insight, strength of

---

* The Eliots are distantly related to the Adams family. Eliot referred jokingly to
Uncle John (John Adams, the second President and father of John Quincy Adams)
when he praised the American Cantos in a letter to Pound (1 Jan. 1931).

will, endurance, and a readiness to recognize the reality of the unseen, but he had not much gift of vision. He craved a lifetime burning in every moment, but had to accept a lesser course of 'trying'. Yet it was this acceptance of the common lot that made his mature poetry more accessible than the merciless clairvoyance of the early verse. He strove to content himself with right action, and not to hope too hard that saving grace would come to fill the waiting vessel of perfected conduct. But Eliot's was a God of pain, whose punishment, until the last eight years, was almost the only sign of the absolute paternal care.

The irony of Eliot's life was that he was unsuited to the model life of saints. He was simply too self-conscious to be a saint. Yet his struggle to subdue intellectual pride, his almost savage intolerance, proved the fertile matter of his poetry. There remains the paradox of a man who wished to be saint above poet, but who became all the greater as poet for his failure to attain sainthood. He fell back on another goal, to be God's agent, and as public spokesman he achieved an extraordinary authority. His pronouncements are still repeated as truths from on high. The prophetic role, like the Puritan rigour of introspection, came most directly from America, as well as the challenge of a terrifying nature where man measures himself in the face of an immeasurable power that is and was from the beginning.

Eliot's career circled back so that the sources of his own life, the Mississippi and Cape Ann, became the source of all life. Despite his adaptation to England, his adoption of English religion, manners, and clothes, and despite his marriages to English women, his poetry led him back to 'the source of the longest river', and to the silence the child heard between two waves of the sea.

The 'Bellegarde' Fragment and the Notes for Murder in the Cathedral

In the Houghton Library, Harvard, there are eighteen pages of pencil notes for *Murder in the Cathedral*. Eliot's brother, Henry Ware Eliot, jun., rearranged the order of Eliot's notes when he made a typed copy that would dovetail with the final text of the play. Fortunately, he kept a record of the page numbers of the original order, so that it has been possible to reconstruct the sequence of ideas for the play and, significantly, the poems that Eliot associated with it, as it evolved in his mind between December 1934 and May 1935.

Page 1. The manuscript of 'Rannoch by Glencoe' (published in Oct. 1935) which was clipped together with the following three pages of outline. The manuscript of 'Rannoch' shows very little change: the poem seems to have come remarkably whole. Eliot used one line about the starved crow in the final text of *Murder*.

Pages 2–3. Eliot jotted an outline sequence of scenes. Its brevity is unlike Eliot's more detailed scenarios for his other plays. Initially, there was to be less of the chorus; there were two other characters, Herbert of Bosham and John; and, most interesting, no Tempters as yet.

Page 4. Outline of time scheme for each scene. On the back of page four Eliot jotted five names of contemporary writers, numbered one to four. These, I think, provided the germ of the four Tempters: Wells, Russell, Lawrence, and (conjoined) Huxley and Babbitt.

The 'Bellegarde' Fragment. One page of pencil manuscript for a sketch is on the same paper as the other seventeen pages of the *Murder* manuscript but, Henry Ware Eliot notes, it was received separately about two months later. On the bottom half of the page, Eliot includes lines from the speech of the second Tempter (beginning 'Power possessed grows to glory . . .'), following six lines which were a revised extract from a separate typescript (with a few pencil lines added in the margin) which Eliot called 'Bellegarde'. Henry Ware Eliot included the two typescript pages of the original 'Bellegarde' fragment with the *Murder* manuscript. Though not aesthetically significant, the 'Bellegarde' fragment may be the earliest germ of *Burnt Norton* and, therefore, of *Four Quartets* (in the sense that the 1914 fragment 'So through the evening' might be said to be the germ of *The Waste Land*). If so, 'Bellegarde' is important not only as a link between two major works but as a suggestive autobiographical statement, with its Jamesian sense of lost love, and Eliot's own sense of impotence when the moment of love fades: a strange quick switch from leaping delight to loss. Over-analysis reads into delight the thin, illicit snatching at the pleasures of imaginative self-aggrandisement.

Pages 6–8. A try-out of some lines for the Chorus beginning 'Seven years and the summer is over'. It seems that as soon as he put pencil to paper, the Chorus came easily.

Pages 9–10. Eliot went on from 'Bellegarde' with the words of the second [Tempter]. The word, Tempter, does not itself appear. These men are still represented solely by their numbers.

Page 11. Plan for the fourth [Tempter]. The complete idea is here.

Page 12. Eliot then worked on the scene between Becket and the Knights, leading to murder. He started with the climactic moment of the scene: Becket's last defiant and submissive words.

Pages 13–14. Chorus, reacting to murder with its sense of a land defiled.

Page 15. Eliot tried out here the voices of the Knights as yet unnamed: taunting voices, tipsy voices, chanting in quatrains, just before Becket's climactic defiance.

Page 16. The defences of what are called, at first, Chairmen (not Knights). Eliot practises the tone of the voice, the style of talk, in the case of the first Chairman, a bland, disarming after-dinner style. Shocking mischief, he says easily. This is the verbal guise of the decent chap. I think he got this easygoing tone through the Chairman before creating his medieval parallel, the first Tempter.

The second Chairman assumes the style of reason. The audience is assumed to be prejudiced in the Archbishop's favour. The insidious appeal is to fair-mindedness: put yourselves in our place.

The third was to be young, tipsy, noisy. His self-defence is that it was unpleasant, and he got nothing out of it.

The fourth is subtle, as befits the parallel to the fourth Tempter. 'Who killed the Archbishop?' he will ask.

Page 17. Becket's declaration that the Law of God is above the Law of man. Here Eliot grasped the essential polarities of the play. This came to him, logically, after the Chairmen's defence of the temporal order.

Page 18. Eliot planned a coda of adoration of God, thanksgiving for the blood of martyrs which creates holy places, and acknowledgement of responsibility for all the evil in the world. This was to be followed by the Chorus's prayer for mercy.

This manuscript outline shows that Eliot went straight into the words of the play. He was thinking, from the outset, in the rhythm of the play's poetic line.

The Composition of The Family Reunion *1934-9*

THERE are at least ten discernible layers of composition following Eliot's first reference to a new play, along the same lines as *Sweeney Agonistes*, in a letter to Hallie Flanagan in February 1934. The layers suggest that the play was brewing in the mid- rather than late-thirties, and that he struggled with it much more than with *Murder in the Cathedral*, where he got quickly into the vein of the verse, and which seems to have needed only a sketchy scenario. In the case of *The Family Reunion*, Eliot types draft after draft. The smooth look of the typescripts can be deceptive: there are many telling changes. Eliot submitted drafts to five people for comment: E. Martin Browne, Ashley Dukes, Emily Hale, John Hayward, and Frank Morley.

1. Typescript scenario (Houghton). There are no names for the characters. The Furies are to be one man and two women in evening dress. The play ends when the hero decides to seek his purgation.

2 Unfinished draft (King's) with no names. Here Eliot first works out the scene between Harry and Mary.

3. Additional scenario, with names (Houghton). This consists of one typescript page on Part I, and two fascinating pages of rough but detailed pencil notes for Part II. The central idea is the process of de-possession. When Harry goes to pack, the ending trails off in uncertainty.

4. Three pages of pencil notes for a scene between Mary and Downing near the end of the play (Houghton). These notes were filed with the manuscript of *Murder in the Cathedral*, and are on the same paper as Eliot's preliminary pencil notes for that play. It is probable that these first four stages of composition are much earlier than has been supposed, between February 1934 and the time that he wrote *Murder* (winter-spring 1935).

5. After a gap of about 18 months, Eliot began to give full attention to the play on his return from New England late in 1936. There is a typescript draft of Part I, dated 1937, with notes by Hayward. (Houghton: called 'Typescript A').

6. A complete typescript draft was given to Emily Hale (who presented it to the Houghton Library in 1960: 'Typescript B'). He considered as titles, 'Follow the Furies' or 'Fear in the Way'. Here Agatha speaks of Harry's possible sanctification.

7. Complete typescript draft, with notes by Hayward, and dated 1937-8 (Houghton: 'Typescript C'). In this draft, Eliot struggled with Harry's

speech about his divided self (II. ii, p. 102) that went back to early notes (see 3). He changed all the verbs from present to past tense, possibly to distance Harry's emotions of contamination and dissociation. It was to this draft that Eliot probably referred in three letters to Pound of 19 Dec. 1937, 17 Feb. 1938, and 21 Feb. 1938. In the first of these he says that the play was three-quarters written, and would be finished by about Easter. At this point he declined to say more about it, glossing his family motto (*tace aut face*) as: say nothing and saw wood. By February he was prepared to say that he thought *The Family Reunion* a lot better than *Murder in the Cathedral* and, in the last of these letters, announced that he had finished, and would let the draft rest for a while.

Typescripts A, B, and C seem very similar, which suggests how patiently Eliot retyped and revised the play.

8. Hayward's draft (King's) dated 28 September 1938, was called the 'first' draft. It is really a fairly late draft.

9. The Working Draft, dated 1938 (Houghton). This draft is the same as 8, but with comments by Emily Hale, Martin Browne, and Frank Morley. Two marginal suggestions from Emily Hale led to two major changes.

First, she suggested that Mary's rebellious outburst came at the wrong point in the play, too late. Eliot shifted the speech to the second scene of the play. Since the speech was, in its original form, more insistent, the effect of the shift would have been to give to Mary's fate an importance which Eliot clearly did not wish to develop. He cut down her speech, making her tamer, less vocal, more polite: a woman who would submit to the waiting-and-watching role. Martin Browne and Morley had also urged Eliot, in vain, that Mary should be developed, or that the relation to Harry should have more substance. Following Martin Browne's criticism, Eliot made a memo to himself to get Mary to arrange flowers which, Morley was quick to point out, was far too feeble a gesture, but Eliot kept it. Emily Hale's more tactful pressure, later in 1938, led Eliot in effect to play her down rather than up.

Emily Hale's other major suggestion (endorsed by Martin Browne) was that Harry's mission be brought to a stronger climax. She wrote on the script: 'chance for Harry's explanation of Furies as he *now* sees them and to strengthen scene between Amy and himself.' The result was an additional dialogue in II: ii. beginning with Amy's question, 'But why are you going?' and ending with Harry's announcement of his 'election' to 'follow the bright angels'.

The Houghton Library has a sequestered correspondence between Emily Hale and Eliot about the play.

10. Finally, there is the play published at the same time as its first performance in March 1939.

Abbreviations

In the source notes the following abbreviations have been used:

App.   Appendix.

AW   *Ash Wednesday*, 1930 (see *Collected Poems*).

Beinecke   Beinecke Library, Yale University.

Berg   The Berg Collection, New York Public Library.

BN   *Burnt Norton*, 1935 (see *Collected Poems*).

CC   T. S. Eliot, *To Criticize the Critic: Eight Essays on Literature & Education* (London: Faber, 1965; New York: Farrar, Straus & Giroux, 1965, repr. Noonday-Farrar, 1968*).

CFQ   Helen Gardner, *The Composition of* Four Quartets (London: Faber, 1978).

CP   T. S. Eliot, *Collected Poems 1909-1962* (London: Faber, 1963; New York: Harcourt Brace, 1963*).

CPy   *The Cocktail Party*, 1949 (see *Collected Plays*).

DS   *The Dry Salvages*, 1941 (see *Collected Poems*).

EC   *East Coker*, 1940 (see *Collected Poems*).

EEY   Lyndall Gordon, *Eliot's Early Years* (Oxford and New York: Oxford University Press, 1977).

E.H.   Emily Hale.

E.M.B.   E. Martin Browne.

EMB   E. Martin Browne, *The Making of T. S. Eliot's Plays* (Cambridge, England: Cambridge University Press, 1969).

ES   *The Elder Statesman*, 1958 (see *Collected Plays*).

facs. *WL* *The Waste Land: A Facsimile and Transcript of the Original Drafts Including the Annotations of Ezra Pound*, ed. Valerie Eliot (London: Faber, 1971; New York: Harcourt Brace, 1971*).

FQ   *Four Quartets*, 1943 (see *Collected Poems*).

FR   *The Family Reunion*, 1939 (see *Collected Plays*).

HM   'The Hollow Men', 1925 (see *Collected Poems*).

Houghton   Houghton Library, Harvard University.

J.H.   John Hayward.

King's   King's College Library, Cambridge University.

* Editions used in text. In source notes, when both English and American publishers are cited, the first cited is the one used in this book.

Notes

CHAPTER I. A NEW LIFE

I *'Nothing but...'*. Letter to Bonamy Dobrée, quoted by Dobrée in 'T. S. Eliot: A Personal Reminiscence' in *T. S. Eliot: The Man and His Work*, ed. Allen Tate (NY: Dell, 1965), 79.

2 *as Lot in Sodom*.... T.S.E. to Pound (19 Dec. 1934). Beinecke Library, Yale. All subsequent references to T.S.E.'s correspondence with Pound are to letters in this collection.

lone, last child. *EEY*, ch. 1.

student year in Paris. *EEY*, ch. 3.

'almost a definite moment of acceptance...'. *Dante* (1929), *SE*, 237. Dante said, 'I have set my feet in that region of life beyond which one cannot go with intent to return.' *Vita Nuova*: XIV.

the 'unread vision...'. *AW*: IV.

a call. *Marina, CP*, 106.

light in an English garden. *BN*: I.

beautiful, uplifted. Letter from C. E. Dexter Morse to the present author.

'life' for a poet. *Shakespeare and the Stoicism of Seneca* (1927), *SE*, 117.

'Where is the Life...'. *The Rock*: Chorus I, *CP*, 147.

'the recognition of the reality of Sin...'. 'Baudelaire' (1930), *SE*, 378.

'reality'. *BN*: I.

4 *'Consumed...'*. *LG*: IV.

events beyond record. I have lifted the phrasing of Carolyn Heilbrun who, in a *New York Times Book Review* (10 Feb. 1985), understood precisely this problem and possibility in biography.

'that the man who's been successful...'. Draft of *ES* owned by Valerie Eliot. Quoted *EMB*, 318.

Virginia Woolf on Eliot. Letter to Vanessa Bell (18 May 1923). Quoted by Ronald Bush, *T. S. Eliot: A Study in Character and Style* (NY: OUP, 1983), 104.

mother's poems. *EEY*, ch. 1.

read about the ordeals of the saints. *EEY*, ch. 3.

a lifetime burning. This idea, which was to find full expression in *EC*: V, originates in an unpublished poem, 'The Burnt Dancer', dated June 1914. Berg.

5 *'crowskin'*. HM: II.

'Let me also wear ...'. HM: II. See also *AW*: II: 'And I who am here dissembled ...'.

Hawthorne's Holgrave. *The House of the Seven Gables*, ch. 12, 'The Daguerreotypist'.

'I was still the same ...'. *LG*: II.

'The Captain'. Osbert Sitwell's memoir, cited by John Pearson, *Façades: Edith, Osbert, and Sacheverell Sitwell* (London: Macmillan, 1978), 239.

'I grow old...'. 'The Love Song of J. Alfred Prufrock', *CP*, 7.

6 *'That is a life'*. 'A Note on War Poetry', *CP*, 215.

Old Buffer of the clubs. He joined a good many: the Oxford and Cambridge Club; the Burke Club, a Tory dining club; The Club, an eighteenth-century foundation mainly for peers, but including John Betjeman and Desmond MacCarthy; later, the Garrick Club and the Athenaeum.

praying in the train. M.T.'s diary (25 June 1952). PRS.

'The horror! the horror!' This was the original epigraph to *WL*. See *facs. WL*.

7 *'the poet, who...'*. 'Yeats', *OPP*, 299.

8 Shakespeare and the Stoicism of Seneca. Published 22 Sept. 1927. *SE*, 107–20.

Helen Gardner suggested. ... Conversation with the present author at Eynsham, late March 1985. Dame Helen Gardner was the author of *The Art of T. S. Eliot* (London: Cresset, 1949) and *The Composition of Four Quartets* (London: Faber, 1978) as well as of many other distinguished works. She was professor of English at Oxford and edited the *New Oxford Book of English Verse*. She died in 1986.

'What every poet starts from ...'. *SE*, 117.

with William Force Stead. 'Literary Reminiscences' (29 April 1940). Unpublished holograph memoir of T.S.E. in response to questionnaire by Dr Osborn, Osborn coll., Beinecke. Because some of this memoir is incorrect, Helen Gardner refused to edit it, but she did believe and like this particular anecdote.

'May Morning'. See *EEY*, ch. 3.

sending red roses. Letter to Conrad Aiken (21 Nov. 1914), Huntingdon Library, California.

9 *with dark hair*. ... Looks recalled by Marie McSpadden Sands (Scripps

College '31) who became close to E.H. in 1932–3 when she designed sets for her productions. Letter to the present author (8 Sept. 1986).

1908. T. S. Matthews, *Great Tom* (NY: Harper & Row, 1973), 140.

like another son to Edward Everett Hale. E.H. To Ricardo Quinones (2 Aug. 1965), who reported this in letter to the present author (29 Sept. 1986).

10 *portrait of E.H.* I am indebted to C. E. Dexter Morse for a photograph.

Adeline Moffat. See *EEY*, ch. 2.

E.H. acting A Backward Glance. *Great Tom*, 146.

E.H.'s family connections. Letter from Caroline Willington (n.d.), Scripps College Archives. Denison Library, Claremont, California.

noble fantasy. This notion was presented to Scripps students during a talk on Eliot in Dec. 1932, and reported in the College newspaper.

11 *Harvard academics*. 'Mr Apollinax', *CP*, 23.

E.H.'s drama courses. Archives of Concord Academy, Concord, Mass. where E.H. taught in the mid-1940s. I am indebted to the English teacher, Philip McFarland, for these facts.

her first post. Information from Megan Sniffen-Marinoff, College Archivist, The Colonel Miriam E. Perry Goll Archives, Simmons College. Information on E.H.'s various posts also from Abbot Academy where she taught from the late 1940s to 1957. I am grateful to Margaret F. Crouch, Librarian at Phillips Academy, Andover, Mass.

collection of photographs. Smith College Archives, Northampton, Mass.

formal first exchanges. These first letters are not sequestered with the bulk of the letters at Princeton, which are not to be unsealed until 2019. E.H. did not class these with the main body of Eliot's letters because, for her, they preceded their understanding. For a full discussion of this correspondence see ch. 4.

12 *Dante's reunion with Beatrice*. *Purgatorio*, Cantos xxx and xxxi.

'comprehends, enlarges . . .'. *SE*, 223.

autobiographical. Letter to Pound (29 Dec. 1929). Beinecke Library, Yale.

'Olive-crowned . . .'. *SE*, 224.

discussed with Stead. Stead, 'Literary Reminiscences', op. cit.

in Burford. T.S.E. wrote to her c/o Mrs R. H. Gretton, 'Calendars', Burford in Sept., and once again on 6 Oct. to an unknown address. Princeton.

confided to Stead. Letter (30 Dec. 1930), Osborn coll., Beinecke. All subsequent references to T.S.E.'s correspondence with Stead are to letters in this collection.

'A very dear friend of mine . . .'. Quoted in *Great Tom*, 148.

final part of A W. A W was published on 24 Apr. 1930.

13 *'life-giving'. A W*: II.

sailing and divine intimations. See WL: V, *Marina*, and *DS*: III.

'exile'. A W: IV.

golden-rod. A W: VI.

'Who . . .'. A W: IV.

'We would see a sign!' T.S.E. took these words from a sermon by the seventeenth-century Anglican, Lancelot Andrewes. *CP*, 29.

some emotions have been purified. . . . See T.S.E.'s discussion of Shakespeare's late heroines, Perdita, Miranda, Imogen, and Marina in an unpublished talk, 'The Development of Shakespeare's Verse', King's College, Cambridge.

draft of Marina. Bodleian Library, Oxford.

had to go back to Mass. Letter to Stead.

Casco Bay, Maine. T.S.E. to McKnight Kauffer (24 July 1930). Letter owned by Grace Schulman, and described in her 'Notes on the Theme of "Marina" by T.S. Eliot'.

enough of a Southerner. . . . T.S.E. to Stead (20 June 1930).

14 *Robert Lowell. Collected Prose of Robert Lowell*, ed. Robert Giroux (NY: Farrar, Straus & Giroux, 1986), 181.

embodiment of old Boston. Confirmed by Isabel Fothergill Smith and Margaret Ann Ingram, colleagues in 1932–4 at Scripps College. See also *The Diary of Virginia Woolf*, 4 (27 Nov. 1935), ed. Anne Olivier Bell (London: Hogarth; NY: Harcourt, 1982), 355, and her *Letters*, vol. 5, no. 3084, ed. Nigel Nicolson and Joanne Trautmann (London: Hogarth; NY: Harcourt, 1979), 446.

'the sublime vision . . .'. 'The Poet' in Ralph Waldo Emerson, *Selected Prose and Poetry*, ed. Reginald L. Cook (NY: Holt, Rinehart, 1950, repr. 1964), 331.

'First Debate'. Notebook, Berg Collection. Eliot dated this poem 1910. See *EEY*, ch. 2.

three martyr poems. 'The Death of Saint Narcissus' (1915) is the only one published (in *Poems Written in Early Youth* (London: Faber, 1967; NY: Farrar, Straus & Giroux). 'The Burnt Dancer' (dated June 1914) and 'The Love Song of Saint Sebastian' are in a folder of miscellaneous manuscripts in the Berg Collection.

sweet brown hair. A W: III.

'of memory'. A W: II.

15 *pivotal poem.* A. V. C. Schmidt, 'Eliot's Intolerable Wrestle: Speech, Silence, Words and Voices', *UNISA English Studies* (Pretoria, 1983), 17–22.

earliest section. This became part II of *AW*.

'*The love of man and woman...*'. Dante, *SE*, 234-5.

'*sublimation*'. Ibid., 235.

imparadisa la mia mente. *Paradiso*, Canto xxviii, l. 3: '*quella che'mparadisa la mia mente.*' I am grateful to Gwen Watkins for locating this quotation.

draft of earliest section. Sent to W. F. Stead. Osborn Coll., Beinecke Library, Yale.

'*the impossible union*'. *DS*: V, *CP*, 199. See Schmidt, op. cit.

'*I mean the turning away...*'. 'Views and Reviews', *New English Weekly*, vii, 8 (6 June 1935), 152.

16 *love's essence in memory*. The phrase is lifted from the *Vita Nuova*.

conversations with Mary Trevelyan. PRS.

This '*has given me...*'. E.H. to President Jaqua, Scripps College Archives.

Scripps College. Information from Lorraine Havens whose husband, Paul Havens, was an early member of the English faculty.

17 *made a ceremony.* ... Recalled by Margaret Ann Ingram (Scripps 1931) who was Assistant Registrar while E.H. was at Scripps. Letter to the present author (1 Sept. 1986).

Laurabel Neville Hume's recollections. Letter, Scripps Archives.

18 *Marie McSpadden Sands's recollections*. Letter to the present author (8 Sept. 1986).

Goldoni. Report on rehearsals in college newspaper, 7 Nov. 1932. Scripps Archives.

Lady Gregory. ... I am indebted to Mrs Hume for sending me a copy of her write-up on the Siddons Club for 1932-3 in *La Semeuse*.

review of E.H. as Lady Bracknell. *The Scripture* (15 May 1933).

It was not long. ... Lorraine Havens, letter in the Scripps College Archives.

on Edward Lear. His talk on Lear is reported in *The Scripture*. See also William Baker's reconstructed account in 'T. S. Eliot on Edward Lear', *English Studies*, 64 (1983), 564-6.

19 '*bitter period*' and '*man of extremes*'. *The Scripture* (12 Dec. 1932).

Vivienne lost touch. She recalls this date some years later in her diary, Bodleian Library.

Virginia Woolf to T.S.E. Letter (15 Jan. 1933) *The Letters of Virginia Woolf*, vol. 5, 150-1, in reply to a letter from T.S.E. in Nov. 1932.

E.H. waiting. Lorraine Havens heard this from her husband who went to the station with Emily Hale. He had once met Eliot at Oxford, and had offered to drive him to the home of Mary Eyre which had been loaned to Eliot for his stay.

visit to Balboa Island. Described by Marie McSpadden Sands in letter to the present author, op. cit.

The US had done him good. T.S.E. to Pound, dated Vigil of Ascension Day, 1933.

From America he wanted. . . . T.S.E. to P. E. More (18 May 1933). More Papers, Princeton University Library.

20 *'somewhere else'*. T.S.E. describes his affinities with More in 'Paul Elmer More' *Princeton Alumni Weekly* (5 Feb. 1937) and in a letter to More (11 Jan. 1937). More papers, op. cit.

felt like Alice. To P. E. More (18 May 1933). More Papers, op. cit.

describing the Cabots. Recalled in Virginia Woolf's letter to T.S.E. (15 Jan. 1933), *The Letters of Virginia Woolf*, vol. 5, 150-1. Richard Clarke Cabot was Professor of Clinical Medicine and Professor of Social Ethics at Harvard University. Ellery Sedgwick (who married Mabel Cabot) was Editor of *The Atlantic Monthly*. They belonged to the uppermost crust of Boston society.

a wild woman of Providence. T.S.E. to Virginia Woolf (March 1933). Berg.

'I met you first at Spring Street'. Copied out for Virginia Woolf in letter dated Twelfth Night, 1935. Berg.

Eliot prolonged his stay. Vivienne expected him back in May according to a signed statement she extracted from him a year before. Bodleian Library.

King's Chapel. This is the oldest pulpit in America still in use where it was established in the seventeenth century. It had been an Anglican church, but after the Revolution became the First Unitarian Church of Boston. There, on 1 Dec. 1932, T.S.E. gave a talk on the Bible.

portrait of E.H. in the hall. Recalled by C. E. Dexter Morse in letter to the present author.

21 *family reminiscences*. Henry Ware Eliot to Marianne Moore (6 June 1936), cited by Bush, op. cit., 183.

'Emily and Mr Eliot...'. Letter to the present author (1 Aug. 1977).

weekend in the Berkshires. Ibid.

'New Hampshire'. Published Apr. 1934 together with 'Virginia'. *CP*, 138.

attended his address. Mrs Elsmith's letter, op. cit.

Frank Morley. 'A Few Recollections of Eliot', Allen Tate's coll., 103-7.

'He is 10 years younger'. (10 Sept. 1933) *The Diary of Virginia Woolf*, vol. 4, 178.

7 December. T.S.E. to Virginia Woolf. Berg.

Kensington. T.S.E. to Virginia Woolf (31 Oct. 1933). Berg.

22 *incognito*. T.S.E. to Pound (Vigil of Ascension Day, 1933). Beinecke.

making poetry pay.... This was a note that T.S.E. added to Stead's 'Literary Reminiscences', op. cit., in 1955.

Eliot's 1935 report. Copy in Eliot Collection, Houghton Library.

23 *T.S.E. to Pound on allusions.* (12 Jan. 1934). Beinecke.

T.S.E.'s letters of rejection. Recalled by Brigid O'Donovan, 'The Love Song of Eliot's Secretary', *Confrontation* (Fall/Winter, 1975).

letter to Edouard Roditi. (10 Aug. 1929). I am grateful to Prof. Roditi for allowing me to read T. S. E.'s letters to him. The letters are in the Department of Special Collections, Research Library, UCLA.

advised Allen Tate and joked. T.S.E. to Tate (22 June 1926; 26 Mar. 1943), Tate Papers, Princeton.

a standard of civilization. Kathleen Raine to Leonard Clark (14 Feb. 1965). Berg.

Stead once witnessed.... 'Literary Reminiscences', op. cit.

24 *John Hayward.* Many of the following biographical details come from a vivid obituary in the *Annual Report*, King's College (Nov. 1965), 30-3.

his voice and puffing. Francis Maynell, obituary in *The Book Collector* (winter 1965).

the favoured age. Desmond Flower, obituary, ibid.

George Rylands. Obituary, ibid.

acted a bevy of prisoners. Annual Report, op. cit. The details that follow are lifted almost verbatim.

joined 'the Biblioboys'. A. N. L. Munby, obituary, *The Book Collector*, op. cit.

light verse. The verses were privately printed in 1939 in a volume entitled *Noctes Binanianae* (referring to John Hayward's flat in Bina Gardens). Copies in King's and the Houghton Library.

25 *Vivienne refused.* Vivienne Eliot, Diaries, Bodleian Library.

Hayward to Morley. Hayward–Morley Correspondence, Letter XI (Feb. 1940). King's. Quoted *CFQ*, 32.

26 *'the pattern'. MC*, I, *Plays*, 17.

Nehemiah as model for the American Puritans. Sacvan Bercovitch, *The Puritan Origins of the American Self* (New Haven: Yale, 1975), 63: 'Nehemiah became the favorite ... *exemplum* of the colonial clergy.'

competition on ancestors. T.S.E. to Virginia Woolf (Apr. 1934). Berg.

Anabase. (London: Faber, 1930; NY: Harcourt, 1938, repr. 1949), 73. A letter from T.S.E. to Edouard Roditi (4 Apr. 1928) says that he had completed the translation about a year before.

27 *'depravity's despair'.* 'What Dante Means to Me' (1950), *CC*, 134.

'His despair...'. 'The *Pensées* of Pascal', *SE*, 364.

'alone with the Alone'. Quoted by T.S.E. in 'Lancelot Andrewes' (1926), *SE*, 308.

a new poetic language. Helen Gardner suggested that Eliot's new style began in *WL*: V, in an interview for a BBC 'Bookmark' programme on Eliot in Sept. 1984. Unfortunately, the director cut the remark.

'*Donne belonged*...'. *SE*, 309.

'*in the spiritual hierarchy*', *SE*, 310.

28 '*precise*'. Shakespeare, *SE*, 115.

December 1934. In Dec. T.S.E. discussed the play during a weekend visit to E.M.B. *EMB*, 55.

no noble-minded Thomas More. *Church Times* review (June 1935), donated to the Houghton Library by the Revd John Carroll Perkins.

a bit of the author as germ for the character. 'The Three Voices of Poetry', *OPP*, 102.

Martin Browne. *EMB*, 35.

29 '*All my life*...'. *MC*, II, *Plays*, 43.

earliest pencil notes for MC. Houghton Library. See App. I.

'*To the Law of God* ...'. *MC*, II, *Plays*, 46.

Matthiessen's review. 'TSE's Drama of Becket', *Saturday Review* (12 Oct. 1935).

'*the pale New England morality murder*'. *Diary*, 4 (Dec. 1935), 356. I am indebted to Ursula Werner for pointing this out in her Oxford thesis on the literary relationship of T.S.E. and V.W. (1987).

To want sainthood.... I have lifted this felicitous and accurate sentence from Roger Lewis's winning essay for the Chancellor's English Essay Prize at Oxford University (on 'The world is but a school of inquiry').

Thomas a 'lap ahead'. Letter from T.S.E. to E.M.B. (Shrove Tuesday 1935) quoted in *EMB* (Supplement to 1970 reprint), 349.

Eliot told his brother.... Letter (28 Apr. 1936) when *MC* was to come to the US. Henry Ware Eliot includes an extract from this letter with a typescript of *MC* in the Houghton Library.

30 *told P. E. More*. Letter (2 June 1930). Princeton.

shaft of sunlight. *MC*, I, *Plays*, 12.

September 1934. This is the likely date of T.S.E.'s visit to Burnt Norton. See below p. 45.

'*I have had a tremor of bliss*'. Part II, *Plays*, 44.

Bertrand Russell as ex-teacher. See *EEY*, ch. 3.

1927 Criterion *review*. (Aug. 1927), 177-9.

31 '*the enervate* gospel of happiness'. 'Thoughts After Lambeth', *SE*, 323-4.

'*What chiefly remains*...'. *SE*, 324.

'*Samson in Gaza*...'. Part I, *Plays*, 24.

T.S.E. on Babbitt. Review, *Criterion* (Aug. 1927) op. cit. and letter to the *Bookman* dated 31 Mar. 1930 (copy enclosed in letter to P. E. More).

A Primer of Modern Heresy. This is the subtitle of *After Strange Gods* (London: Faber, 1934) based on lectures at the University of Virginia in 1933.

'*I am concerned...*'. Ibid. 56.

'*... It may operate...*'. Ibid. 57.

The Tempters conduct Becket. ... From Roger Lewis, op. cit.

32 *Just as Becket faced his Tempters.* ... D. E. Jones showed the parallels between Tempters and Knights in *The Plays of T. S. Eliot* (London: Routledge, 1960), 61-2.

Eliot discussed with his brother. ... Letter (28 Apr. 1936). Extract included with a typescript of *MC*. Houghton.

Eliot challenges the audience's immunity. From Roger Lewis, op. cit.

33 *Holmes. MC* contains a reference to A. Conan Doyle's tale, 'The Musgrave Ritual', one of Sherlock Holmes's early cases, related to Watson. Grover Smith discovered the allusion in *T. S. Eliot's Poetry and Plays: A Study in the Sources and Meaning* (Univ. of Chicago, 1950, repr. 1971), 194.

mentioned to his brother. Letter, op. cit.

pathetic. T.S.E. to Sydney Schiff (4 July 1935), Schiff Papers, British Library. All Vivienne's and T.S.E.'s letters to Sydney and Violet Schiff are in the British Library.

'*that moral activity which* disentangles'. Poe, 'The Murders in the Rue Morgue', *Tales of Mystery and Imagination* (NY: Heritage, 1941), 336. I am grateful to Roger Lewis (op. cit.) for this apt quotation.

Eliot told his brother. Letter, op. cit.

the Mercury. This and the following details about the subsequent history of *MC* come largely from *EMB*.

34 '*That is perhaps the greatest surprise*'. London Letter to the *New Yorker* (13 July 1935) from 'Samuel Jeake, Jr'.

partitioned. This is not like a Greek chorus.

the mystery of corruption. ... I owe these phrases to Sarah Edworthy.

The Times. There is an excellent collection of reviews—of all T.S.E.'s plays— in the Houghton Library.

35 MC *in an air-raid shelter. EMB*, 154.

MC *in the basement of Lloyds Bank.* E.M.B. to T.S.E. (3 July 1941), quoted in *EMB*, 155.

'*one of the most "shared" performances...*'. Ibid.

MC *at Kelham.* 1947. Photographs in the Houghton Library.

Brooks Atkinson's review. New York Times (26 Apr. 1953). Copy in Houghton.

36 *T.S.E. thought Donat the best.* ... M.T.'s diary for Apr. 1953. PRS.

the moment that pierces one.... Plays, 43.

took Eliot no more than four months. T.S.E. said on Irish broadcasting in Jan. 1936 that the play took four months. A. Walton Litz, Introduction to T.S.E.'s 'Tradition and the Practice of Poetry', *Southern Review* (Oct. 1985), 875.

lips that would pray. HM: III.

'between the rocks'. AW: V.

'Shadow'. HM: V.

37 *'DA ... Datta ...'.* WL: V.

fount. AW: IV.

'I am afraid...'. Pound, Cantos xxix and lxxviii, *The Cantos* (London: Faber 1975), 145, 481. I am grateful to A. Walton Litz for identifying Eliot here.

Thomas Hooker. Quoted by Patricia Caldwell, *The Puritan Conversion Narrative: The Beginnings of American Expression* (Cambridge University Press, 1983), 91.

'new verse'. AW: IV.

John Cotton. In *Christ the Fountain of Life* (1651), quoted by Caldwell, 92.

T.S.E. at King's Chapel. Unpublished address before the Women's Alliance on 'The Bible as scripture and as literature' (dated 1 Dec. 1932). Houghton. Bequest of the Revd John Carroll Perkins. I am grateful to Mrs Valerie Eliot for permission (in 1975) to see this.

38 *'which surely no man...'.* 'Thomas Heywood', *SE*, 158.

'a puritan at heart'. Eileen Simpson, *Poets in their Youth: A Memoir* (1982; repr. London: Picador, 1984), 131.

'a smack of the Puritan temper'. Review (June 1935). Donated to the Houghton Library by the Revd John Carroll Perkins.

'hellish'. Plays, 42.

'We are soiled...'. Plays, 48.

'enjoys feeling disgust'. 'History or Poetic Drama?', *Me Again: Uncollected Writings of Stevie Smith*, ed. Jack Barbera and William McBrien (London: Virago, 1981), 148-52.

that nerve. 'History or Poetic Drama', op. cit.

39 *More accused Eliot of Calvinism.* T.S.E. refers to this in a letter to More (10 Aug. 1930). Princeton.

Eliot accused More of heresy. T.S.E. to More (17 Feb. 1932). Princeton.

Eliot's view of hell. T.S.E. to More (2 June 1930). Princeton. *Inferno*, canto III.

later that summer. T.S.E. to More (10 Aug. 1930). Princeton.

Psalm 130. Address on the Bible, op. cit. This psalm was eventually read at Eliot's funeral.

'a man with a mission'. Unpublished autograph memoir of Lady Ottoline Morrell (dated 1 May 1938). Beinecke. Stead notes here that T.S.E. made his remark about Providence more than once.

'*new life*'. Chorus IX, *CP*, 168.

looked to Isaiah and Ezekiel. T.S.E. to P. E. More (7 Nov. 1933). Princeton.

T.S.E.'s own Bible. King's College, Cambridge.

'*Fear not...*'. Isaiah 43: 1.

40 '*The Word of the* LORD ...'. Chorus III, *CP*, 155.

'*The Witness*'. Chorus I, *CP*, 148.

'*an inherited disposition ...*'. T.S.E. to Aldington (8 Oct. 1923). An extract from this letter was printed in the Univ. of Texas Exhibition pamphlet (1961).

'*Let me go forth, O Lord!*' Charlotte Champe Eliot. Hayward Bequest, King's.

decent godless people. *The Rock*, Chorus III.

'*The desert is squeezed...*'. Ibid., Chorus I.

'*the American writing in English...*'. 'Tradition and the Practice of Poetry', a talk given in Dublin in January 1936, published in the *Southern Review* (Oct. 1985), 873–88, with an Introduction and Afterword by A. Walton Litz.

Sir Herbert Read. 'T.S.E.—A Memoir', Allen Tate's coll., 30.

Whitman defined the American poet. ... Preface (1855) to *Leaves of Grass*, *Complete Poetry and Collected Prose* (NY: The Library of America, 1982), 9.

'*Let us affront...*'. 'Self-Reliance', *Selected Prose and Poetry*, op. cit., 174.

41 *Andrew Eliot on 'a generation of vipers'*. Easter day sermon, 1766. Copy in the Eliot coll., Houghton Library. Eliot himself recalled this phrase in letter to M.T. (26 Jan. 1948), PRS, and in a letter to Pound (4 Dec. 1936).

admired grandfather. T.S.E. mentioned his admiration to M.T. (26 Jan. 1948). Letter quoted in PRS.

a classmate. James Freeman Clarke, in his Journal (May 1839). Quoted in obituary in Hayward Bequest, King's.

the classic American sermon, the Jeremiad. See Sacvan Bercovitch, *The American Jeremiad* (Univ. of Wisconsin, 1978).

more as a moralist. See excellent article on Eliot's criticism by Ronald Schuchard: '"First-Rate Blasphemy": Baudelaire and the Revised Christian Idiom of T. S. Eliot's Moral Criticism', *ELH*, 42 (Summer 1975).

'*I speak as a New Englander*'. *After Strange Gods*, 16. T.S.E. repeated this self-characterization as New Englander in a letter to Pound (dated Childermass, 1937).

'*the dark ages before us*'. 'Thoughts After Lambeth' (1931), *SE*, 342.

'*of cords...*'. *Song for Simeon* (1928), *CP*, 101–2.

'*... set down ...*'. *Journey of the Magi* (1927). *CP*, 100. See Alan Weinblatt's stimulating ideas on language in 'T. S. Eliot: Poet of Adequation', *Southern Review* (Oct. 1985), 1118–37.

The prophetic role. See 'Towards a Christian Britain', *The Listener* (10 Apr. 1941), 524–5: Eliot said that the idea of a Christian society would appear 'in the lives of prophets' men who have not merely kept the faith through the dark ages but who have lived through the mind of that dark age, and got beyond it. Prophets, he went on, are not always recognised as such in their own lives, 'but it is through them that God works to convert the habits of feeling and thinking . . . to which we are all more enslaved than we know.' *Desmond MacCarthy. The Listener* (9 Jan. 1935).

42 *Charles William Eliot urged T.S.E.* . . . Recounted by Harry Levin, 'Old Possum at Possum House', *Southern Review* (Oct. 1985), 1008-11.

'Hidden under the heron's wing'. Folder of miscellaneous poems, Berg. For further discussion, see p. 159. See also *EEY*, ch. 3.

43 *T.S.E.'s rooms*. Described by Virginia Woolf, *Diary*, vol. 4 (31 Mar. 1935), 294.

the Sisters of St Elizabeth. T.S.E. told M.T. years later, PRS.

'Denying . . .'. *Animula* (1929), *CP*, 103.

'a spectre . . .'. Ibid.

'simple soul'. Ibid.

Eliot wrote to Mrs Perkins. *CFQ* supplies the dates of T.S.E.'s letters to Mrs Perkins, and also quotes from this correspondence owned by Dr Donald Gallup, Eliot's bibliographer.

according to Jeannette McPherrin. Letter, Scripps College Archives.

Hidcote Manor was 'the one I loved'. Letter to Mrs Perkins, quoted *CFQ*, 36.

'A Country Walk'. Princeton.

44 *Stamford House*. Some information came from the present owner, Catherine Devas, for which I am grateful.

'to feel "at home" . . .'. Letter to Mrs Perkins (30 Sept, 1935), quoted *CFQ*, 35.

E.H. wrote to Scripps in August. Scripps College Archives.

45 *'My weekend . . .'*. Quoted *CFQ*, 35.

'autumn heat'. T.S.E. was always precise about seasons. If he wrote 'autumn' it is likely that it *was* autumn. See his letter to J.H. about a line in the first draft of *LG*: '"Autumn weather" only because it *was* autumn weather . . .'. He goes on to say that autumn also provided a link with *Burnt Norton*, 'La Figlia Che Piange', and 'New Hampshire'. It is significant that the latter, which is a poem of spring or early summer, not autumn, was linked by T.S.E. with other Emily Hale poems.

46 *'Footfalls echo . . .'*. *BN*: I. All subsequent references to *BN* come from this opening section, unless indicated.

'They'. An acknowledged source for *BN* in a letter from T.S.E. to John Hayward (5 Aug. 1941). *CFQ*, 39.

The garden has remained as it was. I first visited Burnt Norton with Helen Gardner and a group of her students in June 1974, in brilliant sunshine, and again with my husband on a mellow autumn day in early September 1986. The former visit was much in mind as Dame Helen had died, and I was writing an obituary. The garden had not changed, and was still deserted.

47 *'Bellegarde' sketch*. Sketch is T.S.E.'s word in a letter to his brother. Henry Ware Eliot, jun. placed the fragment, together with 17 pages of MS jottings for *Murder in the Cathedral*, in the Houghton Library. The fragment is on the same paper, but he notes that it was sent to him some two months later. It consists of one page with six lines (which T.S.E. tried in vain to work into the play) and two other pages, the unfinished 'Bellegarde' sketch itself. See App. I.

rose-garden encounter in FR. II. ii, *Plays*, 106-8.

'leaping pleasures'. Quotations come from the six lines that T.S.E. tried to adapt for *MC*, quoted *EMB*, 44.

48 *'Memory and desire'*. *WL*: I. This section was written in 1921.

'looking into the heart of light...'. Ibid.

'un-being'. *BN*: V.

'Quick now, here, now, always -'. *BN*: V.

'So long...'. Sonnet 18: 'Shall I compare thee to a summer's day.'

its scenarios go back to 1934-5. See ch. 2 and App. II.

49 *'news'*. I, ii, *Plays*, 82-3.

'I only looked...'. II, ii, *Plays*, 106-8.

T.S.E. explained further to Martin Browne. Letter quoted in full, *EMB*, 107-8.

50 *Eliot remarked to P. E. More....* Letter (Shrove Tuesday, 1928).

when they meet.... Dante (1929).

most autobiographical play. I once discussed this with Richard Ellmann, who agreed.

'Thibet of broken stones'. *FR*, II. ii. *Plays*, 104.

CHAPTER 2. THE MYSTERY OF SIN

51 *'the Mystery of Iniquity'*. *The Rock* (London: Faber, 1934), 84, repr. *CP*, 169.

'a bag of ferrets'. V.W., *Diary*, 3 (8 Nov. 1930), 331.

tried to separate. V.W. to Lady Ottoline Morrell (6 Sept. 1932) *The Letters of Virginia Woolf*, vol. 5, 99: 'I hope the separation is complete and final, as it promised to be when I last had news.'

a friend. Roger Sencourt, *A Memoir of T. S. Eliot* (NY: Dodd, Mead, 1971), 151.

52 *'the reality of Sin'*. Op. cit.: 'a recognition of the reality of Sin is a New Life' ('Baudelaire').

'become first capable of Evil'. *After Strange Gods*, 60.

in an essay. 'Baudelaire', *SE*, 380.

asked P. E. More. Letter (28 Apr. 1936). Princeton.

in Charlottesville. T.S.E. was giving the Page-Barbour lectures at the University of Virginia.

'*New Hampshire*'. T.S.E. stayed in NH just before he sailed for England in June 1933. 'Cape Ann' was later (1935), but expresses a similar quickening.

'*Iron thoughts...*'. 'Virginia' (published 1934).

53 *witch-hangers*. Letter to Pound (8–10 Dec. 1933). Beinecke.

Hawthorne's fable. 'Young Goodman Brown'.

'You don't see them ...'. Orestes in *Choephoroi*. The first scene was published in the *Criterion* (Oct. 1926) and the second in Jan. 1927, with the epigraphs repeated, *CP*, 111. On 9 December 1932 T.S.E.'s audience at Harvard was given a picture of a poet with 'ghastly shadows at his back' (*UPUC*, 69). He refers here to Coleridge, but his repeated use of such shadows suggests its personal import.

'*haunted by a demon...*'. 'The Three Voices of Poetry', *OPP*, 107.

Eliot's favourite Hawthorne. 'The Hawthorne Aspect' [of Henry James], *Little Review* (Aug. 1918), 47–53.

'*the violent death...*'. *The House of the Seven Gables*, ch. 1 (London: Dent; NY: Dutton), 18.

54 *witch*. According to the drafts, a witch passed a curse on Great-Uncle Harry. Houghton Library.

physically incompatible. See *EEY*, ch. 4.

'*As to Tom's mind...*'. Draft or copy (8 Dec. 1935) in Vivienne Eliot's Day Book (1935–6). Vivienne Eliot's Papers are in the Bodleian Library, Oxford.

hair stretched out tight. see *WL*: V.

'*Hysteria*'. Eliot put the place and date of composition on both Hayward's copy of his poems and on Harold Monro's, *CP*, 24.

'*Ode*'. In *Ava Vos Prec* (London: Ovid; NY: Knopf, 1920).

'*horror of life*'. 'Cyril Tourneur', *SE*, 166.

'*dying to propagate...*'. 13 Apr. 1936 in Day Book, 1935–6.

red-eyed scavengers. 'A Cooking Egg', *CP*, 37.

Hope Mirrlees. V.W., *Diary*, 4 (12 Nov. 1934), 261.

Hope Mirrlees recalled. BBC TV programme 'The Mysterious Mr Eliot', *Listener*, 85 (14 Jan. 1971), 50.

55 *nightmare*. Letter to Sydney Schiff (*c.* 1924). British Library.

'*Perhaps not even you...*'. The letter is dated 'Monday' (*c.* 17 Oct. 1922).

'*photography*'. facs. *WL*, 10–13. This draft became *WL*: II.

'*The Death of the Duchess*'. facs. *WL*, 104–7.

'*In the Cage*'. Ibid., 10–11, 16–17. The title is from a story 'In the Cage' (1898) by Henry James.

'*Why do you never speak?*'. *WL*: II, *CP*, 57.

'*Those are pearls...*'. *WL*: II.

56 *voyager or pilgrim*. See *WL*: IV and V.

'wonderful'. facs. WL, 10–13.

'I shall rush out...'. WL: II, lines 132–3.

Theresa Eliot. She said this to Peter du Sautoy. Theresa Eliot was married to T.S.E.'s brother Henry Ware Eliot, jun.

'thrown like an assegai...'. Diary, 4 (10 Sept. 1933), *179.*

57 *Eliot told Russell.* Letters, McMaster Univ., Hamilton, Ont. Cited by Bertrand Russell, *The Autobiography of Bertrand Russell*, vol. 2 (London: Allen and Unwin, 1968), 174.

'He is a Prophet'. Diary (2 Oct. 1935). Bodleian Library.

'a sort of super-being'. Ibid.

Eliot confided to Virginia Woolf. V.W., *Diary*, 3 (29 Apr. 1925), 15.

'drown...'. Letter to Lady Ottoline Morrell, *The Letters of Virginia Woolf*, 5 (22 June 1932), 71.

distorted. See Virginia Woolf, *A Room of One's Own* (London: Hogarth; NY: Harcourt, 1929).

proposal to leave the bank. see *EEY*, ch. 6.

began in about Sept. 1923. In Sept. 1923 T.S.E. wrote to Wyndham Lewis to thank him for encouragement over it. In Sept. 1924 he told Arnold Bennett that he wanted to write a contemporary drama about a furnished flat sort of people. (Peter Ackroyd, *T. S. Eliot: A Life*, London: Hamish Hamilton; NY: Simon & Schuster, 1984, 135, 145.) T.S.E. later said that *Sweeney Agonistes* was written in two nights between 10 and 5 a.m. (A. Walton Litz, *Southern Review*, Oct. 1985, 875.)

'I knew a man...'. CP, 122.

58 *Vivienne's writing.* See *EEY*, ch. 6.

poems. Twelve unbound copies of the poems of Vivienne Haigh Eliot were in existence in 1934 when an inventory was made of the Eliots' belongings. There are isolated poems but no collection of them among her papers in the Bodleian Library.

'Am ill...'. Letter (n.d.). Beinecke.

to Leonard Woolf for advice. Letter (n.d.), Berg. The address (9 Clarence Gate Gdns) proves that it was not later than 1925 when the Eliots moved to Chester Terrace.

draft of a letter. The addressee is not legible. It may not have been sent, or even meant to be sent. Her writing books are in the Bodleian Library.

Eliot defined Vivienne's case. To Leonard Woolf, op. cit.

59 *'curse out'.* Four-page letter to Pound (n.d.). Beinecke.

'took to' trances. Ibid.

might turn vampire. Letter to Pound (27 Dec. 1925). Beinecke.

Little Nell. This was her signature to a note to Pound (n.d.), Beinecke.

'anxious to die'. Letter to Pound (n.d.). Beinecke.

a ts. scenario of Sweeney Agonistes. 'The Superior Landlord' (an early title was 'The Marriage of Life and Death: A Dream'). The exact date of this five-page scenario is uncertain. Michael J. Sidnell has made a persuasive case that T.S.E. wrote it much later, in 1934, under the influence of Auden's *The Dance of Death*. On the other hand, T.S.E.'s own note, 'My typing probably precedes the fragments themselves', is not to be dismissed lightly as, elsewhere, his dating of drafts is invariably accurate. It seems unlikely that, if he had begun reframing *Sweeney Agonistes* as much as eight years later, he would have forgotten this. The concluding fragment he did for Hallie Flanagan's production in 1933 is an odd, tacked-on, flat piece, as though the work had gone dead. Other work which T.S.E. was doing in 1934 was, by then, more overtly religious than 'The Superior Landlord'. For Sidnell's argument, see *Dances of Death: The Group Theatre of London in the Thirties* (London and Boston: Faber, 1984), App. A.

words of Brutus. Ibid.; and see above, p. 51.

60 *a dream*. Part of the original title was 'A Dream'.

Sweeney. The name may derive from Sweeney Todd, the murderous barber, or from the name of two men in the Harvard class of 1910, both respectable: Albert Matthew Sweeney and Arthur Sweeney.

like Hawthorne. Ronald Bush has noted in a ground-breaking essay that 'Fragment of an Agon' is a work steeped in Hawthorne. He sees Sweeney as a descendant of Miriam who provokes murder only to find herself 'remote' from 'all that pertained to [her] past life', and living in moral seclusion. ('Nathaniel Hawthorne and T. S. Eliot's American Connection', *Southern Review*, Oct. 1985).

undeveloped nature. See a contemporary essay, 'Thomas Middleton' (1927), *SE*, 142. T.S.E. adds: 'The possibility of that frightful discovery of morality remains permanent.'

'Dream Songs'. 'Doris's Dream Songs', *Chapbook*, 39 (Nov. 1924), 36-7: I. 'Eyes that last I saw in tears'. II. 'The wind sprang up at four o'clock'. This uses several lines from 'Song to the Opherian' which Eliot published in April 1921, and retained as part of the *WL* manuscript. III. 'This is the dead land' became part III of 'The Hollow Men'.

'sweats with tears'. 'The wind sprang up at four o'clock', *CP*, 134.

lost violent soul. See HM: I.

61 *'perpetual star' and 'Multifoliate rose'*. HM: IV, *CP*, 81.

'The important fact . . .'. 'Eeldrop and Appleplex', *Little Review* (May and Sept. 1917), repr. *The Little Review Anthology*, ed. Margaret Anderson (NY: Horizon, 1953), 104.

golden foot. 'Song', *facs. WL*, 98-9.

'golden vision'. 'Eyes that last I saw in tears', *CP*, 133.

'between two lives'. 'Song', op. cit.

broken image. I am linking broken stone in 'The Hollow Men' with the statue of La Figlia.

62 *'that second kingdom...'*. *Purgatorio*: I, translated by John D. Sinclair (Oxford: OUP, 1939, repr. 1968), 18–19.

river of tears. 'The wind sprang up at four o'clock', *CP*, 134.

Could he cross. ... See HM: IV, *CP*, 81, and 'The wind sprang up at four o'clock', *CP*, 134.

Desmond MacCarthy. Review reported by Michael Sidnell, *Dances of Death op. cit. 106.*

'projected...'. 'Cyril Tourneur', *SE*, 166.

becomes moral by becoming damned. *SE*, 142.

'Beneath the stars ...'. T.S.E. quotes from Beatrice Joanna's magnificent death speech in *The Changeling*. *SE*, 143, 148.

'I sat by Tom'. *Diary*, 4, 260–1.

63 *'Crippen'*. Ibid., 261. The American-born Dr H. H. Crippen poisoned his wife in 1910, and was hanged. Neville Coghill also commented on the play's treatment of the psychology of a Crippen in 'Sweeney Agonistes', *T. S. Eliot: A Symposium*, ed. Tambimuttu and Richard March (London: Frank & Cass, 1948), 84.

'some trait of his own'. 'The Three Voices of Poetry', *OPP*, 102.

unfinished. T.S.E. added an ending for Hallie Flanagan's Vassar production in 1933. But, as Carol H. Smith has pointed out (*T. S. Eliot's Dramatic Theory and Practice*, Princeton, 1963, 62–3) this ending doesn't quite fit the play. T.S.E. never chose to publish it.

on two distinct levels. T.S.E., writing on John Marston (1934), suggested that 'what distinguishes poetic drama from prosaic drama is a kind of doubleness in the action, as if it took place on two planes at once'. T.S.E., *Elizabethan Dramatists* (London: Faber, 1963), 161.

'literal-minded and visionless'. T.S.E. gives this theory, specifically in relation to *Sweeney Agonistes*, in *UPUC*, 153.

Krumpacker. Like the name Sweeney, 'Krumpacker' may derive from a respectable man in the Harvard class of 1910, Walter Krumbeck, who became an educator.

1935 revival. Details from reviews. The best is Desmond MacCarthy's for the *Listener* (9 Jan. 1935).

'If the audience gets its strip-tease ...'. T.S.E.'s facetious 'Five Points on Dramatic Writing' in a letter to Pound (19 Dec. 1937) is quoted by Carol H. Smith, op. cit., 53. Although T.S.E. refers here to *FR*, the same theory would apply to *Sweeney Agonistes*.

popular audience. See 'Marie Lloyd' (1923), *SE*, 405–8.

64 *A razor chase*. Described by Sidnell, *Dances of Death*, 106.

Vivienne's drug-addiction. Statement by Theresa Garrett Eliot (28 Mar. 1970). Houghton.

'nobody to hold one's hand...'. M.T.'s diary (Sept. 1954). PRS.

diary kept during marriage. In 1919. See *EEY*, ch. 4.

description of the wife. Given by chauffer, Downing. *Plays*, 71.

'Why, oh why...'. Stephen Spender, 'Remembering Eliot' in Allen Tate's coll., 51.

It is said. By Amy, I. i. *Plays*, 62.

65 *'She used to go about...'*. Said to M.T. (28 Oct. 1954). PRS.

alcohol and morphine. Ackroyd, 185.

Edith Sitwell. See John Pearson, op. cit., 277.

'how his dying eyes lingered...'. Diary (15 Sept. 1934). Bodleian Library.

'...a lovely clear night'. Ibid. (1 Sept. 1934).

66 *About a month after*. Since Vivienne returned in Feb. 1928, and was away nine months, it is likely that she left England in May 1927.

'My dear Tom...'. Diary (16 Feb. 1935).

plucking his sleeve. E. W. F. Tomlin, 'T. S. Eliot: a friendship', *The Listener*, 97 (28 Apr. 1977), 541.

'A terrible time...'. Diary (31 Jan. 1935).

found her sinister. V.W. to Quentin Bell (26 July 1933), *Letters*, vol. 5, 207. According to V.W., Vivienne gave out that she and Ottoline Morrell had been T.S.E.'s mistresses. There was no truth in this.

'Have you any bees...'. V.W., *Diary*, 3 (8 Nov. 1930), 331.

67 *the Eliots' dinner*. Pearson, 242.

like a patient father. The Thorps dined with the Eliots in 1931. In conversation, Princeton, August 1985.

Evie Townsend. Recalled by Janet Adam Smith, 'Tom Possum and the Roberts Family', *Southern Review* (Oct. 1985), 1057.

Father Underhill. T.S.E. to Stead (2 Dec. 1930). Beinecke.

Conrad Aiken. To Theodore Spencer (31 Oct. 1930), *Selected Letters*, ed. Joseph Killorin (New Haven: Yale, 1978), 162.

'shivering, shuddering'. Ibid.

'A restless shivering...shadow'. *FR*, I, i. *Plays*, 62.

coercive. To Russell. See *EEY*, ch. 6. Cited by Russell, *Autobiography*, vol. 2, 174.

letters to Ada Leverson. Berg.

68 *'leaden' and 'sinister'*. Diary, 3 (8 Nov. 1930), 331.

Edith Sitwell meeting Vivienne. John Pearson, op. cit., 277-8.

'eternal enemy of the absolute'. 'Conversation Galante', *CP*, 25.

'*The Love Song of Saint Sebastian*'. See *EEY*, ch. 3.

69 *white satin and ether*. V.W. to Ethel Smyth (7 Sept. 1932), *Letters*, vol. 5, 100.

'*alas no Hamlet would love her*'. *Diary*, 4 (2 Sept. 1932), 123.

'*We had tea*'. Day Book (1 Apr. 1935). Bodleian Library.

a routine to deal with her. Brigid O'Donovan, 'The Love Song of Eliot's Secretary', *Confrontation*, 11, ed. Martin Tucker (Fall/Winter 1975), 3-8.

70 '*under a crowned effigy*'. V.W. to Francis Birrell (3 Sept. 1933), *Letters*, vol. 5, 222.

'*in December*'. V.W. had a letter from Vivienne on 31 Dec. 1933 which she reported to Lady Ottoline Morrell on that day. Ibid., 266.

'*I look like the little ghost...*'. Diary (9 July 1934). Bodleian Library.

The mills of God. Diary (24 Aug. 1934).

'*state of nervous collapse*'. Diary (12 Dec. 1934). She had been served a court order to warn her in late Nov.

71 '*It hurt me...*'. Letter (16 July 1935). Copy in Day Book.

'*At last the* courage ...'. Mar. 1935.

Another scheme. Diary (9 Jan. 1935).

'*It is too absurd...*'. Diary (13 Mar. 1935).

Eliot was to talk. He spoke on 'What in the practice of a particular art, such as poetry, do we mean by tradition?' He gave a copy of the text to Emily Hale.

72 *offering protection*. 1 Jan. 1935, entered into 1934 Diary.

Another plan. 7 Feb. 1935.

'*Everything was perfectly allright ...*'. 28 Nov. 1935, copy in the Day Book Scrapbook for 1935. Bodleian Library.

73 *Sir Herbert Read*. Allen Tate's collection, 23.

74 *Edward Fox as Harry*. In a London production in the late seventies.

the set pattern of the personal narrative. There is a detailed analysis by Patricia Caldwell, *The Puritan Conversion Narrative*, op. cit. In England in the seventeenth century this test was used by a relatively small number of sectarians. But New England's Puritans, led by John Cotton, adopted it widely.

Eliot and the Anglican Church. See *EEY*, ch. 6.

Vivienne pretended.... The following details come from her 'Notes for Broad' [Mr Broad was her bank manager] in her Day Book, 1936.

75 Daisy Miller. Vivienne had ordered a copy from the Times Book Club on 1 Aug. 1935.

76 '*Vivienne!*'. *Diary*, 3 (8 Nov. 1930), 331.

seven times. In Feb. she went on 1st, 8th, 11th, 19th, 22nd and 28th.

77 '*has had very great friends*'. 'Notes for Broad.'

'*apt to lose her wits*'. Copy of letter.

cables. Though Vivienne persists about a mystery, her Diary records (29 Nov. 1935) that she actually met T.S.E. after his return.

Maurice wrote. Mrs Valerie Eliot, letter to *TLS* (10 Feb. 1984), 139.

78 *attempt at escape*. T.S.E. recounted this to M.T., M.T.'s diary (2 Jan. 1957), PRS.

'*goblin ghost*'. Hope Mirrlees interview, BBC TV programme on 'The Mysterious Mr Eliot', *Listener* (14 Jan. 1971).

recalled with pleasure. Diary (26 Dec. 1935).

'*I* trust *the man*'. Diary (14 Dec. 1935).

79 '*Rannoch, by Glencoe*'. Published 1935. *CP*, 141.

'*Landscapes*' *rehearsals for* FQ. Helen Gardner linked them in *CFQ*, 34.

most ambitious play. *CFQ*, 32.

autumn 1936. In an interview with the *Star* (3 Nov. 1936), T.S.E. said that he was working on a new play. In Nov. 1938 he told V.W. that *FR* had taken him two years off-and-on to write. A draft was read to E.M.B. in Nov. 1937, which means that the first draft was done roughly between Nov. 1936–Nov. 1937. Newspaper cuttings attached to a draft of the play are dated April–May 1937, which may be one time when he worked intensively on it.

very much in love. Recalled in letter to M.T. (2 June 1950). PRS.

A professorship at Harvard. Offered by Professor Theodore Spencer in 1933. Sencourt, 153.

80 '*Waiting . . .*'. *FR*, I, ii., *Plays*, 77.

'*I cannot tell you . . .*'. Sidnell, *Dances of Death*, op. cit., 100, 323.

Sweeney Agonistes the most original thing. . . . T.S.E. to P. E. More (28 Apr. 1936). Princeton.

ten discernible layers of composition. See App. II.

date back to 1934-5. The fourth layer is on the same paper as the MS of *Murder in the Cathedral*, and was kept with it.

'*psychic*'. According to Downing, I, i, *Plays*, 72.

81 *the waiting Mary*. As yet she had no name in the Kings College TS. See App. II for dating and sequence of composition.

additional scenario. App. II: 3.

nightmares. See Ronald Schuchard's account of other moments of horror, at Marlow in 1919 and Périgord in 1920, in his spot-on essay 'T. S. Eliot and the Horrific Moment', *Southern Review* (Oct. 1985).

divided. The 1938 Working Draft speaks of Harry's two lives.

82 '*O that awful privacy . . .*'. *FR*, II, ii. *Plays*, 106.

T.S.E. to Mary Trevelyan. She recorded this conversation in her memoir, PRS, on 2 Jan. 1957. (This was M.T.'s last meeting with T.S.E.)

de-possession. This word is used in draft. Quoted *EMB*, 128.

'*exorcism*'. *FR*, II, i., *Plays*, 101.

three pages of pencil notes. Houghton.

marrying was 'a kind of preparation'. This draft is explicit. Later, T.S.E. made it deliberately vaguer: 'Whatever happened was a kind of preparation . . .'.

Martin Browne praised. T.S.E. read the first complete draft to him on 14 Nov. 1937.

stiff pokers. *Diary*, 5 (22 Mar. 1939), 210.

83 Helen Gardner on Agatha. *The Art of T. S. Eliot* (London: Cresset, 1949), ch. 6, 156.

Janet Adam Smith. *Southern Review*, op. cit., 1065.

'*the chief poker*'. *Diary*, op. cit.

'*a horror of women* . . .'. *EMB*, 107.

present to the mind. Phrases recalled from an article by Alfred Kazin on the ghost sense in American literature (Poe, Hawthorne, James) in the *New York Sunday Times* in about 1969.

delusional insanity. 'Notes on Philosophy': a set of index cards. This is a note under Richard Jeffries' *The Story of My Heart*. Houghton.

84 '*his curious search*'. 'Commentary', *Criterion* (Apr. 1933), quoted by Bush, 183.

dangers 'that look like nothing'. Henry James, Preface to *The American* in *The Art of the Novel*, ed. R. P. Blackmur (1907; repr. Scribner, 1937), 31, 33.

'*as radical as any form of Calvinism*'. 'The Church in the Festival', *Life and Work* (Oct. 1947).

Edinburgh Festival production. At the Church of Scotland's Gateway Theatre. It was presented by the Pilgrim Players as part of a season of Eliot's plays. Henzie Raeburn (wife of E.M.B.) was a success as Agatha. The *Scottish Daily Mail* suggested that T.S.E. might be the greatest British playwright since Shakespeare.

rumour. It is related in an article on *The Cocktail Party* by Geoffrey Parson in the *NY Herald Tribune* (12 Feb. 1950).

85 letter from Margaret Eliot. Cited by Theresa Garrett Eliot, op. cit.

Time. 28 Feb. 1938.

Henry Ware Eliot retorted. *Time*.

the 'accident . . .'. I, ii, *Plays*, 83.

early unfinished draft. King's.

upswing in New Hampshire. See 'New Hampshire' and ch. 1 above, p. 21.

'*vernal equinox*'. Quoted in *EMB*, 111.

86 '*a new world* . . .'. Quoted in *EMB*, 98.

Emily Hale. See App. II.

a long speech of protest. Working Draft, II, ii.

the shift. It was moved to I, ii.

'*lifetime's march*'. Agatha's words, II, ii, *Plays*, 104.

87 *origin of evil.* In one draft it is said that the origin of evil lay behind Harry's particular childhood. In the final draft T.S.E. changed it to 'the origin of wretchedness' (II, ii).

divine messengers. T.S.E. uses the phrases 'divine instruments' and 'divine messengers' in letter to E.M.B., op. cit.

the octopus or angel. 'The Three Voices of Poetry', *OPP*, 110.

'*chosen*'. Agatha, II, ii. *Plays*, 105.

Swedish production. T.S.E. gave this amusing account to M.T. PRS.

88 *advised Pound.* Letter advising Pound on the *Cantos* is dated Michaelmas 1933. Beinecke.

'jolly *corner*'. 'I, i. *Plays*, 60.

Calvin. Institutes of the Christian Religion (2.1.8.), ed. John T. McNeill (Philadelphia: Westminster, 1960), 251.

'*dramatism*'. Frank Morley in Allen Tate's coll., op. cit., 110.

the real purgatorial fire. John Hayward's draft, King's.

89 *like the Disciples.* Letter, *EMB*, op. cit.

'*Follow . . .*'. II, iii. *Plays*, 121–2.

the second draft sent to Emily Hale. The Working Draft of 1938. See App. II: 9.

the heat of the sun. II, ii. *Plays, 111.*

Zossima. Fyodor Dostoevsky, *The Brothers Karamazov.*

sanctification. TS B. Houghton. It follows Agatha's 'Harry has crossed the frontier' speech. This was the first of the two drafts that T.S.E. sent to Emily Hale. She kept it until 1960, when she gave it to Harvard. See App. II: 6.

90 *impeccable Bostonian.* To Ethel Smyth (26 Nov. 1935). *Letters*, vol. 5, 446.

'*rich American snob lady*'. To Clive Bell (4 Dec. 1935). Ibid., 451.

polluted soul. T.S.E. used the word '*pollution*' to E.M.B. *EMB*, 108.

Evening Standard reporting. T.S.E.'s cuttings were pasted on to the flyleaf to Part II of *FR*.

'*across the frontier*'. Agatha, II, iii. *Plays, 114.*

91 '*It was the policy of our ancestors . . .*'. 'Endicott and the Red Cross' in *Twice Told Tales* (1837).

'*a hundred visions . . .*'. 'The Love Song of J. Alfred Prufrock'. *CP*, 4.

'*should die . . .*'. 'Portrait of a Lady'. *CP*, 12.

Eliot remarked to Mary Trevelyan. PRS.

two unpublished talks. 'The Development of Shakespeare's Verse'. King's. The talks were given in Edinburgh in 1937 and repeated in Bristol in 1941. In speaking of Shakespeare's late plays, T.S.E. was theorizing about the play that he himself was writing at the time.

the usual classified emotions. Some of this went into 'Poetry and Drama' (1951) in *OPP*.

strange lands of more than polar darkness. This forecasts *FR*, I, ii., where Harry speaks to Mary of moving from pole to pole in the early Unfinished Draft (App. II: 2). And both talk and play forecast 'the unimaginable / Zero summer' in *LG*: I (1942).

92 *told Michael Redgrave*. *EMB*, 136.

the life of the senses will freeze. These polar regions forecast the deliberate freezing of the body in *EC*: IV (1940).

'cruellest' month. *WL*: I.

the soul's sap. *LG*: I.

'lying voices'. I, ii. *Plays*, 81.

'which I cannot put in order', *FR*, II, i. *Plays*, 98.

MC *during the war*. *EMB*, 154.

failure of FR *daunted T.S.E.* Suggested by Bush, 209.

93 *Harry's exit line*. II, ii. *Plays*, 111. Harry reappears once more, but only cursorily.

The way up and the way down. Epigraph to *BN*, from Herakleitos.

vast and terrible sea. In 1940 T.S.E. planned a sequence of only three poems. *East Coker* and *The Dry Salvages*, planned together in 1940, are closely connected.

CHAPTER 3. THE PERFECT LIFE

94 *'acute personal reminiscence'*. T.S.E. to J.H. (5 Aug. 1941), *CFQ*, 24. All quotations from this correspondence, now at King's College, Cambridge, are cited in *CFQ*.

'things ill-done...'. *LG*: II.

'Kensington Quartets'. T.S.E. to J.H. (3 Sept. 1942), *CFQ*, 26. This letter is bound with the typescripts of *LG*. The manuscripts and typescripts of *Four Quartets* are mainly at King's College, Cambridge. There is also material at Magdalene College, Cambridge, and a typescript of *BN* at the Houghton Library.

'grimpen'. The source was pointed out by Helen Gardner, *CFQ*, 103.

'The poetry does not matter'. *EC*: II.

'the thin milk...'. To William Carlos Williams (1920), *EEY*, ch. 4.

95 *books read at Harvard*. There is a collection of T.S.E.'s books in the Houghton Library, as well as his student notes. (See *EEY*, App. III.)

'Now...'. *EC*: V.

'I saw eternity ...'. 'The World', *The Complete Poems*, ed. A. Rudrum (Harmondsworth: Penguin, 1976).

'*And visions rise ...*'. 'Julian M. and A. G. Rochelle' (9 Oct. 1845) or 'The Prisoner' in *The Complete Poems of Emily Jane Brontë* (NY: Columbia Univ. Press, 1941), 238, 242.

96 *Emerson's essays.* See *EEY*, ch. 2. T.S.E. was steeped in Emerson.

97 *the Word* '*Swaddled with darkness*'. 'Gerontion'. *CP*, 29.

alternation of the prosaic and poetic. In 'The Music of Poetry' (1942), *OPP*, 25 he says that 'no poet can write a poem of amplitude unless he is a master of the prosaic.'

'*In my end ...*'. *EC*: V.

'*In my beginning ...*'. *EC*: I.

'*toward Eternity*' No. 712 in *The Complete Poems of Emily Dickinson*, ed. Thomas H. Johnson (London: Faber, 1970).

'*the unimaginable ...*'. *LG*: I.

98 *middle-aged New Englander.* Lambert Strether in Henry James, *The Ambassadors*.

T.S.E. on Huck Finn. Introduction to the Cresset Library's edition of *Huckleberry Finn* (1950), vii–xvi.

the summer night. EC: I.

99 '*still / Moves ...*'. *BN*: V. This is Eliot's parallel to Keats's Grecian Urn.

'*slip, slide ...*'. *BN*: V.

100 '*Love*'. *LG*: IV.

a distilled concentrate. '... concentration / Without elimination'. *BN*: II.

the infinitude of the private man. 'The Divinity School Address' and *Journals* (7 Apr. 1840), Emerson's *Selected Prose and Poetry*, op. cit., 84, 475.

'*freedom*'. *BN*: II.

love-letter from God. Great Tom, op. cit., 144.

Emily Hale's gift of EC. Great Tom, 147.

'*voices of temptation*'. *BN*: V.

'*in an emotional whole*'. (10 Mar. 1941), *CFQ*, 109.

101 '*vibrations ...*'. 'What Dante Means to Me', *CC*, 134.

'*move in measure ...*'. *LG*: II.

moth. 'The Burnt Dancer', dated June 1914, Berg. See *EEY*, ch. 3.

'*In order to arrive ...*'. *EC*: III.

'*always*'. *BN*: V: 'Quick now, here, now, always—'.

biographical premiss. 'Silence' (June 1910). This idea recurs in *BN*: II: 'At the still point of the turning world.'

Emily Dickinson. No. 443 in *The Complete Poems of Emily Dickinson*, op. cit.

103 '*And the end ...*'. *LG*: V.

Bradford's history. *History of Plimoth Plantation*, repr. *The Puritans: A Source-book of Their Writings*, vol. 1, ed. Perry Miller and Thomas H. Johnson (NY: Harper & Row, 1963), 98–9.

Edward Johnson. *Wonder-Working Providence of Sion's Saviour* (1654), ibid., 145.

'who suffer the ecstasy . . .'. *Marina*. *CP*, 105.

104 *poignantly self-revealing*. Tarantula's Special News Service, Letter XII (Feb. 1940). King's.

'disturbance'. *EC*: II.

a letter of 1935. T.S.E. to E.M.B. (Shrove Tuesday 1935) quoted in *EMB* (1970 reprint), 349.

'creature'. *EC*: II.

outside English tradition. There is some suggestion of a parallel with Yeats but the alignment is forced. T.S.E. appears to draw on Yeats's terms in 'An Acre of Grass'—Yeats's denial of autumnal, wise serenity of age with folly and frenzy—but T.S.E. twists the allusion to fit his own more idiosyncratic case: the ageing man's fear of belonging to another (*EC*: II).

figure of Goodman Brown. Hawthorne's tale, 'Young Goodman Brown', is recalled by certain phrases in *EC*: II: 'in a dark wood . . . / And menaced by monsters, fancy lights, / Risking enchantment.'

discovers sin in a dark wood. Melville said that the tale was 'as deep as Dante'. *EC*, too, makes the connection, linking the opening of the *Inferno* ('In the middle . . .') with the dark wood of 'Young Goodman Brown'.

'canopy'. 'Young Goodman Brown'.

105 *dissolves in a dream*. Barbara Everett, in an interesting BBC talk in 1983 on *EC*, 'The Village of the Heart', said that 'entry to East Coker, in the poem, is the beginning of a dream'. In *T. S. Eliot: Man and Poet*, ed. Laura J. Cowan (US National Poetry Foundation, 1988).

'I am here'. *EC*: I.

T.S.E. and the Sketch of the Eliot Family. T.S.E. mentions in a letter to his brother (7 Feb. 1939) that he had looked it up. Their father, he recalled, had owned two copies.

Sir Thomas Elyot. Author of *The Boke Named the Governour* (1531). See *EEY*, ch. 1.

family motto. *EC*: I speaks of 'the tattered arras woven with a silent motto'.

family fortunes had declined. Mentioned in letter to Pound. Beinecke.

had Cape Ann house in mind. T.S.E. to J.H. (27 Feb. 1940).

'Old men . . .'. *EC*: V.

106 *'O dark dark dark'*. *EC*: III alludes to Milton, *Samson Agonistes* (l. 80), *The Poems of John Milton*, ed. John Carey and Alastair Fowler (London: Longman, 1968, repr. 1980), 349.

'fortunate night'. 'Stanzas' (verses 3–4) preceding *The Ascent of Mount Carmel*.

'*amid the blaze of noon*'. *Samson Agonistes* (l. 80), op. cit.

to liberate the divine image in man. Thomas Merton, *The Silent Life* (London: Burns & Oates, 1957), 27.

'*the drought*'. 'The *Pensées* of Pascal', *SE*, 364.

107 '*most hidden of saints*'. 'St. John of the Cross', *Perspectives*, 4 (Summer 1953), 52-61.

108 '*inoperancy of the world of spirit*'. *BN*: III. T.S.E. here sums up briefly the two 'nights' of St John of the Cross: a dark night of sense, followed by a dark night of the spirit.

saint's chart. The chart accompanies *The Ascent of Mount Carmel*.

'*it is the highest activity* . . .'. Quoted in review by M. C. D'Arcy, *Criterion* (Apr. 1938), 358-9.

'*I said to my soul* . . .'. *EC*: III.

'*Saint Sebastian*'. Berg, op. cit. See *EEY*, ch. 3.

The Rule was severe. . . . E. Allison Peers, The Rede Lecture for 1932, collected in *St. John of the Cross* (Faber, 1946). T.S.E. would have been responsible for Faber publications in theology.

'*animal penance*'. *The Dark Night of the Soul*, Book I, ch. 6.

'*Wait without thought* . . .'. *EC*: III.

interior work . . . *The Cloud of Unknowing* (Harmondsworth: Penguin, 1961).

Undisciplined squads . . .'. *EC*: V.

'*The Lover*'. MS notes for *EC*: IV, *CFQ*, 95. There was no MS of *EC* except for Part IV (T.S.E. to J.H., 23 June 1940).

'*the heart of the matter*'. 10 Mar. 1941 quoted in *CFQ*, 109. *EC*: IV.

109 '*conscious of nothing*'. *EC*: III.

'*I faint with heat*'. *CFQ*, 95.

'*reigns*'. *EC*: II.

'*very un-English*'. T.S.E. to Anne Ridler, *CFQ*, 95.

'*a Jansenism of the individual biography*'. 'Pascal', *SE*, 366.

William Force Stead pictured him. 'Literary Reminiscences' (1940), op. cit., Beinecke.

'*great yellow bronze mask* . . .'. *Diary*, vol. 5, 268.

'*a lifetime burning* . . .'. *EC*: V.

110 '*We can have very little hope* . . .'. 'Views and Reviews: Journalists of Yesterday and Today', *New English Weekly*, xvi, 238. At this very time T.S.E. was writing *EC*.

declined in favour. Tarantula's News Service to Morley. See letters IV, XXVIII.

Barker. Letter IV to Morley (Oct. 1939).

playing chess, etc. T.S.E. to J.H. (27 Feb. 1940).

had to visit houses in his area. . . . T.S.E. to McKnight Kauffer (23 May 1940). Pierpont Morgan Library, New York.

111 *lengthy reports of air-raid practice.* Tarantula's News Service, letter II (Sept. 1939).

Hayward had to try hard. Letter III (Sept. 1939).

'*I believe . . .*'. 'Literary Reminiscences' (1940), op. cit.

'*That was a way . . .*'. *EC*: II.

'*in forgetful snow*'. *WL*: I.

112 *to bath at the Fabers.* V.W.'s *Diary*, 5 (16 Feb. 1940), 268.

'*O perpetual revolution . . .*'. *The Rock*, Chorus I.

'*At the still point*'. *BN*: IV. See 'Coriolan': I (1931) for the first use of this phrase, *CP*, 126.

113 '*three quatuors*'. T.S.E. planned 'three quatuors' J.H. told Morley in letter XI of Tarantula's Special News Service (Feb. 1940). *CFQ* 16–8.

'*Through the dark . . .*'. *EC*: V.

the nurse. . . . Wordsworth, 'Lines written a few miles above Tintern Abbey'. *Lyrical Ballads*, ed. W. J. B. Owen (OUP, 1967), 115.

Ahab. Herman Melville, *Moby-Dick*.

beat obedient. See *WL*: V.

'*these frontiers . . .*'. 'A Commentary: that poetry is made with words', *New English Weekly* (27 Apr. 1939), 27.

the planned approach to grace. Marina.

114 *T.S.E. to William Matchett.* Quoted in *CFQ*, 18.

here or there does not matter. Eliot explained in a letter that this was an abbreviation of 'whether here or there'. *CFQ*, 113.

'*Alone–the ice cap . . .*'. *CFQ*, 111, has not transcribed correctly the pencilled holograph D2 (back of p. 5).

'*be separated*'. *CFQ*, 112.

'*made a deeper impression . . .*'. (1930), quoted by Anthony Thwaite, *Twentieth-Century English Poetry* (London: Heinemann; NY: Barnes & Noble, 1978), 45.

T.S.E.'s memory of the Mississippi in flood. Introduction to *Huckleberry Finn*, op. cit.

115 *rockpool. DS*: I and *UPUC*, 78–9, which recalled an experience 'not so simple, for an exceptional child, as it looks'.

power and terror. T.S.E.'s phrase from the Introduction to *Huckleberry Finn*, op. cit.

The Dry Salvages. Information from *Alluring Rockport*, Sawyer Free Library, Gloucester, Mass.

Eliot and Peters. Leon Little's reminiscences for the *Harvard Advocate*'s T.S.E. memorial issue. Typescript in Houghton Library.

'*the ground swell*'. *DS*: I.

116 '*I suspect...*'. Talk on 'Tradition and the Practice of Poetry' in Dublin (1936), ed. A. Walton Litz, *Southern Review* (Oct. 1985), 883. This is a restatement of Eliot's position in *Shakespeare* (1927): 'To express precise emotion requires as great intellectual power as to express precise thought' (*SE*, 115), and again, more explicitly, 'Poetry is not a substitute for philosophy or theology or religion...; it has its own function. But as this function is not intellectual but emotional, it cannot be defined adequately in intellectual terms' (*SE*, 118).

'*the point of intersection...*'. *DS*: V.

'*an occupation for the saint*'. *DS*: V.

'*between the rocks*'. *AW*: V.

117 *a long narrative which Pound cut. facs. WL*, 62-9. See *EEY*, ch. 5 and App. II.

'*And if Another knows...*'. *facs. WL*, 68-9.

'*Sail forth...*'. 'Passage to India'. The Library of America's Whitman, op. cit., 539. This and the following quotations are from stanza 9.

118 '*significant*'. *DS*: V.

fall flat. Helen Gardner calls the ending 'lame' (*CFQ*, 149). It has been criticized also by Donald Davie and Ronald Bush.

'*dearest him...*'. 'I wake and feel the fell of dark, not day', Gerard Manley Hopkins, *A Selection of his Poems and Prose*, ed. W. H. Gardner (Harmondsworth: Penguin, 1953), 62.

'*a dancer to God*'. 'The Death of Saint Narcissus' in *Poems Written in Early Youth*, op. cit., and *facs. WL*, 90-1.

119 *to '*know the place...*'. *LG*: V.

sea's jaws. *LG*: I.

'Datta, Dayadhvam, Damyata'. *WL*: V.

the timeless pattern of spiritual autobiography. Bunyan's words, quoted by Linda Peterson, 'Newman's *Apologia pro vita sua* and English spiritual autobiography', *PMLA* (May 1985), 300-14.

'*affection*', '*security*'. *DS*: II.

the '*meaning of "mother"* ...'. Scheme for *DS*. MS (Magdalene College Library). *CFQ*, 118.

'*We had the experience...*'. *DS*: II.

120 *mere* '*sequence*'. *DS*: II.

palms, tea-leaves, and psycho-analysis. *DS*: V.

entrails. 'haruspicate', *DS*: V.

Eliot on Freud. 'A Commentary: that poetry is made with words' in *New English Weekly* (27 Apr. 1939), 27, which notes, further, that the 'dramatist must study, not psychology, but human beings' and also himself: 'to what he observes, dissects and combines he must add something from himself of which he may not be wholly conscious.'

'. . . *our own past*'. *DS*: II.

In a draft he uncovers. . . . First draft of *LG*: II. *CFQ*, 228.

'*moments of agony*'. *DS*: II.

notes. *CFQ*, p. 118.

'*the ragged rock . . .*'. *DS*: II. In draft this rock immediately follows the 'torment of others'. Bush (op. cit., 219) plausibly suggests a reference here to Vivienne.

sin brought on him by a woman. 'The bite in the apple', *DS*: II. T.S.E. speaks elsewhere of spitting out the withered apple seed.

121   '*circling fury*'. Draft of BN: V. *CFQ*, 88.

carrion. T.S.E.'s last thought of the Mississippi, in the drafts, is the line (added last) about the river bearing dead Negroes, cows, and chicken coops.

things done to other's harm. Op. cit. T.S.E. alludes to Yeats's lines (from 'Vacillation') in *LG*: II.

a future. 'Now about the future', wrote T.S.E. at the end of his first draft of *DS*: II. This was cancelled in the second draft (*CFQ*, 134).

foresaw even before he experienced love. See *Poems Written in Early Youth* and *EEY*, ch. 2.

'*an equal mind*'. *DS*: III.

Mary Trevelyan's suggestion. PRS.

'*Atonement*'. Drafts of the ending of *DS*: V at King's, Magdalene, and Texas. *CFQ*, 146.

122   *Oct. 1940*. The date of T.S.E.'s move is mentioned in a letter to V.W. (28 Oct. 1940). Berg.

household. Janet Adam Smith, 'Tom Possum and the Roberts Family', *Southern Review* (Oct. 1985), 1061.

Cocky. T.S.E. to M.T. (29 Jan. 1945). PRS. Probably Constance Moncrieff.

Margaret Behrens and her peke. T.S.E. to M.T. (30 Oct. 1944). PRS.

gardener. T.S.E. to M.T. (29 Jan. 1945). PRS.

Enid Faber noticed . . . . J.H. to T.S.E. (7 Jan. 1941). King's.

healthiest life. T.S.E. to V.W. (28 Oct. 1940). Berg.

123   *defeat*. See *LG*.

'*To get beyond time . . .*'. Notes for *DS*: V. Magdalene College Library. *CFQ*, 118.

T.S.E. on Beethoven's A minor quartet. Letter to Stephen Spender (28 Mar. 1931), 'Remembering Eliot', *Encounter* 24 (Apr. 1965), 3–14, repr. Allen Tate's coll.

124 *'not to the ear'*. Like the piper on Keats's Grecian Urn: 'Heard melodies are sweet, but those unheard / Are sweeter . . . / Pipe to the spirit ditties of no tone.' Helen Gardner (*CFQ*, 139) links the voice with the siren women in *The Waste Land* manuscript: IV, whose song 'charmed my senses', but this Keatsian melody is definitely 'Not to the sensual ear'.

'*beyond poetry . . .*'. Unpublished lecture on 'English Letter Writers', delivered at Yale in the winter 1933, quoted by F. O. Matthiessen, *The Achievement of T. S. Eliot*, 3rd edn. (1935; repr. NY: OUP 1959), 90.

'*unimaginable*'. *LG*: I.

'*Thou canst not see my face*'. Exodus 33: 20.

the poetry of the Bible. Unpublished address on the Bible at King's Chapel, Boston (Dec. 1932). Houghton.

the figure of the ten stairs. *BN*: V.

125 '*haunts us like the prayers of childhood*'. Unpublished 1913 essay on the ethics of Kant (Houghton), quoted by Jeffrey M. Perl, 'The Language of Theory and the Language of Poetry: The Significance of T. S. Eliot's Philosophical Notebooks, Part Two', *Southern Review* (Oct. 1985), 1015.

Eliot on Le Spectre de la rose. *LG*: III and letter to J.H.: 'I was thinking of the Ballet', *CFQ*, 202.

126 *high points of his past*. First draft of *LG*: II. See above, p. 120.

Now and in England. *LG*: I.

'*Where prayer has been valid*'. *LG*: I.

10 May 1941. Winston Churchill, *The Second World War*, 3 (London: Cassell, 1950), 41.

127 '*rough road*' *and* '*breaks*'. *LG*: I.

'*the passage . . .*'. *BN*: I.

La Figlia. 'La Figlia che Piange' (1912), *CP*, 26.

maytime-playtime. Drafts of *LG*: I.

128 *from well below the surface*. T.S.E. told J.H. that what might be wrong with the first draft of *LG* was the lack of acute personal reminiscence working well below the surface. *CFQ* 24.

'*the dark dove . . .*'. *LG*: II.

Forster on LG. Entry in his Commonplace Book (4 Jan. 1963), 266–7. King's. Forster was then 85. Facsimile edn. by the Scholar Press, 1978.

129 '*I would feel the need . . .*'. *Quarterly Review of Literature*, 5 (1967), quoted by Ackroyd, 260–1.

'*falling down . . .*'. *WL*: V.

Bertrand Russell's hallucination. Russell, *Autobiography*, vol. 2, 18.

'*Fire without . . .*'. *CFQ*, 168. 'Expel' was an alternative to 'Purge'.

the aftermath of air-raids. T.S.E. to W. T. Levy, *CFQ*, 166.

London after an air-raid. Precisely observed by Leonard Woolf, *The Journey Not the Arrival Matters* (London: Hogarth, 1969), 64.

animated. Letter to V.W. (October [?] 1940). Berg. His tone is a striking contrast to her harrowed descriptions of the ruined City squares in her diary.

130 *Eliot's climactic encounter with his other self*. A. Walton Litz, alert to Eliot's ties with Henry James, has pointed out that it is as if the dramatic encounters of the *Inferno* and *Purgatorio* merge with the self-confrontation in 'The Jolly Corner' (in his immensely suggestive review of *CFQ*, 'From Burnt Norton to Little Gidding: The Making of T. S. Eliot's *Four Quartets*', *Review*, 2, 1980). Eliot refers us to Shelley's meeting with a disfigured Rousseau in 'The Triumph of Life' which, he said in 1950, 'made an indelible impression upon me over forty-five years ago.' ('What Dante Means to Me', *CC*, 130).

first version of the ghost's prophecy. *CFQ* gives the complete first draft of 7 July 1941 in App. A, 225-33.

'*The walls of Poitiers...*'. First draft of *LG*: II. Eliot recalls a heady moment, but there was also, on this vacation, one of horror, described by Ronald Schuchard in the *Southern Review*, op. cit., 1046.

'*autumn*'. T.S.E. to J.H. (5 Aug. 1941), *CFQ*, 29.

1912. The date of 'La Figlia'.

131 *like Pound*. See *EEY*, ch. 5.

J.H. on 'Zero summer'. *CFQ*, 160.

J.H. on 'silence'. *CFQ*, 223: 'He put a cross against "silence".'

'*cost me*'. 'What Dante Means to Me', *CC*, 129.

words that won't decay. *BN*: V.

'*old rooted sin...*'. *CFQ*, 188.

132 *lust and rage*. Yeats, 'The Spur', *Collected Poems* (London: Macmillan, 1958), 359. T.S.E. quoted the poem in 'Yeats' (1940), *OPP*, 302.

'*Vacillation*'. Ibid., 284. The lines are quoted by Helen Gardner and Ronald Bush.

Yeats's fire. See 'Byzantium'. Ibid., 280-1.

'*there is only one remedy ...*'. From a second prose outline of the ghost's revised speech. *CFQ*, 189.

both versions are personal. A. Walton Litz has noted that the pesonal urgency was already there in the last twenty-four lines of the first version. ('The Making of *Four Quartets*', op. cit.).

133 '*daemonic fire*'. *CFQ*, 157.

detachment. *LG*: III. It is hard to see here the distinction that T.S.E. makes between 'detachment' and 'indifference'. It is possible that 'indifference' should be preferred, but its connotations are colder than 'detachment'.

134 '*uncompromising*'. J.H. to T.S.E. (1 Aug. 1941). This letter is quoted in full in App. A to *CFQ*.

The Cloud of Unknowing. Op. cit., 52.

The Imitation of Christ. Thomas à Kempis, Book 2, ch. 8: 'Some Advice on the Inner Life'.

'*the purification of the motive*'. *LG*: III. The first typescript reads 'The perfection of the motive'. *CFQ*, 230.

'*Love*'. '*Love is the unfamiliar Name . . .*'. *LG*: IV.

broke down. J.H.'s frank words to T.S.E. *CFQ*, 234.

'*tongues*'. *CFQ*, 213. The original (MS A) version of Part IV, Magdalene, Cambridge.

'*sign that brands*'. *CFQ*, 213. MS A, Magdalene, Cambridge.

135 'Unprofitable Sin', *etc.* First typescript, *CFQ*, 214.

'*already a kind of presence of the supernatural . . .*'. 'Baudelaire', *SE*, 375.

St Bernard's Sermon. Quoted by Thomas Merton, *The Silent Life*, op. cit., 112–13.

136 '*to spend much more time . . .*'. *CFQ*, 196.

'*Solidad*'. T.S.E. wrote 'Solidos', corrected in *CFQ*, 213.

'*broken king*'. *LG*: I.

'*not wholly commendable*'. *LG*: III.

T.S.E. to Allen Tate. (26 Mar. 1943), Tate Papers, Princeton.

137 *the rescue at the Shambles*. T.S.E. to J.H. (19 Sept. 1942). King's.

'*. . . re-reading the poem . . .*'. T.S.E. to J.H. (5 Aug. 1941). King's.

Eliot's Kipling. A. Walton Litz picked out the telling phrases from Eliot's introduction (repr. *OPP*, 265–94), in 'The Making of *Four Quartets*', op. cit.

138 *the white rose*. Recalled by Hope Mirrlees in BBC TV programme, 'The Mysterious Mr Eliot', op. cit.

history as 'timeless moments'. *LG*: V.

Hegel's *Philosophy of History*. Eliot's copy is in the Houghton Library.

talk on Shakespeare in Bristol. Eliot used the two lectures on the development of Shakespeare's verse, composed in 1937 (see above pp. 91–2), which he revised in July 1941. King's.

Eliot to Martin Browne. (20 Oct. 1942), *EMB*, 158.

Eliot's visit to Sweden with Bishop Bell. These details come verbatim from Roger Kojecky, *T. S. Eliot's Social Criticism* (NY: Farrar, Straus & Giroux, 1972), 150.

hoped to revise LG in the winter. T.S.E. to McKnight Kauffer in New York (29 Aug. 1941), saying that he was putting *LG* aside until winter. Pierpont Morgan Library, NY.

139 *smokescreen*'. J.H.'s word describing the first typescript of part IV. *CFQ*, 235.

'*Who heaped the brittle roseleaves?*' See *CFQ*, 216, which made the link with *BN*. Eliot did the revised versions on a pad called MS C. Magdalene.

voices of two mystics. Eliot made the additions to part III by 17 Aug. 1942. He added the line from *The Cloud of Unknowing* to part V by 27 Aug. 1942.

'*the two mystical extremes*'. T.S.E. to J.H. (2 Sept. 1942). *CFQ*, 70.

LG *resonates into a future beyond the poem*. In 'The Making of *Four Quartets*' A. Walton Litz argues for the closure of *Four Quartets* in contrast with *The Waste Land* which is open-ended. I agree in the sense that Eliot does subdue the private search to the given formula for spiritual autobiography which is final.

140 '*ease*'. *LG*: II.

Eliot to Mrs Perkins. (10 July 1936). He motored from Cambridge. *CFQ*, 35.

141 *A classic language*. Eliot posits a role for the poet as saviour and extender of the language, in a brilliant radio interview on 22 Nov. 1940, published as 'The Writer as Artist', *Listener* (28 Nov. 1940).

beyond character. 'The Development of Shakespeare's Verse.' King's.

142 *cumulative effect*. These are Eliot's words from the above talk on Shakespeare's verse.

'*heard, half-heard . . .*'. *CFQ*, 222.

'*We are born with the dead . . .*'. *LG*: V.

'see'. Conrad stresses this in his Preface to *The Nigger of the Narcissus*.

shedding his life like a husk. Helen Gardner said rightly that *FQ* was autobiographical, but not in the same way as Eliot's earlier poetry.

Truth and Reality. (London: Macmillan, 1911). Eliot's copy in Houghton.

143 *Edith Sitwell to Eliot*. *Selected Letters 1919-64*, edited by John Lehmann and Derek Parker (NY: Vanguard, 1970), 203.

eighteen months later. *FQ* was published in England on 31 Oct. 1944.

'*the fourth is the best . . .*'. *Paris Review* interview, with Donald Hall, repr. *Writers At Work*, ed. Van Wyk Brooks, 2nd series (NY: Viking, 1963).

told Helen Gardner. Interview for the *Sunday Times* (21 Sept. 1958).

'*I rest on those*'. *Paris Review* interview.

'*I stand or fall on them*'. Said to W. T. Levy, in William Turner Levy and Victor Scherle, *Affectionately, T. S. Eliot* (London: Dent, 1968), 41.

'*I have the A minor Quartet . . .*'. 'Remembering Eliot', Allen Tate's collection, op. cit., 54.

'*your heart . . .*'. *WL*: V.

144 *The true artist . . .* T.S.E. quotes from Kipling's story 'The Bull that Thought' in his introduction to *A Choice of Kipling's Verse*, repr. *OPP*, 273.

the function of art. 'Poetry and Drama' (1951) in *OPP*, 94.

Mary Lee Settle. *New York Times Book Review* (16 Dec. 1984), 10.

'*which we can only detect...*'. 'Poetry and Drama'. op. cit., 93.

145 *wise woman*. Eliot called her this in a letter to J.H. (2 Sept. 1942).

CHAPTER 4. LADY OF SILENCES

146 '*reality*'. 'human kind / Cannot bear very much reality'. *BN*: I.

'*Lady of silences*'. *AW*: II.

T.S.E.'s letters to E.H. Princeton University.

acid remarks. This was Helen Gardner's comment after she saw them in the 1970s. It is confirmed by the few letters I have seen.

Bodleian Library. E.H. to T.S.E. (12 Sept. 1963). Copy in Willard Thorp Papers, Princeton. Printed in full below, pp. 182–3.

'*to protect me*'. To Willard Thorp (27 Nov. 1965). E.H.'s correspondence with Willard Thorp is in the Thorp Papers, Princeton.

Peter du Sautoy. 'T. S. Eliot: Personal Reminiscences', *Southern Review* (Oct. 1985), 947–56. Details confirmed in letter to the present author (17 Mar. 1986).

147 *psychological change of life*. Letter t M.T. included in PRS.

'*O God!*' Ackroyd, 284.

shocked. T.S.E. to Violet Schiff (28 Jan. 1947). British Library.

148 '*I have met myself...*'. *CPy*: I, ii. *Plays, 153*.

scenes. M.T.'s diary (28 Oct. 1954). PRS.

strong Welsh shriek. *EEY*, ch. 4.

149 *feelings of guilt*. 'T. S. Eliot: a friendship', *Listener*, 97 (28 Apr. 1977), 541–3.

Lavinia's return. *CPy*: I, iii.

original acted version. Author's TS copy of acting edition with MS corrections, Act II, 90, King's. *Plays*, 176.

'*What is hell?*' *CPy*: I. iii. *Plays*, 169.

'*projections*'. See 'Cyril Tourneur', *SE*, 166: 'characters which seem merely to be spectres projected from the poet's inner world of nightmare, some horror beyond words.'

150 '*The whole oppression...*'. *CPy*: II. *Plays*, 175.

Roderick Usher. 'The Fall of the House of Usher', *Tales of Mystery & Imagination*, op. cit.

macabre fantasies. 'The Love Song of Saint Sebastian'; *Sweeney Agonistes*; *The Family Reunion*. It is worth noting that the first of these precedes Eliot's meeting Vivienne.

'*face that sweats...*'. 'The wind sprang up at four o'clock'. *CP*, 134.

Christopher Sykes. 'Some Memories', *The Book Collector* (winter 1965).

disintegrated. To M.T. (30 Jan. 1947), PRS.

151 '*tensely withdrawn*'. Hans Meyerhoff, *Partisan Review* (Jan. 1948).

Lambert Strether. Henry James's New Englander in Europe (1901).

Sir Herbert Read. Tate collection, 31.

sublime Lady. *AW*; *Marina*.

Eliot believed. T.S.E. to M.T. (2 June 1950). PRS.

'emotionless'. *DS*: II.

152 *catastrophe*. T.S.E. to M.T. (27 Apr. 1949). PRS.

family feeling. Letter to Mrs Perkins (30 Sept. 1935), quoted in *CFQ*, 35.

light verse. Op. cit. Lines from 'Morgan Tries Again' are quoted in *Great Tom*, 142.

'detachment'. *LG*: III.

153 *'so perfect a solution'*. To Willard Thorp (17 Jan. 1965).

'many a passage...'. To Willard Thorp (5 Jan. 1964).

154 *'ambiguous'*. See above, p. 49.

'we do not so much...'. *UPUC*, 34.

'my eyes failed'. *WL*: I.

'I remember...'. This comes from the draft of *WL*: II, *facs. WL*, 12-13.

155 *Notebooks*. *The Complete Notebooks of Henry James*, ed. Leon Edel and Lyall H. Powers (Oxford: OUP, 1987), 112-13. Entry for 5 Feb. 1985.

'Salutation'. Title from the *Vita Nuova*: IV where Dante calls Beatrice 'the Lady of the Salutation'. Published 10 Dec. 1927 in the *Saturday Review of Literature*.

God speaks. Deuteronomy 34: 4; Numbers 25: 52-6.

156 *ditties of no tone*. Keats, 'Ode on a Grecian Urn'. Soundless music is heard also in *DS*: III where a voice descants in the ship's rigging but 'not to the ear'.

'prickly pear'. HM: V.

157 *wife's adultery*. Ackroyd, 84.

Willard Thorp on 'Gerontion'. An excellent lecture (Mar. 1947) at the University of Virginia. Copy in the Eliot collection, Houghton Library.

The Changeling. Source identified by Grover Smith, *T. S. Eliot's Poetry and Plays: A Study in Sources and Meaning*, op. cit., 57, 309.

a general conclusion: a waste land. Eliot wished to print *The Waste Land* preceded by 'Gerontion', but was dissuaded by Pound.

158 *Barbara Gates Burwell*. The daughter of Dorothy Elsmith.

'thing'. Preludes: IV, *CP*, 15.

the 'new years'. *AW*: IV.

Marina. Eliot's title *Marina* derives from Shakespeare's *Pericles*, which ends with a blissful reunion of a long-separated father and daughter. Marina is a figure of absolute purity.

bolt. See Arnold, 'The Buried Life', *The Essential Matthew Arnold*, ed. Lionel Trilling (London: Chatto; NY: Viking, 1949), 124-7.

'*Cape Ann*'. *CP*, 142. Helen Gardner remarked to me that this was 'Emily Hale's poem' (conversation, March 1985).

159 *over the heads.* See Henry James, 'The Jolly Corner', *Selected Short Stories*, ed. Quentin Anderson (NY: Holt, Rinehart, 1957), 335. Eliot alludes to this tale in *FR* I. i. (*Plays*, 60) and, too, with the ghost in *LG*: II. The latter, I think accurate, suggestion was made by A. Walton Litz in 'The Making of Eliot's *Four Quartets*', *Review*, 2 (1980), 14.

vanity. In the draft (Bodleian Library), the humming-bird is a peacock, the traditional symbol of vanity.

'*Hidden under the heron's wing*'. Berg. The poem is written in the post-Paris hand, i.e. after Nov. 1911 and before June 1914. See *EEY*, ch. 3.

the lotus. I am grateful to Andrew Topsfield, Curator of Indian Art at the Ashmolean Museum, Oxford, for information.

'*Difficulties of a Statesman*'. Part II of 'Coriolan'. Published in *Commerce* (winter 1931-2). *CP*, 127-9.

160 '*Tom's head . . .*'. *Diary*, vol. 4, 262-3.

161 *E.H. wrote to President Jaqua.* Scripps College Archives, Denison Library.

Kipling. 'The Ballad of East and West' (1889), *A Choice of Kipling's Verse*, ed. T. S. Eliot (London: Faber, 1941 repr. 1979), 111.

Eliot came at once. *CFQ* notes (p. 35) that T.S.E. wrote on Easter Sunday to thank Mrs Perkins.

time of BN*'s composition.* My dating is conjectural. It could not have been written before 24 Mar. 1935, when Martin Browne read Part I of *MC*. Soon after this, possibly after rehearsals began on 7 May, Browne asked T.S.E. to write the additional lines that were eventually to become the opening lines of *BN*. (See *EMB*, 56 and *CFQ*, 39.)

'*Descend lower . . .*'. *BN*: III.

'*Quick now . . .*'. *BN*: V.

commitment postponed. After Eliot's death, E.H. said in a letter to Willard Thorp (17 Jan. 1965) that the relationship had not been consummated.

'*Quick now . . .*'. *LG*: V.

exploration. 'Old men ought to be explorers', *EC*: V.

162 *writing her off. Diary* and *Letters* op. cit. See above, p. 90.

E.H. to Ruth George. Letter in the Denison Library. Originally printed in the *Virginia Woolf Miscellany.*

164 *August and September.* Dates given in a letter from Valerie Eliot to Mrs Catherine Devas, owner of Stamford House.

E.H.'s long dress. Janet Adam Smith, who was too pregnant to attend this occasion, heard this anecdote from her mother who was present.

165 '*Miss Hale has brought her garden . . .*'. *Great Tom*, 143.

July 1938. T.S.E. sent a letter to Hugh Gordon Porteus on 15 July 1938 from Chipping Campden. Beinecke.

the woman who accompanied Eliot. PRS.

Cat Morgan. T.S.E. wrote E.H. a comic verse in this character in 1937 or 1938.

uncomfortable castle. Janet Adam Smith, in conversation, Sept. 1985.

J.H. reported to Morley. Letter. King's.

166 *Bennett Junior College*. E.H. put the address on a pamphlet by T.S.E. 'Reunion by destruction' (1943) which he sent her. Denison Library.

headmistress. Trustees minutes (28 Sept. 1944). I am indebted to Philip McFarland for finding this and other facts about E.H.

'my wretched way of living...'. E.H. to President Hard of Scripps College (1 Oct. 1945) offering her Eliot collection. Denison Library.

a good sort. Janet Adam Smith, in conversation.

167 *What is a Classic?* Repr. *OPP*, 52–74. The copy T.S.E. sent to E.H. is in the Denison Library.

'destiny'. *OPP*, 64.

Aeneas abandons Dido. *Aeneid*, IV, ll. 542–5.

Aeneas justifies himself. *Aeneid*, IV, ll. 458–9, trans. Allen Mandelbaum (NY: Bantam, 1972), 92.

'projection'. *OPP*, 63.

felt 'a worm'. 'Virgil and the Christian World', BBC broadcast, 9 Sept. 1951, *OPP*, 135–48.

dreamlike scene of parting. Cf. the imagined scene of parting in 'La Figlia che Piange'.

'burning' etc. *Aeneid*, VI, ll. 597–626.

A. Walton Litz. In conversation with the present author.

168 *'used to follow Emily...'*. Letter (1977), op. cit.

Janet Adam Smith. See her delightful reminiscences of T.S.E. in 'Tom Possum and the Roberts Family', *Southern Review* (Oct. 1985), 1057–70. T.S.E.'s correspondence with Michael Roberts is in the Berg Collection.

169 *'have' or 'possess'*. Valentine Cunningham drew attention to these terms in a lecture 'In the Jamesian Cage' which made suggestive connections between James and Eliot.

Her inaudible presence. I am indebted to Elizabeth Garrett for pointing out this kind of relation to a woman in her fine analysis of 'The Buried Life' in her thesis, 'The Poet, the Mirror, and the Fool' (Univ. of Oxford, 1986), 18, 22.

'An International Episode'. *Selected Short Stories*, op. cit., 102.

Theresa Eliot. I am grateful to Professor Eloise Hay for passing on this anecdote, which was told her by Theresa Eliot just before her death.

170 *at Emily's instigation.* Miss Tucker told the trustees: 'It is to her, as you know, that we are wholly indebted for Mr Eliot's coming.' (With thanks, again, to Mr McFarland.)

aged eagle. AW: I. Richard Chase, 'T. S. Eliot in Concord', *The American Scholar,* 16 (Autumn, 1947), 441.

looking up with effort. Ackroyd, 285.

Emily to Lorraine Havens. I am immensely grateful to Mrs Havens for photocopies of the two valuable letters from E.H., in Aug. 1947 and in Sept. 1948, that she has preserved; also for her sympathetic picture of a woman she knew well for a great number of years.

171 *nursed plans.* See below, her offer (8 Jan. 1948) to President Hard to give a public reading of T.S.E.'s poems.

another letter to Lorraine Havens. Written after E.H.'s return from a summer vacation at Grand Nassau.

172 *drafting* The Cocktail Party. According to Browne, T.S.E. was drafting the play between May and Aug. 1948.

'hidden meaning'. Letter to Thorp, op. cit. T.S.E. sent E.H. an undated typescript.

less personal than a poem. 'The Three Voices of Poetry' (1953), *OPP,* 96–112.

well below the surface. See T.S.E.'s comment to J.H., about the problem of *LG* being the lack of personal reminiscence working well below the surface, above pp. 94, 104, 303.

173 *'moments . . .'. CPy,* I, i, *Plays,* 142.

'There was a door'. CPy, I, iii. Ibid. 169.

174 *'the* daimon . . .'. King's. Quoted *EMB,* 184.

shut up. 'Of Individualism in Democracies' in *Democracy in America,* vol. 2, part II, ch. 2, ed. J. P. Mayer (NY: Anchor, 1969), 508.

175 *as did less gifted men.* E.H. to Lorraine Havens, op. cit.

still in love. Letter (2 June 1950). PRS.

'my way of thinking'. PRS.

'If I can only hold . . .'. CPy, I, i. *Plays,* 143.

Charles de Foucault. Described by T.S.E. in a wireless talk, 'Towards a Christian Britain', *Listener* (10 Apr. 1941), 525. He refers to a biography by René Bazin which conveyed the extraordinary 'spiritual quality' of this holy life. 'I think it is through such men as Foucauld that the reborn Christian consciousness comes', he added.

purgatorial trial. Carol H. Smith, *T. S. Eliot's Dramatic Theory and Practice* (Princeton Univ. Press, 1963), ch. 5.

176 *Geoffrey Faber.* Letter quoted in programme notes to John Dexter's 1986 production in London.

177 *against the bent. CFQ,* 15.

178 '*For what happened . . .*'. Act II, *Plays*, 189.

went with Eliot. Dorothy Elsmith told me this in 1977, op. cit.

E.H. at opening night and Theodora's comment. M.T.'s diary (25 and 28 Aug. 1953). PRS.

179 *a man's sense*. . . . T.S.E. to M.T. (2 June 1950). PRS.

Notebooks. 5 Feb. 1895. Op. cit.

Ann Kennedy Irish. Letter, *Abbot Academy Bulletin* (Oct. 1957). I am grateful to Margaret F. Crouch at Phillips Academy, Andover, for sending a copy.

devastated. I am very grateful to Barbara Burwell for a most perceptive description of E.H. Her words were so well chosen that I have constantly used them.

180 *Caroline Willington.* Statement in the Scripps College Archives.

'*shocked and angry*'. Letter from Mrs Eliot to *TLS* (24 Feb. 1984), 191.

letter to Willard Thorp. This and all subsequent letters in the Thorp Papers, Princeton.

hoped to pick up a post. To Thorp (summer 1957).

appeared disturbed. *Great Tom*, op. cit., 149–50.

181 '*I miss the real exchange . . .*'. 22 Nov. 1961.

a little house. . . . E.H. to Ricardo Quinones (23 Jan. 1965), op. cit.

Willard Thorp explained. Conversation in Aug. 1985.

182 *E.H.'s letter to 'Tom'.* A copy survives, sent to Willard Thorp. Princeton.

183 *By November.* Letter to Willard Thorp (29 Nov. 1963).

'*personal*'. See letter to President Hard at Scripps (20 Sept. 1945), Denison Library, which has all subsequent letters to Hard and his replies.

184 '*nothing to say*'. To Hard (8 Mar. 1948).

offered Sweeney Agonistes. This offer, I think, was conditional. In the end she kept it until her death.

185 *address at University College, Dublin.* First printed in autumn 1985 in *Southern Review*, ed. A. Walton Litz, and entitled 'Tradition and the Practice of Poetry'. Professor Litz adds a useful afterword on Eliot and Yeats.

reports from Eleanor Hinckley. To Willard Thorp (17 Jan. 1965).

186 *Mr Dix's compromise.* To Willard Thorp (8 Feb. 1965).

left her some money, etc. I am indebted for these facts to a brief biography written for E.H.'s friends at the time of her death in 1969, and given to me by Mrs Elsmith.

187 *a future mystery.* E.H. to Margaret Thorp (11 Jan. 1965), Thorp Papers.

188 '*watchers and waiters*'. *FR*, I, ii, *Plays*, 77.

mature gentlemen in James. See *The Ambassadors*; 'The Jolly Corner'; 'The Beast in the Jungle'.

189 *Winterbourne*. In *Daisy Miller* (1879). See above, p. 75.

Robert Acton. In *The Europeans* (1878).

'*I think of it...*'. 'The Beast in the Jungle' (1903), Henry James, *Selected Short Stories*, op. cit., 224.

the notion of some infinite 'thing'. 'Preludes': IV. *CP*, 15.

'*Something or other...*'. 'The Beast in the Jungle', op. cit., 223.

'*Christ the tiger*'. 'Gerontion'. Note also the three white leopards, *AW*: II.

'*He hadn't disturbed people...*'. 'The Beast in the Jungle', 227.

privilege. Ibid., 228.

'*the real truth*'. Ibid., 230.

'*a man of extremes*'. Lecture on T.S.E. at Scripps in Dec. 1932. See above, p. 19.

190 '*burst upon the world*'. To Willard Thorp (27 Nov. 1965).

CHAPTER 5. FAME AND FRIENDS

191 *the drink to The Guardians*. M.T.'s diary (5 June 1950). PRS.

'*TS... TS... TS*'. Eileen Simpson, *Poets in their Youth* (1982; repr. London: Picador, 1984), 171.

192 '*the most desperately lonely business*'. PRS: M.T.'s diary, Dec. 1950, on T.S.E.'s return from Chicago.

T.S.E. performing Sherlock Holmes. 'The Adventure of the Reigate Squire' (with thanks to Julie Akhurst Hall). *Great Tom*, 158-9.

'*No-one thinks of me as a poet...*'. Levy, op. cit., 19.

utterly depleted'. Allen Tate's coll., 32.

Desmond MacCarthy. Correspondence in King's.

193 '*Coriolan*'. See above, pp. 41-2.

tapped their beaks in vain. Image from Virginia Woolf's *The Waves* (London: Hogarth; NY: Harcourt, 1931), 181.

'*the private door*'. Act. I. *Plays*, 236.

'*remoteness*'. Act I. *Plays*, 237.

194 *descriptions of M.T.* I am grateful to Janet Adam Smith and Peter du Sautoy for providing clear images.

M.T.'s diary. Extracts from the diary are part of her unpublished memoir of her friendship with Eliot (PRS), which is privately owned.

196 *godfather*. See Janet Adam Smith, 'Tom Possum and the Roberts Family', op. cit.

The Old Curiosity Shop. Chs 36 and 66. To M.T. (19 Dec. 1944). PRS.

became critical of Eliot's seclusion. M.T.'s diary (Good Friday, Apr. 1955). PRS.

197 '*now and in England*'. *LG*: I: 'Now and in England'. *LG*: V: 'History is now and England'.

198 *'prayer, observance...'. DS*: V.

199 *'treat men and women...'.* 'Experience'. *Selected Prose and Poetry*, op. cit., 238. I am grateful to Quentin Anderson for pointing this out, years ago, at Columbia.

had been in love with one woman. T.S.E. to M.T. (2 June 1950). PRS.

200 *psychological change of life.* T.S.E. to M.T. (27 Apr. 1949). PRS. See above, p. 147.

native Calvinism. T.S.E. to M.T. (21 Feb. 1942). PRS.

201 *early London years.* See *EEY*, ch. 4.

final letters to Pound. Beinecke.

Archbishop Temple. He died in the autumn, 1944.

I'll Walk Beside You. (London: Longman, 1945). In 1943 M.T. had considered doing a book of letters which T.S.E. had brushed off on behalf of Faber. The Longman's book was successful.

202 *'fear and horror'.* Ibid., 56.

'For the last four years...'. Ibid. 59.

'mental rehabilitation'. Ibid. 54.

'termites'. T.S.E. used this word in a 1917 letter to Lytton Strachey, where he complains that he was 'sojourning among the termites' (see *EEY*, ch. 5); he used it again to M.T. in Nov. 1955 (PRS).

M.T. at an air-evacuation centre. I'll Walk Beside You, 40–1.

203 *Mrs Millington.* T.S.E. to M.T. (30 Oct. 1944). PRS.

'the horror!' See Ronald Schuchard, 'Eliot and the Horrific Moment', *Southern Review* (Oct. 1985), 1045–56.

204 *'Oh, it's YOU again, Julia'.* M.T.'s diary (24 Nov. 1949). PRS.

Julia 'is me'. PRS (18 Aug. 1949).

Eliot pictured her sailing.... T.S.E. to M.T. (23 Feb. 1948). PRS.

the future of the East.... Ibid.

Eliot asked for tips.... T.S.E. to M.T. (13 Mar. 1949). PRS.

205 *fade. DS*: III: 'the future is a faded song or a lavender spray / Of wistful regret...' For T.S.E.'s memories see above p. 121.

Eliot's rebuke. M.T.'s diary (7 Dec. 1952). PRS.

February-March 1946. T.S.E. moved into the flat in February, J.H. a month later. *CFQ*, 12.

1935. CFQ, 12.

très-loyal serviteur. This is how J.H. signed a letter to T.S.E. (5 Mar. 1941). King's.

206 *bored with all living.* T.S.E. remarked on this in an address to Friends of Rochester Cathedral in 1937, 'Religious Drama: Medieval and Modern' (NY: House of Books, 1954): 'There is a very profound kind of boredom which is

an essential moment in the religious life, the boredom with all living in so far as it has no religious meaning.'

'at home'. See references to T.S.E.'s 1935 letter to Mrs Perkins, pp. 44, 292.

even to his confessors. PRS (in conversation on 27 Nov. 1951).

an old man.... Note to M.T. (6 Oct. 1953). PRS.

in a cage. PRS (20 June 1951). The phrase, in a cage, recalls the original title of *WL*: II: 'In the Cage'.

eleven years with J.H. They lived together from Mar. 1946–Jan. 1957. The chief sources for T.S.E.'s life during these years are PRS; *CFQ*; *The Book Collector* (winter 1965) which contains 'Some Memories', a series of obituaries for J.H.

his lacerating barbs. Nicholas Barker (in *The Book Collector*, op. cit.) is particularly good on the atmosphere in J.H.'s company.

207 *strain*. PRS.

'escape into living...'. *The Confidential Clerk*, I. *Plays*, 236–7.

Winter and summer.... Daily habits from Ackroyd, 276–7.

208 *Tereschenko*. M.T.'s diary (6 July 1953). PRS.

commiserate. M.T. describes a visit to J.H. when T.S.E. was away in Nice in Mar. 1952. PRS.

'He can't help hurting us'. M.T.'s diary (Easter day, Apr. 1955). PRS.

'man of letters'. Kathleen Raine, *The Book Collector*, op. cit.

'Metoikos'. Signature on a paper for the Moot. *Great Tom*, 126. Confirmed in PRS.

told Helen Gardner.... *CFQ*, 13.

wrote from Cambridge.... King's.

209 *illustrated catalogue*. *CFQ*, 12.

ran brilliantly as a dictator. John Carter, *Sunday Times* obituary.

took the Distillers Company to task. Catherine Porteus, *The Book Collector*, op. cit.

'a poem...'. Kathleen Raine, ibid.

'carpentry'. Obituary, *Annual Report*, King's College (Nov. 1965), 30–3.

'Besides a strong personal affection...'. PRS.

210 *He feared nobody*. Obituary, King's College.

'Be witty'. Recalled by Mrs Watkins in conversation, Sept. 1986.

Graham Greene. *The Book Collector*, op. cit.

Janet Adam Smith. Ibid.

211 *'the chill ascends...'*. *EC*: IV.

Hayward's desire. Described sympathetically by Graham Greene, *The Book Collector*, op. cit.

weird, ghostly, Strindbergian. Frances Partridge, *Julia: A Portrait of Julia Strachey* (London: Gollancz, 1983), 207–8.

212 *the first housekeeper*. Recalled by Christopher Sykes in *The Book Collector*.

'confidential clerk' as divine agent. Carol H. Smith, op. cit., 210.

would like to change his name. T.S.E. to M.T. (Oct. 1955). PRS.

'Bonsir Nehemiah'. M.T.'s diary (Oct. 1955). PRS.

adoptive nephew. Signature to a note of Dec. 1955. On another occasion Bonsir was M.T.'s son-in-law.

214 *'I set myself...'*. Preface to PRS.

looking old. (Mar. 1955), PRS.

'he seemed to take fright...'. PRS.

on 27 April 1949. Letter, PRS.

on 29 May 1950. M.T. proposed by letter. PRS.

215 *'Will you be looking in...'*. M.T.'s diary, PRS.

'I never see...'. M.T.'s diary (3 Apr. 1950), PRS.

reply of 2 June. Letter, PRS.

a pain that gnawed at his liver. See *EC*: IV, and Helen Gardner's commentary (*CFQ*, 44–6) showing the allusion to Gide's handling of Prometheus' liver.

on 5 June they had a talk.... PRS.

216 *he no longer enjoyed his love's company*. T.S.E. to M.T. (2 June 1950). PRS.

'THE lady'. PRS (23 July 1950).

'mediocre' contemporaries. M.T.'s diary (2 Jan. 1955). PRS.

Shaw. Ibid. (2 Apr. 1951).

F. R. Leavis. Ibid. (Mar. 1955).

Pound. Ibid. (Mar. 1955).

217 *Muir, Auden, Day Lewis, Sitwell, Marianne Moore*. Ibid. (1 Nov. 1956).

C. S. Lewis's Christianity. Ibid. (23 Dec. 1949).

confessions. M.T.'s diary (27 Nov. 1951, 26 May 1953, and 7 Oct. 1954). PRS.

'I believe in hell...'. Diary, PRS.

'the whole of me...'. M.T.'s diary (26 May 1953). PRS.

over Tower Bridge. This was in Sept. 1955. PRS.

218 *the cage*. See *facs. WL*, 16–17: 'In the Cage' (the cancelled title of *WL*: II).

the home of Mungojerrie and Rumpelteazer. T.S.E. explained to M.T. (Sept. 1956). Diary, PRS.

football games. Recalled by Christopher Sykes in 'Some Memories', *The Book Collector*, op. cit.

Eliot would work the lift.... PRS (30 Nov. 1954).

219 *'I love the economy of Mozart'*. M.T.'s diary (15 May 1947). PRS.

'*After all...*'. M.T.'s diary (30 Nov. 1952). PRS.

221 '*on stilts*'. *Emerson in his Journals* (14 Nov. 1839), ed. Joel Porte (Cambridge, Mass.: Belknap, 1982), 230.

communicates principles. 'The American Scholar', *Selected Prose and Poetry*, op. cit., 67.

'*He judges...*'. 1855 Preface to *Leaves of Grass*, op. cit.

The greatest poet.... 'Goethe as the Sage', *OPP*, 253.

the war had brought.... Preface to *The Dark Side of the Moon* (London 1946).

'*centuries of barbarism*'. Interview in *Horizon* (Aug. 1945).

'*prophetic gloom*'. (London: Faber, 1948; NY: Harcourt, 1949, repr. in *Christianity and Culture*), 185.

222 *speech at Aix-en-Provence*. Made on receiving the degree of Hon. D.és L. Hayward Bequest: 'Miscellaneous Essays & Addresses'. King's.

'*... our own ability...*'. *OPP*, 10.

The Notes *warn....* 91.

letter to Duncan MacCarthy. 14 Nov. 1947. King's.

'*We live in an* impossible *age*'. M.T.'s diary (5 Dec. 1954). PRS.

Gomorrah. Letter to M.T. (St Wenceslas 1948) while on board the s.s. *America*. PRS.

Nineveh. In Apr. 1956 T.S.E. wrote to M.T. that he had no hopes of a Christian Conference arranged by J. O. Oldham and Kathleen Bliss, whose vague aspirations seemed futile in the face of Nineveh.

praying in the Underground. M.T.'s diary (25 June 1952). PRS.

explained this to M.T. Diary (24 June 1944). PRS.

'*spiritual organization*'. Quoted by Ackroyd, 273.

223 '*What is man...*'. Psalm 8.

Eden had not understood. T.S.E. to Pound (12 Oct. 1956). Beinecke. The talk had been delivered on 19 Apr. 1955, and is repr. as 'The Literature of Politics', *CC*, 136–44.

'*Half of the harm...*'. *CPy*: II. *Plays*, 175.

'*I don't hear any voices...*'. Ibid., 185.

'*deranged society*'. 'The Frontiers of Criticism'. *OPP*, 116.

'*chaos*'. *What is a Classic? OPP*, 74.

'*Whig? Tory?*'. Auden's review, *New Yorker* (23 Apr. 1949), 85–6.

'*a voice in Ramah...*'. Ibid.

224 *the prophet has no being*. I am grateful to Dr Rachel Salmon of Bar-Ilan University, Israel, for her persuasive understanding of the prophets.

'*In the year that King Uzziah died...*'. T.S.E. quoted the opening of Isaiah 6: 1 in a letter to M.T. (28 Nov. 1944). PRS.

'*And he laid it upon my mouth . . .*'. Isaiah 6: 7–9.

went against the grain. Helen Gardner said (*CFQ*, 15) that 'in writing plays Eliot was writing, to some extent, against the bent of his natural genius. Essentially he was an explorer, not an expounder . . .'

224 *Mr McKnight*. T.S.E. told this to M.T. MT's diary (2 Apr. 1951). PRS.

Mr Silvero. 'Gerontion' (1919).

Mme Sosostris. *WL*: I.

226 *looked beyond his time*. In *What is a Classic?* (*OPP*, 73) T.S.E. admired 'the dedication of Aeneas . . . to a future far beyond his living achievement.'

'*Nihilism itself becomes boredom*'. Leslie Paul, 'A Conversation with T. S. Eliot', *Kenyon Review*, 27 (1965), 11–21. Recorded in 1958.

227 *into the red Eye of the morning*. Sylvia Plath, 'Ariel', *Collected Poems* (Faber, 1981), 240.

'*the indomitable spirit of mediocrity*'. *CPy*, I. ii. *Plays*, 153.

make the best of a bad job. *CPy*, II. *Plays*, 182.

'*transparent*' *words*. 'Poetry and Drama' (1951), *OPP*, 79. This idea originated in his unpublished Shakespeare lectures of 1937, op. cit.

'*You will forget this phrase . . .*'. *CPy*, II. *Plays*, 182.

'*You've missed the point . . .*'. *CPy*, I, i. *Plays*, 125.

'*There's altogether too much mystery . . .*'. *CPy*, I. *Plays*, 137.

228 *the dog in the night*. 'Silver Blaze' (with thanks to Julie Akhurst Hall).

the immortal hand. Blake's 'Tyger', *Complete Writings*, ed. Geoffrey Keynes, (OUP, 1966, repr. 1984), 214.

provincialism of time. *What is a Classic? OPP*, 72.

'*The Three Provincialities*'. *The Tyro*, repr. *Essays in Criticism* (1951). See also Pound's shared concern in 'Provincialism the Enemy', *Selected Prose 1909-1965*, ed. William Cookson (Faber 1973), 159–73.

as it was for Henry James. See Henry James, 'Nathaniel Hawthorne' (1879). In 'From Poe to Valéry' (1948) T.S.E. said that Poe had 'the provinciality of the person who is not at home where he belongs, but cannot get to anywhere else.' *CC*, 29.

'*Provinciality . . . a vice*'. 'Professional, or . . .', *Egoist* (Apr. 1918), 61.

'*positive literary vice*'. 'Tradition and the Practice of Poetry', op. cit., 882.

229 '*emancipated*'. Essay on P. E. More (1937), op. cit. T.S.E. criticized provincials of their time in a letter to P. E. More (20 July 1934), Princeton.

*Dante the '*least provincial*'*. 'What Dante Means to Me', *CC*, 134–5.

'*insupportable to posterity*'. *The Tyro*, op. cit.

'*In Memory of Henry James*'. *Egoist*, 5 (Jan. 1918), 1. Quoted by Ronald Bush in 'Nathaniel Hawthorne and T. S. Eliot's American Connection', *Southern Review* (Oct. 1985), 924–33.

'history had meaning'. 'Virgil and the Christian World', *OPP*, 148. In this wireless talk on Aeneas in 1951 T.S.E. said that 'for no one before his time except the Hebrew prophets, history had meaning.'

Aeneas as prototype of Christian pilgrim. Ibid. 143-4.

a by-product of his private poetry workshop. 'The Frontiers of Criticism' (1956), *OPP*, 117, and 'To Criticize the Critic' (1961), *CC*, 13.

230 *'impersonality'*. 'Tradition and the Individual Talent' (1919), *SW*, 53, 56-9.

'objective correlative'. 'Hamlet and His Problems' (1919). *SW*, 100.

'dissociation of sensibility'. 'The Metaphysical Poets' (1921), *SE* 247.

a hundred years on. . . . 'To Criticize the Critic'. *CC*, 19.

'I'm surprised we were allowed Milton . . .'. Pearson, *Façades*, op. cit. 385.

'bluff'. 10 Aug. 1929, King's, cited by P. N. Furbank in 'Forster, Eliot, and the Literary Life', *Twentieth Century Literature*, 31 (Summer / Fall 1985).

'icy inviolability'. 'Shorter Notices', *Egoist* (June–July 1918) 87.

'that parlour game'. 'Professional, or . . .', *Egoist* (Apr. 1918), 61.

'called to the seat of judgement'. 'To Criticize the Critic', *CC*, 12.

'not I . . .'. *Sincerity and Authenticity* (Cambridge, Mass.: Harvard; Oxford: OUP, 1972), 8.

canonized and excommunicated. Harry Levin used the phrase in a letter to F. O. Matthiessen in 1934, printed as an appendix to *Memories of the Moderns* (London: Faber, 1981), 243.

231 *tone more English than that of the English*. Chris Baldick, *The Social Mission of English Criticism 1848-1932* (OUP 1983), 110.

introduced Eliot to Bruce Richmond. T.S.E., 'Bruce Lyttleton Richmond', *TLS* (13 Jan. 1961). Richmond was 90 when T.S.E. wrote this piece.

'understanding'. 'The Frontiers of Criticism', *OPP*, 121.

the only criticism that he could recommend. See T.S.E.'s letters to Helen Gardner, Bodleian Library. In Oct. 1949, Helen Gardner had a letter from the Cresset Press quoting T.S.E.'s opinion that 'it seems to me the best book of its kind that has been done'. T.S.E. confirmed this view in a letter to W. T. Levy, *Affectionately, T. S. Eliot*, 105.

T.S.E.'s reservations about source-hunting. His more private remarks were recalled by Helen Gardner in conversation with the present author.

'Yeats'. *OPP*, 299.

'The fact that . . .'. T.S.E. to Philip Mairet (30 Oct. 1956), Austin, Texas. Quoted by Jeffrey M. Perl and Andrew Tuck, 'The Hidden Advantage of Tradition: on the significance of T. S. Eliot's Indic Studies', *Philosophy East and West*, 35 (Apr. 1985), 122.

'the greater expression of personality'. 'Yeats', *OPP*, 299.

232 *'A Note on War Poetry'*. *CP*, 215.

'A poet may believe . . .'. 'Virgil', *OPP*, 137.

'the adjective of some transcendental self '. Quoted by Calvin Bedient, *He Do The Police In Different Voices* (Univ. of Chicago, 1987), 16.

'there is something integral'. UPUC, 88.

this 'inner compulsion'. 'Kipling', *OPP*, 274.

'a consistent view of life'. 'From Poe to Valéry', *CC*, 35.

233 *the whole pattern*. This uses, almost verbatim, T.S.E.'s strictures on understanding Shakespeare in 'John Ford' (1932), *SE*, 170.

his poetry came from America. *Paris Review* interview, op. cit.

'real significance . . .'. 'Stravinsky and Others', *New Republic* (10 Mar. 1926), repr. *T. S. Eliot: The Critical Heritage*, 1 (London: Routledge 1982), 239-40.

a distinctive sense of the past. 'In Memory of Henry James', op. cit.

'American Literature'. CC, 56.

'depravity's despair'. 'What Dante Means to Me', *CC*, 134.

Jansenism and Puritanism. *SE*, 357.

234 *pulsates with the agony . . . .* 'A Prediction in Regard to Three English Authors Who, though Masters of Thought, Are likewise Masters of Art', *Vanity Fair*, 21 (Feb. 1924), 29, 98.

fragments of a greater Reality. Jewel Spears Brooker gives an admirably concise and clear summary of what in Bradley's thought appealed to T.S.E. in 'The Structure of Eliot's "Gerontion": An Interpretation Based on Bradley's Doctrine of the Systematic Nature of Truth', *ELH*, 46 (1979), 314-40.

'fractions are worth more to me . . .'. (Nov.–Dec. 1833), *Emerson in His Journals*, op. cit., 119.

Auden. Introduction to *The Faber Book of Modern American Verse* (1956), 18.

tradition is not inherited. . . . 'Tradition and the Individual Talent', *SW*, 49.

'strong traits . . .'. 'The Custom House', introductory to *The Scarlet Letter*.

'To the high mountain peaks . . .'. *The Scarlet Letter*, ch. 11: 'The Interior of a Heart'.

235 *the difference between a mad and effective writer*. 'The Social Function of Poetry', *OPP*, 9.

'To Carthage . . .'. *WL*: III.

Dante's refining fire. *WL*: V.

the peace that passeth understanding. T.S.E.'s note to 'Shantih', *WL*: V (needless to say, not one of the bogus or distracting notes).

236 *The rebel may appear as social conformist*. T.S.E. was referring to Tennyson, 'In Memoriam' (1936), *SE*, 295.

'When a man . . .'. (9 Dec. 1932), *UPUC*, 73.

Wordsworth. (17 Feb. 1933), *UPUC*, 87.

'a profound spiritual revival'. (9 Dec. 1932), *UPUC*, 80.

'see and hear more'. 'What Dante Means to Me', *CC*, 134.

'*the obligation to explore*'. Ibid.

'*thing*'. 'Preludes': IV.

'*a fringe of indefinite extent...*'. 'Poetry and Drama', *OPP*, 93.

'*unattended*' moments. *DS*: V.

the still point.... *BN*: II.

237 '*The Word in the desert*'. *BN*: V.

Denied the ultimate vision.... I draw here on what T.S.E. says of Virgil (*OPP*, 74) because it seems equally true of himself.

pills and potions. The streak of hypochondria is confirmed by Sir Herbert Read in Allen Tate's coll., 32.

lesion. Medical details given by T.S.E.'s doctor to M.T. in June 1956. PRS.

238 *chrysalis*. The image is derived from T.S.E.'s '2nd Debate between the Body and Soul' (1911). Berg.

feared that he was coming to his end. His doctor told M.T. that the racing heart would have given a panic-stricken sense of approaching death.

'*As for poetry...*'. M.T.'s diary (30 Nov. 1954). PRS.

'*abnormal*'. Diary (June 1956). PRS.

reading Paul Tillich. T.S.E. took a copy of *Systematic Theology* to South Africa in 1950. He remarked to W. T. Levy in 1954 that vol. 1 was one of the profoundest theological books of recent times (Levy, p. 50).

Tillich on self-punishment. He proposed a 'proper human self-love' instead of the 'false' self-love that is connected with self-contempt. *Systematic Theology*, vol. 1 (London: Nisbet, 1953; Univ. of Chicago, 1951), 313.

Tillich on forgiveness. *The New Being* (London: SCM Press, 1956), 48.

239 *torn between duty to God or duty to man*. Letter to M.T. (28 Oct. 1955). PRS.

neurotic depressive. The query is in a talk with M.T. (Sept. 1956). PRS.

'*I, even I...*'. Isaiah 43: 25.

240 '*a peach of a girl*'. M.T.'s diary. PRS.

left to dine alone with Jean Kennerley. T.S.E. to J.H. (5 Aug. 1941). King's.

Monica. Heroine of *ES*.

'*unattached devotion...*'. *DS*: II.

CHAPTER 6. LOVE: THE UNFAMILIAR NAME

241 *Laforgue married*. David Arkell discovered this neat coincidence in his fine biography, *Looking for Laforgue* (London: Carcanet, 1979).

'*thoughts without need of speech*'. Poem, 'To My Wife', printed as a dedication to *The Elder Statesman* (1958). In a revised form it appeared as 'A Dedication to My Wife' in *CP*, 221.

began in Oct.-Nov. 1955. Dating of the composition of the play comes from T.S.E.'s conversations with M.T. PRS.

242 'had *to get to Tom...*'. Interview, *Observer* (20 Feb. 1972).

Queen Anne's School. I am grateful to Dr Rosemary Pountney of Jesus College, Oxford, for details about the school which she attended.

'*I can't get to know her...*'. M.T.'s diary (27 Mar. 1955). PRS.

sudden impulse. Letter to M.T. (28 Oct. 1950). PRS.

243 *a better collection*. Remarked by Peter du Sautoy in conversation (1986).

would dodge into the lavatory. To M.T. Postscript, PRS.

work late. Ibid.

to conceal a deeper failure. From a page of manuscript (n.d.) in Mrs Eliot's possession. *EMB*, 318.

first draft. The first drafts of Acts I and II, as well as the Green and White synopses are at King's. The manuscript and typescripts of Act III are owned by Mrs Eliot.

'*sticky*'. M.T.'s diary (Mar. 1956). PRS.

244 '*stricken*' *and Tomlin*. Tomlin, 'T. S. Eliot: a Friendship', op. cit.

'*cadaverous*'. Donald Hall, *Remembering Poets* (NY, 1978).

looked after his affairs. *EMB*, 316.

'*the ELD ST. begins to unburden his heart...*'. The second, White synopsis for the play. King's. Quoted *EMB*, 310.

introduces a love scene. *EMB*, 317-18.

Her words seem to come from far away. *EMB* links this with Harry's words to Mary in *FR*, I. ii: 'you seem / Like someone who comes from a very long distance.'

'*changing*'. The word was retained in the final version, *Plays*, 298.

'*Love*'. III. *The Temple* (1633). *The Works of George Herbert*, ed. F. E. Hutchinson (OUP, 1941) 188-9.

exquisite courtesy. I am grateful to Kate Lea for this phrase and for explaining the nature of sacramental love in this poem.

245 *web of fiction*. III. *Plays*, 340-1.

'*morbid conscience*'. III. *Plays*, 345.

Claverton ran over... and did not stop. The source of this (a long shot) may be the accident in *The Great Gatsby*, to which Eliot responded with unwonted enthusiasm when Fitzgerald sent him a copy in 1925.

'*emotional situation*'. 'The Three Voices of Poetry', *OPP*, 111.

'*Enrique Gomez*'. 'The Two Unfinished Novels', *Egoist* (Jan. 1918), 3-4. A. Walton Litz made the connection with *ES*.

246 '*in unison*'. 'The Three Voices of Poetry', *OPP*, 109. T.S.E. distinguished speaking in unison from using a character as mouthpiece.

call out his latent potentialities. *OPP*, 102. See discussion of Becket in *MC* in ch. 1, p. 28 above.

'*a pit*...'. The line comes from a rough first draft for *DS*: III. Manuscript at Magdalene College, Cambridge, quoted *CFQ*, 137. The date would have been late 1940, for J.H. received a complete draft of *DS* on New Year's Day, 1941.

as an old man explores. See *EC*: V: 'Old men ought to be explorers.'

completed draft of play Jan. 1958. Letter to William Turner Levy, quoted in Levy, op. cit., 101.

'*I can only say*...'. Ibid.

247 *the blankness of the walls.* Quoted in *EMB*, 319.

'*But have I still time?*' *Plays*, 338.

'*the heinousness*...'. III. *Plays*, 345.

'*spectral existence*...'. Ibid., 341.

It is enough.... Ibid., 340.

once again. In *FR*. See ch. 2, pp. 74, 82, 91 above.

in late Nov. On 25 Nov. T.S.E. told M.T. that he got out his typewriter and did several pages of Act II.

248 '*And more frightening*...'. Kept in Act II, *Plays*, 325.

daring to strip the mask. I have drawn on E.M.B.'s words about the Elder Statesman, *EMB*, 311.

'*One day*...'. Levy, 43.

knit together. Recalled by Gwen Watkins in conversation (Sept. 1986).

249 *pangs.* First draft, King's. Quoted in *EMB*, 315-16.

'*2nd Debate between the Body and Soul*'. Berg. See *EEY*, ch. 3.

the way from.... (Jan. 1861), *Emerson in his Journals*, op. cit., 491.

Monica. I am guessing here about the associations of this name for Eliot. He might well have chosen it quite arbitrarily.

250 *March 1938 T.S.E. told E.M.B.*... Letter (19 Mar. 1938) quoted *in toto* in *EMB*, 106-8.

'*I am only a beginner*...'. *ES*, III. *Plays*, 354.

Act I completed 9 Feb. 1958. EMB, xiv.

'*like the asthmatic*...'. *ES*, III. *Plays*, 355.

More rewriting.... *EMB*, 317.

first production of ES. See *EMB*, 338.

Act III at Edinburgh. EMB, 330-2.

251 '*a new person*'. III. *Plays*, 355.

Peter du Sautoy. 'T. S. Eliot: Personal Reminiscences', *Southern Review* (Oct. 1985), 954.

'*My dear lady*...'. M.T.'s diary (Trinity XVIII, 1956). PRS.

252 '*My dear chap ...*'. Helen Gardner, recalling J.H.'s account to her. In conversation with the present author.

'*I thought...*'. Recalled by Gwen Watkins, who said that several people were there at the time.

felt his helplessness anew. Christopher Sykes, 'Some Memories', op. cit.

morale never recovered. Gwen Watkins, in conversation with the present author.

253 *Graham Greene.* Obituary for J.H., op. cit.

a union.... Peter du Sautoy described the marriage in this way, op. cit., 955. See also the relationship of Charles and Monica in *ES*.

'*a streak of sadism*'. T.S.E. remarked on this comment in *Ushant* in letter to Aiken (7 Nov. 1952). Huntingdon.

would not be pinned. See 'Prufrock', who is 'pinned'. *CP*, 5.

254 *removed acknowledgement to J.H.* Noted in *Great Tom*, op. cit., 124.

He paid his contribution. Hilary Spurling, *Secrets of a Woman's Heart: The Later Life of I. Compton-Burnett 1920-1969* (London: Hodder and Stoughton, 1984), 241.

'*sacrifice others*'. Second draft of Act I, *EMB*, 318: 'In sacrificing himself he's had to sacrifice others.'

Dimmesdale. Nathaniel Hawthorne, *The Scarlet Letter*.

255 '*Explore your own higher latitudes*'. Conclusion (ch. 18) to *Walden*.

spat out the butt-ends.... 'Prufrock': 'Then how should I begin / To spit out all the butt-ends of my days and ways?' *CP*, 5.

'*Love reciprocated ...*'. Interview with Henry Hewes, *Saturday Review* (13 Sept. 1958), 32. Copy in Houghton.

'*None of my books...*'. Recorded by V.W. (25 July 1926) in *Diary*, vol. 3, 99.

'*old man's frenzy*'. 'An Acre of Grass', *Collected Poems*, op. cit., 347.

'*throbbings of noontide.* 'I Look into My Glass', *Wessex Poems and Other Verses* (1898).

the passing affair. See 'Portrait of a Lady' and 'Gerontion' ('adulterated' is, I think, a serious pun: see ch. 4, p. 157 above).

256 *like 'crawling bugs'. facs. WL*, 44-5.

dancing lessons. Photonews.

John Finley's dinner. An account of the evening is given by Harry Levin in 'Old Possum at Possum House', *Southern Review* (Oct. 1985).

unbent to V.W. EEY, ch. 4.

unbent to Iowa students. Great Tom, 154.

correspondence with Groucho Marx. The Groucho Letters: Letters from and to Groucho Marx (NY: Simon & Schuster; London: Michael Joseph, 1967), 154-62.

257 *Groucho to Gummo Marx.* Ibid., 162–34.

258 *child with nurse.* Photograph, Houghton.

entertained Janet Adam Smith's children. 'Tom Possum and the Roberts Family', *Southern Review* (Oct. 1985).

with Ivy Compton-Burnett. Hilary Spurling, *Secrets of a Woman's Heart*, op. cit., 241.

259 *fiftieth anniversary report on the class of 1910.* Copy in Houghton.

'very good mind'. Levy, 98–9.

madly happy. Letter on return from honeymoon. Schiff papers, British Library.

It is a wonderful thing . . .'. Levy, 98–9.

'. . . art and love . . .'. Ushant (Boston: Little, Brown, 1952), 185–6.

told Henry Hewes. Saturday Review, op. cit.

260 *'No peevish winter . . .'.* CP (1963), 221. This is the last poem in *CP*.

'You were the first sympathetic reader . . .'. Letter to Cyril Connolly, quoted in obituary for T.S.E. (10 Jan. 1965) in the *Sunday Times*.

'One insular Tahiti.' Moby Dick, ch. 58.

'The last part . . .'. To Levy, 110.

261 *'a loss of personality'.* Diagnosis by the Unidentified Guest, *CPy*, I. i. *Plays*, 134.

The New Being. Op. cit., 13.

October chill. Letter to Allen Tate (23 Oct. 1957). Princeton.

November fogs. Letter to Tate (26 Nov. 1958). Princeton.

told Pound. Letter (29 Jan. 1960). Beinecke.

cruise to Jamaica. The Eliots travelled on the Santa Rosa (Grace Line). They stayed at the Jamaica Inn, Ocho Rios, Jamaica from 14 Jan.–5 Mar. 1961.

told Vernon Watkins. Letter (26 Apr. 1962). Berg.

bent over. Levy, 126.

said of More in 1937. T.S.E. to Willard Thorp (17 Feb. 1937). More Papers, Princeton.

262 *afraid of death.* M.T's diary (8 Aug. 1949). PRS.

'Death is not oblivion'. To Henry Hewes, op. cit.

envied Joyce. Letter to Pound (28 Dec. 1959). Beinecke.

still spoke of things he wanted to do. Letter to Pound (Nov. 1961). Beinecke.

'feeling'. CC, 20.

'emotional preferences'. CC, 19.

fed emotions. CC, 18.

263 *a paradox of the New England mind.* T.S.E. analyses this in a review of Henry Adams, 'A Sceptical Patrician', *Athenaeum* (23 May 1919). See *EEY*, ch. 5.

Emerson on his aunt. Emerson in his Journals (6 May 1841), op. cit., 253.

'the comfort...'. CC, 23.

'sequence which culminates in faith'. SE, 360.

'the pride of birth ...'. George Herbert, no. 152 in the series, *Writers and their Work* (London: Longman, 1962), 12–13.

unsparing self-examination. Ibid., 13.

temptation to the religious poet. Ibid., 24.

264 *'the fluctuations of emotion...'.* Ibid., 23.

'And now in age I bud again'. From 'The Flower', quoted 25. *Works*, 166.

'Love'. George Herbert, 34.

'convalescence of the spirit'. Ibid., 26.

265 *'The last time I saw him...'. Introduction to a Reading of Poems by T.S.E.* (Univ. of Minnesota, 15 Feb. 1965). Copy in Tate Papers, Princeton.

tenderly. Sykes, obituary for J.H., *The Book Collector*, op. cit.

'He was–my dear–friend'. Helen Gardner recalled this in conversation, 1985.

telephoned Kathleen Raine. Obituary, op. cit.

chose Beethoven's 7th. Said this to M.T. (23 Dec. 1949). PRS.

Stravinsky's setting. Dedicated to T.S.E. in 1962.

Thou hast granted my request.... 'Praise' II, *The Temple. Works*, 146.

Emily Hale's letters. Thorp Papers, Princeton.

266 *service for T.S.E. at Harvard.* E.H.'s letter to Willard Thorp.

'little brown people'. Nanu Mitchell, in conversation.

267 *'She never recovered...'.* Information from Humphrey Carpenter.

Vivienne as Daisy. Daisy Miller (1879). See p. 75 above.

Emily as May. 'The Beast in the Jungle' (1903). See p. 189 above.

Valerie Eliot like Alice Staverton. 'The Jolly Corner' (1909).

playing a part in his obituary. ES, II. *Plays*, 324.

C. Day Lewis. Obituary for *The Times*, written in 1946 with Hayward's help. Revised by Hayward in 1959. Drafts in King's.

T.S.E.'s photo of Poets' Corner. A picture postcard. Houghton.

next to Tennyson.... Described thus in a letter from Valerie Eliot to Allen Tate (17 Jan. 1967). Tate Papers, Princeton.

'And what the dead had no speech for...'. LG: I.

'Though our outward man perish...'. The Lesson came from 2 Corinthians 4: 16.

268 *'for the things which are seen...'.* Ibid. 4: 18.

'Can a lifetime represent a single motive?' Prose summary for *LG*: III on scribbling pad (Magdalene 'MS A'), quoted in *CFQ*, 197.

'unimaginable'. LG: I.

the 'life of a man of genius'. 'The Classics and the Man of Letters' (1942), *CC*, 147.

269 *Eliot in Sweden.* T.S.E. to Marian Eliot (18 Dec. 1948). Bodleian Library. The Swedish girls who burst into his room were celebrating St Lucy's Day.

destiny, mystery. In 'Virgil and the Christian World' (1951), *OPP*, 144, T.S.E. said: 'The concept of destiny leaves us with a mystery.'

feelings beyond the nameable. 'Poetry and Drama', *OPP*, 93.

'the deeper unnamed feelings...'. UPUC, 155.

270 *art* makes *life, makes importance.* In a letter to H. G. Wells (10 July 1915), James wrote: 'It is art that *makes* life, makes interest, makes importance...'. Henry James, *Letters*, ed. Leon Edel, 4 (Cambridge, Mass.: Belknap, 1984), 770.

'metamorphose'. Shakespeare and the Stoicism of Seneca (1927), *SE*, 117. See also 'Yeats' (1940), *OPP*, 299, where he speaks of the impersonality 'of the poet who, out of intense and personal experience, is able to express a general truth; retaining all the particularity of his experience, to make of it a general symbol.'

'a Catholic cast of mind...'. 'Goethe', *OPP*, 243.

271 *'destiny'.* I am using phrases from *What is a Classic?* because it seems to me that T.S.E. has a special sense of affinity with Aeneas.

peculiar detachment from all environment. I have drawn on 'Kipling' (1941) where, again, there seems a particular affinity.

the extremist. E.H.'s description of T.S.E. See ch. 1, p. 19.

'The loneliness of home...'. 'The Rest Cure', 18. King's. Quoted in *EMB*, 320.

His youth was interred.... Draws on *What is a Classic?*

'He wasn't a bit like an Englishman'. BBC programme, 'The Mysterious Mr Eliot', op. cit.

came from America. T.S.E. was interviewed in the NY apartment of Mrs Cohn (of the House of Books) by Donald Hall. *Writers at Work*, op. cit.

'fare forward...'. DS: III.

Whitman's voyaging. 'Passage to India', stanza 5, The Library of America's Whitman, op. cit., 534.

set formula. Edmund S. Morgan, *Visible Saints: The History of a Puritan Idea* (Cornell Univ. Press, 1965), 91: 'The pattern is so plain as to give the experiences the appearance of a stereotype.'

at home in America before 1830. See *EEY*, ch. 1: letter to Herbert Read (1928).

272 *'What a debt...'.* 'The Method of Nature' (1941). I am indebted to Faith Williams for pointing out these words in her outstanding unpublished dissertation, 'Young Emerson as a Religious Writer' (Columbia University, 1973), 9.

Increase Mather. Quoted in *Visible Saints*, 147.

outpost. Ibid., 112.

'For Thine is the Kingdom'. HM: V.

Whimpering. '*Not with a bang but a whimper*', HM: V.

the devil of the stairs. *AW*: III.

election. T.S.E. used this word in *FR* (II, ii, *Plays*, 111), and in relation to the notion of 'destiny' in 'Virgil and the Christian World', *OPP*, 144.

273 '*trying*'. 'Who are only undefeated / Because we have gone on trying'. *DS*: V.

too self-conscious to be a saint. I am indebted to Alison Shell for a similar remark in a first-year tutorial on Eliot.

the prophetic role and introspection. The Puritans adopted the modes, of course, from the Old Testament.

is and was from the beginning. *DS*: I.

'*the source of the longest river*'. *LG*: V.

Acknowledgements

I AM grateful to the late Maurice Haigh-Wood for permission, given in 1976, to quote from his sister Vivienne Eliot's papers.

My greatest debt is to the late Dorothy Elsmith of Woods Hole, Mass., who was a good friend of Emily Hale. She contacted me in the summer of 1977 to say that my guesses in *Eliot's Early Years* had been right, and in a spirit of the utmost loyalty and discretion offered details about Emily Hale's relationship with Eliot. I met Mrs Elsmith twice in 1977–78, once in London and once in Oxford, and then, after her death, her daughter Barbara Gates Burwell gave me a further incisive and memorable description of Emily Hale. I also benefited from Willard Thorp, whose wife Margaret had been a lifelong friend of Emily Hale. Her correspondence with Professor Thorp, which has to do with Eliot's thousand-odd letters to her, was the most exciting find, and I am grateful for the permission to quote from the Thorp papers.

A large batch of Emily Hale material, full of useful dates, was provided by Judy Harvey Sahak, Librarian and Assistant Director of the Ella Strong Denison Library in Claremont, California. Judy Sahak was nothing less than a co-researcher, with her ingenuity for sources beyond the official papers, like a Scripps College magazine of the early thirties, and she identified photographs of Emily Hale by the reappearance of a certain elegant pair of shoes. She also put me in touch with friends of Emily Hale who had striking memories, above all Lorraine Havens, who gave me copies of two valuable letters in which Emily describes her changing relationship with Eliot in 1947 and 1948. Other Scripps friends who shared wonderfully clear memories were Marie McSpadden Sands, Laurabel Neville Hume, and Margaret Ann Ingram.

The biographer Humphrey Carpenter, in Oxford, kindly allowed me to read his aunt, Mary Trevelyan's unpublished memoir of her twenty-year friendship with Eliot. Readable, detailed, and highly intelligent, it gives a fascinating close-up of Eliot in a period when his fame in the forties and early fifties seemed to preclude close ties.

Helen Gardner had an unsurpassed understanding of Eliot's work and character, and many of her casual comments have lingered in my mind. A. Walton Litz, another fine Eliot scholar, gave, as ever, excellent advice. As a Columbia student, in 1972, I was grateful for his genial encouragement to pursue research, the findings of which were bound to irritate critics and reviewers of settled opinions. I also have valued his continued encouragement to pursue Eliot's American background, in particular the ties with Henry James. As regards the American family background, Mary Eliot in Boston was both helpful and reassuring about my sense of Eliot's bonds and his awareness of Puritan forebears. Eliot's friend and Faber colleague Peter du Sautoy gave me lunch in April 1986 at one of Eliot's haunts, the Russell Hotel, and with grave, discreet judgement, described Eliot in later years. Another acute picture of the later years came from Gwen Watkins.

Once again, I must thank Dr Michael Halls, Modern Archivist at King's College, Cambridge, this time for his help with the enormously valuable John Hayward Bequest, which contains the bulk of Eliot's later literary manuscripts (from the drafts of *Sweeney Agonistes*, written 1923–6, to those of *The Elder Statesman*, written from 1956–8). Other librarians who have been helpful are James J. Lewis, Curator of the Houghton Library, and an assistant, Susan Halpert; Ann Van Arsdale of Princeton's Special Collections; Sara S. Hodson, Assistant Curator of Literary Manuscripts at the Huntingdon Library; Mark Gentry at the Beinecke Library, Yale; Mary Clapinson, Keeper of Western Manuscripts in the Bodleian Library, Oxford; librarians in the manuscript room of the British Library; and last, but not least, Dr Lola Szladits, curator of the choice Berg Collection in the NY Public Library.

I am grateful for permission to quote from the following copyright material: *The Making of T. S. Eliot's Plays* by E. Martin Browne, reprinted by permission of Cambridge University Press. T. S. Eliot's *Collected Poems 1909-1962*, copyright 1936 by Harcourt Brace Jovanovich, copyright © 1963, 1964 by T. S. Eliot; *Selected Essays*, copyright 1950 by Harcourt Brace Jovanovich, Inc, renewed 1978 by Esme Valerie Eliot; from *Complete Poems and Plays 1909-1950* (HBJ, 1952; Faber, 1969), all reprinted by permission of Faber & Faber Ltd., and Harcourt Brace Jovanovich, Inc. Excerpts from *The Waste Land: A Facsimile and Transcript of the Original Drafts, Including the Annotations of Ezra Pound*, edited and copyright © 1971 by Valerie Eliot, reprinted by permission of Faber & Faber Ltd., and Harcourt Brace Jovanovich, Inc. Excerpts from *On Poetry and Poets* and *To Criticize the Critic*, are reprinted by permission of Faber & Faber Ltd, and Farrar, Straus & Giroux, Inc. Excerpts from Helen Gardner, *The Composition of the Four Quartets*, copyright © 1978 by Helen Gardner, are reprinted by permission of Faber & Faber Ltd., and Oxford University Press Inc. Excerpts from *The Groucho Letters: Letters from and to Groucho Marx* copyright © 1967 by Groucho Marx are reprinted by permission of Simon & Schuster, Inc. Three quotations from William Force Stead, in the Osborn Collection, are reprinted by permission of The Beinecke Rare Book Library, Yale. Excerpts from *The Diary of Virginia Woolf*, Vol. 3: 1925–1930, Vol. 4: 1931–1935, edited by Anne Olivier Bell, copyright © 1980 and 1982 respectively by Quentin

Bell and Angelica Garnett and *The Letters of Virginia Wolf*, Vol. III: 1923–1928, Vol. V: 1932–1935, edited by Nigel Nicholson and Joanne Trautmann, copyright © 1977 and 1979 respectively by Quentin Bell and Angelica Garnett, are reprinted by permission of The Hogarth Press on behalf of the estate of Virginia Woolf and the Editors, and Harcourt Brace Jovanovich, Inc.

Seven people were kind enough to comment on the typescript or on particular chapters: Willard Thorp and Lorraine Havens confirmed the accuracy of the portrait of Emily Hale in chapter 4; Humphrey Carpenter checked and corrected details about Mary Trevelyan in chapters 5 and 6; A. Walton Litz looked at the whole book; Andrew Topsfield, Curator of Indian Art at the Ashmolean Museum, corrected misconceptions about Indian scriptures; Roger Press commented on style, as did Kate Lea who gave meticulous attention to detail, and also helped to sort out matters of Anglican theology after welcoming teas in her cottage in Beckley.

I am also grateful to Catherine Devas for showing me Stamford House in Chipping Campden, and to Viscount Sandon for allowing several visits to Burnt Norton and providing historical details. Pam Woodward typed, yet again, with speed and accuracy, and the Trudeau Institute in the Adirondacks provided ideal conditions for summer work: comfort on the edge of the wilderness, solitude without loneliness.

While writing this book I benefited from the judgement of my daughter, Anna, and from the help of first-rate editors, Kim Scott Walwyn, Judith Luna, and Jeff New in Oxford, and Jonathan Galassi in New York. Once again my husband, Siamon Gordon, performed the essential 'caesarian operation'.

Biographical Sources

THIS bibliography is not meant to be comprehensive. It is a selection of materials for a biographical approach to T. S. Eliot. For a wider bibliography, see the source notes for this book and the bibliography in F. B. Pinion's *A T. S. Eliot Companion: Life and Work* (London: Macmillan, 1986).

UNPUBLISHED SOURCES

The unpublished sources are so abundant and widely scattered that it is unlikely that any one scholar could cover them completely. To venture on this research is to realize the extraordinary coherence of Eliot's career and, at the same time, its unfamiliar aspects, so that a freshly researched study will differ quite quickly from the more derivative books on this author. A prevailing myth is that research is made impossible by current restrictions. No scholar should be deterred, for though a few manuscripts and typescripts may not be seen—mainly those at the Houghton Library—the vast majority are available, notably the two major collections of literary manuscripts: those of the early years in the Berg Collection in the New York Public Library, and those of the later years in King's College Library, Cambridge University.

The largest unpublished source is Eliot's letters, the majority of which, though dispersed across Great Britain and the United States, are open to scholars. Eliot was too guarded, on the whole, to be a great writer of letters, but there are some more confidential batches: to Virginia Woolf (in the Berg); to Bertrand Russell (in the Russell Archive at McMaster University, Hamilton, Ontario, largely to do with Eliot's difficulties in his first marriage); and to his Harvard friend Conrad Aiken (at the Huntingdon Library, California). The early letters to Aiken tell us what Eliot was writing during the most obscure period of his life, the years immediately before his first publication in 1915, and there are tantalizing plans for a sequel to 'Prufrock' in which the speaker will attend, not a tea-party, but a masquerade. He will go as St John the Divine, wearing only underwear. The letters after 1916 are uninteresting with the exception of a letter of 1952, acknowledging Aiken's autobiographical novel, *Ushant*. Faber's rejection of Aiken's poetry in the early thirties was obviously a source of grievance, as was Eliot's much greater fame. Eliot's letters sounded like attempts to keep the friendship up, mostly, it appears, unsuccessfully. Aiken was also scornful of Eliot's becoming a Christian, but some warmth seems to have returned with the arrival of Valerie Eliot.

The letters that are vital to an understanding of Eliot's creative and religious development—the two go together—often come in small, isolated groups. There are the few letters to Aiken from the Continent in the summer of 1914. Then, Eliot's letters to William Force Stead form a background to his growing attachment to Anglicanism during the twenties, his conversion, his first confession, and his acceptance of celibacy. These letters are in the Osborn Collection in the Beinecke Library at Yale. There, too, are Stead's 'Literary Reminiscences', dated 29 April 1940, holograph notes on Eliot's character in response to a questionnaire by Dr Osborn. Though there are minor inaccuracies, two reported exchanges with Eliot on the subject of love (with Emily Hale in mind) do sound true. The third small group which has literary importance are twenty-two letters to Paul Elmer More, the Princeton theologian, from 1928 until More's death in 1937. The most fascinating of these letters (in the More Papers, Princeton University Library) debate the nature of hell, and one late letter acknowledges an unusual similarity in their lives.

There are numerous other batches of letters to people of less importance to Eliot. The Humanities Center at Austin, Texas has mopped up a fair quantity but, though enormous and no doubt useful, this Eliot collection is less discriminating than that of the Berg which, under its curators, the late John D. Gordan and Dr Lola Szladits, has amassed only the gems in Eliot's papers, amongst them the early notebook and folder of miscellaneous poems, and *The Waste Land* manuscript.

Eliot's letters reflect, as good letters do, a different relationship with each correspondent. His letters to Virginia Woolf reflect her enjoyment of this form, and her style of playful vivacity. His letters to Pound (in the Beinecke) reflect, in turn, Pound's bristle and contempt. His letters to More reflect the latter's theological depth and their common interest in spiritual autobiography. Another group of letters, to Sydney Schiff (who wrote under the name Stephen Hudson), from 1919 to 1943 (in the British Library) have, from the start, a rare note: open and affectionate. In relative unguardedness, these letters might be classed with those to More and Virginia Woolf, but of the three they are the most natural since Eliot has no wish to make an impression, whereas with Virginia Woolf he wanted to be amusing, and with More, to be the most serious of converts. The naturalness with Schiff came partly from the fact that both had wives who suffered from chronic illness. Vivienne's letters show that she enjoyed her own relation to the Schiffs, who treated the young Eliots with a sympathy that was not reserved for Eliot alone. It was a couple relationship, and perhaps the only genuine one that Eliot and Vivienne shared. Another reason for the special tone of these letters is that Schiff seems to have replaced Pound as Eliot's literary mentor when Pound left England. Eliot's letters in 1920–1 confide work plans, and reveal that he was showing Schiff work in progress.

Though Eliot was adept at taking on the colouring of his correspondents, Pound's Brer Rabbit language was wearing to keep up, and Eliot imitated, with more success, the Southern drawl of Allen Tate (in the Tate Papers, Princeton). Eliot's later letters to Pound blend American humour with weary exasperation over futile efforts to defuse Pound's epistolary outbursts and invective. Eliot could not treat him as he did the younger Faber authors—with kindly consideration—for Pound was his senior by a few years, with a prior claim to fame. Eliot could never forget what he owed to Pound, and Pound never relinquished the right to prick Eliot's ambition of taking on the colourless cover of the English gentleman. As Pound saw it, the other Faber poets, like Auden, Spender, and Wallace Stevens, were his inferiors, and he only allowed Faber to publish him as a personal favour to Eliot and Morley. On 25 January 1934 Eliot tried to divert the tide of Pound's letters with the humorous complaint that his main occupation at Faber was now to superintend a department devoted to correspondence with Mr Ezra Pound.

His letters to Pound have the atmosphere of the literary marketplace. Most are about the minutiae of the literary life—rivals, money, reviewers—and reflect moods of aggression, particularly in the earlier letters with their masculine bravado, misogyny, and anti-Semitism. After 1936, Eliot resisted the continued virulence of Pound's anti-Semitism, and on 13 August 1954 let fly one furious rebuff to the effect that, although Pound was at liberty to continue with personal insults, Eliot would tolerate no further insult either to his nationality or to his religion, which included the Jewish religion. This letter was signed T.S.E. instead of the usual Tp (Tom possum). Pound, delighted to have provoked this steam, reaffirmed his attachment to the long friendship.

Three central batches of letters are restricted but, in each case, it is not impossible to gain some insight into the ties they represent. The largest, and probably most important, batch of letters, approximately a thousand to Emily Hale from about 1930 to 1957, is sealed at Princeton until 12 October 2019. Emily Hale's letters to Eliot may have been destroyed (see ch. 4), but fortunately a letter of 1947 to Lorraine Havens, describing a crisis in their relationship, has survived, as have a good number of her letters to Willard Thorp, which give some idea of the relationship from her point of view. The latter are in the Thorp Papers at Princeton, which include, too, a copy of Emily Hale's final letter, sad in its restraint, which she wrote to Eliot in September 1963.

His letters to two other close friends, John Hayward and Mary Trevelyan, are restricted at King's College and the Houghton, respectively. Though the Hayward correspondence is officially closed until 2000, it is possible to see those crucial letters which had to do with the composition of *Four Quartets*, and Mary Trevelyan included a great number of Eliot's letters to her, or extracts from them, in her unpublished memoir of their friendship.

This memoir, 'The Pope of Russell Square, 1938–58', intersperses these letters with narrative commentary and accounts of conversations (drawn from Mary's diary), providing a unique close-up of Eliot during his most inscrutable years of fame in the late forties and early fifties. Well-written, highly readable, and splendidly detailed, it will undoubtedly be published sooner or later, but cannot appear in its entirety until Faber brings out a full edition of Eliot's letters. The typescript is owned by Mary Trevelyan's nephew, Humphrey Carpenter, and niece, Kate Trevelyan.

Because Eliot drew so constantly on his life, especially his inner life, as a source for his writing, the earlier drafts and evolution of his works have a special interest. The scenarios and drafts of Eliot's plays, *Sweeney Agonistes*, *The Family Reunion*, *The Cocktail Party*, *The Confidential Clerk*, and *The Elder Statesman* (of the last, the scenarios and first two Acts), are part of the Hayward Bequest at King's. In Eliot's early years, many of his drafts were handwritten; in later years he tended to work directly from a few rough notes onto the typewriter. Some of these rough notes have survived. There are those for the *Quartets* in King's and Magdalene College, Cambridge, and another, longer set for *Murder in the Cathedral* in the Houghton Library (see App. I).

The scenarios and drafts of *The Family Reunion* are divided between King's and the Houghton: they reveal ten stages of composition (see App. II) of this most autobiographical of Eliot's plays. Eliot consulted Emily Hale at one stage, and her marginal comments may be seen at the Houghton, but their correspondence to do with the play is sequestered. Available, though, at the Houghton, and thoroughly absorbing, are E. Martin Browne's scrapbooks on different productions of Eliot's plays.

Of the unpublished essays, Eliot's address on the Bible, in the historic King's Chapel in Boston on 1 December 1932, is the most profound, with its distinctions between scripture and literature, and its suggestiveness for Eliot's poetic search for the Word. This typescript was donated to the Houghton Library by Emily Hale's uncle, the Revd John Carroll Perkins, who was, at the time of Eliot's talk, minister of the chapel.

Hayward collected several of Eliot's other unpublished addresses, which are now at King's College, Cambridge. It is often assumed that, amongst these, the Clark Lectures (at Cambridge University, 1926) are the most important, but I find them less exciting than two lectures on

'The Development of Shakespeare's Verse', delivered at Edinburgh University in 1937 (the remarks on *Hamlet* being pertinent to the composition of the intensely introspective *Family Reunion*). He repeated the (revised) lectures at Bristol in 1941, and gave the carbons to Emily Hale, who later gave them to Harvard. Necessary to our understanding of Eliot's dramatic aims are his theory, given here, of the ultra-dramatic, and his comments on the challenge of poetic diction. Some points from these lectures went into 'Poetry and Drama' (1951).

Hayward also collected and bound the drafts of *Four Quartets*. These are well documented by Helen Gardner in *The Composition of* Four Quartets (London: Faber, 1978), but she overlooked one draft of *Burnt Norton* which Eliot sent to Frank Morley in New York, and which is now at Harvard. The draft had additional lines at the end (see ch. 3), cut on Morley's advice. The extant drafts of Eliot's other mature poems are fairly polished, with only the odd notable variant or epigraph. I suspect that, in some cases, he destroyed earlier drafts, as is likely in the case of *The Confidential Clerk*, which Hayward labelled a first draft but appears close to a final one.

Eliot's first wife left her diaries to the Bodleian Library, Oxford. They are less significant for the early years, for all but one were written either before or after she lived with Eliot, but the diaries of the thirties do contain many memories (perhaps distorted, and to be read with caution), copies of letters, and a detailed account of the years of separation— wholly, of course, from Vivienne's point of view. The diaries, taken together, are a fascinating document of moods, character, and behaviour. The library also has drafts and fragments of her attempts at fiction and poetry in the twenties, some of which Eliot published in the *Criterion*.

PRINTED SOURCES

Eliot's essays in spiritual biography, 'The *Pensées* of Pascal', 'Baudelaire', 'Paul Elmer More' (in the *Princeton Alumni Weekly*, 5 Feb. 1937), the account of Charles de Foucault (in 'Towards a Christian Britain', *Listener*, 10 Apr. 1941, 524–5), and *George Herbert* (no. 152 in the series, *Writers and their Work*, London: Longman, 1962), together with the collected editions of poems and plays, and in particular *The Family Reunion*, are more revealing of his inner life than any existing memoir or biography. For a curious self-characterization, see his 'Eeldrop and Appleplex: I', *Little Review*, 4 (May 1917), 7–11, and also the strange 'Ode', published once only, in *Ara Vos Prec* (London: Ovid, 1920).

Donald Gallup's *T. S. Eliot: A Bibliography* (NY: Harcourt, 1969) is the indispensible guide to printed works, particularly useful for its accurate year-by-year listing of uncollected critical articles, of introductions to books by other authors, and of books containing letters from Eliot. The bibliography shows what a prolific reviewer he was in early years, what a frequent commentator and speaker in later years. There is a vast body of criticism that has remained for some decades unread by new generations of Eliot's admirers, and many distinguished thoughts lie buried in obscure and, for many, unobtainable journals. One has only to leave the well-trodden paths of the volumes of selected criticism to find fresh approaches to Eliot through his own words. Two outstanding but almost unknown pieces of the mature years are 'A Commentary: That Poetry is Made with Words', *New English Weekly*, 27 (Apr. 1939), which provides a gloss on *Four Quartets*, and a stimulating exchange on language with a radio interviewer, Desmond Hawkins, on 22 November 1940, printed as 'The Writer as Artist' in the *Listener* (28 Nov. 1940), 773–4. These views on the writer's duty to his language lie behind *Little Gidding*: V.

Eliot often talked more freely to children. Two obscure school addresses are interesting for their reminiscences: one at Milton Academy, Milton, Mass., on 17 June 1933, which is printed in the *Milton Graduates Bulletin*, 3 (Nov. 1933), 5–9; the other at the centennial of the Mary Institute, St Louis, on 11 November 1959, which is printed in *From Mary to You* (St Louis, 1959), 133–6. See also an informal interview with Eliot in the *Grantite Review*, 24, no. 3 (1962), 16–20. There were two full-scale interviews in Eliot's later years, the first with Helen Gardner, 'The "Aged Eagle" Spreads His Wings: a 70th-Birthday Talk with T. S. Eliot', *Sunday Times* (21 Sept. 1958). This gives an intelligent survey of the whole career, dominated by Eliot's conviction that the difference between his pre- and post-conversion poetry had been exaggerated by critics. A year later, Donald Hall did the fine *Paris Review* interview, containing Eliot's other telling assertion—also ignored for the next two decades—that his poetry came from America. This interview is reprinted in *Writers at Work*, ed. Van Wyck Brooks, 2nd series (NY: Viking, 1963). Eliot also reminisced, this time about his family in St Louis, in a 1953 address, reprinted in *CC*, 'American Literature and the American Language'. Occasional recollections may be found in his various introductions to books by other writers. For memories of America, see his Preface to E. A. Mowrer, *This American World* (London: Faber, 1928) and his Introduction to the Cresset edition of *Huckleberry Finn* (1950).

There have been numerous memoirs by people who knew Eliot. The best have been cameos which do not venture beyond immediate knowledge. An amusing collection was edited in honour of Eliot's sixtieth birthday by Tambimuttu and Richard March (London: Frank & Cass, 1948), containing lively memoirs by Conrad Aiken ('King Bolo and Others'), Clive Bell ('How Pleasant to Know Mr. Eliot') and Wyndham Lewis ('Early London Environment'). Another good collection was edited by Allen Tate after Eliot's death, *T. S. Eliot: The Man and his Work* (NY: Dell, 1966; London: Chatto, 1967), with interesting memoirs by Frank Morley, Sir Herbert Read, Bonamy Dobrée, and Robert Giroux. Amongst the many fine articles in the *Southern Review*'s Eliot issue, ed. James Olney (Oct. 1985), Janet Adam Smith has a delightful reminiscence of Eliot, showing his domestic aspect, in 'Tom Possum and the Roberts Family'; in the same issue Harry Levin recalls Eliot at Harvard, and Peter du Sautoy, Eliot as fellow-publisher. Mr du Sautoy gives a picture of Eliot's happiness in his second marriage, when their friendship was at its height. One of the liveliest memoirs came from Hope Mirrlees in an interview for the BBC TV programme, 'The Mysterious Mr Eliot', printed in the *Listener* (14 Jan. 1971), 50.

There are numerous books and articles which contain portraits of Eliot, amongst the best Bertrand Russell's *Autobiography*, vols. 1 and 2 (Boston: Little, Brown, 1967–9; London: Allen & Unwin); Ezra Pound, *Selected Letters* 1907–1941, ed. D. D. Paige (repr. NY: New Directions, 1971); Humphrey Carpenter, *A Serious Character: The Life of Ezra Pound* (NY: Houghton Mifflin; London: Faber, 1988); Humphrey Carpenter, *A Serious Character: The Life of Ezra Pound* (US: Houghton Mifflin; London: Faber, 1988); A. Walton Litz, 'Ezra Pound and T. S. Eliot', *Columbia Literary History of the United States*, ed. Emory Elliott (NY: Columbia Univ. Press, 1988), 947–71; and Leonard Woolf, *Downhill All the Way* (NY: Harcourt, 1967; London: Hogarth, repr. OUP). A less known but vivid image of Eliot as a newcomer to London's literary scene may be found in Iris Barry, 'The Ezra Pound Period', *The Bookman* (Oct. 1931). Witty anecdotes of Eliot as an undergraduate may be found in Donald J. Adams, *Copey of Harvard* (Boston: Houghton Mifflin, 1960), and Conrad Aiken, *Ushant* (Boston: Little, Brown, 1952). There is a rather snide picture of angelic coldness in Richard Aldington's *Life for Life's Sake* (NY: Viking, 1941). Finally, some rare close-ups of Eliot may be found in Vivienne Eliot's sketches: 'Letters of the Moment—I and II', *Criterion*, 2 (Feb. and Apr. 1924), 220–2, 360–4; '*Thé Dansant*', *Criterion*, 3 (Oct. 1924), 72–8; 'A Diary of the *Rive Gauche*' and '*Necesse est Perstare?*', *Criterion*, 3 (Apr. 1925), 425–9, 364; and '*Fête Galante*', *Criterion*, 3 (July 1925), 557–63.

There are several full-length memoirs, all written with an uneasy blend of effusion and condescension. They are based on no more than a slight acquaintance with the man, and show little feeling for his work. They are *Affectionately, T. S. Eliot* by William Turner Levy and Victor Scherle (NY: J. B. Lippincott, 1968); Robert Sencourt, *T. S. Eliot: A Memoir* (NY: Dodd; London, Garnstone Press, 1971); and T. S. Matthews's *Great Tom* (NY: Harper; London: Weidenfeld & Nicolson, 1974). The latter is full of inaccuracies, but it does uncover the important relationship with Emily Hale, and has collected some genuine facts about her.

E. Martin Browne's *The Making of T. S. Eliot's Plays* (Cambridge: Cambridge University Press, 1969, repr. with supplement, 1970) is a special kind of memoir which recalls Eliot's work in the theatre. It has immensely valuable information about the evolution of his plays, backed by reports of conversations and abundant quotation from Eliot's drafts and letters, though, for all this, the book is less perceptive than Carol H. Smith's unsurpassed *T. S. Eliot's Dramatic Theory and Practice* (Princeton: Princeton University Press, 1963).

H. W. H. Powel, Jun. did pioneering biographic work in his Brown University master's essay, 'Notes on the Life of T. S. Eliot, 1888–1910' (1954), followed by John Soldo with his informative Harvard dissertation, 'The Tempering of T. S. Eliot 1888–1915' (1972). The first full-length biography was Peter Ackroyd's deft and readable *T. S. Eliot: A Life* (London: Hamish Hamilton; NY: Simon & Schuster, 1984). An imaginative source is still Herbert Howarth's *Notes on Some Figures Behind T. S. Eliot* (NY: Houghton Mifflin, 1964; London: Chatto, 1965). In a class of its own is Valerie Eliot's Introduction to her admirable edition of *The Waste Land Manuscript*, which gives the biographical background from 1914–22. This is biographical work of a high order, designed to last, where facts are selective and direct the reader towards the work.

For those whose definition of biography would include the inner and imaginative life, it is appropriate to mention three critical articles that provide acute insights into different aspects of Eliot's mind. Ronald Schuchard's 'T. S. Eliot and the Horrific Moment' and Ronald Bush's 'Nathaniel Hawthorne and T. S. Eliot's American Connection' both appeared in the Eliot issue of the *Southern Review* (Oct. 1985). The other outstanding essay is by A. V. C. Schmidt, 'Eliot's Intolerable Wrestle: Speech, Silence, Words and Voices', *UNISA English Studies* (Pretoria, 1983), 17–22, which examines Eliot's struggles with language in his search for the ineffable Word. A final suggestive piece is Paul Elmer More's 'Marginalia: I, *The American Review* (Nov. 1936), including a spiritual biography which, Eliot told him in a letter of 11 Jan. 1937, was more like his own than that of anyone he had known, particularly More's sentence: 'I have often wondered what line my experience might have taken had I been brought up in a form of belief and a practice of worship from which the office of the imagination and of the aesthetic emotions had not been so ruthlessly evicted.' More explores the Calvinistic inheritance, the attractions of 'pure spirituality' in the religious philosophy of India, scepticism in relation to conflicting impulses in some obscure region of the soul, the call, and a final state on 'the border' of the unknown.

Index